AF564675

GANDHI IN TWENTY-FIRST CENTURY

GANDHI IN TWENTY-FIRST CENTURY

Edited by
DR. ASHU PASRICHA
Department of Gandhian Studies,
Panjab University, Chandigarh

Foreword by
DR. JAI NARAIN SHARMA
Professor and Hon. Director,
Gandhi Bhawan
Department of Gandhian Studies
Panjab University, Chandigarh, and
President, Indian Society of Gandhian Studies

DEEP & DEEP PUBLICATIONS PVT. LTD.
F-159, Rajouri Garden, New Delhi-110027

GANDHI IN TWENTY-FIRST CENTURY

ISBN 978-81-8450-350-0

Typeset by S.S. COMPOSERS
3190, Mohindra Park, Shakur Basti, Delhi-110034.

Printed in India at MAYUR ENTERPRISES
WZ Plot No. 3, Gujjar Market, Tihar Village, New Delhi-110018.

Published by DEEP & DEEP PUBLICATIONS PVT. LTD.
F-159, Rajouri Garden, New Delhi-110027.
Phones: 25435369, 25440916
E-mail: ddpbooks@yahoo.co.in • ddpubs@gmail.com
Showroom:
2/13, Ansari Road, Daryaganj, New Delhi-110002 • Telefax: 23245122

Contents

DR. JAI NARAIN SHARMA
Professor and Hon. Director,
Gandhi Bhawan
Department of Gandhian Studies
Panjab University, Chandigarh, and
President, Indian Society of Gandhian Studies

Foreword

We have hailed Gandhi as Prophet, Crusader and Liberator but he has been seldom properly and critically understood. No doubt, he has been eulogized, romanticized and even mythologised but hardly conceptualized and rationalized. This is because there has been a general apathy among the intellectuals in our country who have only vague notions about Gandhi's relevance. This is indeed a tragedy that intellectuals have yet to get adequately stimulated to go into the works and ideas of world's greatest son since Socrates, Buddha and Jesus. This gulf between the intellectuals and Gandhi remained wide for more than one reasons. The Indian Society of Gandhian Studies aims at bridging this gulf and also wants to bring the Gandhian academicians and activists closer.

The Indian Society of Gandhian Studies was formed in pursuance of a resolution adopted at the Conference on "Studies in Gandhian Thought" convened by Gandhi Bhawan, University of Allahabad from 2nd October to 4th October, 1972 by Acharya J.B. Kripalani and Jayaprakash Narayan. While inaugurating the Conference, Kripalaniji stressed the need of studying the ideas, thoughts and methods of Gandhi for they are more relevant today than ever before.

The top intellectuals of our era like Acharaya J.B. Kripalani, Jayaprakash Narayan, Pyarelal, U.N. Dhebar, K.M. Munshi, G. Ramachandran, J.K. Mehta, Gunnar Myrdal, Mother Teresa, R.P. Mishra, Ram Jee Singh, etc. have been closely associated with this organization.

The business of the society is conducted by an Executive Committee consisting of a President, 3-Vice-Presidents, 1-General Secretary, 1-Associate Secretary,

1-Treasurer, 1-Local Secretary, 1-Managing Editor and 6 members all elected for 2 years. The Society has organized a number of national and international Seminars on many vitally important topics. It holds its Annual Conference with specific themes.

The following is the detail of the activities of the Society uptil now:

Sr. No.	Year	Conference	Place	President	Secretary
1.	1972	Inaugural	Allahabad	Professor B.R. Sexena	Professor J.S. Mathur
2.	1973	1st	Allahabad	Professor B.R. Sexena	Professor J.S. Mathur
3.	1974	IInd	Allahabad	Sri. Sumitra Nandan Pant	Professor J.S. Mathur
4.	1975	No Conference		Sri. Sumitra Nandan Pant	Professor J.S. Mathur
5.	1976	IIIrd	Allahabad	Sri. Sumitra Nandan Pant	Professor J.S. Mathur
6.	1977	IVth	Patiala	Sri. Sumitra Nandan Pant	Professor J.S. Mathur
7.	1978	No Conference		Smt. Mahadevi Verma	Professor J S. Mathur
8.	1979	Vth	Madras	Smt. Mahadevi Verma	Professor J.S. Mathur
9.	1980	VIth	Muzaffarpur	Sri. Jainendra Kumar Jain	Professor J.S. Mathur
10.	1981	No conference		Sri. Jainendra Kumar Jain	Professor J.S. Mathur
11.	1982	VIIth	Calcutta	Sri. K. Arunachalam	Professor J.S. Mathur
12.	1983	No Conference		Sri. K. Arunachalam	Professor J.S. Mathur
13.	1984	No conference		Sri. K. Arunachalam	Professor J.S. Mathur
14.	1985	VIIITh	Gauhati	Professor V.V. Rao	Professor J S. Mathur
15.	1986	IXth	Allahabad	Professor V.V. Rao	Professor J.S. Mathur
16.	1987	Xth	Gandhigram	Professor V.V. Rao	Professor J.S. Mathur
17.	1988	XIth	Bhagalpur	Professor V.V. Rao	Professor J.S. Mathur
18.	1989	XIIth	Kottayam	Sri. Devendra Kumar	Professor Ramjee Singh
19.	1990	XIIIth	Sewagram	Sri. Devendra Kumar	Professor Ramjee Singh
20.	1991	XIVth	New Delhi	Sri. Devendra Kumar	Professor Ramjee Singh
21.	1992	XVth	Madurai	Sri. Devendra Kumar	Professor Ramjee Singh
22.	1993	XVIth	Ladnun	Professor Ramjee Singh	Professor S.Jeyapragasan
23.	1994	XVIIth	Kanyakumari	Professor Ramjee Singh	Professor S.Jeyapragasan
24.	1995	XVIIIth	Jammu	Professor Ramjee Singh	Professor S.Jeyapragasan
25.	1996	XIXth	Jabalpur	Professor Ramjee Singh	Professor S.Jeyapragasan
26.	1997	XXth	Latur	Professor Ramjee Singh	Professor M. Maharajan
27.	1998	XXIth	Varanasi	Professor Ramjee Singh	Professor M. Maharajan
28.	1999	XXIIth	Dharwad	Professor D.N. Pathak	Professor M. Maharajan
29.	2000	XXIIIth	Aurangabad	Professor D.N. Pathak	Professor M. Maharajan
30.	2001	XXIVth	Ahmedabad	Professor D.N. Pathak	Professor Jai Narain Sharma
31.	2002	XXVth	Madurai	Professor D.N. Pathak	Professor Jai Narain Sharma
32.	2003	XXVIth	Sri Nagar	Professor J. Pandey	Professor M.S. Dadage
33.	2004	XXVIIth	Pondicherry	Professor J. Pandey	Professor M.S. Dadage
34.	2005	XXVIIIth	Nagpur	Professor Himanshu Bouorai	Dr. Anil Dutta Mishra
35.	2006	XXIXth	Varanasi	Professor Himanshu Bouorai	Dr. Anil Dutta Mishra
36.	2007	XXXth	Latur	Professor R. K. Mani Tripathi	Dr. Anil Dutta Mishra
37.	2008	XXXIth	Chandigarh	Professor R. K. Mani Tripathi	Dr. Anil Dutt Mishra
38.	2009	XXXIIth	Ladnun	Professor Jai Narain Sharma	Professor K.S. Bharathi

There are two ways of promoting Gandhian Thought, by reaching out to the masses and by approaching the intellectuals. Gandhian activists are trying to realize the former. But this is not enough. Unless we win the devotion of the articulate minority particularly in the world of both formal education and mass education, we will be on the beaten track.

Realizing that Gandhi's thought and actions emanated from his characterstic total view of life, the society has constantly tried to promote the study of Gandhian thought at the level of Universities as a separate and an independent discipline. But because of the apathy of both the academic and power elites, only about half a dozen Universities in the whole country started Gandhian Studies as separate discipline and that too only at the Post-Graduate level. The urgent need of the time is to introduce this subject at both Post-Graduate and Under-Graduate level in whole of the country.

Gandhian Studies Centres were established in various Universities and Colleges precisely for this purpose and also as a part of the broader endeavour to preserve the memory of the 'Father of the Nation' and transmit a very crucial element of Indians intellectual heritage to the new generation. The idea was not to create one more teaching department or research center to existing numerous departments in the University and Colleges, but to go beyond rituals and mere theoretical presentation and work for honest introspection and serious restructuring of our national priorities to achieve the social, political and cultural goals for which the Mahatma lived and died for. The expectations from the centers were very high but it is generally admitted that many of them failed to live up to the great expectations for variety of reasons.

There are several factors, which contributed to this state of affairs. The marginalisation of Gandhian Studies is largely due to the fact that it never got due attention or the required support from the powers that be. A comparative study of the finances made available for the propagation of Gandhian Studies through Universities and the funds made available to other similar programmes show that Gandhian Studies were never a priority area in our scheme. There is probably no point in blaming any one agency for this sorry state of affairs. There is urgent need of promoting Gandhian Studies as a subject and strengthening the Gandhian Studies Department and Centres in the country and abroad.

The Department of Gandhian Studies, Panjab University, Chandigarh organized a Three Day International Seminar for this purpose from 28-30 January 2009.

All the Gandhian Studies Centres, recently opened by University Grants Commission; the various departments of Gandhian Studies in the country and Indian society of Gandhian Studies, which has an effective membership of nearly eight hundred (800), Gandhian activists and scholars as its members from India and abroad were invited. The purpose was to provide a common platform to all the Gandhian academicians, activists and officials of University Grants Commission so that the problems can be discussed at length, properly analyzed and remedial measures and effective steps could be taken.

There was an overwhelming response from the scholars from India and abroad. The Conference was inaugurated by Shri T.N. Chaturvedi, former Governor of Karnataka and former Auditor and Comptroller General of India while the Valedictory address was given by Professor R.P. Mishra, noted Gandhian and former Vice-Chancellor of Allahabad University, Allahabad.

The present volume contains the selected papers presented in the conference. Dr. Ashu Pasricha, a budding scholar and an authentic interpreter of Gandhian Philosophy was assigned the task of editing the volume. She has done a wonderful work. I congratulate her on her endeavor.

Chandigarh JAI NARAIN SHARMA

List of Contributors

Aditya Angiras, Lecturer, Department of Hindi, VVBIS & IS, Sadhu Ashram, Hoshiarpur, Punjab.

Poonam Bawa, Professor, Director, Centre of Women Studies, Jain Narain Viyas University, Jodhpur.

H.S. Rathore, Professor, Director, Gandhian Studies Centre, Jai Narain Viyas University, Jodhpur.

Arvind Adityaraj, Lecturer, Post-Graduate Department of Political Science, College of Commerce, Patna, Bihar, Magadh University, Bodhgaya.

Ganesh Prasad, Reader & Head, Political Science Department, G.V.P.G. College, Risia, Bahraich.

Anand Kumar, Lecturer, Political Science, Government P.G. College, Sitapur (U.P.).

Sanjeev Kumar, Assistant Professor, Department of History, Government College, Naraingarh (Haryana).

K.D. Chopade, Retd. Professor, Shivaji Colony, Parbhani, Maharashta.

Ram Naresh Thakur, Head of Department, P.G. Department of Economics and Director, Gandhi Study Centre Samastipur College, Bihar.

Surendra Roy, Chhathu Rai College, Kishanpur, Samastipur, Freelance Journalist, Samastipur, Bihar.

Himanshu Shekhar, Reader, P.G. Department of Economics, C.M. College, Darbahnga.

Hemlata Jha, Middle School, Loha, Madhubani.

D. Nirmala Devi, Reader, School of Gandhian Thought & Development, M.G. University.

Shyam Chandra Gupta, Lecturer, Department of Commerce, J.N. College, Nehra, Darbhanga.

Kamal Manohar, Department of Political Science, H.P. University, Shimla.

Hossien Nemat Zadeh Gara, Iran.

Bedi, B.S., Custom Office, Ludhiana.

Dayanidhi Prasad Roy, Professr, L.N.M.U., Darbhanga.

Reena Roy, At+Po.-Patory, Samastipur, Bihar.

Ranjit Kaur, Research Scholar, Department of Gandhian Studies, Panjab University, Chandigarh.

Manoj Rajan, Department of Gandhian Studies, Panjab University, Chandigarh.

Ramesh Kumar, Assistant Professor, Department of History, Government College, Naraingarh (Haryana).

Tawinder Kaur, Department of Gandhian Studies, Panjab University, Chandigarh.

Sheeja O.K., Lecturer, Department of Philosophy, University of Calicut, Kerala.

Amit Narula, Assistant Professor, Department of English, Gobindgarh Public College, Alour (Khanna).

Kusum Narula, Professor, Department of English, A.S. College For Women, Khanna (Distt. Ludhiana).

Parmod Chauhan, Development Officer, LIC, Shimla.

Ranjana Bhardwaj, Research Scholar, Department of Ancient History, Culture & Archaeology, Panjab University, Chandigarh.

Suresh Kumar Soni, Lecturer, Govt. Post-graduate College, Bilaspur, HP.

Seema Pasricha, Department of Gandhian Studies, Panjab University, Chandigarh.

Kusum Solanky, JRF (UGC), Department of Gandhian Studies, Panjab University, Chandigarh.

Monica Sharma, Assistant Professor, Department of History, Kanya Maha Vidyalaya, Jalandhar.

Ranju Devi, JRF (UGC), Department of Gandhian Studies, Panjab University, Chandigarh.

Sumit Narula, Lecturer, Department of Mass Communication, Amity University.

Ranjan Bala, Head of Political Science Department at Malwa College, Bondli, Samrala (Punjab).

Kiyanoush Ghalavand, Iran.

Introduction

The three day International Conference under the aegis of the Indian Society of Gandhian Studies was organized by Department of Gandhian Studies, at Gandhi Bhawan, Panjab University. 225 delegates (176 outside and 49 from Chandigarh) across the country and abroad attended the Conference.

In the Inaugural session, Professor J.N. Sharma, Organizing Secretary & Chairman, Department of Gandhian Studies welcomed the delegates and put forth the need of such conference in the modern world to reduce the tension among nations and need to spread the teachings of Mahatma Gandhi to solve the global issues. He has also expressed his deep sense of appreciation for Acharya Shri Mahapragya on whose recommendations Jai Tulsi Foundation, Kolkata, Professor Javed Alain, Chairman, ICSSR, New Delhi and Professor Raghvalu and Dr. S.V. Prabhath, IAS, Chairman, NCRI, Hyderabad, Shri. B.S. Bedi, Ludhiana and Professor R.C. Sobti, Vice-chancellor, Panjab University, Chandigarh for the financial support. Dr. Sharma further stated that Acharya Shri Mahapragya was very kind enough that he deputed Professor B.R. Dugar to represent him in the conference. Dr. S.V. Prabhath, IAS, Chairman, National Council for Rural Institute, Ministry of Human Resource Development, Government of India, Hyderabad had very kindly agreed to be the Guest of Honour in the inaugural function but due to some mishap in the family he could not attend.

In his welcome address Professor J.N. Sharma stated that Gandhian Studies Centres were established in various Universities and Colleges for the promotion of Gandhian Studies and also as a part of the broader endeavour to preserve the memory of the 'Father of the Nation' and transmit a very crucial element of Indian intellectual heritage to the new generation. The idea was not to create one more teaching department or research center to existing numerous departments in the University and Colleges, but to go beyond rituals and mere theoretical presentation and work for honest introspection and serious restructuring of our national priorities to achieve the social, political and cultural goals for which the Mahatma lived and died for. The expectations from the centers were very high but it is generally admitted that many of them failed to live up to the great expectations for variety of reasons.

There are several factors, which contributed to this state of affairs. The marginalisation of Gandhian Studies is largely due to the fact that it never got due attention or the required support from the powers that be. A comparative study of the finances made available for the propagation of Gandhian Studies through Universities and the funds made available to other similar programmes show that Gandhian Studies were never a priority area in our scheme. There is probably no point in blaming any one agency for this sorry state of affairs. But certainly there is urgent need of promoting Gandhian Studies as a subject and strengthening the Gandhian Studies Department and Centres in the country and abroad.

In his Key note address, Shri T.N. Chaturvedi, an internationally acknowledged scholar, Ex-Governor, Karnataka and former Comptroller and Auditor General of India elaborated the moral values of Mahatma Gandhi and appealed to audience to make them their part and parcel of life. He further stressed, "primarily to youth, to inculcate the Gandhian values and try to emulate those in their life." In modern times, the Gandhian philosophy has been eroded with the passage of time and there is an utmost need to revive the Gandhian Institutions with more vitality with limited resources", says Chaturvedi. "With change in Political scenario and Economic conditions, the complexity in society has also increased, resulting in the more importance of Gandhian thought ever before", adds Chaturvedi.

He further stated that Gandhi was a many-sided personality. The outward simplicity of his life and his single-minded devotion to truth cloaked innumerable deep currents of ideas, disciplines, loyalties and aspirations. He was at once saint and revolutionary, politician and social reformer, economist and man of religion, educationist and satyagrahi; devotee alike of faith and reasons, Hindu and inter-religious, nationalist and internationalist, man of action and dreamer of dreams. He was a very great reconciler of opposites and he was that without strain or artificiality. He loved greatly and accepted unreservedly that truth can reside in opposites. No one has yet understood objectively his complex and magnificent personality. We have all come too much under the spell of the astonishing integration and unity of the man within himself. It was Rabindranath Tagore who once wrote that those disciplines are the most complex, which finally lead to the utter simplicity of a great song. One has only to look at those who learn music to see the daily grind of hard discipline through which they must pass before they bring out a soulful song. Gandhi's life was one long and ceaseless saga of endeavour in which he added, bit-by-bit and piece by piece, to his stature culminating in the advancing fullness of his personality. There was nothing mystic or miraculous about his development and growth, from a common man into the unsurpassed Mahatma of our history. It is open to each one of us to see how he advanced, step by step, gathering innumerable fragments of truth one by one and piecing them together in the crucible of his life, ready to look at facts, understand their significance, face any consequence in the pursuit of a cause, suffer any penalty for a mistake, recover lost ground again, but always advancing, open-minded and without fear and dedicated selflessly to reach and hold the truth of a matter at any cost. He was, therefore, not born a Mahatma. He grew into one. He was a common man who pulled himself up to most uncommon heights. He was no god, but became a god-man. Gandhi knew this about himself and that was why he called his biography, "The Story of My Experiments with Truth". Experimentation was one of the deepest passions of his life. He experimented with food, health and cure, clothes and dress, politics and economics, education and reform, organization and revolution, ethics and spirituality, with almost everything that his life knew as part of life. With relentless logic and courage he broke new ground in every direction and yet had the depth and width of mind to separate defeat from success, the false from the true, the unreal from the real and to integrate all his aims and achievements into the unity of his personality.

Dr. Samani Mangalpragya, Vice-Chancellor, Jain Vishwabharati University, Ladnun, Rajasthan, explained Mahatma Gandhi's technique of Non-violence and truth at a length to establish peace in the society. Non-violence is a holistic concept and can play a major role in channelising our energy for peace establishment efforts. According to her "Non-violence is the only solution for caste, religion and sectoral violence." She emphasized that the root cause of non-violence is poverty and psychological stress which can be cured through Training in Non-violence.

The challenges of our time have become so multifarious, multidimensional and mind boggling that no clear direction seem to be emerging. What is more they give us contradictory and conflicting horizons. Cynicism, frustration, hopelessness and darkness are near to be unavoidable. Man finds himself under the severe strain and is compelled to reassess his environment, nature, culture and future. Humanity is at the crossroads. It is really here hope signals have to be explored. In such a situation the course indicated by the unerring fingers of the Father of the Nation should come as a solace to all those who seek happiness, real prosperity and goodwill for all.

Professor R.K. Manitripathi, President, Indian Society of Gandhian Studies stressed that if proper justice is to be done to Gandhi's thought, it must be considered in its entirety and in its proper setting in Indian conditions of the time and the problems he had to solve. The local and temporal over-emphasis, wherever it exists, must be toned down to bring out the proper relation of the parts to the whole scheme of his thought and philosophy. Any point or points under-emphasised must be clearly brought out. Sometimes gaps must be filled to make the thought and the expression consistent with the whole scheme. Often, the local colour has to be toned down to bring out a universal principle. Above all, the whole thought has to be correlated to Gandhi's own conduct and life.

Like every great reformer the Mahatma's thoughts are greater than his words and arguments. Often his conduct is more revealing and eloquent than the arguments he advanced for a particular course of action. In studying him, therefore, note must be taken not only of the spoken or written word but also of his life, the way he faced and met critical situations, organized institutions and behaved towards friends and opponents. His public and private life were an open book. Therefore, his writings must be studied along with it. The writings alone may not bring out the full implications of his philosophy of life, individual and social. Further, one must rely on one's own intelligence, knowledge and experience for a proper understanding of Gandhi's ideas, policies and programmes.

In his Presidential Address, Professor R.C. Sobti, Vice-Chancellor, Panjab University, laid down the emphasis to solve the current issues and problems through Gandhian methods, not only in words but also in action. Professor Sobti further stressed that Mahatma Gandhi has been hailed as a prophet, a crusader and liberator but he has been seldom objectively analyzed and understood. No doubt, he has been eulogized, romanticized and even mystified but hardly conceptualized and rationalized. This is because there has been a general apathy among the intellectuals in our country who have only vague notions about Gandhi's relevance. This is indeed a tragedy that intellectuals have yet to get adequately stimulated to go into the works and ideas of world's greatest visionary since Socrates, Buddha and Christ.

In the Valedictory function Professor J.N. Sharma, Department of Gandhian Studies, Panjab University, Chandigarh highlighted the achievements of the three day International Conference. He again thanked Acharya Shri Mahapragya, Dr. Samni Mangal Pragya, Professor B.R. Dugar and Shri S.K. Dugar of Jai Tulsi Foundation, Kolkata; Professor Javed Alain, Chairman: Dr. Prahlad Singh, Deputy Director, ICSSR, New Delhi; Dr. S.V. Prahbath, L-kS. Chairman and Professor Raghavalu, NCRI, Hyderabad and Professor R.C. Sobti, Vice-Chancellor, Panjab University for the financial help which made this conference possible.

He expressed his gratitude and appreciation for the

leading role Professor R.P. Mishra, former Vice-Chancellor of Allahabad University and Honorary Director of the program, and Prof. D. Gopal, Coordinator of the program, have played in introducing Gandhian Studies in the IGNOU-GSDS project and making it a great success. But for them, the project would have neither been conceived nor implemented. He also thanked all the academics from different parts of the country who have come to take part in this International event.

Professor Sharma further acknowledged with thanks the interests the Chairman of Indian Council for Rural Institutions, Hyderabad (NCRI) and Professor Raghavalu are taking in Gandhian Studies and Rural Regeneration.

The Chief Guest Professor R.P. Mishra highlighted the need for Gandhian and Peace Studies Departments and Centres in India and abroad and said that in this violence prone World Gandhi is the only alternative. He discussed threadbare the current political, economic, social and enviromnental situation in the world in general and India in particular, called upon all individuals, groups, and countries to tread the Gandhian Path of Truth and Non-violence for that is the only sure means to make this world a better place to live. Professor Mishra vowed to join hands with likeminded people and organizations to sensitize the younger generation in whose hands the future of humanity lies with Gandhian values of Truth and Non-violence by educational and all other possible means. He requested the UGC, universities and colleges, Central and State departments of education to implement Gandhiji's Basic Education Philosophy from primary to post-graduate level within a period of five years.

He emphasized that the following nine resolutions passed by the ISGS should be forwarded by Professor Jai Narain Sharma, President, ISGS to the concerned persons and authorities for action.

Resolution No. 1

All members of the ISGS, hereafter referred to as Society, should adhere to the Gandhian values in their personal as well as professional life. They should lead a life that inspires others; they should be role models for others especially the youth. All members of the Society should pledge to follow the Gandhian path.

Resolution No. 2

All Gandhian institutions (University Departments, NGOs, and others) resolve their internal conflicts peacefully and follow the Gandhian way of conflict management and resolution. They must present themselves as examples for others to follow.

Resolution No. 3

The Ministry of Human Resource Development should launch at least one Mahatma Gandhi University in each state of the country (in larger states like UP and Maharashtra, there could be two). All Universities and Colleges should open Centers of Gandhian Studies and Peace and introduce relevant aspect of Gandhian Studies as an elective subject in all social science disciplines (Example: Gandhian Economics in Economics). These Centers should select a village as a field laboratory.

Resolution No. 4

All political parties of India should adhere to the following principles:

(a) They should not give tickets to persons with criminal background;
(b) They should not divide the society on the basis of caste and religion;
(c) They should introduce internal party democracy;
(d) They should get party accounts audited;
(e) They should vow to check the growing menace of corruption; and
(f) Each MLA, MP should develop at least one village in his constituency as Gandhi Gram with all necessary infrastructure, employment opportunities and social welfare measures.

Resolution No. 5

India should redefine development as a multi-faceted process aimed at enhancing the quality of life of all (Sarvodaya) and making the best use of natural and human resources of the country. Inner development is more important than outer development. Unfortunately, inner development is being neglected and over-emphasis is being placed on material and technological advancement unmindful of its implications for natural environment and human personality. The Society commends the 7-H model of integrated development of all aspects of human life:

HEAD	Intellectual development through Nai Talim;
HEART	Character building by inculcating Gandhian values;
HAND	Training in at least one skill;
HEALTH	Sustainable health through healthy living;
HOME	Happy Home with strong family ties;
HABITAT	Clean environment, and
HARMONY	Harmonious relations among people of different regions, religions and political affiliations.

Resolution 6

The government of India to save the Gandhian institution from getting into wrong hands. After the sad demise of noted Gandhian Smt. Nirmala Deshpande, the Harijan Ashram. in Delhi appears to be in disarray. Lot of land donated by people over 50 years ago is being usurped by unscrupulous people. A committee should be appointed by the Ministry of Culture to look into this issue and suggest measures to improve the working of Gandhian institutions funded by the government of India.

Resolution No. 7

All Planning Agencies (national, state, district, block and city/village) should aim at creating a Rural-urban society in India. Development should not be city-centric. It should aim at integrated development of villages, small towns, intermediate size cities and large cities in a manner that there are enough livelihood opportunities in villages as well as cities of various sizes. This is the only way to check the distress migration from villages to cities. Greater emphasis need to be laid on self-employment at the local level through agro-industrial development.

Resolution No. 8

All State Public Service Commissions should introduce Gandhian Thought and Peace as a compulsory paper for various examinations and tests they conduct to select candidates for state services.

Resolution No. 9

The Association thanks Prof. Rajsekharan Pillai, Vice-Chancellor of Indira Gandhi Open University, New Delhi, Prof. D. Gopal, Co-ordinator, Gandhian Studies Programme, IGNOU, New Delhi and Dr. Savita Singh, Director, Gandhi Smriti and Darshan Samiti, New Delhi for rendering yeomen's service to the nation by launching a very comprehensive and innovative program of Gandhian Studies and Peace. This program consists of courses leading to Certificate, Diploma, Master Degree and M.Phil, and Ph.D. in Gandhian Studies and Peace. It is by far the most comprehensive program ever carried out in the world. It has been planned to convert this program into virtual university accessible to all no matter where they are through computers.

The current volume is an effort to bring forth the selected papers presented during this International Conference in different sessions. I was assigned the task of editing the volume.

Dr. Aditya Angiras, in his paper, highlighted that Gandhi has been remembered in history because of his campaigns for seeking the ultimate truth and by using the weapons of truth, love and non-violence to win autonomy for India. But Gandhi said that "no one is competent to offer Satyagraha unless he has a living faith in God." And the Bhagavad Gita, to which he would always turn for inspiration, is the allegorical description, not of a Satyagraha campaign, but of the quest of the human soul for union with the Supreme-Master. Further, according to Srimad Bhagwad Gita, the outward work that Gandhi did in liberating India and uplifting the oppressed classes is of no more importance than the work of a meek forager, while Gandhi himself ceaselessly reiterated that no work is superior or inferior. It was this quest for God that determined Gandhi's every action and we should remember that when he said Truth is God, it did not mean only devotion to the Supreme Soul since more important for him was devotion to the inner Light that the Rishis of India and the authors of the Upanishads experienced themselves while leading a normal human life.

Professor (Ms.) Poonam Bawa and Professor H.S. Rathore in their joint paper, emphasised on that the educational institutions may employ suitable methods of developing peace education which should be in total harmony with the working of the institution. In every subject, every material and in every activity we shall find a way of developing in students a deep awareness and sensibility of peace. Gandhi stood for total peace and tolerance: "The sun of ahimsa keeps away all the dark realities of hatred, envy and dislike. Ahimsa shines high up in the realm of education. No one can hide in like the sun." Gandhian education is basically an education for peace and tolerance that would clear the way to truth and love. The aims, the principles, the concepts and the methods of education can be oriented to develop peace in the individual as well as in the Nation.

In the fast emerging global scenario moral values, ethics, spirituality, family values, religious insights have all seemed to have lost their place and values is highlighted by Dr. Arvind Adityaraj. Ethics and morality appear to be out of tune with the ethos of the global village. Globalization has thrust to the forefront. Deterioration of the nation-state, leading to global integration mostly on the strength of economic prosperity of the industrially rich and developed nations have led to a situation where vast iniquities that divided small minority of haves from he huge majority of have-nots. The economic liberalization and the technological automation threaten to widen further the existing economic, social, political and cultural disparities. Global justice will be far cry unless bold initiatives are undertaken, to overcome these disparities.

Dr. Ganesh Prasad and Dr. Anand Kumar in their paper made an attempt to analyse the various facets of Gandhi's multidimensional personality, to cover his formative years; his struggle against racism and imperialism to discus his attitude to religion and the partition of India, to elaborate his public life and the relevance of his political and economic thought in the twenty-first century and to conclude that Mahatma Gandhi is the most influential Indian of the twentieth century whose shadow continues to loom large over the country even sixty years after his death. He struggled and dreamt of a India free not only from the yoke of the British rule but also free from the evils of poverty, illiteracy, untouchability with all its citizens enjoying equally the fruits of freedom and prosperity and the resurging popularity of 'Gandhigiri' is proof of Gandhi's continuing relevance in the twenty-first century.

Dr. Sanjeev Kumar, a budding historian in his presentation emphasised that Gandhi's recognition as a major political leader was not the result of a continuous accretion of power. His rise to influence was an erratic process, and he followed no predictable route to fame, as so many of his contemporaries had done through the law courts, legal and political associations and local administration. By early 1918 Gandhi had emerged from the comparative obscurity of his first years back in India by leading three local satyagrahas.

He further said that the fact of the matter was that Gandhiji was leading a mass movement in which every section made its own contribution. As we have seen that Gandhiji wanted a millennial change a society free from vestiges of all forms of exploitation. And hence the Marxist attack on his class bias is off the mark. In his personality as well as in his ideas he had transcended all these limiting categories, of class, caste, region and religion. With the passage of time some of his ideas are appearing to be more and more relevant. He summed up by saying, Gandhiji made seminal contributions not only to our freedom struggle but also to a new world civilisation.

Professor K.D. Chopade highlighted the influence of Gandhi on Cesar Chavez who is also known as a Mexican Gandhi. Being a Mexican and worked for the benefit of Mexican farm worker in Gandhian way, he is called by his follower as Mexican Gandhi. He was leader of migrant farm workers in United States of America. Cesar has started his carrier as a farm worker.

India along with abroad is passing through all round unrest such as terrorism, the nuclear war, regional wars, etc.

is rightly expressed in the paper by Dr. Ram Naresh Thakur and Dr. Surendra Roy. According to them due to above problems, India as well as the whole world has come in the state of fear and havoc, etc. creating turmoil in the world. It seems that the brutality has dominated over the humanity. Barbarian activities, malice sense, etc. have been inherited in the psyche of selfish persons that has created several problems.

Dr. Himanshu Shekhar and Dr. Hemlata Jha, highlighted Gandhi's revolutionary concept of satyagraha is based on the simple weapons of truth and non-violence unleashed an indomitable moral force should be the vital weapon by which the world can get rid of from all ills. Gandhi's mantra not only aroused Indians to free themselves from colonial oppression and social injustice, but inspired millions of people all over the world in their quest for freedom, justice and a life of dignity we feel that this is the only weapon by which the world can get command over all the ills. In such circumstances Gandhian Studies becomes necessary.

Dr. D. Nirmala Devi, emphasised that in order to bring about a state of International Peace and Co-operation Gandhi wanted India to take a leading role. For him, India is a land of duty (Karmabhumi). India is an ancient land with moral weapons and has been a votary of if non-violence and moral force in international relations. Therefore, it should remain a relevant force in international relations on the basis of its moral strength rather than its military strength. It is for the leaders and people of India to come up to such tasks by developing their moral qualities.

Dr. Shyam Chander Gupta, argued that polity must be fearless, full of equality, providing protection to all eternal values and only then it can be pro-people. In can accord apt dimension to development. Man can contribute to world peace only in such a system of government along with gaining his goal. Government should be welfaristic to people and above being non-violent as enunciated by Mahatma Gandhi. Gandhian principle of non-violence is very much significant in modern system of government from this point of view. This significance is likely to be of permanent nature perpetually.

Dr. Kamal Manohar, studies that the concept of non-violence assumes a peculiar character in the Gita. Non-violence and violence depends wholly upon the circumstances. The decision between the two, is a thorny problem for, *"kim karma kim akarme, ti kavavo, py atra mohitah"*—ages too are perplexed as to what is action, what inaction. Tilak has referred to the dilemma of Hamlet in arising at the decision. Right sense of action is clouded with the conflicting duties raging in the mind of the doer. Non-violence has been accepted as a moral principle but moral principles are not an end in themselves. It is only through religious devotion to one's duty, that one can attain the highest bliss.

Dr. Hossien Nemat Zadeh Gara, an Iranian scholar agreed that no doubt Gandhi was influenced by the ethical doctrines of Buddhism and Jainism. But he gave Ahimsa an active political context as an instrument for militant social action. He gave the doctrine of Non-violence a revolutionary intent and direction. He gave to the future generation a direction, an aim, a way of life; from political to personal conduct, from economics to ethics. Gandhi's moral force was Non-violence. And we have reasons to believe that Non-violence in spirit and action is the only solution to the ever conflicting and changing world order. Non-violence as a moral value is ever relevant for mankind for its expected survival in the future to come.

Shri B.S. Bedi, stressed that non-violence is not a mechanical performance. It is the finest quality of the heart and comes by training. It takes a fairly strenuous course of training to attain to a mental state of non-violence. In daily life it has to be a course of discipline though one may not like it, like for instance, the life of a soldier. But I agree that unless there is hearty co-operation of the mind, the mere outward observance will be simply a mask, harmful both to the man himself and others. The perfect state is reached only when mind and body and speech are in proper co-ordination. But it is always a case of intense mental struggle.

Professor Dayanidhi Prasad Roy and Dr. Reena Roy, agreed that today, excessive consumerism is ruining the world. Gandhian advocated the principle of sustainable consumption, by considering the basic needs of large masses of poverty stricken people in the world. It condemned the proliferation of green and asserted that there is enough on this planet, for the fulfilment of the needs of every one but not enough for the satisfaction of the ever growing greed of the people. Elimination of misery and destitution from this planet occupies the central place in the vision of Gandhian world order.

Ms. Ranjit Kaur, admitted that in India, Gandhi's view of education has not received as much attention as it deserves. In fact he and his ideas have always been in controversy because of one reason or the other. And so is the case with his thoughts on Education. With the help of education, Gandhi wanted to evolve the complete man in us, which God has created in his own image. The educational system, with English as the medium of instruction introduced by Britishers, was to provide clerk for the company and not to stimulate initiative or skill in production. That education not only isolated educated from the masses but also made their bookish knowledge hardly of any practical use.

At that time Gandhiji thought that the only way of saving the nation was to revive village economic life and to relate education to it. This education was to be based on village occupations and young generation was to be trained to use their brain and brawn simultaneously, effectively and efficiently.

Dr. Manoj Rajan, pointed out that Gandhi always set high standards for printing words and was of the view that it is the only platform where you address the mass society in one go and educate them for their legal rights. The most potent weapon to revolutionize the society, Gandhi visualized its importance in early stage of his life and makes it a part and parcel of his plan of action. Journalism, which is a discipline of gathering, writing and reporting news, and more broadly it includes the process of editing and presenting the news articles, fascinated everyone and the man of the millennium Mohandas Karamchand Gandhi was not an exception. The power of his communication was so forceful that whatever he said and wrote made an everlasting mark on reader's mind and his approach to journalism was totally devoid of any self-interest. None of his contemporary or afterwards ever used the media so forcefully to ponder over the general issues that concerned the society. He knows the importance of communication and used it to shape the opinions and mobilizing the people.

Shri Ramesh Kumar, is of the opinion that the history of politics in India during last three decades has been profoundly influenced by the three forces of nationalism, socialism and Gandhism. Mahatma Gandhi began his political career in India in the early thirties dedicated to the realization of certain well defined political goals comprehensively described as Purna Swaraj. He started his leadership as a nationalist, though as time passed he constantly enlarged the scope of his nationalist philosophy. This finally emerged as sarvodaya and acquired the official, sanction of the Indian National Congress as its philosophy of political action and corporate life. Gandhi transformed nationalism from being a mere politics of protest to a consistent philosophy of life.

Ms. Tawinder Kaur, argued that Gandhi's economic ideas are perfectly consistent with his metaphysical and ethical presuppositions. According to him the whole gamut of man's activities constituted an indivisible whole and therefore, he did not draw any distinction between economics and ethics and considered that economics as untrue which ignored, or disregarded moral values. It was this insistence of Gandhi on the indivisibility of economics and morality that prompted some economists to consider his economic system to be a path that leads to non-economic goals. Gandhi considered the introduction of moral values as a regulating factor in economic matters an extension of the law of non-violence in the domain of economics. "True economics", wrote Gandhi, "never militates against the highest ethical standard, just as all true ethics to be worth its name must at the same time be also good economics... true economic... stands for social justice, it promotes the good of all equally including the weakest and is indispensable for a decent life." The end sought in a non-violent economic order is happiness combined with full mental, moral and spiritual growth.

Dr. Sheeja O.K. stressed that the modern man is living

in a world which is advancing with an unprecedented growth of industrialization and technological progress in all spheres. The dynamics of heavy industrialization and technological progress have far-reaching effects on the modern society. There are some major issues in the modern world, such as ecological imbalance, terrorism, crisis caused by violence and wars, communal riots and so forth.

Shri Amit Narula and Kusum Narula, in their joint presentation argued that the thought, philosophy and the message of Gandhi are very much relevant today. We must say they alone constitute the only positive factor which can save the modern civilization which is heading for a disaster. We witness a sure and certain dilution of higher values of life in the scheme of our lives. Permanent values of service before self-sacrifice before hoarding and concern for others are fast dwindling and their place is being taken by selfishness, greed, opportunism, deceit, cunning and falsehood. Gross materialism is eating into the vitals of society and a certain agnostic attitude is in evidence almost everywhere. Even family lies are being broken, love is losing ground to hatred, distrust and suspicion.

Mr. Parmod Chauhan, is of the opinion that Western democratic societies have seldom been stronger. Their dangerous totalitarian opponents have been vanquished; their technology continues to move at a dizzying pace; their citizens are living longer, are more literate, and generally enjoying a higher standard of living than earlier generations; their models of the economy and polity have been one dominant, and their culture is becoming globalized. The West has put its stamp on the world: modernity and modernization provide the standards by which we understand success and failure.

Dr. Ranjana Bhardwaj highlighted that Mahatma Gandhi followed the principle of Non-violence. Consequently it could be possible to keep the country integrate. He gave the message of peace, amity, brotherhood, equality, untouchability to the world. He was also against the ethnic discrimination in some parts of the world. So Mahatma Gandhi adopted this teaching of Non-violence and gave us fruits of his legacy of principle of Non-violence.

Dr. Suresh Kumar Soni, reveals that Gandhi actively fought against odds and evils, which hampered the growth, well-being and advancement of man. He relentlessly worked to establish a just and equitable socio-political and economic environment for the fulfilment of man and mankind. He believed in complete and comprehensive development of human being. His concern was not merely to seek material development of man but also to attain his moral and spiritual perfection. From the above, it is clear that the various tenets of Gandhian thought signify the spirit of humanism, which has its basis in reason, self-purification, morality, ethics and love for humanity, and truth that is God.

Dr. Seema Pasricha, argued that the Gandhian Philosophy of political change on all counts, emerges as the most satisfactory and flawless theory or change. It encompasses the ages but does not let even a split-second escape out of its ambit. It aims at the transformation of the individual with the simplification and purification of the state apparatus. It is neither uncontrolled change nor selective change. It is neither change at whirlwind speed nor mere reformism at sluggish snail's pace speed. It is the Charkha theory of change, requiring patience and perseverence, deft touch and delicate handling. It touches all points and covers entire life. It is because of this life theory of change with its non-violence, Satyagraha and truth that Gandhi's deep political philosophy with its deeper implications has to be universally realised. Wherever the Gandhian laws of life are contravened in individual, national or international life, man has to pay very dearly for his transgressions.

Ms. Kusum Solanky, is of the opinion that an analysis of Gandhi's fundamental ideas further reveals that in Gandhi's social order based on justice and equality, there was no place for competitor and confrontation between man and woman and he did want women to ignore their duty as housekeepers, mothers, moulders of future generation and builders of the nation. But at the same time he did not put any limit on their role in practice. They very fact that he invited woman to take part in public and political life of the country even in 1920s and 1930s postulates that he believed in complete gender equality and considered women fit for all types of activities outside home. His call to parents not to kept their daughters utterly ignorant and illiterate and bring them up only for purpose of marriage, to girls to get education and to remain unmarried and to be economically independent provide ample evidence of his belief in equality of the sexes. In his Ashram he treated men and women as equals.

Dr. Monica Sharma highlighted the contribution of KMV in the field of education in North India is nowhere more evident than in this contribution of Lala Devraj, who was even honoured for this work. He not only wrote most of the books himself but also arranged for their publication and distribution. Some of these books were later translated into Marathi, Telugu and Gujarati. In 1904, the Punjab and Central Provinces recommended some of these texts for their schools. This was a triumph for their schools. This was a triumph for the KMV concept of women education.

Ms. Ranju Devi, argued that Gandhiji felt that India is a one Nation and every unit must have this realization. He, therefore, believed that whatever differences exist should be obliterated and every unit should feel one with the other. In fact, on the demand of the nation all must appear with the one voice. For this the atmosphere of oneness has to be created. This cannot be achieved unless: (1) the inequality existing in the society is obliterated; (2) violence is eschewed; and (3) the foreign power is removed

Mr. Sumit Narula, emphasised and made aware of the fact that Non-violence is a science. It does not mean just sitting around feeling good about the world. Without analysis, research and proper training you can't practise it. We have constructed a perfect violent defense system. But we haven't put so much as one dollar a day aside, on systematic training in non-violent defense.

And there is such a defense. In USA we have the Civilian-based Defence Association, where Professor Gene Sharp has been doing research on the issue for over 30 years. In The Politics of Non-violent Action, a regular encyclopaedia on non-violence, he systematically describes 198 specific actions, including historical examples. The Indian Society of Gandhian Studies founded by Acharya J.B. Kripalani and Lok

Nayak Jayaprakash Narain. Currently, under the Presidentship of Professor Jai Narain Sharma, Department of Gandhian Studies, Panjab University is doing tremendous job towards spreading Gandhi's principles and how they can be used in our day-to-day life.

Dr. Ranjan Bala highlighted that in a world pervaded with violence and terror, the struggle for peace and security must begin in everyday life. Peace and security have always been among humanity's highest value, for some supreme end. The concept of peace and security is as old as human knowledge of society. The quest for peace and security has been a central motive in the life of man from the first moment of his entrance in the worldly scene. Mankind has been searching for an ideal society, where men can lead a happier, worthier and more rewarding life. Peace and security continues to be a powerful wish, desire and a passion with millions as well as a conviction deeply felt and aspired too. All nations long for it. Leaders negotiate for it yet it remains most elusive than ever.

Mr. Kiyanoush Ghalavand, another Iranian scholar argued that the true characteristic of faith is not to deny the hostility of the world, but to recognize it and to believe in spite of it! Faith is a battle. And our non-violence is the most desperate battle. The way to peace is not through weakness. We do not fight violence. No much as weakness. Nothing is worthwhile unless it is strong, neither good nor evil. Absolute evil is better than emasculated goodness. Moaning pacifism is the death-knell of peace; it is cowardice mid lack of faith. Let those who do not believe, who fear, withdraw. The way to peace leads through self-sacrifice.

I sincerely apologise to the learned scholars whose papers could not be included in the present volume.

I am grateful to Professor J.N. Sharma, President, ISGS for entrusting this task to me. I am also thankful to Professor R.P. Mishra, Former Vice-Chancellor, Allahabad University, Allahabad, Professor R.N. Pal, Pro-Vice-Chancellor, Professor D. Gopal, Coordinator, Gandhian Studies Programme, Indira Gandhi National Open University (IGNOU), New Delhi for encouraging me to undertake this task.

I am also grateful to Professor K.S. Bharathi (Nagpur,

Maharashtra), Professor B.R. Dugar (Ladnun, Rajasthan), Professor S.K. Sharma, Chairman, Organising Committee of the Conference and Secretary to Vice-Chancellor, Panjab University, Chandigarh, Professor Surya Kant, Professor Wilheim Zoltan (Hungary), Professor R.K. Manitripathi, former President of ISGS (Gorakhpur), Professor Ramjee Singh (Bihar), Professor M.S. Dadge (Latur, Maharashtra), Professor Nakade, former PVC (Latur, Maharashtra), Professor R.S. Yadav (Kurukshetra University, Kurukshetra), Professor R.P. Dwivedi (Varanasi), Professor S. Andiyapan (Madurai), Professor Himansu Bourai (Srinagar, Uttarakhand), Professor Pushpa Motiani (Ahmedabad, Gujarat), Professor Anurag Gangal (Jammu University), Professor Narender Dogra (Punjabi University, Patiala, Punjab), Professor Rajendra Chuahan (Shimal, Himachal Pradesh), Professor Raj Singh (Hissar, Haryana), Professor H.S. Rathore (Jodhpur), Professor Madhukarshyam Chatturvedi (Jaipur University, Jaipur, Rajasthan), Professor Sheila Rai (Jaipur, Rajasthan), Professor Ram Binod Singh (Bihar) and Dr. A.D. Mishra (New Delhi).

Lastly, I am also grateful to Shri G.S. Bhatia, my publisher for his consistent zeal in printing and publication of this volume.

Chandigarh ASHU PASRICHA

Dynamics of Gandhian Thought

Aditya Angiras

Soft dark and rather large protruding eyes having glasses, a small frail man, with a thin lean face, his head covered with a little white cap, his body clothed in a coarse white cloth, barefooted who generally had a staff in his one hand always has nothing striking about him except his whole expression of "infinite patience and infinite love." There is an almost childlike simplicity in him[1] as his manner is gentle, refined and courteous even when dealing with adversaries[2] having impeccable sincerity.[3] He is modest and unassuming, almost timid and hesitant in making an assertion yet one may feel his indomitable spirit through the actions he did. He makes no compromises at any stage and never tries to hide a mistake since he is not afraid of admitting having been done something wrong. Diplomacy is unknown to him; he shunned oratorical effect and never thinks about it. He feels at ease only in a minority, and is happiest when is in meditative solitude, where he can listen to: his "still small voice" within.[4]

Mohandas Karamchand Gandhi, (1869-1948) was a major political and spiritual leader of India during the independence movement who pioneered non-violent, civil disobedience, which figures still in many of the human rights movements of the 20th century. The title attributed and associated with Mohandas Karamchand Gandhi is Mahatma which has been coined from Sanskrit language for representing the "Great Soul." Born in 1869, in Porbandar in the state of Gujarat into a Vaishya (merchant class) family, Gandhi was married at the age of 13 to Kasturba. He was an average student who studied law in England from 1888 to 1891. Before leaving India, his mother made him promise that he would abstain from meat, alcohol and sex. The years passed soon and Gandhi was back in Mumbai. After returning to India, it was time for his first and only case as a lawyer in India, and the man stood ineptly tongue tied in court. The writing was on the wall, and Gandhi lost the case. His uncles packed him off to South Africa in 1893 to work for an Indian merchant involved in a civil suit. The turning point in Gandhi's life began in South Africa where he found himself in the midst of an intimidated and oppressed Indian community that was the butt of racial discrimination. Aware of his own shortcomings, Gandhi struggled to overcome personal inhibitions, and worked towards uniting the South African Indians to protest against discrimination and racial bias done to them by the South African Government. After a few brief spells in prison, he succeeded in getting the local governance to relax it's laws for the first time in 1908, then again in 1914. He withdrew his children from a government school and established a farm at Phoenix in 1904 where he endeavored to build a community based on the combined philosophies of John Ruskin, Leo Tolstoy and Henry Thoreau whom he called a true American. Around the same time, he started a correspondence with Tolstoy. In 1906 he took a vow of celibacy. He lived in South Africa for 20 years and it would not be out of line to believe that the nature of his work in South Africa inspired him to achieve the near impossible back home, where Gandhi was already a name to reckon with.

He inclined towards abstract asceticism and believed in Thoreau's philosophy of complete self-reliance and the dignity of labor, wearing a khadi and a shawl that he had woven for himself. The spinning wheel that he worked on religiously every day is profoundly symbolic of the Mahatma and his beliefs to this day. Deeply hurt by the unyielding caste system in his country, he worked throughtout his life for the upliftment of Harijans. He dreamt of a free and self-reliant India, where Christians, Hindus, Muslims and Harijans would live in total peace and harmony and work towards a better world. Perhaps the most profound of his philosophies was his quest for the inner truth, an untainted non-sectarian truth, universal in appeal. Probably he understood that supreme truth remains relevant in every time to come and thus found this very aspect in non-violence. He believed and practiced non-violence in thoughts, words, and actions that leapt from love for mankind that lay beyond the continent of calculations and rewards a personal philosophy inspired by the Bhagavad Gita considered as perhaps the most lucid representation of Hinduism, and by many as the most sacred book of the Hindus. Gandhi not only represented the best rudiments of Hinduism, but, on the contrary, was also interested in implicating them at social and ethical levels for reforms[5] as he understood that these are sometimes applied and interpreted to keep the poor and oppressed peoples in a permanent state of powerlessness as he saw the quandary of poor farmers and laborers which indicated the widespread discrimination between the ruler and the ruled class of the then India. Thus by using the force of Indian National Congress and personal belief, Gandhi tried to alleviate the common people from poverty, fought for the liberation of women, and tried to end the caste system by using the term "Harijan" which literary means "the people of Lord Supreme." Although Gandhi remained committed to non-violence forever even in the most adverse situations in his life which is in accordance with surmons of Upanishads as he was a student of Hindu philosophy since his proclamation indicates "I call myself a Sanatani Hindu, because I believe in the Vedas, the Upnishads, the Puranas and all that goes by the name of Hindu scriptures and therefore in incarnations and rebirth; I believe in the varnashrama, dharma in a sense, in my opinion strictly Vedic, but not in its presently popular crude sense. I believe in the protection of cow ... I do not disbelieve in murti puja."[6] He did not disbelief other religions but treated all of them at the same ground. Thus a person, who lived in simplicity by organizing an ashram that was self-sufficient in its all needs, used rigorous fasts for self-purification (as suggested by Patanjal Yoga Sutram) as well as a means of protest. Although one of his foremost concerns was improving the status of India's lower classes and drawing the poor and the marginalized into the mainstream of freedom struggle, but on contrary to this, his other concern was self-purification by practicing the different teaching of Upanishads. According to Gandhi "Hinduism as I know, it entirely satisfies my soul, fills my whole being ... When doubts haunt me, when disappointments stare me in the face, and when I see not one ray of light on the horizon, I turn to the Bhagavad Gita and find a verse to comfort me; and I immediately begin to smile in the midst of overwhelming sorrow. My life has been full of tragedies and if they have not left any visible and indelible effect on me, I owe it to the teachings of the Bhagavad Gita."[7] Each day he held a morning and evening prayer meeting, first at his ashram in Sabarmati, then at Wardha. The ashram hymns included Hindu prayers Bhajanavali along with "Rock of ages", "Abide with me", "Who would true valor see", and of course, his favorite Christian hymn "Lead, kindly light" which shows his unbiased nature for seeking the selfpurification and pacification for others and this thought, in particular, is driven by the Vedic concept of "Vasudhaiva Kutumbakam." According to Gandhi, God and dharma are inseparably linked, and both are combined with emancipation. Religion and politics, thus according to Gandhi, could not be divided into different categories. Dharma and emancipation, according to him, were the social concepts and not the individual ones as he perceived in the Sri MadbhagadGita Lord Krishna (The supreme soul) is a friend who comes to Arjuna during his distressing event of his life. Truth, as Gandhi believes, is no impersonal absolute is not a substitute for God. Truth clarifies what God meant when he used the term. It is a perpetual source of power coming from the inner self. Hence his use of the word Satyagraha represents the truth force. As he explains himself "Its root meaning is holding onto truth, hence truth force. I have also called it love force or soulforce."[8]

It is quiet difficult to attribute any of the philosophical schools of Hindu philosophy to Gandhi in particular as his belief is in an ultimate unity between God and the universe. He describes this very ideology by saying "I subscribe to the belief or the philosophy that all life is in essence one and that humans are working consciously or unconsciously towards the realization of that identity. The belief requires a living faith in the Supreme Soul who is the ultimate arbiter of our fate."[9] Elsewhere he iterated "Man's ultimate aim is the realization of God, and all his activities, social, political and religious have to be guided by the ultimate aim of the vision of God. The immediate service of all human beings becomes a necessary part of the endeavor, simply because the only way to find God is to see him in his creation and ultimately become one with it. This can only be done by rendering selfless service for all. I am part and parcel of the whole and I cannot find the Supreme Soul apart from the rest of humanity."[10] The search for salvation or liberation as Gandhi perceived, can not be attained if one is be selfish. Thus his criticism of the sannyasin who left society, including his family, to pursue his own spiritual journey is obvious since his ideal is King Dashratha and Pravahini of Upanishads who led the normal family life and attained salvation. He is a true Vaishnava (devotee of Vishnu) who counts the suffering of others as his own suffering as his song celesta indicates.[11] His idea of "Ram Rajya" is also based on these very lines of Indian thought process.

Gandhi has been remembered in history because of his campaigns for seeking the ultimate truth and by using the weapons of truth, love and non-violence to win autonomy for India. But Gandhi said that "no one is competent to offer Satyagraha unless he has a living faith in God."[12] And the Bhagavad Gita, to which he would always turn for inspiration, is the allegorical description, not of a Satyagraha campaign, but of the quest of the human soul for union with the Supreme Master. Further, according to Sri Madbhagwad Gita, the outward work that Gandhi did in liberating India and uplifting the oppressed classes is of no more importance than the work of a meek forager, while Gandhi himself ceaselessly reiterated that no work is superior or inferior. It was this quest for God that determined Gandhi's every action and we should remember that when he said Truth is God, it did not mean only devotion to the Supreme Soul since more important for him was devotion to the Inner Light that the Rishis of India and the authors of the Upanishads experienced themselves while leading a normal human life. Thus Gandhi's work and message must be understood through SriMadBhagavad Gita and other Upanishads that had been providing the basic inspiration on the way of working.

When Harijan recommenced it's publication, Gandhi's words came like a tonic to the oppressed class. Somehow he was always utterly right, right because no fleck of self-pride or incredible supernatural revelation spoilt the purity, simplicity and courteousness in what he wrote. We find the very intimate detail of the inner life as a great public character and spiritual genius, from childhood until death in his own words and writings through his collected works published by V.B. Kher in three volumes, entitled "In Search of the Supreme", Gandhi's words on the spiritual aspect of life as well as his own "Experiments with Truth", there is also Pyarelal's "Mahatma Gandhi: the Last Phase", which gives the intimate details of his quest for the ultimate truth during the last years.

All the work is transient in nature, and Gandhi's is no exception and each one has his own work to do, and it is our own work, however humble, that both Gandhi and the Sri Madbhagwad Gita would have its fulfil, and it is of the Mahatma's message in connection with our ordinary lives, that I would say something. "It is better to do your own duty however imperfectly than assume duties of another person, however successful; prefer to die performing your own duty; the duty of another will bring you great spiritual danger."[13] What is our own duty in this context it needs a bit of the clarification here at this juncture.

Under the ancient Hindu system of division into castes, or more correctly Varnas, a man's work was determined by the hereditary calling of his father's profession in the history of India under British regime. The son of a sandal maker must become a sandal maker himself and a woman of course learned only the domestic arts according to the station in life of her father. Gandhi's ideas concerning caste system underwent considerable modification as his experiments with Truth proceeded and in the end he would probably have agreed that a man's proper work must be ordained by his nature. He never gave up the idea of the need for division of labor and from the beginning he started asserting that no work was superior or inferior[14] as it becomes evident from "My experiments with truth." He also consistently asserted that the work done for a livelihood must be done as a duty, and should not be governed by the law of money making or one's own pleasure It must never be changed for the sake of making a better livelihood.[15] But on contrary to this he asserted that one's bread and butter work does not prevent one's engaging in public service also.

It must be understood that there is no question of superiority and inferiority, neither is there any importance and room in attaining success or failure. Success and failure are not in our hands, for all actions are the result of the working of the three gunas "and take place in time by the interweaving of the forces of nature"[16] as Sri Madbhagwad Gita states and only the deluded man acts like the Doer.

Gandhi's own work has been very successful in gaining autonomous government for India since it was attained without committing any violence or shedding a single drop of blood. It was accomplished even without hatred for the others with surprising result that a person with a passport of the conquering race is welcomed everywhere as a friend. It should be mentioned that Gandhi was influenced from the Vedic saying "We should see everyone with the friendly passion."[17]

Gandhi was unutterably cast down at the failure of his efforts to instill love and non-violence, shows that even up to shortly before his death he had not wholly absorbed into his being the Gita teaching and his own also that success and failure are of no account. It was only by fasting that he was able to purify his mind of depression and regain the equilibrium of a Vedic Rishi. But the very fact of this human weakness and ability to overcome it inveriably makes his teaching more helpful than that of the Rishis who are said to have dwelt always on the Himalayan heights in perfect serenity.

Those who have not absorbed the Srimad Bhagwad Gita's teaching that success and failure are of no account must find it hard to accept the truth that the "matchless weapon" of satyagraha that Gandhi brought into use is already being forgotten. When Martin Luther King started the desegregation movement in United States, he did not consciously copy Gandhi's methods. The movement came into being of its own accord, and only after it was fully launched did its leader remember back to his reading of, Gandhi and see the likeness of Gandhi's methods to his own. Thus it is that all work, say both the Sri Madbhagwad Gita and Gandhi at every cost should be offered to the Lord or the Supreme Soul, as a sacrifice, something to be made holy because it is done as a service to all without making any discrimination.

When the universe was created, simultaneously the law of sacrifice, the opposite to creation, was brought into being, For, the universe is composed of pairs of opposites.[18] The law of sacrifice is universal; and it is only at his peril that man tries to exclude himself from the working of this law. In the East it seems to be almost a universal custom to recognize that this law applies to man, by symbolically offering food to the God before partaking of it oneself.

Gandhi's interpretation of ch. 7 v. 17 is very interesting from the above said point of view. This verse describes the man dearest to God. It has been translated according to own personal understanding since Annie Besant had translated it as "The wise, constantly harmonized, worshipping the one"; whereas Mukherjee as "The wise, ever steadfast, fired by a single purpose" and Isherwood and Prabhavananda as "The man of spiritual discrimination." On the contrary Edwin Arnold as "He who is intent upon the One" and Mascaro as "The man of vision" whereas Radhakrishnan as "The wise one who is ever in constant union with the Divine and whose devotion is single minded." But Gandhi said it is "Those who know what they are about and for whom service to others is something they cannot do without."[19] Again in the Eighth Chapter, Gandhi's interpretation of the bright fortnight of the moon is the path of selfless service.

Complete surrender to the Supreme and universal love towards all of the creation are the culminating notes of the Sri Madbhagwad Gita. "Who burns with the bliss and suffers with the sorrow of every creature within his heart, making his own each bliss and each sorrow .... He who in this oneness of love, loves me in whatever he sees, wherever that man may live, in truth this man lives in me."[20]

But the culminating note of Gandhi's teaching was Truth. Truth is doubtless implied in every chapter of the Gita, but its necessity is never made explicit. Truth is not one of the things that Krishna describes himself as being.

The reason behind, according to me, is that Sri Madbhagwad Gita came into existence when people were simpler and there was greater harmony between the conscious and subconscious mind, which latter was brought into daylight, as it were, by dreams and myths which to people in those days were real. When Sri Madbhagwad Gita talks about the sacred fig tree of Aswattha, "the everlasting rooted in heaven, its branches earthward, its leaves a song of the Vedas",[21] this may be merely a pretty fancy to us but to people of the age of the Gita it was real because it was part of the collective subconscious which dream life showed to be a fact.

Thus it can be said that the driving force behind every action of Gandhi was Indian socio religious texts like Sri Madbhagwad Gita and Vedas, which form the core of Hindu way of life, accompanied with the righteous thought process of other religions.

Notes and References

1. As C.F. Andrews says, "He laughs like a child and adores children."
2. "Few can resist the charm of his personality. His bitterest enemies become courteous when confronted with his beautiful courtesy." (Joseph J. Doke)
3. "He is not a passionate orator; his manner is calm and serene and he appeals particularly to the intelligence. But his serenity places the subject he discusses in the clearest light. The inflexions of his voice are not varied, but they are intensely sincere. He never makes any gestures with his arms, in fact he rarely even moves a finger. But his luminous words, expressed in terse, concise sentences, carry

conviction. He never abandons a subject before he feels that he had made it perfectly clear." (Joseph J. Doke)

4 *Young India,* March 2, 1922. The dates cited in the notes of this volume refer to the date of publication of Gandhi's articles in *Young India.*

5. Gandhi's song celestial is 'Vaishnav Jan to tene Kahiye.........

6. *Young India,* June 10, 1921.

7. *Ibid.,* June 8, 1925.

8. *Ibid.*

9. *Ibid.*

10. *Ibid.*

11. "Vaiashnava Jan tene kahiye ...."

12. V.B. Kher, In Search of the Supreme, III, p. 343.

13. *Ibid.*

14. Upanishads never stressfullv asserted on the caste svstem in ancient India as we find satya kam Jabal, a non-Brahmin became Brahmin after accepting the truth.

15. V.B. Kher. In Search of the Supreme, 11, p. 211.

16. Bhagavad Gita, Isherwood's translation, p. 58.

17. YajurVeda 36.18

18. SriMadbhagwad Gita, ch. 3; Kher, III, p. 236.

19. Kher, III, p. 236.

20. Mascaro's tr., ch. 6. v. 3 1.

21. Sri Madbhagwad Gita 15.1 & 15.2.

Rediscovering Gandhi Education for Truth and Non-Violence

POONAM BAWA AND H.S. RATHORE

Paying tribute of Mahatama Gandhi on his 75th birthday, Albert Einstein wrote: "Generations to come, it may well be, will scarcely believe that such a one as this ever in flesh and blood walked upon this earth."[1] Gandhi today has become a universal symbol more than anything else of the supreme principles of truth, love, non-violence, justice and human brotherhood. The world is found more and more lacking in these values to colossal degrees and we are being overcome by a realization that these values alone can redeem the world from a state of increasing degeneration. No other techniques are found to be more potent than the Gandhian techniques generated from these principles of human conduct, and this realization is leading Gandhi to ever greater recognition.

E. Stanley Jones calls Gandhi "the voice of the dumb millions."[2] Gandhi has become for us Indians not a mere national hero as the Father of the Nation, but a living voice exhorting us and inviting us to renew our commitment to build a nation of physically and spiritually free persons. Increasing problems leave us in ever greater bondage and Gandhiji's voice is a liberating voice, provided Indians and the world at large are willing to renew their commitment to truth and brotherhood. We are rediscovering Gandhi as the powerful light that is capable of shining over the whole modern world with the potent rays of spiritual integrity and spiritual revolution. One of the most valuable legacies Gandhi has left to posterity in his life and teachings are crystallised in satyagraha and non-violence. These great principles are envisaged to help modern world contemplate and practice truth and love penetrating all life's activities.

Mahatama Gandhi is rediscovered today in his intense devotion to world peace and political and religious tolerance based on the brotherhood of man. As George C. Marshall says, Gandhi "was one of those rare spokesman for the conscience of all mankind."[3] He has become again the voice of mankind for a livable world of peaceful co-existence that is facing nightmare threats, Gandhi is the need of the day, not only for Indians but for the entire world on the face of overwhelming problems. He saw the redemption of the world through the weapons of humility and simplicity and showed Indians that these values can be more powerful than empires.

Gandhi is in several ways rediscovered by Indians and the world at large. It may be called a rediscovery because the spirit of interest and enthusiasm in everything related to Gandhi has come to be a recent thing. The Gandhian thoughts and trends, and all the values that he held as precious for himself, for the Nation and the world lay hidden in the annals of decades without receiving adequate recognition, when he lived he reached people through direct contact, action and example, coming down to and moving in the midest of the people for whose freedom he dedicated himself. After his death, independent India almost transformed Gandhi into a myth, a legend and a classsic example of national herosim. The country found not much worthy of practicing in its march to sophistication and modernism. That was indeed a great tragedy.

India in particular and the world at large are

rediscovering Gandhi. This is a lingering and slow process, but an inevitable one. The vision of Mahatama Gandhi is a vision of salvation for the country. The greatness of the Gandhian message has been tested on the anvil of decades. Gandhiji's greatness is not supposed to be mummified for the sheer pleasure of keeping it. It is a living greatness and living and evolving message. The most characteristic aspect of Gandhi's teachings is that he did not merely preach his message for the world but he lived it every moment of his life. As K.L. Gauba says, "Gandhi, the man of destiny, born to emancipate his country first emancipated himself by the conquest of desire and fear."[4]

GANDHI AND WORLD PEACE

Gandhi in all his undertakings proved himself to be one of the greatest messengers of peace the world has witnessed and peace becomes the quintessence of his political philosophy. It is Gandhi's contributions to world peace that the world at large has aptly recognized in him. Gandhi showed the world not only the goal of peace but the supreme method of achieving world peace. George C. Marshall writes, "In his devotion to peace and tolerance of the brotherhood the Mahatama was one of those rare spokesman for the conscience of all mankind."[5] Peace and tolerance, for Gandhi, were the supreme means for the realization of Truth and Love which were identical to the Ultimate End of man. Gandhi's spiritual, political and economic tenets were permeated by the principle of peace. In the light of peace alone could the human being witness truth.

Gandhi developed his world-view against the background of a world of violence. Violence by the foreign rule, economic violence against the poor, political violence against the down-trodden and underprivileged, educational violence against the illiterate and the backward and above all the violence of war and crime. Gandhi's message of peace took all its sharpness and sensitivity against this background of violence. He says, "What you gain by violence will be lost by greater violence."[6] Gandhi recognized violence as the root cause of all evils and all evils are thus reducible to violence against the spirit of truth. Hence for him non-violence or ahimsa becomes the only path to truth and only solution to the problems of life-individual, social and national. Hence ahimsa has the great role in the framework of Gandhian thoughts. Thus non-violence becomes identified with peace. Peace becomes the true and the positive way to the realization of truth.

Peace becomes an international goal in the framework of Gandhism. Today peace is the catch-word in international relations because the world has come to realize more than ever the vital role of peace in the very survival of mankind. At the time of Gandhi's assassination Earl Warren wrote, "The assassination of Gandhi removes from the world by a cowardly act a powerful force for the world peace. Gandhi was essentially a man of peace."[7] The world recognized Gandhi's contribution to world peace in ways more than one. Gandhi professed his love of the British, the Americans and the Europeans as a whole at the same time he deplored the violent sophistication and advancement of the West. Gandhi loved the British but hated their ways. He writes recalling his role in the Boer War of 1899. "I felt that I demanded the rights as a British citizen it was also my duty to participate in the defense of the British empire." Based on this conviction Gandhi formed the Peace Corpse which consisted of 1100 members to provide relief work. Gandhi's love of the British was part of the great and universal drive he had for peace. Gandhi always set his eyes on world Peace as the foundation on which to build a world of truth and love. He says, "Once we accept truth and love as the foundations of our existence, then we have discovered the foundations of the unity of humanity."[8] The unity of humanity can be based only on the principle of peace as the necessary condition for the development of truth and love in the hearts of men. Gandhi saw the message of Christ as a unique expression of peace in the world: "I want the help of especially Christians to strengthen my conviction in non-violence because thousands of them believe that the message of Christ is the message of World Peace and good will."[9] Gandhism stands for international peace. It is only through peace that the world can move in the path of truth towards God.

EDUCATION FOR PEACE AND TOLERANCE

Gandhian peace is an individual value. Just as truth and ahimsa begins with the individual and get realized in the individual, peace is a great value that should begin with the individual and become the basis for the development, other social and psychological attitudes. Edmond Taylor remarks, "This has produced the great Gandhian personality a combination of inner peace arising from a more total integration of all elements in the personality than most men achieve."[10] The development of the spiritual personality takes place in total integration with the psychological attitudes. We find this integration revealed in the Gandhian personality. Peace becomes not only a goal but also a condition for self-realization. Peace becomes the necessary condition for the spiritual development of the individual. For this reason the sages and rishis of ancient times desired total isolation in their encounter with God. Peace in the individual is identified with divine presence in the religions. For Gandhi peace becomes an individual value of great significance.

Gandhian spirituality is founded on peace. Gandhi says, "In violence we exhibit not the spirit but the brute in us."[11] The spirit can be realised and nurtured only in a state of non-violence that is peace. All aspects of spirituality that can be practiced by the individual and can lead to God are based on peace in the individual as a condition for divine light. God's light in truth and love will shine on the individual only in a state peace. Spirituality is the realization of truth and the vision of God through prayer, sacrifices and spiritual exercises that were so dear to Gandhi. He says, "Ahimsa is the only means to the realization of truth...... A perfect vision of truth can only follow a complete realization of ahimsa."[12] Peace is a state of complete non-violence in the individual, society and nation. Gandhian spirituality can be realized and developed only within the framework of peace that should reign in the individual. Where there is no truth there cannot be peace and where there is no love, again there cannot be peace. Peace in the genuine sense would thus become the co-principle of truth and love.

Man's tolerance of one another's wrongs, tolerance and

forbearance of social differences is fundamental to Gandhian thoughts. Tolerance is basic to the survival and progress of individuals, society and the nation. Dwight Macdonald says, "He practiced tolerance and love to such an extent that he seem to have regarded the capitalist and the garbage man as his social equal."[13] Tolerance is a fundamental Gandhian virtue that makes the Gandhian ahimsa a most potent thing. Tolerance becomes a refinement of the most powerful principal of ahimsa. In a country like India more than anywhere else tolerance becomes central value for different reasons. India is a divided country with fundamental religion-philosophical and cultural separatism. This separatism is reflected most in our Hindu-Muslim and other communal rivalries and parochial tendencies. Gandhi saw that these communal rivalries would be a death-knell to the survival of this country. Gandhi's experiences after the partition immensely proved how malicious and terrible communalism in India could turn out to be. The Hindu-Muslim massacres after the partition compelled Gandhi to undertake a fast unto death, which he stopped on assurance from leading members of different communities that the bloody rivalries would be stopped at once.

Against this background tolerance is felt to be a very fundamental value in this country. Today tolerance is a constitutional value as an attitude fundamental to the democratic practices in this country. Tolerance and the fundamental right are absolutely correlated. It requires tolerance on the part of one individual to recognize the democratic right of another. It requires tolerance similarly to recognize the constitutional rights communities. This recognition equities forbearance which we call tolerance in this context. The rights of individuals and communities call for tolerance on the part of other individuals and communities. Here tolerance becomes a positive virtue and enters into the very realm of ahimsa or love. Martin Luther King writes, "We will return good for evil. We will love our enemies. Christ showed us the way, and Gandhi showed us how it could work."[14] Tolerance becomes love in its positive directions and Gandhi carries it to the logical extreme of loving one's enemies in line with the teachings of Jesus

Christ. Tolerance as a constitutional value with reference to the fundamental rights takes the direction also of justice. It is merely allowing the other the necessary justice that he naturally deserves. Gandhi says, "My experience has shown me that we win justice quickest by rendering justice to the other party:[15] Tolerance becomes justice paid in equal measure to those who owe it under a given social set-up.

FUNDAMENTALS OF EDUCATION

Peace and tolerance are fundamental goals of education. Education considered from whatever viewpoint ends up in a rediscovery of peace at the very root of all formations and developments. Education aims primarily at helping the individual achieve a state of psychological, social and spiritual balance or equilibrium. In other words the individual discovers, in the process of education, a self-balanced in the right attitudes towards himself, society and God. This constitutes the state peace in the individual. It is a process of developing the self-in these attitudes. The individual becomes capable of comparing and contrasting his own potentials and achievements with those of others not in a spirit of negative and unhealthy competition but in truth and love. This amounts to the development of peace within oneself. Peace in the right sense is not a negative state of lack of conflicts and problems within oneself. Peace is a positive and dynamic state of integrating in the right manner the diverse elements, conflicts and problems in the personality and obtaining a holistic state of quiescence. In Gandhi's own words this becomes a successful search for truth: "A successful search for truth means a complete deliverance from the dual throng such as love and hate, happiness and misery."[16] It is not the cancellation of diverse elements but the harmony and integration of these elements that constitute peace in the individual as part of the development of his personality.

Education aims at promoting peace in the nation. Development of attitudes of peace in the individual leads to collective endeavors for peace in the nation. This has dimensions. On the one hand education ensures that the individual grows up in full awareness of the significance of peace at the national level, and on the other hand education attempts to direct this individual awareness to actual peace at the national level. Through the right orientations of educational content and methods and through the provision of learning experiences the awareness and a feeling of urgency for peace at the national level can be developed. Peace and tolerance go hand in hand. Peace can be regarded as the end and tolerance as the means and the method. Education should help students to price the value of peace and tolerance more than anything else.

Once Gandhi was asked by a student: "What can students do to create Hindu-Muslim unity?" Gandhi answered, "The way is simple. Even if all the Hindus turn out to be hooligans and begin insulting you, you should not stop considering them your brother is blood."[17] Gandhi had no excuse and compromise for the principle and his admonition took an absolute nature. That show the level of greatness and the depth of sincerity he attached to these principles. Gandhi made it clear that education has vital role to play in developing peace and tolerance in all the affairs of the country, especially at all the levels of decision-making. The process of developing an intense awareness of peace permeates all level and all aspects of education. It is not possible for education to have separate stream of 'peace education' long with other subjects and disciplines. But education should be in a clear position to integrate peace values with all other aspects of the curriculum.

Gandhi saw the evil practice of untouchability as a major obstacle to the practice and realization of peace and tolerance in the real sense of the words in several parts of India. Untouchability reigned supreme even in the days of Gandhi and he remained conscious in creating the necessary wave against these evil practices: "National schools should be capable of spreading the message of charka, unite the Hindus and the Muslim, educate the untouchables and thus remove from schools the curse of untouchability."[18] The practice of untouchability grieved Gandhi to the depth of his personality. Education is the only solution of this practice if it is still persisting in any form in any part of the country. Ways in which one community considers another as inferior is another form of untouchability and this practice comes directly opposed to the ideal of peace and tolerance. Obstacles of the ideal of peace and tolerance crop up in different ways. Very often people fail to recognize that such ways have anything to do with the maintenance of peace and tolerance. Education has the sacred duty to safeguard the values of peace and tolerance from all such lapses that may occur in the individual, society or nation.

Education aims further at international peace, and tolerance at the level of nations. The Gandhian message of peace has gathered significance more than ever on the face of the growing arms race between world powers. The modern world has the ever growing feeling that humanity is moving towards a nuclear end. The nuclear holocaust has to be averted. Gandhi's efforts for peace in the world can be regarded as the only solution to divert such a holocaust. Norman Thomas says, "If ever men achieve a world peace, to no single man will it owe a greater debt than to Mohandas K. Gandhi."[19] Gandhian education recognizes Gandhi's role in developing international peace and attempts to include the value of international peace and tolerance as an internal component of education. The very existence of the United Nations symbolizes international peace and promotes all international peace negotiations. Studies on the UN has been made a vital component of the school syllabus with a view to developing an awareness of the problem of international peace in students. Again, education can attempt to synthesize the Gandhian teachings on peace with the efforts of the UN to render the knowledge of the students and their attitudes more powerful.

Peace becomes part of personality development from all perspectives. Peace-attitudes are part of the individual's spiritual personality in his attempts to move towards Truth as the ultimate Goal. Education for Gandhi is "the all-round drawing out of the best in the child and man-body, mind and spirit."[20] This 'best' for Gandhi is in fact 'the inner voice of Truth.' The strengthening of this inner voice of truth, as all the Gandhi's personal experiments consisted of, is actually the strengthening of peace in all its different perspectives.

Gandhi says, "one person who can express ahimsa in live exercises a force superior to all force of brutality."[21] Peace in the individual becomes the expression of ahimsa as peace and ahimsa are inseparable. A character well founded on peace will exercise the attitudes of truth and ahimsa to other. Peace and tolerance provide a link between personalities of individuals within a given social set-up. Peace at the individual level would thus become the flowering or blossoming of the personality. Based on this Gandhi tells students, "If your education is substantial, then it should permeate to the neighborhood and exercise its influence."[22] The odour of peace in the individual cannot help permeating to outside the individual and exercise the right influence.

Education for peace and tolerance receives high priority in a world that is facing serious nuclear threat. Educational goals in all their diversities have a dimension of peace with reference to the individual, society and nation at large. These goals require a coordination to bring home the full importance of peace and tolerance. Peace is a value that should achieve integration with other values in education. Peace is an attitude that requires development along with other important attitudes to produce holistic personality. Peace becomes a principle that is capable of providing the necessary directions in the individual's attitudes towards himself, society and the nation. Education and Gandhism becomes a harmonious whole at the level of peace.

The concept of peace is also part of the content of science education. Science aims not at the destruction of mankind nor dose it orient itself to purpose of violence. It is a fact that the world has been employing the inventions and discoveries of science and technology for purpose of war and destruction. It may also be said that most intense research into certain areas of science took place during the World Wars as well as it takes place as part of the arms-race by world power. All the same no genuine scientist orients his genius for war and destruction. Science education has great scope for developing in the students great convictions regarding the peaceful applications of science and technology. These convictions are based on the fact that science and technology fundamentally aim at the progress of humanity and the strengthening of civilization as well as making this world a better place for man to live in.

Peace becomes a content of social science and culture studies. The teaching of social science at the school level naturally indulges the way India from time immemorial symbolized peace. The background of Hinduism, Buddhism and Jainism and all the religious innovations and movements emphasized peace as a principal value to be cherished on this land. The very social structure of this country is based not on rivalry but on peaceful co-existence as compared to the social structure of the West. Peace has been the most cherished value of several kings and emperors who ruled over this great land. The great principle of dharma or righteousness that govern all socio-economic interactions of traditional India is centered on peace and tolerance. Education through social sciences constitutes, thus, one of the most potent means of inculcating and developing in students a love of peace and tolerance. This value can be perpetuated in them through the variety of learning experiences that can be generated in the framework of such studies.

Peace becomes the content of Gandhian education more than in any other aspect. Gandhi's orientations is education have been fashioned after developing everything that would help the realization of a whole set of related values, attitudes and perspectives. Peace is fundamental to these orientations. Gandhi's thoughts and personality become synonymous with the ideals of peace. Teaching Gandhism in one way or other, developing Gandhian thought through educational experiences would all amount to dealing with the concept of peace and tolerance.

Educational for peace basically requires a development of the peace consciousness as a necessary atmosphere in academic institutions. This requires a general pattern or framework of learning experiences, work experiences and co-curricular and extra-curricular involvements for providing an ever greater and well-organized awareness of peace. Efforts can be made to keep outside the scope of the institution violence of any form. Gandhi says, "We have to make this training school (the Basic school) a school for winning freedom and for the solution of all our ills, of which the primary one is our communal troubles. And for this purpose we shall have to concentrate on non-violence..... All problems are, therefore, to be solved non-violently."[23]

Peace consciousness can be developed as part of peace education through the method of culture studies for tolerance: Instead of developing a communities and cultures, efforts can be made in education to promote peace-based culture studies. Considerable cultural interaction can be made possible at the level of education and promote better understanding between communities with diverse cultural experience. A sense of acceptance and appreciation of the culture concepts, cultural values and practice of other communities will make peace education a fruitful endeavor. As part of these culture studies tours and visits to culture centres, religious centres and functions of importance can be organized in such a way as to promote the value and urgency of peace and tolerance among communities based on Gandhian ideal. Inspite of ideological disagreements with the practice of other communities, students must have the necessary training to see things in a new perspective of peace and tolerance. It is most usual to be critical of other cultural practice only because these are just different and not opposed. Peace education enables us to overcome this tendency and see things in the new perspective.

Inter-religious experiences will constitute another method of promoting peace education. Gandhi says, "The communal unity is not confined to the Hindus and Muslims only, it extends to all, including the Englishman........ That is the message of non-violence."[24] Educational institutions will be able to provide students with religious experiences that belong to the different religions in our country. This effort must be based especially on those prayers, function and ceremonies that have a universal, human significance and can be easily acceptable to members of other communities. Exposure to such religious services will enable student to develop a clear sense of sympathy attraction as well as reverence for the religious viewpoint of other communities. These experiences can be chiefly in the form of simply prayer services and reading sessions based on scriptural texts that belong to the different religions. These sessions may be conducted by the staff and the students belonging to the school or by guest-participants who can be invited from the community. It is most important again that these experiences should develop the basic spirit in them rather than merely add an item to the already burdened syllabus.

Educational institutions may employ suitable methods of developing peace education which should be in total harmony with the working of the institution. In every subject, every material and in every activity we shall find a way of developing in students a deep awareness and sensibility of peace. Gandhi stood for total peace and tolerance: "The sun of ahimsa keeps away all the dark realities of hatred, envy and dislike. Ahimsa shines high up in the realm of education. No one can hide in like the sun."[25] Gandhian education is basically an education for peace and tolerance that would clear the way to truth and love. The aims, the principles, the concepts and the methods of education can be oriented to develop peace in the individual as well as in the Nation.

Notes and References

1. Einstain, Albert, In Norman Consist (ed.), p. 164.
2. Jones, Stanley, In Norman Consist (ed.), p. 132.
3. Marshall, Norman Consist (ed.), p. 96.
4. Gauba, K.L. The Assassinalim, p. 305.
5. Marshall, J.C. In profiles, p. 96.
6. *Harijan*, 10 Feb. 1940.
7. Wassen, Earl, In profiles, p. 216
8. *Harijan*, 3 February 1940
9. *Harijan*, 10 March, 1940
10. Toylar, E., In profiles, p. 72.
11. An Auto biography, p. 256.
12. *Ibid.* p. 382.
13. Macdonald, D., In profiles, p. 110.
14. King M.H., In profiles, p. 89.
15. An Auto biography, p. 136.
16. *Ibid.*, p. 261.
17. *Harijan*, 28 April 1946.
18. Towards New Education, p. 21.
19. Thomas, N., In profiles, p. 166.
20. *Harijan*, 14 July 1937.

21. Gandhi, M.K., In profiles, p. 45.
22. To the Students, p. 173.
23. *Mahatama*, Vol. 4, p. 96.
24. *Mahatama*, Vol. 7, p. 96.
25. To the Students, p. 146.

Challenges of Globalization and the Gandhian Alternatives

ARVIND ADITYARAJ

Mahatma Gandhi (1869-1948) was not a methodical philosopher but a man of action and a leader who commanded considerable influence over men. Like Buddha and Socrates, Gandhi stressed only certain basic values and did not systematically elaborate the essential philosophical postulations and the sociological, political and economic implications of his theories at an advanced intellectual level. However, he certainly had emphatically put forward certain fundamental ideas for the regeneration of man and the reconstruction of society and politics and in this sense he could be regarded as a moral, social, economic and political thinker. His greatness laid in his towering character, his political moral leadership, his inner intuitive experiences and his messages of truth and non-violence. He was also a prolific writer of force and power. His writings touched almost all the social, educational, cultural, economic and political problems of the contemporary world. Although not a system-builder in the academic sense of term, Gandhi had expressed many ideas, which are highly relevant to the modern age.

CONTEMPORARY WORLD SCENARIO

The fast emerging global socio-political and scientific sequence of events is a convincing reminder of the speed with which the forces released by science and technology and aided by human greed has dismantled almost at one stroke all humanity hitherto believed invincible. The socio-economic and political set-up all over the world has undergone tremendous changes during the last two decades and a new culture has taken over. Traditional values and concerns seem to have been replaced by a new set of attitudes and life style, which are steeped in materialism and consumerism and are propagated by the champions of unlimited material progress in an organized manner. All of a sudden, economics has overshadowed all other branches of human endeavour. The most frightening aspect of the whole development is that man is nowhere in the reckoning now and has been pitiably reduced to the status of a consumer. Human, ethical and moral values have been seized by those who believe that economic growth is the real index of power. While the power of money was never underestimated anywhere, never before in human history every thing is being measured in terms of per capita income and G.N.P. (gross national product) or the relative purchasing power or such other material considerations.

The rise in the materialistic and consumerist culture has led to the callous indifference shown to mother earth. There has been an over exploitation of nature as if there is inexhaustible wealth hidden beneath the surface. Environmental pollution has resulted in the rise in earth's temperature. The warnings and spirited campaigns undertaken by the various environmentalist groups to stop many of the harmful steps taken by the governments of affluent countries receive practically little attention. Hence, in a world increasingly enamoured with technology and conspicuous consumption on the one hand and giving into violence on the other, it is high time that the humanity should rediscover the Mahatma.

THE LEGACY OF MAHATMA GANDHI

Gandhi did not receive any formal training in economics, nor did he study much economics on his own. He had probably read Adam Smith's classic Wealth of Nations and he turned to the serious study of Karl Marx only in his 75th year. Since moral considerations weighed heavily with Gandhi in everything he did, his economic ideas were no exception. However, from his scattered writings and pronouncements a consistent body of knowledge in economics has been carved out which is named as "Gandhian Economics" and which has contemporary relevance, remarkable originality and the attributes of an analytical contribution of a high order.

It is widely accepted that the core of the legacy Gandhi left for humanity, is that he taught the world that truth is greater than all worldly possessions and that slavery, violence, injustice and disparities are inconsistent with truth. What Gandhi left is a carefully evolved vision of an organically sound and naturally supportive and respecting independent world order. The six decades of Gandhi's public life in six continents, spearheading various movements for a social and political environment, demonstrated with convincing sincerity a revolutionary zeal for change; change with consent; hitherto unexplored in national and international politics. Hence, Gandhi was totally against the usual violent methods associated with revolutions. He offered a package of alternatives to humanity. By his insistence on non-violence to violence, persuasion and reconciliation to end hostilities, trusteeship to end economic injustices, improvement of the lot of the depressed sections by abolishing factors that perpetrate social inequities, ending man's tyranny on nature by respecting nature as the protector of human race, limiting one's wants and developing equal respect for all religions, Gandhi offered humanity the blue print for a holistic vision. Gandhi convincingly demonstrated through ashram experiments the use of alternative sources of energy, appropriate technology, etc. In short, an ardent practitioner of truth that he was, Gandhi showed the humanity that there are workable alternatives which will be creative and sustainable. However, Gandhi on several occasion said that he was not trying to teach anything new. According to him truth and non-violence are as old as hill.

Gandhi warned against a series of social and political turmoil, ecological devastations and other human miseries that might arise unless modern civilization takes care of nature and man tries to live in harmony with nature and tries to reduce his wants. He cautioned in strong words that consumerist tendencies and callous indifference to values will not help humanity to progress towards peace. Hatred of all forms, exploitations of all types are actually negation of humanity's basic right to exist. The Gandhian legacy of simple living in conformity with the basic rhythm of life, typifies the age-old wisdom of humanity. Gandhi tries to convince humanity that war never solved any problem. Thus in Gandhi we have a world leader, who dreamt of a warless world and promoter of a social order, where exploitation and injustice will not become the dominant tendencies. While talking about the relevance of Gandhi, Martin Luther King Jr. (1929-1968) expressed his opinion in these words: "Gandhi was inevitable. If humanity is to progress, Gandhi is inescapable. He lived, thought and acted inspired by the vision of humanity evolving towards a world of peace and harmony. We may ignore Gandhi at our own risk."[1]

Mahatma Gandhi, as early as in 1908, in his landmark work Hind Swaraj pointed out that unprincipled growth will land humanity on the brink of disaster. The evil that we are to fight is within us and that we are ignorant of it is the basic problem. This can be possible only if we adopt a holistic vision of life and ensure equality and justice, which presupposes the simple truth that each individual is unique and we should respect his individuality and let him maintain his uniqueness and what applies to an individual, should apply to a nation or at a global level. He further wrote; "I must confess that I do not draw a sharp line or any distinction between economics and ethics. Economics that hurts the moral well being of an individual or a nation is immoral and therefore, sinful."[2] This indicates that "sustainable development", the buzzword among the environmentalists these days, requires both biological and cultural diversity, which in turn is inescapably linked to justice and compassion, towards each other and to the nature.

GANDHI ON CAPITALISM

Gandhi was never reconciled to the capitalist system of production and technological growth. He criticized the inequities of capitalism at a time when the capitalist economy had not yet become the dominant aspect of the total economy of India and that indicates his foresight.[3] The dominant factor for his opposition against capitalism was that it was based on the policy of exploitation of labourers. Gandhi regarded labour force as the most vital factor in the production. He in the 7 September 1947 edition of *Harijan* wrote; Labour is far superior to capital. Without labour, gold silver and copper were useless burden. It was labour which attracts precious ore from the bowels of the earth."[4] Besides, Gandhi saw in capitalism the evils of social polarization between two opposed social classes - the capitalists and the labourers. This results in strikes, lockouts, sabotage and hence there is a marked decline of social spirit. Gandhi felt that in his ideal state this social antagonism would be replaced by increasing co-operation and mutual reciprocity.[5]

Gandhi was a firm believer in the ideals of socialism, but was thoroughly opposed to socialism of Marxian type. Apart from the use of violence for the attainment of their goal, Gandhi was against the communistic notion of bringing all the means of production under public ownership. According to him by doing so, the socialists create enormous concentration of power and they have not evolved a satisfactory method of dealing with such situation. The theory of Trusteeship was Gandhi's answer to the problem on the one hand of concentration of wealth among the capitalist and on the other concentration of power in the state. In a nutshell, the theory of Trusteeship holds that all possessions including one's talent and mental excellence belong to the society and those who have these possessions should hold them in trust for society. His concept of Trusteeship is based on the Isha Upanishad, which asserts that God is the owner of the world and that we own nothing. In the words of Gandhi; "the rich man will be left in possession of his wealth, of which he will use what he reasonably requires for his personal needs and act as a trustee for the remainder to be used for society. In this argument, honesty on part of the trustee is assumed."[6]

GANDHI'S IDEA OF VILLAGE REPUBLIC *VIS-À-VIS* GLOBALIZATION

Globalization is an umbrella term for a complex process, which is systematically restructuring the interactive phases among nations by breaking down barriers in the area of culture, commerce, communication and several other fields of endevour.[7] The most likely fallout of this ongoing process of globalization is that its advantages move from top to bottom. As the real effects of economic globalization on any country's economy is yet to crystallize fully, on the basis of certain initial trends one can derive the conclusion that it may largely benefit the urban affluent and only marginally the rural or urban poor. But it may also happen that the benefits dry up before reaching the bottom. This is a universal phenomenon and no country is exception to it. This has led to a rise in the cases of poverty, hunger and unemployment throughout the globe. Besides the foregoing, ills of globalization include;

(a) Violation of human rights of the developing countries,
(b) In the name of bringing prosperity, resorting to plundering and profiteering,
(c) Going for cultural assimilation via cultural imperialism,
(d) Export of artificial wants, and
(e) Little care for nature, ecology and environment.

Mahatma Gandhi's economic thought is the polar opposite of what today's consumerist society stand for. The foundation of all his social and economic solutions was based on the concept of Sarvadaya, the welfare of all. Gandhi's philosophy is religious and spiritual, economic and political questions are seen from the moral and humanistic perspective. The welfare of the human beings and not of systems or institutions is the ultimate consideration. In fact, economics should not be separated from the deep spiritual foundations of life. This can be best achieved, according to Gandhi, when every individual is an integral part of the community; when the production of goods is on a small scale; when the economy is local; and when homemade (Swadeshi) handicrafts are given preference. These conditions are conducive to a holistic, spiritual, ecological and communitarian pattern of society.

THE GANDHIAN CONCEPT OF 'VILLAGE REPUBLIC'

As Gandhi was against the massive concentration of economic power among a handful of individuals, in his economic model he favours economic decentralization and hence villages become the basic economic units. His idea of Gram Swaraj (village self-rule) aims at developing villages in a manner which retains and strengthens those components of the village ethos, which deserve to be retained and strengthened. According to the idea of Gram Swaraj, each village should be basically self-reliant, making provisions for all the necessities of life- food, clothing, clean water, sanitation, housing, education and so on, including government and self-defence and all socially useful amenities required by a community. His vision of independent India was not that of a nation state, but a confederation of self-governing, self-reliant, self-employed people living in village communities, deriving their right livelihood from the products of their homesteads. Maximum economic and political power- including the power to decide what could be imported into or exported from the village would remain in the hands of the village assemblies.[8] According to the principle of swadeshi, as propounded by Gandhi, economic dependence on external market forces could make the village communities vulnerable. A village must build a strong economic base to satisfy most of its needs and all members of the village community should give priority to local goods and services. In other words, each village should be a microcosm of India a web of loosely interconnected communities.

Gandhi considered such villages so important that he thought they should be given the status of "Village Republics."[9]

Gandhi believed that the village community should embody the spirit of the home—an extension of the family rather than a collection of competing individuals. Gandhi's dream was not of personal self-sufficiency, not even family self-sufficiency, but the self-sufficiency of the village community. The British believed in centralized, industrialized and mechanized modes of production. Gandhi turned this principle on its head and envisioned a decentralized, homegrown, hand crafted mode of production. By adopting the principle of production by the masses, village communities would be able to restore dignity to the work done by hands. In Gandhi's words: "...not mass production but production by the masses."[10] In fact, mass production is only concerned with the product, whereas production by the masses is concerned with the product, the producers and the process.

GANDHI ON INDUSTRIALIZATION AND THE USE OF HEAVY MACHINERY

Global industrial society, as opposed to society made up of largely autonomous communities committed to the principle of "swadeshi", is unsustainable. Dr. E.F. Schumacher, author of the classic critique on modern economics, Small is Beautiful, who called Gandhi the greatest "People's Economist", says; "Gandhi abhorred the industrial civilization because it was based on callous exploitation of non-renewable resources. It made bodily welfare the sole object of life, which reduced man to nothing but a clever animal."[11] Gandhi's experiences in self-control and disinterestedness led him to pronounce: "Civilization consists not in the multiplication of wants but in the deliberate and voluntary reduction of wants." His alternative to the massive industrialization was the formation of village industries and crafts, primarily spinning and weaving of Khadi. Spinning would be a way of supplementing the meager income of a villager. It also gave self-determination to one of life's necessities—clothing. Today Khadi makes only one percent of the textile industry of India, it however employs nearly two million people.

The driving force behind mass production is the cult of the individual. In contrast, a locally based economy enhances community spirit, community relationships and community well being. Mass production leads people to leave their villages, their land, their crafts and their homesteads and go to work in the factories. Instead of dignified human beings and members of the self-respecting village communities, people become cogs in the machines, standing at the conveyor belt, living in the shanty towns and depending on the mercy of the bosses. Then fewer and fewer people are needed to work, because the industrialists want greater productivity. The masters of money economy want more and more efficient machines working faster and faster and the result would be that men and women would be thrown on the scrap heap of unemployment. Such a society generates rootless and jobless millions living as dependants of the state. On the other hand in the Gandhian idea of production by the masses, the machine would be subordinated to the worker; it would not be allowed to become the master, dictating the pace of human activity.

Gandhi's attitude towards machinery changed considerably with the passage of time. In 1908, he writes in his classic Hind Swaraj (Chapter XIX); "Machinery is the chief symbol of modern civilization, it represents a great sin. I cannot recall a single good point in connection with the machinery........It is necessary to realize that machinery is bad, we shall then be able to gradually do away with it." Increasingly he began to realize that it is not machinery as such that is evil but the social condition under which it is used. In the 12 February 1938 issue of *Harijan* he wrote; "If I could produce all my country's wants by means of 30000 people instead of 30 million? I should not mind it, provided that the 30 million are not rendered idle and unemployed." Gradually Gandhi began to see that under proper condition of social control, even large scale machinery could be used in such a way as to serve the villages and their crafts and not destroy them as they did in the past in the absence of social control. He wrote in the 27 January 1940 issue of *Harijan;* "I do visualize electricity, ship building, iron works, machine making and the like existing side by side with village handicrafts. Hitherto, industrialization has been so planned as to destroy the village crafts. In the state of future it will subserve the villages and their crafts.

The position that Gandhi came to hold on machinery was quite close that of Marx. In the absence of social control machinery causes unemployment and leads to exploitation of labour and the destruction of artisan. Hence, the indiscriminate proliferation of machinery is harmful, however, under proper social control; machinery could confer many benefits on society. In other words, instead of the use of the large scale technology in an arbitrary manner, Gandhi was in favour of large scale technology in few sectors co-existing with small scale technology and handicraft.

Gandhi knew that with the globalization of economy, every nation would wish to export more and import less to keep the balance of payment in its favour. As a result there would be perpetual economic crisis, perpetual unemployment and perpetually discontented, disgruntled human beings. In communities practicing swadeshi, economics would not dominate society. Beyond a certain limit, economic growth becomes detrimental to human well-being. Contrary to the modern world view that the more material goods you have, the better your life would be, Gandhi said: "A certain degree of physical comfort is necessary but above a certain level it becomes a hindrance instead of a help; therefore the ideal of creating an unlimited number of wants and satisfying them seems to be a delusion and a trap. The satisfaction of one's physical needs must come at a certain point to a dead stop before it degenerates into physical decadence."[12] Besides, in this age of globalization, the economists and industrialists fail to see when enough is enough. Even when countries reach a very high material standard of living, they are still caught up with the idea of economic growth. The global economy drives people towards high performance, high achievement and high ambition for materialistic success. This results in stress, loss of space for personal and family relationships and loss of spiritual life. Gandhi realized that in the past life in India was not only prosperous but also conducive to philosophical and spiritual development. Swadeshi for Gandhi was the spiritual imperative. In order to protect their economic interest, countries go to war—military war as well as economic war. There cannot be real peace in the world if countries would look at each other as sources of raw materials or as markets for finished industrial goods. The seeds of war are sown with economic greed. Throughout history one finds that the pursuit of economic expansion consistently leads to military adventures. In the words of Gandhi; "There is enough for everybody's need, but not for anybody's greed." Swadeshi is thus a prerequisite for peace.

CONCLUSION

Though set in the Indian socio-economic context, Gandhian philosophy is certainly considered as a universal and timeless philosophy. It is regarded that the ideals of truth and non-violence, which underpin the whole philosophy, are relevant to all mankind. It embodies numerous Western influences to which Gandhi was exposed at different points of time in his life. His philosophy upholds the ideal of a just and equitable society. His social order has been described as "communism minus violence." However, Marxists traditionally do not accept the Gandhian model because of what they regarded as his 'bourgeois' outlook. Gandhi rejected the Marxian concept of violent class conflict and regarded the centralization of political and economic power in the hands of the state as counter productive to the development of a non-violent society. Nevertheless, Gandhian philosophy, particularly the concept of Sarvodaya does contain many socialist sentiments. His thoughts have been likened also to the concepts of Utopian Socialism and Philosophical Anarchism.

In the fast emerging global scenario moral values, ethics, spirituality, family values, religious insights have all seemed to have lost their place and values. Ethics and morality appear to be out of tune with the ethos of the global village. Globalization has thrust to the forefront. Deterioration of the nation state, leading to global integration mostly on the strength of economic prosperity of the industrially rich and developed nations have led to a situation where vast iniquities that divided the small minority of haves from the huge majority of have-nots. The economic liberalization and the technological automation threaten to widen further the existing economic, social, political and cultural disparities. Global justice will be far cry unless bold initiatives are undertaken to overcome these disparities. Robert Hart in his famous essay Gandhi and the Greens: Road to Survival writes; "At the critical period in the history of the world, humanity's only ultimate hope for survival lies in the worldwide movement for grass root reconstruction on Gandhian lines."

Notes and References

1. Varughese, Suma, Looking for Gandhi: Life Positive, Available at http://:www.Lifepositive.com/Spirit/masters/mahatma-gandhi/gandhi.asp
2. Radhakrishnan, N., Gandhi in the Globalized Context: The Transnational Foundation for Peace and Future Research, Available at http://:www.transnational.org/forum/meet/2003/Radhakrishnan-Gandhi.html
3. Varma, V.P., Political Philosophy of Mahatma Gandhi and Sarvodaya (Patna: Bharati Bhawan), 1994, p. 109.
4. *Ibid.*, p. 110.
5. *Ibid.*
6. *Harijan*, 25 August 1940.
7. Globalization; Wikipedia the Free Encyclopedia, Available at http://www.en.wikipedia.org/wiki/globalization
8. Kumar, Satish, Gandhi's Swadeshi—The Economics of Permanence. Available at http://www.squal.net/caravan/icc-en/krrs-en/ghandi-econen.htm
9. *Ibid.*
10. *Ibid.*
11. Varughese, Suma, Looking for Gandhi: Life Positive, *op. cit.*
12. Kumar, Satish, Gandhi's Swadeshi—The Economics of Permanence Satish, *op. cit.*

The Gandhian Gospel and its Relevance to the 21st Century

GANESH PRASAD AND ANAND KUMAR

The present paper is an attempt to analyse the various facets of Gandhi's multidimensional personality, to cover his formative years; his struggle against racism and imperialism.. to discus his attitude to religion and the partition of India, to elaborate his public life and the relevance of his political and economic thought in the twenty-first century and to conclude that Mahatma Gandhi is the most influential Indian of the twentieth century whose shadow continues to loom large over the country even sixty years after his death. He struggled and dreamt of a India free not only from the yoke of the British rule but also free from the evils of poverty, illiteracy, untouchability with all its citizens enjoying equally the fruits of freedom and prosperity and the resurging popularity of 'Gandhigiri' is proof of Gandhi's continuing relevance in the twenty-first century.

Gandhi occupies a great place in the history of world. He is one of the most talked and most debated personalities and wields everlasting influence over the posterity. Gandhi is the least understood among the few great men that the world has produced.[1] Even those who claim to be his followers do not seem to have grasped the true meaning of his message. Since his martyrdom in 1948, a number of writers have written on Gandhi. Some of his close followers have described Gandhi essentially in terms of his emphasis on satya ahimas apariggraha and other moral principles which have been emphasised throughout history by all great men, and have, on that basis characterised him as a Saint. The essence of Gandhi his philosophy of technique of non-violent action that he evolved to very near perfection, or his thinking and place in contemporary political thought, particularly in terms of the thinking on development has continued to elude our grasp.

Gandhi symbolised a harmony between thought and action an almost flawless harmony, the depth of which it may be difficult to comprehend. He was not essentially a philosopher or a political thinker. He was a man of action who reacted with vigour to every critical situation of political, social, religious or cultural conflict tht he was faced with and tried to resolve it by truthful and non-violent means. The formulation of his thinking, prior and subsequent to action taken by him in a particular situation before him localised in time, space as well as in surroundings rather than an outcome of his philosophy, in the sense in which philosophy is a deliberately evolved system of thought it is this characteristic of redeting to a particular situation in a particular way and, naturally, each being a different. A situation, different kind of response which has introduced in his thinking and action and element of dynamism and, therefore, of unpredictability, with regard to the strategy that he would evolve in the context of the space and time and the specific situation which demanded it.[2]

Commenting on the methods and techinques of Gandhi, A.L. Basharn goes on to argue that Gandhi himself learned much from the West methods of civil disobedience and passive resistance from Thoreau, for instance, and the concepts of the dignity of labour and social reform as did Jawaharlal Nehru and other younger leaders in their attachment to socialism and large scale industrialization.[3] But there was also a deliberate turning back to the indigenous and the traditional. Gandhi advocated swadeshi ('one's own county'), by which he meant the use of indigenous and local institutions as well as Indian made goods'[4] and fostered the use of the traditional Indian spinning wheel, the charkha; he invoked Hindu and Jain concepts such as ahimsa (non-violence) and tapasya (self-inflicted suffering); and called for harted or the cessation of business activity, a traditional means of persuading the authorities to modify what the protesters regard as oppression.[5] Through his celibacy (brahmacharya) and asceticism Gandhi was invoking extraordinary, super physical powers in which tens of millions of his countrymen beleive deeply.[6] Much of Gandhi's success in attracting a vast following was due to his use of concepts such as moksha, symbols and parables drawn from the stories of Rania and Prahlada, of institutions (even the Muslim Khilafat), and of techniques like the hartal which were already part of the consciousness of various Indian groups.[7]

Analysing the basic tenets of Gandhian attitudes Louis Fischer says that Gandhi was guided by reason not as generally believed by emotions. He says, 'Mankind can not live by logic alone, but also needs poetry,' he once wrote. Gandhi frequently left the field of sensory perception and rational mental processes for that middle zone of faith, instinct, intuition and love, but he never wandered away from it into the refereed realm of mystic massages, miracles hallucinations, prophecy and other unaccountable manifestations of mind and body. "Whilst he did not rue out the athenticity of supra-sensuous phenomena", says one of his closest disciples, 'he very strongly disapproved of pursuing them.' He judged men and events by the criteria of cold fasts and invited others to judge him rationally. He did not wish to influence people by mystic radiation. His estimate of himself was practical success. He told Muriel Lester, an Englishwoman, that he never heard a voice, saw a vision, or had some recognized experience of God. No mystic experience has been vouchsafed to him. His guide was reason on the wing of faith.[8]

This exposition revals that Gandhi was never guided by emotions. His emotions were dominated by rationality and intellect. The fabric of Gandhian thought was woven, besides many other sources by Gita. M.V. Kamath says that for all that, Gandhi writes: "The Gita is not an aphoristic work; it is a great religious poem. The deeper you dive into it, the richer the meanings you get, it being meant for the people at large, there is pleasing repetition. With every age the important words will carry new and expanded meanings. But its central teaching will never vary. The seeker is at liberty to extract from this treasure any meaning he likes so as to enable him to enforce in his life the central teachings.[9]

Gandhi was a versatile personality. He was an embodiment of thougth and action blended as a whole. He was a seer and not devoid of practical notion of life. He tried his best to run the people of the country on the lines of righteousness and pity. He was radical in all spheres of life. Though writers and commentaters on Gandhism may or may not be convinced with this assertion. It is here congruous and relevent to discuss the role and performance of Gandhi during his struggle against the colonial rule in India. As we know "that Gandhi's struggle in South Africa prepared him for the future plans of liberating his mother land after returning home. He succeeded in doing the same.

Now it is proper to look into the universal teaching of Gandhi. Though Gandhi was like some other great persons, a child of his age but he perceived the future and tried his best to diagnose the malady of the Indian society of his time. Gandhi thought that it "was impossible for driving out the Britishers by violence from Indian soil because it was a gigantic force against which we could not use weapon and manpower. Gandhi was practical therefore he advised his people to adopt the technique of non-violence and satayagraha. Later on, these technique became universal all over the world. Gandhi thought about religion. His concept of religion was not as it is taught in the scriptures of any religions found in India. His teachings regarding the building of modern India were quite in consonance with the traditional wisdom and morality.

B.R. Nanda produces the whole picture of Gandhi's

personality and his influence on the posterity in the following terms. He says 'I am not built for academic writing', Gandhi wrote. 'action is my domain.' He was constantly trying to understand the world around him, but he was not content with interpreting it; he wanted to transform it. His 'mission' was to convert even Indian whether he is a Hindu, Muslim or any other, even Englishman, and finally the world to non-violence for regulating mutual relation. His ideas grew out of his experience: they were, as he was, went to say, experiments with truth: theory was usually the handmaiden of practice. When he spoke or wrote, he did not make a conscious effort to be consistent with what he has said earlier. Indeed, one can discern the evolution of some of his ideas; he was as he loved to put it, growing from 'truth to truth'. The vast corpus of Gandhian thought, recording as it does the day-to-day and indeed hour to hour response of the Mahatma to men and events over half-a-century, lacks the architectural symmetry of the philosophic edifices built in the privacy of the study by Marx, Weber, and Freud.[10]

B.R. Nanda again writes that Gandhi's ideas did not fit into neat categories was, not the only barrier between him and his contemporaries. To the British, indeed to most Europeans, he remained an enigma till the end, not only were they unable to appreciate the cultural context of his ideas, he touched them on a tender spot: their racial prejudice and the vested interests of the Empire. A few exceptional individuals, such as Romain Rolland, Albert Einstein, and C.F. Andrews, expressed their admiration of Gandhi but the common image of the Mahatam in Europe and America oscillated between that of a whimsical saint and a wily politican. Stanely Jones has recorded how in the 1930's Gandhi was a semi joke with the people of the West. An English Quaker; Johan S. Hoyland, rooted in 1931 that satyagraha was looked upon in the West as ridiculous and undignified. Working class audiences when told about it characterized it as "grown-up sulks." More educated audiences regard it with cold disfavour. It is took exotic, too unconventional, in a word, too Christian for us.

It was not only the British who were baffled by the Mahatmas ideas. J.B. Kripalani recalls that when Gandhi retuned from South Africa in 1915 he struck him 'rather as an ecentric specimen of an England returned educated Indian'. Of the Indian leaders of the time, none was closer to Gandhi than Gokhale, but even he laughed at many of the opinions experessed in Hind Swaraj and told Gandhi, 'After you have stayed in India your views will correct themselves.'[11]

Gandhi's philosophy of life is well explained in the words of Raghavan Iyer as follows: "It is only through daily moral choices and sagacious employment of limited resources in the social sphere that individuals sustain their inherited and acquired entitlements. For this very reason, the divisive and dangerous notion of exclusive ownership is systematically misleading and at worst, a specious and subtle form of violence. This engenders assertive rights or claims, and even privillged access, that far exceed the legitimate bounds of actual human need even though protected by statutory law or social custom. It also obscures the generous bounty of nature and the potential fecundity of human resourcefulness and innovations, which together can readily provide enough for all inhabitants of the globe, only each person would hold in trust whatever he has to meet his essential needs, without profligate excess or any form of exploitation. This is the basic presupposition behind Sarvodaya's, non-violent socialism, which is as old as the communal sharing taught by Buddha and Christ.[12]

That Gandhi was saint in the tradition of Nanak and Kabir, Chaitnaya and Tiruvallur, who worked unceasingly for human equality in their respective regions of activity through leading a life of devotion and continous preaching, and on a Fanzer scale, in the tradition of Buddha and Mahavira, Christ and Muhammad, whose meassage was for the whole of humanity cannot be doubted. But Gandhi was a politician also, a politician who commanded all the tactics and strategies that make a politician successful, though different in methods from those followed by most of the politicians. In Gandhi's personality there is a unique combination of the great heights to which saints as well as politicians can rise. Gandhi is one of the great saints that the world has produced because he knew the true meaning of religion and life. He is also one of the great politicians, because he knew the full meaning and significance of political power.[13]

THE PRINCIPAL IDEAS AND PRINCIPILES OF GANDHI

The ideas and theories of Gandhi that shook the world may be seen as follows:

1. Non-violence and Ahimsa

Gandhi was basically neither a politician nor a political thinker. He was a seeker after Truth and had developed the conviction early in life that truth could be reached only through Non-violence. Non-violence for Gandhi was linked up with Truth. Truth was the end. Non-violence was the means of reaching it. It was "not nerely a negative step of harmlessness" but "a positive step of love, of doing good even to the evil doer."

Indira Rothemlund writes that Gandhi had on abiding faith in the unfailing power of non-violence and the ultimate victory of truth. It is out of this faith that Gandhi evolved satagraha which continues to be relevant to this day. For instance, the achievements of the Polish Solidarity, though very limited, serve to revive our hopes in the efficacy of satyagraha movements in resisting authoritarianism while the potency of the Gandhian satyagraha is thus recognized, the stringent requirements of, or demands on, the satyagrahis are seldom appreciated. From what follows, it would seem that nothing short of a form of 'religious' or spiritual commitment on the part of the satayagrahis would suffice.[14] Gandhi was the greatest exponent of the doctrine of ahimsa or non-violence in modern times, but he was not its author. Ahimsa has been part of the Indian religious tradition for centuries: Hindu, Jain, and Buddhist, it was Gandhi's genius that transformed, what had been an individual ethic, into a tool of social and political action. This he did in the course of his twenty-year long struggle against racialism in South Africa.[15]

2. Satyagraha as a Political Method

Satyagraha (truthful action), Gandhi's enduring contribution to political thought and practice, is derived from the Vedic concept of binding truth. He used the word God as standing for Truth (satya). His concept of satyagraha emphasized not only satya but also the means of holdings on to it. In this he draws upon the entire Indian tradition, from the vow (vrata) as implied in the invocation of Rta of the Vedas to the Sat-Brahman of Vedanta, from the detached action of the Bhagavad Gita to the ahimsa of the Buddha.

In Gandhian thought and practice, religion and politics are inseparable. In Hind Swaraj, in reply to a question, he writes: "your argument tends to show that there must be complete divorce between politics and religion or spirituality. This is what we see in everyday life under modern conditions. Passive resistance seeks to rejoin politics and religion and to test any one of our sections in the light of ethical principles.[16]

In his Satyagraha in South Africa, Gandhi himself described the doctrine of satyagraha thus:

> "The worlds rests upon the bedrock of satya or truth, Asatya meaning untruth also means non-existent, and satya or truth also means that which is. If untruth does not so much as exist, its victory is out of the question. And truth being -that which is can never be destroyed. This is the doctrine of satyagraha in a nutshell."[17]

Can conflicts, individual, intergroup and international, be resolved through the power of love and truth, non-violently? This is the central question that has to be raised in an estimate of satyagraha as a political method. Satyagraha, as a science, is yet young according to Gandhi. He wrote: 'I have no set theory to go by'.[18] I have not worked out the science of Satyagraha in its entirety.[19] and Satyagraha, as conceived by me is a science in the making:[20] In other words, there are some lacunae in the theory, as will be seen below, nevertheless, as it is we shall be justified in thinking with Smuts that the principle of suffering to move the sympathy and gain the support of others for the cause one has at heart-where ordinary political methods of reasoning and persuasion fail is 'Gandhi's distinctive contribution to political method.'[21] This may be of two type, individual satyagraha and mass satyagraha.

In short, satyagraha itself assumes the character of a

vow. And it also assumes the character of ahimsa, since non-vioione was another pre-requisite: it commanded action. Since the 'karmoyoga' as recommended by the Bhagavad Gita was also a prerequisite. The Mahatma sums up these prerequisites by saying that satyagraha-leader must be a 'man of God who will compel reverence and love even of the opponent by the purity of his life, the utter selflessnes of his mission and the breadth of his outlooks.[22]

3. Gandhi's Notion of Religion

It is a curious paradox that though Gandhi's attitude to religion holds the key to the understanding of his life and though, its nuances and significance have often been by his admirers as well as his critics. That he should have been misunderstood deliberately misrepresented by his political opponents was only natural. Few British critics would have gone so far as Archbishop Cosmo Lang, who in a letter to Lord Irwin, described Gandhi as a mystic, fanatic and an anarchist'[23] Gandhi was a firm believer in the theory of religious tolerance. He said that there was no rivalry among religions. Gandhi's views on religion has been well summarised by A. Appadorai in following terms:

Gandhi is equally clear that religion cannot be divorced from politics: in his view those who say that religion has nothing to do with politics, do not know what religion means, Religion according to Gandhi, means 'the permanent element in human nature which counts no cost too great in order to find full expression and which leaves the soul—restless until it has found itself, known its Maker and appreciated the true correspondence between the Maker and itself'.[24] The separate religions—Hinduism, Islam, Christianity, Buddhism—are different roads converging to the same point. Even as a tree has a single trunk, but many branches and leaves, so there is one true and perfect religion, but it becomes many as it passes through the human medium. The Allah of the Moslems is the same as the God of the Christians and the Isvara of the Hindus. Living faith in this God means acceptance of the idea of a brotherhood of mankind. It also means equal respect for all religions. 'After long study and experience,' Gandhi says, 'I have come to the conclusion that (1) all religions are true; (2) all religions have some error in them.'[25] All faiths consititute a revelation of truth but all are imperfect and liable to error. Hence the necessity of tolerance which does not means indifference to one's own faith, but a more intelligent and purer love for it. Tolerance gives us spiritual insight, which is asfar from fanaticim as the north pole from the south. True knowledge of religion breaks down the barriers between faith and fiat. Gandhi comes to the conclusion that in reality there are as many religions as there are individuals, and, therefore, religion is essentially a personal matter and if we succeed in confining it to the personal plane, unnecessary conflicts would be avoided in our political life.[26]

4. Gandhi's Theory of Power

Power is generally associated with violence. Political power can be won through non-violent action—this was Gandhi's message for humanity. Gandhi was not a utopian. He did not reject political power nor did he, like the anarchists, try to abolish it. He could see that it was necessary to wield political power in order to counteract the political power of the adversary—which could be done only by bulding up countervailing political power the major difference between him and most of the other leaders being that he tried to cultivate political power through non-violent means. One might make a distinction between the two views regarding the basic nature of political power. On the one side there is what has been described the "monolith theory" of power which assumes that the power of a government is a relatively fixed quantum, a 'given', a strong, independent, durable, self-reinforcing, and self-perpetuating force. This theory leads to the view that power is based on violence and can be overthrown only by greater violence. This is taking a narrow view of power. On the other hand, there is view that government or any system for that matter, in order to be effetive has to depend on the peoples goodwill, decisions and support. Non-violent action, as Gene Sharp has pointed out is based on the second of these views: that governments depend on people, that power is pluralistic, and that political power is fragile because it depends on many groups for reinforcement of its power sources. Relying on destructive violence to control political power is regarded by theorists of non-violent action as being just as irrational as attempting to use a lid to control steam from acauldron, while allowing the fire under it to ablaze uncontrolled. Gandhi took this view of power—of power being rooted in society. He believed that the roots of political power reached beyond and below the formal structure of the State into the Society itself.[27]

5. Gandhi's Theory of Democracy

It is worth mentioning here for the purpose of understanding the Gandhian thought according to Ronald J. Tercheck democracy was instrumental to his larger goals of non-violence and freedom, and did not receive more attention in Gandhi's writings because he did not believe that political solutions could be understood apart from soical and economic relations. If the institutional foundations of society promoted inequalities, dependency and fear, political system would reflect these defects. The reason for this conclusion in Gandhi's works is not the Marxist rationale that the political system merely reflects the interests of the ruling class. The problem was more complicted for Gandhi, who was willing to acknowledge the potency of concentrated wealth but who insisted that economic inequality was not the sole or even the most important challenge to freedom. Modernization, stratification, industrialization, and urbanization presented obstacles to a sustained non-violent society where freedom was respected. And they could be important obstacles to the demorcatic prospect as well.[28] The early dynamic concept of democracy was replaced after the Second World War by static concept, as we find in the writings of Michel. Mannheim, Aron. Schumpeter and others, who seem to indentify democracy with elite rule sanctioned by periodical elections. Gandhi never regarded competitive political parties as necessary for democracy—he might even have regarded, as the sarvodaya thinkers be political parties as detrimental to the growth of democracy.[29]

6. Gandhi's Concept of Freedom and Responsibility

Gandhi's insistence that freedom and responsibility

linked is hard on narrow individualism: it acknowledges that freedom is essential but Gandhi then logically concludes that if we are free, we must account for our own action. Freedom without responsibility is a contradiction in terms for Gandhi. We may want to join the two together, but Gandhi condemns us to recognize the realities of freedom, that is, the responsibilities of freedom. Someone cannot be free from Gandhi's perspective, who does not, account for his actions or who dismisses unintended consequences. Gandhi's idea of freedom is well expressed in following terms of Ronald J. Terchek to talk about morally autonomous agents means we must talk about free agents. And this is what Gandhi pursued in his politics. 'No society.' He insisted, can possibly be build on the denial of individual freedom. It is contrary to the very nature of man. Just as man will not grow horns or a tail, so will he not exist as a man if he has no mind of his own. For Gandhi, free choice meant that men and women should not be constrained by physical coercion, economic power, government, or social position. But more than choice is involved with freedom: Gandhi continually connected duty with freedom and held that everyone was responsible for the choices he made.[30]

7. Gandhi and Political Theory

Even though not a political philosopher in the traditional sense of the term. Gandhi made a great contribution to political theory by evolving and suggesting the most effective means for bringing about the most effective change in the state and the society. Political theory, as Joan Bondurant has pointed out, is concerned both with the ends of political action and the means of achieving them. Traditional political thought, assuming a separation of ends and means has emphasized its major concern with the ends at the cost of means. The challenge of Gandhi's political thought centres upon the necessity of reconciling ends and means through a philosophy of action. The contribution, however, as Joan Bondurant points out, "has not been alone to the development of a social and political method. It extends further into the realm of political thought and challenges the substantial presuppositions of the mainstream of political theory."[31]

8. Gandhi on War

The motive power of Nazi and Fascist aggression was the desire to carve out new empires, and behind it all was a ruthless competition to annex new sources of raw materials and fresh markets. In Gandhi's opinion, wars were thus rooted in the overweening greed of men as also in the purblind tribalism that placed nationalism above humanity. In the ultimate analysis, to shake off militarism, it was necessary to end the competitive greed and fear and hatred which fed it.[32]

9. Gandhi on Untouchability

Gandhi's views on untouchability is very important. He believed in traditional system of stratification of society. Therefore, men standing on the lowest stratum of society were main concern of his thought because the prevailing system of untouchability was taken to be the cure of the Indian society. Gandhi's methods of uprooting untouchability were different than that of Dr. Ambedkar

10. Apart from the View Expressed above Gandhi Profounded many other Theories

His theory of trusteeship is much important because it devises a novel technique of econorm. Gandhi emphasised that the teeming millions of Indian society can have the bread and butter when they would be guided by the concept of trusteeship. Gandhi also advocated that industrialization is not the solution of the problem as obtained in India, hence the adaptation of small industries are the only solutions in increasing the economic status of the downtrodden people in India.

With due respect to the above exposition of the Gandhian gospel and teachings reveals that there are parochial and universal elements in his message. So long as the Gandhian relevance in 21th century is concern, the following points may be noted. They are:

1. After his death. Gandhi seemed to have had a somewhat better prospect of being understood when some of the barriers to understanding that

existed during his lifetime diasppeared. After the liquidation of colonialism, the life and thought of its principal antagonist could be seen in the West without imperialist blinkers. Besides, some of the complacency and even arrogance that unlimited vistas of progress inspired in the developed countries earlier during this century have begun to wear off. It is becoming increasingly clear that while science and technology have provided mankind tremendous service they are likely before long (to use the words of Andre Malraux) to present their bill, and the bill is going to be heavy. The looking of nuclar proliferation and ecological devastation have had a chastening effect. Grave social stress, the by-products of a runaway technology and unbridled economic growth, have caste a shadow on the long-term viability, and even wisdom of the western economic modle. In several Third World countries, even when vast scientific, industrial, and financial infrastructures have been built up and GDPs significantly increased, the great majority of the population has not been lifted out of the mire of poverty and still remains on the periphery of the processes of economic development.

2. Gandhi's views on industrialization came in for much criticism in his own time. He avowed opposite on not to machinery as such, but to the 'craze for machinery': but such qualifications do not alter the basic fact of his scepticism about the industrial civilization as it has evolved in Europe and American over the past two hundred years. Gandhi insisted that as the supreme consideration was man, 'the machine must not atrophied the limbs of man. The mad rush for wealth must cease and the labourer must be assured not only of a living wage, but a daily task that is not a mere drudgery.' When he referred to the possibilities of machinery—'mastering' or 'enslaving' man. Gandhi seemed to his

contemporaries guilty of indulging in hyperboles. However, we now know how real the dangers of runaway technology are. In his Technological Society, Jacques Ellul launched a powerful onslaught on the domination of man by 'technique'. This onslaught was carried further by Herbert Marcuse in his One Dimensional Man, and by Jurgen Habermas in his Towards A Rational Society, who have shown how technique instead of being the slave has become the master of man. Because of the search for the most efficient way of optimizing some abstract utility or goal of the organization, there is an increasing reliance on 'systems' and hierarchical bodies with their prescribed outlines and features. The management of the industrial society thus becomes a 'system' that leaves little scope for choice and judgement of the individual and often excludes judgements about values because these values cannot be verified by appeal to experimental data, it is this 'manipulation' of man in the industrialized society that alarms thinking of men and women. As Ivan IIlich points out in his Tools for Conviviality the hypothesis of the makers of the industrial revolution was that machines can replace slaves, but 'the evidence show that used for this purpose, machines enslave men'.

3. Gandhi had the prescience to see that in the relationship between was likely to loose; that what he really needed was tools to work, rather than tools to work for him. 'Pandit Nehru wants industrialiation'. Gandhi told an Amercan businessman in 1940, 'because he thinks that if it is socialized, it would be free from the evils of capitalism. My own view is that the evils are inherent in industrialism, and no amount of socialization can eradicate them.' The tremendous growth of technology since Gandhi's time has revealed that large-scale industrialization has inevitable concomitant: the alienation of man

which is not essentially related to the nature of political system. A recent writer has indeed suggested that Karl Marx may have been aiming at the wrong target; at capitalism rather than large-scale organization of industry.

4. The intractability of the socio-economic problems in the developing countries, and the emergence of new tensions and dangers in the affluent. West are inducing a mood of introspection and sending thoughtful men back to Gandhi. This process of reappraisal was perhaps best epitomized in the case of Aldous Huxley. In Jesting Pilate, Huxley wrote that to 'one fresh from India and Indian spirituality Ford seemed a greater man than the Buddha. At about the same time, in a letter to his brother, Julian Huxley, he ridiculed Gandhi as one 'who plays he ascetic with his loin cloth'. In Do What You Will (1936) he criticized Gandhi's advocacy of a rural economy based on handicrafts and argued that it would amount to a 'massacre', as the rising population could be fed and clothed only by large-scale industrialization.
5. Ten years later, the wheel had come full circle. In Science, Liberty and Peace (1945) Huxley argued that the record of Gandhi's achievements was not irrelevant to the historical and psychological situation of the industrial West'. He echoed Gandhian doubts on industrialism, which made life fundamentally unliveable for all and suggested that scientists should work on small-scale machinery, cooperatives, and natural sources of energy like the sun and the wind. In one of his novels Huxley spoke through one of the concrete and cosmic facts of real people and the inner light.' Then finally, in the 'Gandhi Memorial Peace Number' of Visva-Bharati Quarterly, October 1949 Huxley wrote: 'Gandhi's social and economic ideas are based upon a realistic appraisal of man's nature and the nature of his position in the universe. He knew, on the one hand, that he

cumulative triumpha of advancing organization and progressive technology cannot alter the basic fact that man is an animal of no great size, and in most cases of very modest abilities. On the other hand, he knew that these physical and intellectual limitations are compatible with a practically infinite capacity for spiritual progress. For this amphibious being on the borderline between the animal and the spiritual, what sort of social, political, and economic arangements are the most appropriate. To this question Gandhi gave simple and eminently sensible answers. Men, he said, should do their actual living and working in communities of a size commensurate with their bodily and moral stature; communities small enough to permit of genuine self-government and the assumption of personal responsibilities, federated into large units in such a way that the temptation to abuse great power should not arise. The lager a democracy grows, the less real becomes the rule of the people and the smaller is the say of individuals and localized groups in deciding their destinies.[33]

6. Given the circumstances, one wonders whether, if there was no Gandhi in the first quarter of the 20th century, there would have been need to invent one. What is true and has seldom been contradicted is that the times proclaim the man. In 1940, Britain needed Winston Churchill, not Neville Chamberlain. In 1920, India needed Winston Churchill, not Neville Chamberlain. In 1920, India needed someone other than Bal Gangadhar Tilak (who was by then dead anyway) and that was Gandhi. Given India's long and painful history, would anybody, apart from a Gandhian, have been able to successfully combat the British?

Many questions remain unanswered. Could Gandhi have internalized his quest after the Supreme and led the

Congress in secular terms? Then he would not have been a Gandhi. Could he have staunch to his quest but remained outside politics like a latter day Sala Tukarama or Kabir? Then India would have been berefit of a leader. Has Gandhi been really instrumental in changing Indian society. Indian society would have changed even without a Gandhi because of the onset of technology and globalisation. All these issues may be highly debatabel but what connot be denied is the impact that Gandhi has had on people all over the world and the legacy he has left behind. It is a validation of Gandhi's philosophy, that across the world social activists and leaders have chosen to follow his prinicple of militant non-violence. Martin Luther King Jr. was greatly influenced by Gandhi's ideology of non-violent social protest. The Dalai Lama has acknowledged the inspiration he has received from Gandhi's teachings. Nelson Mandela and Aung San Suu Kyi have fought oppressive regimes drawing upon Gandhi's legacy.[34]

Lastly Einstein said that in so far as he succeed in keeping himself from the shackles of selfish desire, it is......akin to that which possessed the religious geniuses of all ages'. Among these geniuses, Einstein included Gandhi. He believed that the moral qualities of its leading personalities 'are perhaps of even purely intellectual accomplishment'. His tribute to Gandhi paid sixty-two years ago in 1939 can scarcely be improved upon:

> A leader of his people unsupported by any outward authority: a politician whose success rests not upon craft nor the mastery of technical devices. but simply on the convincing power of his personality: a victorious fighter who has always scorned the use of force and inflexible consistency, who has devoted all his strength to the uplifting of his people and the betterment of their lot: a man who had confronted the brutality of Europe with the dignity of the simple human being and thus all times risen superior.

Generations to come, it may be, will scarce believe that such a one as this ever in flesh and blood aiked upon this earth.[35]

Lastly it may be submitted with respet that Gandhi exerted farmiciable influence and everlasting impact on the succeeding generations. After his death also in his life time a voluminuos literature was produced on him. He was variously interpreted. Much debate was made around his concept of religion and his theory of non-violence. It will be concluded that Gandhi's great achievement was to evolve and practise a non-violent method for conflict-resolution at the beginning of the twentieth century which proved to be the most violent century in the annals of mankind. In the first half of the century, which almost synchronized with Gandhi's entire public life, there were two devastating world wars with a colossal loss of life. In the second half we were spared of the catastrophe of a third world war, but the 'cold war' between two rival ideological-cum-military blocs brought the world to the verge of an atomic holocaust: only a 'balance of terror' between them kept the peace. However, their rivalry led to localized conflicts, instigated or fanned by the Superpower, largely in Third World countries. In 1995, the then United Nations estimated that between 1945 and 1994 there had been 127 conflicts with 22 million casualties in comparison to 88 conflicts during the first half of the century. Gandhi offered a non-violent alternative to this recurring cycle of hatred and violene. Beginning his public life in the hostile environment of South Africa, he discovered that in an imperfect and changing world, conflicts of interest within and between countries were inevitable. His technique of satyagrah sought reconciliation through dialogue and compromise, but if justice was denied, it provided for a confrontation, but it had to be a non-violent confrontation. Webster's Third New International Dictonary aptly sums up this technique as one of achieving social and political reform by means of tolerance and active goodwill coupled with firmness in one's cause expressed through non-violence, passive resistance and non-co-operation.[36]

SUMMARY

The present paper is an attempt to analyse the various facets of Gandhi's multidimensional personality, to cover his formative years; his struggle against racisim and imperialism, to discuss his attitude to religion and the partition of India, to elaborate his public life and the relevance of his political and economic thought in the twenty-first century and to conclude that Mahama Gandhi is the most influential Indian of the twentieth fist century whose shadows continues to loom large over the country even sixty years after his death. He struggled and dreamt of a India free not only from the yoke of the Brtish rule but also free from the evils of poverty, illiteracy, untouchability with all its citizens enjoying equally the fruits of freedom and prosperity and the resurging popularity of 'Gandhigiri' is proof of Gandhi's continuing relevance in the twenty-first century.

Notes and Refeences

1. Sharp, Gene, Gandhi as a Political Strategist (Boston: Porter Sament Publishers, Inc.), p. xiv, cited in S.P. Verma, Modern Political Thinkers (New Delhi: Vikash Publishing House Pvt. Ltd.), 1996, pp. 365-66.
2. Bose, N.K., Studies in Gandhism (Calcutta: Indian Associated Publishing Co.), 1947, p. 366.
3. Basham, A.L. (ed.), The Illustrated Cultural History of India (Oxford: Orford University Press), 2007, p. 259.
4. See 'Swadeshi' (14 February 1916) in Speeches and Writings of Mahatma Gandhi (Madras: Natesan Publishers), 1933, pp. 336-44; also see *Young India*, 3 December 1919, p. 8.
5. Basham, A.L., "Traditional Influences on the Thought of Mahtma Gandhi", in R. Kumar (ed.), Essays on Gandhian Politcs: The Rowlatt Satyagraha of 1919 (Oford: Oxford Univesity Press), 1971, pp. 17-42; Bose, N.K., Studies in Gandhism, *op. cit.*
6. Basham, A.L., The Wonder that was India (London: Oxford University Press), 1956, pp. 244-46.
7. *Ibid.*, p. 260.
8. Fischer, Louis, The Life of Mahatma Gandhi (London: Harper Collins Publisher), 2008, p. 307.
9. Kammath, M.V., Gandhi a Spiritual Journey (Mumbai: Indus Source Books), 2007, p. 151.
10. Nanda, B.R., In Search of Gandhi: Essays and Reflections (New Delhi: Oxford University Press), 2007, p. 254.
11. *Ibid.*, pp. 254-55.
12. Iyer, Raghavan (ed.), The Essential Writings of Mahatmm Gandhi (New Delhi: Oxford University Press), 2005, p. 2.
13. Verma, V.P., Modern Political Thinkers, *op. cit.*, p. 368.

14. Rothermund, Indira, Gandhi's Satyagrah and Hindu Thought (Deutsch; Thomas Pantharn), Kenneth L. Deutsch (ed.), Political Thought in Modern India (New Delhi: Sage Publications), 1986, p. 297.
15. Nanda, B.R., In Search of Gandhi: Essays and Reflections, *op. cit.*, p. 247.
16. *Young India*, 3 September 1925, Also in The Collected Works of Mahatma Gandhi, Vol. 10, p. 248.
17. Banerjes, Surendranath, A Nation in Making: Being the Reminiscences of Fifty Years of Public Life (New Delhi: Oxford University Press), 1925, p. 285.
18. *Harijan*, 23 October 1937.
19. *Ibid.*, 24, September 1938.
20. *Ibid.*, 27 May 1939.
21. Radhakrishnan, S. (ed.), Mahatam Gandhi: Essays and Readings of His Life and Work (London. Allen and Unwin), 1949, p. 285.
22. Gandhi, M. K., Hindu Dharma (Ahmedabad: Navajivan Publishing House), 1950, p. 109.
23. Chatterjee, Maraaret, Gandhi's Religious Thought (London: Allen and Unwin), 1983, p. 90.
24. *Young India*, 12 May 1920.
25. Sabarmati, 1928, pp. 17-19 cited in Selections from Gandhi by N.K. Bose (Ahmedabad: Navajivan Publishing House), 1948, pp. 226-27.
26. Aradorai, A., Inian Political Thinking in the Twentieth Century. An Introductory Survey (New Delhi: South Asian Publishers), 1987, p. 152.
27. Verma, S.P., Modern Political Thinkers, *op. cit.*, pp. 369-70.
28. Terchek, Ronald J., Political Thought in Modern India (Deutsch: Thomas Panthan), 1986, p. 309.
29. Terchek, Ronald, J. (ed.), Gandhi and Democratic Theory (Deutsch: Thomas Panthan), 1986, p. 325.
30. *Ibid.*, p. 313.
31. Verma, S.P., Modern Political Thinkers, *op. cit.*, p. 383.
32. Nanda, B.R., In Search of Gandhi: Essays and Reflections, *op. cit.*, p. 248.
33. *Ibid.*, pp. 259-61.
34. Kammath, M.V., Gandhi a Spiritual Journey, *op. cit.*, pp. 194-95.
35. Nanda, B.R., In Search of Gandhi: Essays and Reflections, *op. cit.*, p. 26.
36. *Ibid.*, pp. 249-50.

Gandhi and Indian Nationalism

SANJEEV KUMAR

Born on 2 October 1869 at Porbandar in Gujarat, Mohandas Karamchand Gandhi was educated both in India and in the UK. What distinguished him from his fellow students was not his brilliance or studiousness but his truthfulness and a deep sense of rectitude. But what, in fact, changed his own fate, as well as the fate of Indian people, was his visit to South Africa, in 1893, to pursue a legal case on behalf of one of his clients. That was the time when racial discrimination against the Indian community, was at its worst. And the Indian community, comprising primarily indentured labour, low-grade servicemen and some businessmen, was hardly in a position even to raise their voice, not to talk of offering any resistance to it. In the course of his travel, Mohandas himself was subjected to racial discrimination but unlike other Indians he refused to pocket personal insults. Instead, he decided to resist it irrespective of its costs and consequences. He did not take it only as his personal insult, instead he interpreted it as a direct attack on the dignity of the entire Indian community. He organised the

Indian community and launched many struggles against racial discrimination. It was in the course of one of these struggles that he 'invented' and perfected the instrument satyagraha. Ultimately, on the face of a long drawn struggle, the African Government conceded some of the major Indian community demands.

The South African experience and his prolonged stay and struggle therein enriched his life in several ways. He had found a new weapon (satyagraha) to resist injustice both at the individual and societal level; learnt the art of leading a life of an exemplar; developed a unique capacity to feel the pulse of the people and prepare them for self-suffering and sacrifice. And he also developed a deeply held secular outlook despite being rooted in religious and spiritual experiences. With such a rich and varied experience, he was back to India in January 1915. On the advice of his political Guru, Gokhale, he spent a year travelling throughout India to familiarise himself with the people of India and their problems. He attended the Lucknow Congress (1916) but had hardly any big role to play there. Meanwhile, his name and reputation earned during his South African struggle had not gone unnoticed in the country. His speech at Banaras Hindu University in 1916,[1] in which he condemned the entire Indian elite including the Indian Princes for leading a life of ease and opulence when the people are being grinded in poverty, had reached every nook and corner of the country. Soon Gandhiji was invited to Champaran, Bihar, and he himself witnessed the conditions of peasants suffering at the hands of the Indigo planters of European origin. Having examined their problems, he launched a struggle which ultimately resulted in some relief for the Champaran peasantry. Subsequently, he led two more local struggles Kheda peasant satyagraha and Ahmedabad mill-worker's strike. In all these local struggles, he successfully demonstrated the efficacy and effectiveness of the weapon of satyagraha. This was followed by the Rowlatt Satyagraha in 1919, which was the first national struggle led by Gandhiji and that brought him at the national scene. He was greatly moved by the Jallianwala Bagh massacre and also by the genuine grievances of the Indian Muslims against the British, for their mishandling of the Turkish Caliph question. All these events provided the background to the launching of the Khilafat and Non-Co-operation Movements in 1920.[2]

Gandhi's recognition as a major political leader was not the result of a continuous accretion of power. His rise to influence was an erratic process, and he followed no predictable route to fame, as so many of his contemporaries had done through the law courts, legal and political associations and local administration. By early 1918 Gandhi had emerged from the comparative obscurity of his first years back in India by leading three local satyagrahas. These campaigns, though 'sub-political' by the standards of modern style Indian politics, gained him both a local following in his home territory of Gujarat and across the subcontinent in Bihar, and wide public esteem as a saintly worker and a humanitarian righter of 'wrongs'. Although these assets had political potential, none of the politicians considered that Gandhi was a serious contender for power in their world, and the debacle of the Rowlatt satyagraha seemed to confirm such an assessment of Gandhi. His first all India satyagraha came to nothing and its violent side effects were diametrically opposed to those the peace loving Mahatma had intended.

By the second half of 1918 his public repute was at such a low ebb as a result of this and of his recruiting campaigns that it appeared that in a few months his attempt at intervention in all India politics had squandered the capital accumulated through slow, constructive work in the localities. Yet the Rowlatt satyagraha, despite its failure, showed that the new leader with his simple technique of passive resistance and his rallying cry of a fight to the finish against 'wrongs' inflicted by the government, was capable of mobilizing wide sections of society who felt a variety of discontents often unrelated to the question at issue, though he could neither control those he roused nor channel the energy they generated. However, by the end of 1920 this erratic leader had regained his lost ground, declared himself a committed politician, captured control of the Congress and persuaded it as a body to adopt his plan of non-co-operation, in stark contradiction of its former policies.[3] Gandhi's dramatic assertion of dominance depended on his championship of the Khilafat and Punjab 'wrongs', which succeeded where his campaign against the Rowlatt 'wrong' had failed. It secured him an all India following and manoeuvred the politicians into a position of weakness which played into his hands.

A new leader was able to seize power because the bonds uniting the politicians were so weak and because their range of supporters was so limited. When the foundations of Gandhi's strength are analysed it becomes evident that he relied on people who were outside the political nation as it had existed in relation to Congress politics. The members of that nation were the western educated, largely from the three Presidencies which had earliest felt and responded to the educational and administrative penetration of the West, and had evolved a political style well suited to gaining the goals to which they aspired, namely place and influence in the administration, and equality of status and opportunity with their rulers whose educational equals they now were. Gandhi's supporters in Congress by contrast were men from areas such as Gujarat, U.P., Bihar and the Punjab, merchant groups and Muslims, all of whom had been rare participants in Congress affairs, either because they lacked the necessary skins or because they had ambitions which Congress politics could seldom satisfy and fears which Congressmen could not assuage. But Gandhi's campaigns had touched them all by 1920 and in him they thought they saw a leader who could voice their aspirations and remedy their grievances in a way the western educated had not done.

Such new support not only gave Gandhi votes in Congress: it also gave him leverage among the existing politicians who saw that he was a power to be reckoned with. They were themselves so divided by regional differences and personal rivalries that they could not close up their ranks against him; and enough of them judged that support for Gandhi was the most profitable option open to them to give him control over their main political institution. However, by early 1922 Gandhi had proved himself unable to control the new forces which had brought him to power. The new participants in politics, who had acted as subcontractors for Gandhian non-co-operation in their own areas and groups, pursued personal or sectional ends through his technique of satyagraha instead of following his central plan, and as non-co-operation disintegrated. Gandhi also lost the leverage he had acquired among the former political leaders. Only Goal saved him from a fall from power as ignominious as his rise to power had been startling.

The phenomenon of the philanthropist's emergence as a political leader forced contemporaries to wonder if Gandhi had changed radically, and the debate has continued since whether the great soul was transformed into a scheming wording, whether the Mahatma and the politician co-existed uneasily in the one man, or whether the religious devotee consciously used the weapons of this world in the pursuit of higher goals. Sir Harcourt Butler at the time, for example, took the simple way out and judged Gandhi to be a politician. "I am afraid that I cannot attribute any honest motive to that man. He is behind and above all a slim politician."[4] Lord Reading, on the other hand, thought he was 'a religious enthusiast' who was forced further and further along the slippery path of politics until there was a clash within him between the saint and the politician as his influence increased, as it undoubtedly did and very largely in consequence of what Indians regarded as his saintly character and life, he gradually found himself the leader of a political party ready, for a time at any rate, to follow him blindly ... his power grew, but equally he had to meet all the difficulties of a political combination ... I have always thought that he became more the politician than the holy man and in the former capacity had to say and do things which were not strictly compatible with the latter."[5]

Gandhi, however, saw no dichotomy in his life, nor any inconsistency between his old and new activities. Before 1919 he had been merely a peripheral participant in politics, venturing into that realm only when he felt he had to forward the causes which were his life's work the immediate service of his fellow men by righting 'wrongs' inflicted on them, and the wider service of his country by promoting his ideal of true Swaraj, when Hindus and Muslims, and high and low castes would live together in harmony, where the corruptions of modern civilization would have been purged out of society, and where the relationship of British and Indian would be one of partnership rather than subjection. From 1919 onwards the actions of the rulers and the attitudes of Indian politicians convinced him that part time political action combined with local, constructive work was not enough if he was to continue the service he had in mind. After the Rowlatt satyagraha he saw that power on an all India level might be within his reach and he consciously entered the ranks of the politicians, challenging them in their own citadel of Congress. His aims had not changed but the arena of his actions had broadened. Nor did Gandhi feel that he was a religious worker making temporary use of the weapons of the world. Satyagraha saved him from having to wrestle perpetually with the problem of reconciling the use of bad means for the attainment of good ends, because in it he believed he had found the perfect technique of conducting conflict. It was to him both means and end, because if properly followed it transformed its exponents into men capable of ruling themselves and searching for truth, without violating their opponents integrity by force of any kind. On the occasions when satyagrahis abandoned his ideas for violence he stopped his campaigns rather than permit in his name the use of methods which would vitiate the goal by corrupting the protagonists.

Gandhi deliberately set out to challenge the established politicians after 1919, but how far he consciously tapped new sources of strength in an attempt to oust them is a question almost impossible to answer. There is no evidence that Gandhi had in mind any plan for a political career: he was drawn into politics when his ideals demanded that he should pursue them in this arena of public life. Neither is there any proof that he consciously went out to groups and areas beyond the political nation in a considered campaign to undermine the existing leaders and build up support for himself. Rather, the accident of his birth in Gujarat, his experience in South Africa of working among low castes, traders and Muslims, and his belief, held since the first decade of the century, that ordinary Indians were being enslaved by modern civilization through the instrument of the raj and their compatriots educated in western style, trained him naturally to turn to people the politicians had left out of account.

It is tempting to argue from Gandhi's successful reliance on new participants in politics that his rise to power was accompanied by a total transformation of Indian politics. An investigation of non-co-operation shows far greater numbers than ever before participating in a political campaign, coming from areas and groups the older politicians had barely touched, and pursuing goals very different from those of the earlier politicians, because they were as relevant to the lives of the new political participants as council places and entry into the civil service were for the western educated. An analysis of Congress after the reform of its constitution in 1920 shows a similar 'transformation'. Membership figures soared, the organization was extended almost throughout British India to all the previously backward areas, the Muslims and Sikhs received places on the A.I.C.C. reflecting more accurately their proportion of the population.[6] However, the eruption of a new leader with his allies and his policies worked no permanent transformation in the structure and goals of Indian politics or of its participants. Gaol saved Gandhi's face but limited his room to manoeuvre and regain power, and late in 1925 the Secretary of State, Lord Birkenhead, was able to write, 'Poor Gandhi has indeed perished, as pathetic a figure with his spinning wheel as the last minstrel with his harp, and not able to secure so charming an audience!'[7] A section of the Congress reverted to the old tactic of council entry at the next election, and the number of Congress delegates declined sharply from 4,728 at the 1921 session to 3,848 in 1922, and 1,661 in 1923.[8] Moreover, after the collapse of non-co-operation and the abolition of the Khilafat in 1924 by the Turks themselves, the Hindu-Muslim alliance disintegrated, and Muslim attendance at Congress dropped. Within two years of Gandhi's imprisonment Congress members and their policies were reminiscent of the closed shop politics of the early Congress rather than the Gandhi dominated sessions of 1920 and 1921.

The net result of the political ebullitions of 1920-22 was not a radical restructuring of political life, the pursuit of totally new goals or the removal from political leadership of the western educated elite of the Presidencies. Much of the old structure, geared to the old goals, remained, because it was one real avenue to power in Indian public life. Many of the Presidency leaders retained their positions, because however much Gandhi denigrated the sources of their influence they were important men in public life and had never completely lost their grip in their home regions. The difference between politics before and after non-co-operation lay not in the transformation of the political nation in relation to nationalist politics, but in the extension of the groups which formed that nation and the reorganization of Congress to accommodate the new participants and their aspirations. The doors of modern politics were opened not to the 'masses' or even to all those who had participated in non-co-operation, but to the western educated of the once backward areas and to some vernacular literates from town and countryside who had acted as subcontractors for non-co-operation or found themselves on voters' lists for the first time in 1919, and saw in nationalist politics post-Montague and Chelmsford and post-Gandhi a means of forwarding and protecting their interests.

Such a conclusion is less dramatic than the assumption which has often been made that Gandhi's emergence as a leader was the dawn of an era of the mass politics of nationalism, as the Mahatma by his charismatic leadership harnessed the feeling of the masses to the political skill and ambition of the educated. Yet it is more realistic. This investigation of the nature of Gandhi's appeal and the extent to which charisma could elicit a political response, and of the sources and stability of Gandhi's political power, shows how difficult it was for Gandhi to make any direct political outreach to wide sections of Indian society. Public life was far more complicated than such an interpretation of the Mahatma's actions would suppose. The essence of politics was organization to exercise power in public life, and power in a diverse society such as India often involved the clash of interests. To expect even such a novel leader as Gandhi to be capable of a direct political appeal to the masses is to deny the complexities of public life and to forget the very real barriers which confined the actions of earlier politicians and convinced them that any extension of the range of their political allies was dangerous, if not impossible. Even Gandhi needed a powerful organization of his own, and failing that a strong network of subcontractors who would organize and control for him in the places where his personal writ did not run: when he had neither he was as powerless as they had been.[9]

A realistic assessment of Gandhi's role in politics must look behind the image of the Mahatma reaching out to the masses however satisfying that is to the nationalist hagiographer, for it does not do justice to the complexities of Indian society or consider the relationship of Gandhi's leadership to changes which were occurring independently of his actions. The evidence suggests that instead of working out from an assumption that participation in modern politics must of necessity spread to increasing numbers, or from the concept of Indian nationalism, and trying to trace a progression from elite to mass involvement in the nationalist movement in which Gandhi is the key figure, an understanding of what actually happened comes only from beginning at the grass roots, from investigating the component parts of Indian public life, the relationship of the parts with each other and Gandhi's place in those relationships.

The all India activities of those western educated Indians who formed the backbone of the early Congress and earned the name of nationalists were only one mode of political action in the subcontinent. The men who evolved such a political style did so because their education introduced them to examples of similar styles in the experience of the West and because it was able to win them many of the prizes they coveted. However, if politics in its wider sense is the aspiration to exercise power in the community and the development of techniques to achieve this end, it follows that different political modes were likely to emerge as men sought access to sources of power different from those the western style politicians aspired to control. Such different layers of political action were visible in India as people became aware that society was changing under the impact of British rule and as a result of growing contact with the West, though most of the resulting struggles for power were 'sub-political' by the standards of the nationalist politicians who specialized in the manoeuvres of councils, congresses, deputations and the press. The landholders, for example, played their type of politics through loyal collaboration with the raj combined with a customary manipulation of their tenants, while wealthy traders and urban magnates did likewise in the towns, securing the ear of the Collector while extending their influence through networks of patronage among client groups. At a lower level villagers played out their own struggles for power, using the weapons of caste, faction and village office. Such groups were outside the political nation in terms of nationalist politics and rare participants in Congress activities, because Congress was not an arena in which they could contend for the prizes which mattered to them.

Nationalist politics were only an elegant surface veneer, the most sophisticated political layer beneath which were a host of struggles for power, no less real to the contestants and no less political because the style of action evolved by western educated politicians was irrelevant to them. The educated politicians inhabited a limited political world, but they were safe within it provided it remained isolated from the struggles occurring simultaneously at other levels of public life. To reach out to those involved in other modes of politics was generally unnecessary and always difficult for them, because they had few pawns to offer which were relevant to those other political games. However, should their isolation end, through their own volition or because of external pressure, they risked an eruption of latent forces into their political calculations.

Gandhi's rise to power was made possible by events which put an end to the isolation between the different layers of politics. The war and its ramifications in public life produced a situation where various groups were no longer satisfied with the political made to which they had been accustomed, and developed aspirations which could only be fulfilled or grievances which could only be remedied by activity in other arenas of politics. One direct effect of the war was to push up prices and dislocate the economy in most parts of India, prompting cultivators, industrial workers and businessmen to seek new means of redress, and focusing the discontent of all groups on the raj, which attempted to mitigate economic hardship by imposing unpopular restrictions on traders and businessmen, yet proved singularly incapable of holding down the spiral of prices which hurt the bulk of the population. Because the war found Britain and Turkey on opposite sides it also disturbed a large number of Muslims and made them amenable to new forms of political agitation.

But the indirect effects of the European conflict on Indian public life were the most far reaching. By forcing the British into a tight corner where they sorely needed Indian collaborators if they were to hold their Empire the war was the occasion for a re-division of power in public life through constitutional reform. Once it became clear that considerable power was to be devolved to Indian hands through the Montague Chelmsford Reforms a multitude of groups who had seen little to be gained from participating in the politics of councils and congresses realized that the rewards and losses would be so great in that political arena that they could not afford to be left out. Landholders, businessmen, peasants, caste groups, religious leaders, all realized that modern style politics would impinge increasingly on their local positions as power was devolved, and that they would have to learn its ways if they were not to lose out to other groups of their fellow country men. The Reforms not only raised the stakes in nationalist politics: by extending the franchise they also gave leverage in such politics to once backward or uninterested people. The politicians in turn recognized that they would have to extend the range of their political allies if they were to retain power in the changing situation. Thus the war years saw the breakdown of many of the barriers between the different political arenas, making it both possible and profitable for previously latent groups to erupt into the old limited world of western style politics.

Gandhi was singularly well equipped to take advantage of such a situation of latency by his ideology, his simple and adaptable technique of satyagraha, by his experience of working with varied groups in South Africa, and, as a stranger to Indian politics, by his freedom from those ties with any one group or area which had tended to curb the activities of earlier leaders. The eruption of participants accustomed to lower layers of politics into the modern all India political arena was first visible when Montague toured India. It was strikingly clear when Gandhi temporarily changed the rules of the political game in that arena by introducing non-co-operation. People from once backward groups and areas seized on non-co-operation as a means of expressing their grievances and promoting their interests, and Gandhi rose to prominence as he played the role of mediator between the various levels of political aspiration and activity. In 1920-22 he did on an all India scale what he had done in Bihar and Gujarat in 1917 and 1918.

After March 1922 many of the new participants reverted to their former political modes. As prices dropped, as the Khilafat agitation died down, and as non-co-operation collapsed, their incentives and opportunities for new forms of political activity declined. The latent subsided into comparative quiescence, except for the few who were incorporated into the political nation. However, Gandhi by his temporary exploitation of latent forces in political life spelt out for himself and the other politicians a crucial problem which was raised by the devolution of power to Indian hands. The prospect of power was divisive in a plural society where there was no consensus about ultimate aims. Non-co-operation showed the dangers of clashes between conflicting aims when people outside the old political nation became aware of changes in the locus of power in the community and were given an opportunity to express their fears and ambitions.

The abandonment of non-co-operation and the partial return to old style politics shelved the problem temporarily, but as the British continued on the path of constitutional reform it became increasingly acute. Gandhi and the political leaders realized all too clearly that they could not just reach out to the masses with the gospel of nationalism and expect unconditional support any more than the earlier politicians could have done, because different groups interpreted the 'nation' in different ways or had other foci for their loyalty.

Congress leaders tried to make nationalism a unifying ideal, promising nearly all things to nearly all men when Swaraj was obtained, hoping thereby to bind together the diverse groups with their often conflicting interests which made up society in the subcontinent. To a certain extent they succeeded, but the partition of the country and the fissiparous tendencies which have plagued both India and Pakistan since independence demonstrated that their success was neither complete nor permanent.

Gandhiji's role in the freedom struggle, can be clearly understood under the following eight sub-headings:

(i) Unmasking of the ugly face of British imperialism;
(ii) Satyagraha as a new weapon for national struggle;
(iii) Secular foundation of Indian nationhood and Hindu-Muslim unity;
(iv) The Congress in a new avatar;
(v) Constructive work: a new dimension of revolution;
(vi) Work through legislatures and local self-government bodies;
(vii) A dream for a new India; and
(viii) A dream of new civilization.

UNMASKING OF THE UGLY FACE OF BRITISH IMPERIALISM

It is true that ever since its inception in 1885, the leaders of the Congress were engaged in the task of disrobing British imperialism to its nakedness. They attempted to pull down three pillars which held the edifice of the British rule in India: benevolence, rule of law and its invincibility. One of the basic justifications of the British rule in India was its supposed benevolent character as ordained by providence. The early nationalists like Dadabhai Naoroji, M.G. Ranade, R.C. Dutt and Gopal Krishna Gokhale were the first to refute this British claim. And they, through their writings and speeches, proved beyond any reasonable doubt that the British rule had brought nothing but misery and mass pauperisation in its trail. In the light of their exposure, the British rule looked more like a curse rather than a boon from the hands of Providence. It was another matter that the liberals did not translate their intellectual investigation into actual political demands. This was followed by the Extremist's bold tactics to expose the facade of the British rule being based on the pillar of the rule of law. Tilak, Aurobindo, Lala Lajpat Rai and Bipin Chandra Pal and other Extremist leaders, through their self-invited sufferings, exposed the brutal and lawless character of the British rule. Whenever these leaders were awarded long term imprisonment or were deported from the country, the illegal character of the British system stood exposed and self-condemned, making its claim of ruling India by law to appear as a sham. But, perhaps despite their best efforts, the Extremists could not take the battle of Swaraj to the court of the common people. The armed revolutionaries pulled down the third pillar of the British claim of their being invincible. A small band of armed revolutionaries challenged the mightiest Empire on earth, and through their death defying acts instilled a sense of deep fear among the British rulers, while injecting at the same time a sense of fearlessness among our own people. Thus, through their daring acts, they exposed the soft underbelly and the Achilles' heel of the British Empire. But their activities were confined to certain pockets of the country and there too only among a small section of the society. They could not establish live contacts with the larger masses.

Then came Mahatma Gandhi like a political hurricane and shook all the above mentioned three pillars of the British imperial rule to their foundation. During the period from 1919 to 1922, he thoroughly exposed the brutal, authoritarian nature of the British 'lawless laws'. What was more, he brought the masses along with him to see the ugly face of the British Empire. By all-round exposure of the British ugly face, he weakened the moral fiber of the British rule and limited its capacity, to a great extent, to indulge unashamedly in acts of oppression and suppression. That limitation of the British 'steel frame' and Gandhiji's utter defiance instilled a sense of fearlessness among our people. That was demonstrated by the fact that in every subsequent national movement more and more people participated making self-invited suffering and defiance as an order of the day. The benevolence, rule of law and invincibility, the three pillars of the British imperial rule, were shaken by Gandhiji to their foundation. Thus, he made the British rule appear both morally and materially untenable.

SATYAGRAHA AS A NEW WEAPON FOR THE NATIONAL STRUGGLE

As we know, in the pre-Gandhian era that there were three major schools of thought, each using its brand of armoury against the British. Law, popular pressure and guns were the three weapons being used by the Moderates, the Extremists and the armed revolutionaries respectively. By 1918-19, all three weapons used by different schools had lost their cutting edge. By the end of the war the revolutionary movement had been curbed, controlled and tamed by the strong armed tactics and use of brutal force by the British. The liberals were virtually in disarray and, in fact, lost all their sheen as they appeared as a willing partner in the implementation of half-hearted and half-baked measures of self-government, i.e. the Act of 1919. Tilak's Home Rule Movement had failed to take a popular form and was primarily confined to certain pockets of western India. By 1918-19, Annie Besant had started dragging her feet and was avoiding a head-on collision with the British. In brief, the country was groping for a new leader and new sudarshan chakra. What gave urgency to this national need was the national disillusionment caused by the inadequacies of the Act of 1919 and brutalities displayed by Rowlatt Act and subsequent Punjab happenings.

It was in such a situation that Gandhiji appeared on the national scene with his sudarshan chakra of satyagraha in his hands. Besides, he was no greenhorn political activist. He was an old warhorse with an experience of two decades of struggle in South Africa. Having invented, experimented and perfected his own sudarshan chakra of satyagraha he had the self-confidence of a master warrior of non-violent struggle. Thus, in the eyes of the people he entirely fitted the bill of a new saviour of the nation. For Gandhiji, satyagraha was based on truth and non-violence. It was much more than boycott or passive resistance. It was to posit soul force against the brute force. It was no weapon for the weak. It was a weapon of the strong, willing to undergo self-invited sufferings but not to accept any act of injustice. The underlying idea behind it was that one will resist every act of injustice, irrespective of cost and consequences (neither will we kill nor will we accept any act of injustice). The beauty of satyagraha is that it leaves behind no trail of bitterness and personal animosity, as it is based on the principle of 'resist the evil but not the evil doer'.[10] Thus, it uplifts all the parties involved in a disputation both morally and spiritually. It puts a limit on the ferocity of counter attack. If the other party crosses the Lakshman Rekha of oppression, it would fall in its own eyes. What is more, it can be used by the lowliest of the low and the weakest of the weak against the highest of the high and the mightiest of the mighty. Gandhiji used his sudarshan chakra of satyagraha in all national struggles as well as at the local level—at Champaran, Kheda, Ahmedabad, Bardoli and many other places. Gandhiji never considered satyagraha as a stale and stagnant concept: it was a dynamic and growing phenomenon ever acquiring new dimension and new meaning. Examine this: The same Gandhiji who withdrew the Non-Co-operation Movement on the issue of violence at Chauri Chaura refused to condemn people's violence during the 'Quit India Movement'. He even refused to censure Jayaprakash Narayan who was leading an underground movement, which went against the Gandhian principle of open defiance and resistance. It is this ever growing and ever dynamic aspect of satyagraha, which had made it so popular all over the world. It has remained as the brahmastra of all those who might be physically and materially weak but strong and invincible spiritually.

The point of no condemnation of people's violence during the Quit India Movement needs a little more elucidation. To that end, one can raise a number of direct questions. Was the Mahatma losing his faith in the efficacy of non-violence or was he willing to take to another path as a part of his apatdharma (contingency) and more than willing to deviate from his nityadharma of non-violence. The answer to these questions is an absolute negative. For him non-violence was a part of his being. On a personal level, there was no question of deviation from the path of non-violent resistance. It may be recalled that even while launching civil disobedience in 1930-32, he had made it clear that stray cases of violence would not make him withdraw the movement. That was truer of the Quit India Movement which was being launched in the nature of a people's rebellion, unlike the Non-Co-operation Movement which he withdrew after the Chauri Chaura incident. But, the Quit India Movement, was not to be the Congress-led movement, but a people's movement. He knew it more than anybody else that the entire population could not be made to develop absolute faith in non-violence. Hence, the only alternative was not to launch any movement till the entire population was trained in non-violent resistance. This was an impossible proposition. Besides, the prime aim of the Quit India Movement was nothing less than independence of the country. The same was made clear when he addressed the AICC meeting of 8 August 1942, which endorsed the Quit India Movement. Giving a clarion call to his countrymen he said: 'Every one of you from this moment consider yourself a free man or woman and act as if you are free. I am not going to be satisfied with anything short of complete freedom. We shall do or die. We shall free India or die in the attempt'.[11]

It is clear from the above statement that the nature, dimensions and the objective of the Quit India Movement radically differed from the earlier Gandhian movements. It was nothing less than a call total rebellion within the broad framework of non-violent resistance. Besides, the government unleashed tremendous violence against people who responded to this unprecedented challenge in whatever way they could. And that is why the Mahatma blamed the government and its 'leonine violence' for people's acts of resistance which might not be considered non-violent, which is why he refused to condemn the people and their leaders who took to violent resistance. He was so convinced of the Government's responsibility for unleashing violence during the Quit India Movement that when it came out with a pamphlet 'Congress responsibility for the disturbances during 1942-43', he challenged the Government to initiate trial of the detenus and produce evidence so that they could defend themselves and prove their innocence in the court of law. As an unimpeachable proof of his total faith in non-violence, he undertook a 21 day fast during February March 1943 to resist the false propaganda of the government that the Mahatma and his Congress had bid goodbye to the principle of non-violence during the Quit India Movement. The letter which he wrote to the Viceroy on the eve of his epic fast is worth quoting: "It (the fast) is on my part meant to be an appeal to the Highest Tribunal for justice which I have failed to secure from you. If I don't survive the ordeal I shall go to the judgement seat with the fullest faith in my innocence. Posterity will judge between you as, a representative of an all powerful government and me as a humble man who had tried to serve his country and humanity through it."[12]

It is clear from the above analysis that the Mahatma had not lost his faith in non-violence. Nor was he willing to take to other means as a part of his apatdharma. So convinced was he about the 'leonine violence' of the government that he refused to censure his compatriots for any deviation from the non-violent path as a response to 'leonine violence' of the government.

A question is often asked whether the weapon of satyagraha could be used against a more authoritarian and totalitarian regime like those of Hitler and Stalin. Admittedly, it would be much more difficult. But in our view if there is a group of determined satyagrahis, no power on earth, however brutal and inhuman it might be can withstand their moral onslaught on their unjust system. Thus satyagraha has the potential to be used in all conditions and all eventualities, the only precondition being a pure will and an iron determination to use it.

SECULAR FOUNDATION OF INDIAN NATIONHOOD AND HINDU-MUSLIM UNITY

The Indian Congress, from its very inception was committed to lay down a secular foundation for Indian nationhood. It tried to encompass and represent all communities in the country. In fact, no one raised any doubt against the secular credentials of the Moderates. Even Tilak, whose secular credentials were doubted primarily on account of his mass mobilisation techniques of Ganesh Puja, joined hands with Jinnah to sign the Lucknow Pact, which started a new era of Hindu-Muslim bonhomie.

Gandhiji took Hindu-Muslim unity to new heights. He had impeccable secular credentials since his South African days even though he always asserted that he was a Sanatani Hindu. In fact, his religious world view was that if one is rooted in his own religion, it provides a good base for respecting others' religion. After coming to India he virtually made Hindu-Muslim unity as one of the basic principles of his belief system. Thus, in his Ashram Bhajanawali he picked up relevant passages from scriptures of different religions, which used to be recited during his prayer meetings. When the Indian Muslims initiated the Khilafat Movement, he extended whole hearted support to their cause. Muslim leaders like Muhammad Ali and Shaukat Ali enthusiastically participated in the Non-Co-operation Movement launched by Gandhiji. For a while it seemed that a firm foundation for Hindu-Muslim unity had been laid down. But soon things took a new turn and communal riots started the country during 1923-24. Gandhiji made Herculean efforts through the All Parties Conference and the Nehru Report to find an amicable solution for the communal tangle. But ultimately nothing much came out of it. And Jinnah ended as a Muslim communal leader by presenting a 14 point package for the Muslim community. Gandhiji made another attempt at the Second Round Table Conference to thrash out a solution for the communal problem but he failed on account of the intransigence of the Muslim leadership. The poor performance of the Muslim League in 1937 and its failure to enter into a coalition government with the Congress, made Jinnah more intransigent, and in 1940 he ended by propounding the two-nation theory and demanding a separate homeland for the Muslims. Soon after his release from jail in May 1944, Gandhiji entered into a serious dialogue with Jinnah and even went to the extent of accepting the idea of Pakistan-based on Rajagopalachari's (CR) formula. But this was not acceptable to Jinnah and hence the talks ended in a fiasco.

The Cabinet Mission Plan tried to keep the country united but it ultimately collapsed on the issue of compulsory grouping of Provinces and the sovereignty of the Constituent Assembly. This plunged the country into the biggest communal carnage. Gandhiji rushed from one place to another, viz., Calcutta, Noakhali, Bihar, and Delhi in a singular effort to extinguish the fire of communal carnage. That was the highest water mark of his secular credentials. He was assassinated by a fanatic on the ground that he favoured Muslims. If secularism became one of the main pillars of the Indian constitution, Gandhiji's life and work was perhaps the greatest contributory factor to it. In brief, Mahatma Gandhi played a singular role in laying secular foundation of our country. He lived and died for it.

THE CONGRESS IN A NEW AVATAR

Gandhiji was aware that a re-organised and re-vitalised Congress was a precondition for launching the Non-Co-operation Movement on the national scale. He knew that the Congress since its inception had been what one of prominent leaders had called, a three day tamasha. As such it had hardly any organisation at the grass roots level and hence its capacity to mobilise the people for any struggle was limited. Hence at the Nagpur Congress held in 1920, Gandhiji proposed a number of changes in the Congress both at its ideological and organisational levels. The new objective of the Congress was 'the attainment of Swaraj by peaceful and legitimate means'.[13] Thus it underlined the inherent right of the people to agitate and even defy laws so long they could remain peaceful and would be willing to pay the price for defying the laws. But a much more important question was how to make the Congress a fighting organisation in the absence of which no programme, however radical it might be, could be implemented. On the initiative of Gandhiji, the Nagpur Congress made major changes in the structure and the nature of the Congress organisation. Some of these changes were as follows:

(i) The provincial Congress committees were to be

organised on a linguistic basis and not on the basis of British made Provinces, which more often than not, were conglomeration of a number of linguistic groups.

(ii) The total strength of membership of the All India Congress Committee was increased but a ceiling of 350 memberships was also imposed.

(iii) For a better deliberation of the issues, it was decided to hold the Subject Committee meeting two or three days before the general session. That would contribute towards a better decision-making process in the general session.

(iv) A Working Committee comprising 15 members including the president, secretary and treasurer was to be constituted, which would carry on the day to day work of the Congress. Besides, it would also ensure continuity of work.

(v) The Congress was to be organised from the grass roots level to the national level with regular active membership. To enable even the poorest of the poor to apply for the membership of the Congress, only a nominal fee of four 'annas' (a quarter of a rupee) was introduced.

All this resulted in the complete overhauling of the Congress organisation making it a fit and fighting organisation. Besides, the Congress was made a fully democratic organisation in which everyone had a right to present and press for his particular viewpoint. Mahatma Gandhi maintained a peculiar relationship with the Congress. On many occasions, particularly during the national struggle, he would get authorisation from the Congress to take all major decisions on his own. Even after, 1934, when he, on his own, ceased to be a Congressman, it was he who would decide about the timings as well as issues on which the national struggle would be fought. And for taking such decisions on his own, he primarily depended on his 'inner voice' rather than formal decisions of the organisation. But this was no authoritarianism as his 'inner voice' was not based on his whims and fancies but based on a well thought out strategy and real will of the people. As he had the uncanny knack of feeling the pulse of the people as well as the Congressmen spread all over the country, his decisions were never off the mark. Whether it was the Civil Disobedience Movement or the Quit India Movement, millions responded to his call and participated in his movements risking all that they had. It was his unique leadership quality which always held him in good stead making people repose their faith in him. Even those who differed with him could never challenge his integrity and sincerity. Another issue he tackled was that of finding the whole timers for the national work. The people who left schools, colleges, law courts and services became the mainstay of the national movement. Many of them did not care to earn their livelihood or raise a family. It is they who worked as the standing army of the national movement. In brief, we may say Mahatma Gandhi took the Congress to the grass roots level, revitalised it at every level, built up an army of whole time workers and imbued them with a deep sense of purpose and commitment to the national cause. By any standard, this was an unparalleled performance in historical terms.

CONSTRUCTIVE WORK: A NEW DIMENSION OF REVOLUTION

One of the basic problems of the Marxian revolutionary movement is how to bring about social change till the state power is captured by the working class. The Marxists have solved this problem by asserting that all reformist programmes are reactionary, as they divert the attention of the working class from the main task of smashing the bourgeois state and, thereby, capturing the state power. The basic weakness of the Marxist thinking is that all attention is focused on the institution of the state which, ultimately, results in the emergence of the totalitarian state. What is more, in the process the sinews of civil society are weakened, virtually giving the wielders of the state power total freedom to act as they wish. Gandhiji was sceptical of the institution of the state. For him, the state as by its very nature smacks of authoritarian violence posing a serious threat to the liberty of individuals. In fact, he stood for a weak state and strong civil society. In keeping with his basic principled stand, he assigned a big revolutionary role to the constructive programmes both in the pre-revolutionary and post-revolutionary period. In the wake of the withdrawal of the Non-Co-operation Movement, he came out with a string of constructive programmes: Khadi work, development of village industries, national education, the removal of the untouchability and Hindu-Muslim unity. Subsequently, he set-up a single purpose organisations like All India Spinner Association, Adimjati Sevak Sangh and *Harijan* Sevak Sangh and a host of other organisations. He also encouraged and helped in setting up of thousands of Ashrams largely manned by constructive workers. Gandhian constructive programmes played a crucial role in the national movement in several ways. In the first place, the string of constructive programmes extended support and succour to the thousands of freedom fighters, particularly when the national struggle was at its low ebb. In fact, during the pause, they were resting, recuperating and gathering strengths as well as establishing live contacts with the people through various programmes. Thus, constructive programmes were of great help in consolidating as well as expanding the national movement. Second, they provided hardcore cadres at the time of the national struggle. In any mass movement, the common masses come and fight for a while and then go back to look after their hearths and homes. Thus, the real strength of any mass movement is sustained by whole time workers. But that raises the question of their maintenance and new opportunities for continuous work. Mahatma Gandhi, through his constructive work related institutions and Ashrams, not only succeeded in raising a big army of workers but also trained them and made them real vanguards of the movement. Third, constructive programmes significantly contributed to uplift of the weaker sections of the society. In the process they strengthened the social fabric of civil society, while making solid contributions to social revolution.

WORK THROUGH LEGISLATURES AND LOCAL SELF-GOVERNMENT BODIES

Mahatma, Gandhi himself was no great admirer of legislative work. Hence, even after the withdrawal of the Non-Co-operation Movement, he insisted on the continued boycott of the legislative bodies. But soon after 1924-25 he accepted the initiative taken by C.R. Das and Motilal Nehru, who had earlier set-up the Swaraj Party. The Swaraj Party was permitted by the Congress to pursue their work in legislatures which, in turn, performed an outstanding work by making the dyarchy almost dysfunctional for a while. In fact, there was an inherent contradiction in the basic policy of the Swaraj Party. In their struggle with the 'no changers' who favoured the continued boycott of the legislature, the Swarajists did argue that their primary motivation for the Council's entry was to take the battle of Swaraj to the enemy's camp with the ultimate objective of wrecking the system from within. However, the lure of the office, ultimately, led to its split and decline. But, the credit goes to the leadership of Motilal Nehru that the Swarajists were back to openly join the battle of Swaraj under Gandhiji's leadership. Subsequently, the Congress itself with the blessings of the Mahatma, participated in the 1937 elections and even formed governments in a number of Provinces. But Congress, refused to be co opted by the establishment and, in fact, they their power position either to expose the iniquities and injustices inherent in the system or to extend help or relief to the people. But when the time for struggle came, those engaged in legislative work, without any hesitation, plunged into the movement putting their heart and soul in it even by sacrificing their ministerial positions. In fact, through their enhanced stature, acquired through their legislative work, they only drew more people to the movement but also forced the British to deal with them with greater respect, partly out of fear and partly out of genuine respect.

A DREAM FOR A NEW INDIA

In the pre-Gandhian era, there was not much clarity

about the kind of India our people would like to build up in the post-independence era. One of the major contributions of Mahatma Gandhi was that he had a vision and dream for a 'new' India. For him a radical social transformation leading to a revolutionary change in the status and living conditions of the Daridranarayan was to be a real touchstone for the India of his dream. He was firmly of the opinion that in such an India there would be no distinction of the rich and the poor, and the high and the low.[14] Besides, there would be no discrimination on the basis of caste, creed, religion, region and sex. It would be a society totally free from exploitation of man by man. He was so much committed to the principle of equality among men that he was totally opposed to any distinction between mental and physical work. In fact, he propounded his theory of bread labour which, in plain language meant that everybody, whatever may be his educational and professional qualifications, would have to put in some amount of physical labour to earn his bread. He stood for a self-sufficient village republic, looking after its needs to the maximum extent. Being a philosophical anarchist he favoured the concept of minimal state so that it did not infringe upon the liberty of the individual. He did not favour total abolition of the institution of private property, and, in fact, favoured a system of trusteeship in which the rich would retain their property but would look upon themselves as the trustees rather than the owners of these properties. He did not favour big machines, though he was not opposed to machines *per se*. In a word, India of Gandhiji's dream would be what he called Ram Rajya. As such, he stood for a millennial change. It is a different matter that independent India took a different road to development. But now sensitive people all over the world are rediscovering him and finding some of his ideas rather more relevant for the twenty-first century.

A DREAM OF A NEW CIVILISATION

In his Hind Swaraj and even in his subsequent writings Gandhiji was critical of the Western civilisation which he called 'Satanic'. For him vices like violence, exploitation, materialism, capitalism, inequality, ecological imbalances, racialism, consumerism and imperialism were inherent in the very nature of the Western civilisation.

After rejecting the modern civilisation he attempted to present an outline of a counter culture, which he called Ram Rajya. Ram Rajya is self-rule of an individual. For that, man has to reduce his needs to bare minimum. Many people have not fully grasped the deeper meaning of Ram Rajya as conceived and conceptualised by Gandhiji. For him, Ram Rajya was not the rule of any king. In fact, it has nothing to do with the state. For Gandhiji, Ram Rajya meant rule of Dharma, rule of justice. And above all it meant self-rule by an individual upon himself. For that man has to reduce his needs to the bare minimum. In fact, he never talked of Ram as an individual; for him Ram is a metaphor and an abstract concept, which stood for justice, equity, self-sacrifice, concern for others, etc. He always maintained that in every human heart both Ram and Ravana live.[15] Ravana stands for selfishness, subjugation of others, naked show of strength, grabbing worldly things to the maximum extent. On the other hand, Ram stands for selflessness, sacrifice, self-denial, self-rule and a deep sense of justice.

In spite of the clear enunciation of the secular nature of the concept of Ram Rajya by Gandhiji, it always remained an anathema, nay even a red rag, to the Muslim communalists. They deliberately gave it a Hindu connotation to beat Gandhiji with a communal stick. Even the fact of immense popularity of the Ramayana story among the Muslim masses of Indonesia did not deter them from imputing to it a communal tinge. For Gandhiji it was nothing but of good, just, and equitable rule. In other words, it was a real people's promise of justice for everybody.

Mahatma Gandhi made a number of contributions to the Indian struggle for independence. But there was no dearth of his critics even during the days of the freedom struggle. Though Hindu-Muslim unity ever remained as a basic article of his faith, yet he had his critics from both the sides of the line. According to Jinnah and the Muslim League he was an ardent Hindu and a thorough Congressman who wanted to dominate and subjugate the Indian Muslims. On the one hand Jinnah totally rejected Gandhij's secular credentials; on the other, Hindu fanatics attacked him for being pro Muslim and primarily responsible for promoting Muslim communalism in India. They even held him responsible for the partition of the country. In fact, one of the Hindu fanatics, Nathu Ram Godse, assassinated him on this very count. In our view, these biased attacks from both sides of the line, only prove his secular credentials. Jinnah divided the country because Gandhiji was nothing but a Hindu and Godse killed him because he favoured the Muslims. His impeccable secular record during 1946-47, his death defying courage to stand in the midst of the communal carnage without making any discrimination between Hindu and Muslim crowds is a living witness to the courage of his convictions nay, his undying faith. He lived and died communal amity.

A second line of attack comes from the Marxists. The nitty gritty of their criticism has been that Gandhiji had a class bias in favour of the rich and propertied classes. They further argued that his theory of trusteeship is nothing but a clever ploy to help the propertied classes. They also accuse him of being soft on British imperialism, always ready to compromise, including the last one for the independence of the country. They also attack some of his basic ideas like self-sufficient village, minimal state, theory of trusteeship, his concept of bread labour, etc., either as too idealistic or too backward looking. The Marxists including the Communist Party of Soviet Union and the Comintern revised their own assessments of Gandhiji several times. Not only that the Communist Party of India at times came to the fold of the national movement and at other times it drifted away from it. At times, they even openly opposed it, as in the case of the Quit India Movement. These inconsistent stands and their changing assessments of the Gandhiji led national movement took away much of the sting from their criticisms. Some of the problems which Gandhiji identified in the Marxist line of thought like the totalitarian nature of the state and total suppression of individual liberty, have been proved to the hilt by subsequent developments of the communist societies. Gandhiji's view that mere abolition of private property would not necessarily result in an exploitation free social order, has also been proved by historical developments.

The fact of the matter was that Gandhiji was leading a mass movement in which every section made its own contribution. As we have seen that Gandhiji wanted a millennial change a society free from vestiges of all forms of exploitation. And hence the Marxist attack on his class bias is off the mark. In his personality as well as in his ideas he had transcended all these limiting categories, of class, caste, region and religion. With the passage of time some of his ideas are appearing to be more and more relevant. To sum up, Gandhiji made seminal contributions not only to our freedom struggle but also to a new world civilisation.

Notes and References

1. Collected Works of Mahatma Gandhi (New Delhi: Publications Bureau, Ministry of Information and Broadcasting, Government of India), Vol. XIII, 1918, pp. 210-16 (hereinafter CWMG).
2. Sharma, Jai Narain, Power, Politics and Corruption: A Gandhian Solution (New Delhi: Deep and Deep), 2004, p. 12.
3. Brown, Judith, Gandhi's Rise to Power (Cambridge: Cambridge University Press), 1972, p. 353.
4. *Ibid.*, p. 354.
5. *Ibid.*
6. Krishna, Gopal, "The Development of Indian National Congress as a Mass Organisation 1918-1923", The Journal of Asian Studies, Vol. XXV, No. 3, 1966, pp. 413-30.
7. Hyde, H. Montgomery, Lord Reading: The Life of Rufus Isaacs (London: George Allen), 1967, p. 389.
8. Krishna, Gopal, "The Development of Indian National Congress as a Mass Organisation 1918-1923", *The Journal of Asian Studies, op. cit.*, p. 418.
9. Sharma, Jai Narain, Power, Politics and Corruption: A Gandhian Solution, *op. cit.*, p. 129.
10. *Young India*, 11-08-1920, pp. 3-4.
11. *CWMG*, Vol. LXXVI, 1942, pp. 391-2.
12. *Ibid.*, Vol. LXXVII, 1943, pp. 58-60.
13. Sitarammaya, History of the Indian National Congress (Bombay: Padma Publications Ltd.), Vol. I, 1947, pp. 50-56.
14. Sharma, Jai Narain, Alternative Economics (New Delhi: Deep and Deep), 2003, pp. 45-7.
15. *Harijan*, 23-06-1946, pp. 186-7.

Cesar Chavez: Mexican Gandhi

K.D. CHOPADE

INTRODUCTION

Cesar Chavez who is also known as a Mexican Gandhi. Being a Mexican and worked for the benefit of Mexican farm worker in Gandhian way he is called by his follower as Mexican Gandhi. He was leader of migrant farm workers in United States of America. Cesar has started his carrier as a farm worker. Farm workers migrated from Mexico or imported by labour contractor were suffering from lot of injustices about wages, working hours, inadequate residential facilities, etc. Due to lack of labour union, Growers were exploiting farm workers. Great Depression of 1929 aggravated difficulties of these workers. Being farm worker Cesar Chavez had first hand experience about all this exploitation. In 1935 US Government has passed the National labour Relation Act guaranteeing workers right of Organization and Collective bargaining right. This helped Cesar to start his Organizational activities. All these activities were based on Gandhian ways, i.e. Non-violence, strike, picketing, fast, etc. It adds the instances happened in 1965 which compel Cesar to start his movement. In which two instances are important, (1) President Kenedy's approval for civil rights to black and Dr. Martin Luther King's (Jr.) march to protest that states refusal to follow federal law, (2) President Johnson's growing commitment to Vietnam under cut his domestic reform.[1]

LIFE AND WORKS

Before going in details of Gandhian ways adopted by Cesar, it is interesting and important to know something about his life and mission. Cesar was born on 31st March 1927 in migrant Mexican farm worker family at Arizona state of USA. Cesar mother Juana Cesar taught him Morality, Non-violence, Truth and Humanism. His mother always told him that one has to struggle with difficulties to get better life. Man should not be afraid of struggling for aims and objectives. She herself studied Mahatma Gandhi and she was very much influenced by thoughts and working of Gandhi. Her ideas of non-violence were very strong and perfect. She explains if someone slap you, you should allow him to slap on the other side, suppose he is cruel enough he will slap on other side, but after other slap what is next ? that person will be automatically ashamed of his behaviour. Cesars mother and the personality of Dr. Martin Luther King (Jr.), who made Cesar the follower of Gandhian thought.

Cesar learned from the prescdents of Dr. Martin Luther King (Jr.) and Mahatma Gandhi. It should be no surprise to them that Cesars methods for creating mass movement on behalf of social justice resembled those of these two leaders more specifically Cesar was able to organize the farm worker and to bring other to support their cause through three mobilizing techniques used by Gandhi and King.

(1) The generation of pride in group identity
(2) The mobilization of religious freely on behalf of a policy
(3) Practice of Non-violence.[2]

Cesar entered in public and social life in June 1952.

Freed Ross recruited Cesar in to Soul Alinsy's Community Service Organization (CSO). Cesar holds house meetings and voter registration drives. In 1958 he was promoted as General Director of CSO. In Feb. 1960 he conducted first activity of Gandhian impact. He arranged 'Dharana' at Greensborough for protecthon of Civil Rights of the Workers. On 31.03.1962 Cesar started student Non-violence Coordination Committee. Cesar resigned from CSO on dispute over organization. 30 Sept. 1962 Cesar along with Dolores Hureta formed the National Farm Workers Association (NFWA). Eagle Flag and Slogan Si se puede (yes, we can) had been accepted. On 16.09.1965 on Mexican Independence day Cesar arrange first strike at Vineyard in deleno to protest against low wages. To draw attention towards deleno strike Cesar Chevaz led a march from beleno to State Capital Sacremento. Which took 25 days to cover 450 miles. In August 1966 Cesar went on fast for 13 days to pray for victory in the on going conflict for worker jurisdiction with the Teamster company. Again on 14 August 1968, he told his followers, he was going to fast until their commitment that they are not going to be commiting violence. Cesar went on fast for 25 days to draw attention to the grape strike. Senator Robort Kennedy's pursuaded him to broke fast, Dr. Martin Luther King (Jr.) also sent a telegram and congratulate him to brake the fast on 10th March 1969. Indocalixo march was conducted by Cesar to focus the attention of the people living nearby strike areas. To protest against law controlled farm workers rights of strike and Boycott, Cesar went on fast for 25 days in 11.05.1972. From 15.04.1973 Cesar started strike for labour working on Grape Vineyard and from 01.09.1973 Boycott movement was started at Gallo Vineyard. 22.02.1975 Gallo Boycott in energized with a march on Modesto City, this Boycott movement continued for 3 years. In 1984 Cesars UFW declared a new Boycott on grapes on July 1988 Cesar went on fast for 36 days to protest against use of pesticides on grapes. All his fasts after unnoticed, he never declared his fast in daily routine. After 3-4 days due to weakness his colleague knows that Cesar is obscene sent during fast. Cesar use to consume water only. He took a march from San Joaquin to Coachilla to protest against the low wages, to the farm workers. 23.04.1993 Cesar died. In 1994 US president Bill Clinton posthumanously awarded the presidential medal of freedom to Cesar.

POWER OF NON-VILENCE

In his life Cesar preferred Gandhian way for the movement organized by UFW. Strike, boycott, picketing, fast and march are observed by Cesar to justify the demands made by UFW for farm workers. Cesar described that "to us Boycott of grapes was the most near perfect of non-violent struggle because Non-violence also requires Man's involvement." The Boycott demonstrated to the whole country. The whole world, that people can do by non-violent action."[3] Further Cesar says that "non-violence is the abstract concept is a very difficult thing to comprehend or explain. I had read a lot, but all of it was in abstract." It is difficult to carry the message to people who are not involved in non-violence must be explained in context. People equate Non-violence with inaction with not doing anything and it's not that at all. It's exactly the opposite of it. But Gandhi never said "not to do any thing." Gandhi said exactly the opposite. He said "do something offer your life."[4]

Cesar largely influenced by Gandhi and his philosophy, he always thought about Non-violence in context of farm labour and UFW. Cesar clarified that by and large people oppose violence so when government or growers (farm owners) use violence against us, i.e. farm workers. We strategize around it.

We can respond non-violently because that swings people to our side that gives us our strength, therefore, the workers have to understand Non-violence. Cesar classified that Gandhi ones said he had rather have man be violent than be a coward. I agree if he is coward, then what good is he for any one? But it is our job to see that he is not a coward, that is really the beginning point of our training.[5]

Like Gandhi Cesar protested against violence when two workers were shot dead in August 1973 in the firing made for the protection of grower, at that time Cesar immediately called off the strike and called for Boycott. Cesar was also strong believer of non-violence. This organization (UFWA) is more nearly a cooperative that a Union and incorporates earlier ideas of 19th Century.

While helping farm labour in the struggle for civil rights Cesar carefully developed his ideas about strike. His ideas a 'Doul' strike were based on two basic principles "Non-violence and use of outside help. Realizing that out sides were more able and ready to stand out against pressures than local people." Cesar made full use of a wide range of civil rights and religious group. Like Gandhi, religion played an important role in Cesar's struggle. The symbolic invocation of the Virgin of Guadalupe (Mexican goddess) attracted Mexican American to the NWFA as well as there were common progress at the time Cesar on fast, labours use to attended these prayers along with their family members. Place of fast became a small village.

In Feb. 1968 Cesar embarked on what would turn out to be 25 days fast. He regards the fast as both an act of moral protest and an attempt to organize worker. Cesar explain that Non-violence extracts a very high price from one who practices it.

But once you are able to meet that demand then you can do most things provided you have a time. Gandhi showed how a whole nation could be liberated without army. This is the first time in the history of the world when a huge nation occupied for over a century, achieved independence by Non-violence. This speech delivered by Cesar at the conclusion of his 25 day fast. Concluding the speech Cesar said "Knowing of Gandhi admonition that fasting is the last resort in place of sword during a most critical time in our movement."

STRIKES AND FAST

Cesar known for strikes, he called, which create general awareness among the farm workers about their rights. Among these strikes Deleno Grape Strike (1965) is mot important. When California growers received temporary dispensation from labour department to harvest the grape crop to pay the 1.40 Dollar per hour. Meanwhile for same work Filipino worker received 1.25 Dollar per hour. Mexican American is getting 1.10 Dollar per hour. This discrimination in wages caused for the strike. After 10 days raise in wages and equal wages formula was accepted by grower and after that strike was called off.

But later grower refuse to pay new rates of wages. After general meeting on 16th September 1965 worker voted for strike and Deleno grape strike begins. Deleno grape strike covered 400 square miles area and involved thousands of workers. The tremendous job of organizing picket line to patrol the field fall to inexperienced farm workers and urban volunteers working side by side. Union started to convince workers to join strike. Union has observed that growers have hired police and police were ready to arrest union workers. In later days grower hired goons from cities, violence was a constant possibility, but Cesar avoid violence. After March to state capital Sacramento on 7th April 1966 strike ended successfully.

Second strike also shows Cesars love for Non-violence and his affection towards Gandhian philosophy. AT Giummara grower company site, as usual there had been violent incidents on the picket line. Several packing sheds of company had been burned down. Increasingly, Cesar felt that violence could end only in destruction of the strike. Once UFW was associated with violence. It would lose its public support. Cesar hit upon a ways of demonstrating his commitment to the principle of Non-Violence, a fast and he began his fast and told to the union members that he was going to fast until the members made up the mind, that they were not going to be commiting violence."[6] And ultimately members were ready to stop violence.

Fast which was point of discussion for long period was happened due to the organizational competition between Cesar's UFW and Teamster. Since 1972 Cesar started a campaign and by majority voting UFW got recognisation of the workers. But April 1973 growers from Coacholla and Dleno announced that they had signed contracts on the Teamster. Cesar immediately called for strike putting out most the UFW worker from the fields to intimidate the strike. The Teamster recruited goons and started threatening violence. On June 1973. Modesto-based Gollo Winery signed contract with Teamster. Cesar announced boycott of all Gallo Wines. Throughout June and July violence erupted in the strike area. Two of the members of UFW were killed by Teamster goon. Immediately Cesar called on all members to fast for 3 days. At this instance Cesar told that it must be a time to think again about violence and Non-violence.

In these three instances of strike apart from the capacity and ability Cesar had not committed any violence or provoke for violence. He prefers fasting and Non-Violence only.

On July 1968 at La Paz, Cesar started a fast to protest pesticides usage. Generally Cesar's fast is unnoticed to his members. Use of pesticide on grape is poisonous and he propagate the point and public supported Cesar which caused for nation-wide support to Cesar. On 22nd August, i.e. after 36 days he ended his fast. As an expression of support Jesse Jackson a Presidential candidate and actor Martin Sheen and Roast Blake, later fasted for 3 days to keep dive the chain of suffering.[7]

All these instances of strike Boycott, picketing and fast shows Cesars intensity and integrity towards rights of farm worker and Gandhian philosophy.

Notes and References

1. Richard Grisward and Richard Gracia, Cesar Chavez Triumph of Spirit.
2. *Ibid.*
3. Peter Skerry Mexican American The Ambivatent Ministry.
4. *Ibid.*
5. *Ibid.*
6. Michell E. Houle: Cesar Chevez.
7. Richard Grisward and Richard Gracia: Triumph of Sprit.

Significance of Non-Violence for Peace

RAM NARESH THAKUR AND SURENDRA ROY

India along with abroad is passing through all round unrest such as terrorism, the nuclear war, regional wars, etc. Due to above problems, India as well as the whole world has come in the state of fear and havoc, etc. creating turmoil in the world. It seems that the brutality has dominated over the humanity. Barbarian activities, malice sense, etc., have been inherited in the psyche of selfish persons that has created problems.

TERRORISM

Terrorists are creating different kinds of troubles to the already troubled world of today. They have violated every standard set forth by the system of global code of conducts in several areas. Many big and small terrorist oriented organizations are collaborating with different culprits (Miscreants, Criminals, Mafias, etc.) who work against the calin and peace of the countries and therefore against global peace in general. Several bomb blasts by the terrorists in every corner of the world have shaken the entire world. There are sundry examples of these misdeeds of terrorists before us whether the attack on Arnerican World Trade Centre or attack on the Indian Parliament, or bomb blasts in metro Railway in London. In India, Maoists, ULFA, Islamic Terrorists, etc. have killed thousands people so far. There are national and international unsocial elements behind these terrorist activities. It cannot be ignored that impotency and carelessness of central and provincial governments are also main causes of this problem.

TERRORISM IN INDIA

India has been suffering from terrorist episodes time and again which disturb the peace and development of the country. It has become the profession of some misguided youths of some countries. The solution is only the Gandhian way. Recently very strong bomb blast took place, in the Indian Ambassy in Afghanistan. Before it Govind Mandir of Jammu and Akshar Dham Mandir of Gujarat were adversely affected by these heinous crimes of terrorist attacks. Just now Bangaluru and Ahmedabad have been attacked by the terrorists. From 2005 to 2008 16 attacks of terrorist groups took place in India. In this period there became 68 blasts in which 557 persons were killed and 1,379 innocent persons were injured.

As United States says Iran, Bangladesh, Palestine, Sudan, Libya, North Korea, Cuba, Iraq, and Syria have frequently been supporting terrorism. For instance, since the year 1988 when the Pam Am 103 was bombed by Syria and the number of several hijackings took place, etc. In Dec. 1999, the hijacking of Indian Air lines' Airbus to Kandhar, Afghanistan from Kathmandu, Nepal airport had drawn the attention of the world.

The Nuclear War: During the last fifty years armed conflicts among the countries of the world have claimed appropriately twenty seven million lives. It is estimated that civilians represent eighty five percent of casualities, with a majority of being children and the elders.

Thousands of nuclear weapons have been produced so

Terrorist Attacks in India

(From 2005 to 2008)

Sl. No.	*Dates*	*Place*	*State*	*Blast*	*Killed*	*Injured*
			2005			
1.	28 July	Johnpur	U.P.	1	14	79
2.	29 Oct.	Delhi	Delhi	3	61	200
			2006			
3.	7 March	Varanasi	U.P.	3	20	100
4.	14 April	Delhi	Delhi	2	Nil	13
5.	8 Sept.	Mumbai	Maharastra	3	38	100
			2007			
6.	28 Feb.	Panipat	Haryana	2	68	125
7.	18 May	Hyderabed	Andhra Pradesh	1	16	50
8.	11 July	Mumbai	Maharastra	7	150	300
9.	25 Aug.	Hyderabad	Andhra Pradesh	2	42	50
10.	11 Oct.	Ajmer	Rajasthan	1	2	17
11.	15 Oct.	Ludhiana	Punjab	1	7	32
12.	19 Nov.	Civil Court	U.P.	6	13	40
			2008			
13.	1 Jan.	Rampur	U.P.	Nil	8	00
14.	13 May	Jaipur	Rajasthan	9	68	150
15.	25 July	Bangaluru	Karnataka	8	1	9
16.	26 July	Ahmedabad	Gujarat	19	49	114
		Total		68	557	1379

far and deployed all over the world. There are more than 2,200 such weapons, equal, to 5,000 Hiroshima available even after signing several arms control agreements. A technically well equipped nuclear missile called MX (Missile

Experimental) can reach any part of the world in less than 30 minutes and destroy completely 140 well developed cities like Tokyo, Washington, Moscow and London. There are almost hundred MX missiles with US. In addition, there are also air launchers, submarine launchers and ballistic missiles which are put in alert by nuclear countries such as Israel, North Korea, Argentine, and Brazil, etc. Those countries are having ambitious plans to produce and deploy such weapons in near future.

Therefore, of all the human challenges the threat of nuclear war has been one of the major and dangerous one that bothers the leaders of the world. Today the magnitude with which the nuclear weapons are made and deployed in and around the world is increasing, staggering and remaining as one of the biggest problems to be solved first in the present millennium. The world has witnessed, as noted various nuclear weapons deployed on the land, sea and in the outer space.

Third world countries like India, Israel, Pakistan, Argentine, Brazil, North Korea, Iran and Iraq are developing fast this missile technology. Some of them have world's involvement. The Americans are now, as they argue, planning to develop yet another system known as National Missile Defent (NMD) or Theatre Missile Defeno (TMD) in order to defend their nations and their friendly countries in case of missile attack launched by any country in the world.

Regional wars: Apart from the global war scenario the regional wars are also being considered as one of the biggest problems of mankind in the world. Many wars were fought in the world regions. Till the end of the cold war there were almost fourteen full scales wars and several major armed conflicts took place due to civil, economic and religious differences in the world, specially Europe, South America and Africa were the worst affected regions in this respect. For instance, in Africa alone 1.7 million people were killed because of regional wars. It is notable that such wars are also affecting the worst those countries like Sri Lanka which has been involved in war for the last seventeen years killing millions of people in the ethnic conflicts between Sinhlese and Tamil separatists.

As is the case with Angola where more than 5,00,000 people were killed, millions were displaced due to wars among people. In Algeria battle between Muslim fundamentalists and the government have killed millions of people. In Sudan, too, the civil war that began in the year 1956 taking the life of millions. Since 1984 war is going on in Turkey between government and Kurdish minority people killing thousands, people. Since 1989 Afghanistan, Colombia, Chechnya, Indonesia, Peru are the countries facing several wars with groups of people.

Several methods have been adopted to solve above terrorist activities and malicious conflicts but they have been proved in vain so far. Mahatma Gandhi, the father of the nation, had presented a method as peace oriented, non-violence before India as well as abroad. It is true that Mahatma Gandhi was not any psychologist or philosopher or expert. Reality is that he used to find out any fact relating to any problem particularly peace through non-violence from his realization.

The basis of Gandhism is non-violence only and Gandhi's life is dedicated for upholding Ahimsa, Every religion revolves around Ahimsa and it is the supreme religion, avoids bloodshed practically recognizing the right of life even for the animals adopt vegetarian food. The views of Gandhi on non-violence are all the more nearer to other philosophies such as Jainism and Buddhism. It is true that non-violence is an essential condition of human existence and basis of non-violence is mutual understanding and co-operation.

We should have firm belief in Gandhi's non-violence. Eminent Gandhians have been thinking for a long time to start Gandhi institutes to propagate Gandhi's ideology. We should not believe in propaganda as the world generally understood and held the view that the most effective method of the furtherance of a cause is living example provided by the purity and usefulness of the life of the devotees. Those of us, therefore, who want the Gandhian ideology to live and flourish must try to purify our lives and gain for our cause in the favour of men by giving them love and selfless service.

It is true that there is scope for those types of institutes, which are essential now. We are yet to bring with him and bequeathed to us. We are witness to its dynamic power exhibited in winning independence for us with the weapons of 'Ahimsa' without shedding a drop of blood. But the extension of the vital principle of 'Ahimsa' to the solution to the affairs of the world in general could not be taken in hand in his life time. He was waiting to see it fully established in his own country before it could be taken up out side. Had he lived up to the age of 125 years, as he used to say that he wanted to do, he would have had time to canalise world force for world peace, but that was not destined to be. He was snatched away from us very soon after the attainment of his immediate objective, the freedom of India. Unfortunately the last two years of his life were occupied in allaying the forces of evil, which had their full sway in our country in a manner unprecedented in history. This unexpected phenomenon in a country which took pride in the legacy of the great principles of peace and good-will inherited from time immemorial from great sages hurt him and his zest for living ceased to exist. He has gone but his mission is still with us, and it is for us to push it in such a way as to turn in into a world peace.

It is the duty of those of us who had privileged of close association with him and who knew him in the radiance of his life to gather all that he left scattered in such a way as to collect it for the guidance of the generation to come and the world out side. If this work of organization is not taken up immediately it will not be done at all, as the number of his close associates are doing fast. In a few years they will have passed away and no one will then be left to this significant work.

The Sarvodaya Samaj is already there. These institutes can serve as a wing of the Sarvodaya Samaj. Though these institutes, it is proposed particularly to approach the intellectuals and the leaders and through them to affect every aspect of national life with the colour of Gandhian thought. These institutes are expected to produce new literature, drama, music, paintings, dance and poetry saturated with the Gandhian ideology. It is proposed to start a college for the study of Gandhian thought and literature and to have chairs for the teaching of Gandhian thought in the Universities.

Gandhiji dreamt of creating a new world of love and peace, friendship and co-operation. He wanted to destroy forces of exploitation and his method of doing so was through moral forces and reformation of the individual. His all constructive works are directed to the end. Khadi and Charkha, Gram Udyog and *Harijan* Seva, all led to the same goal.

His last great conception of 'Nai Talim' was a masterstroke for the attainment of the same goal of revolutionizing society. He brought forward a scheme in which no distinction was made between the rich and the poor, the urban and the rural people. The children in early life had to be taken in hand and educated alike in the same way. They were taught to respect and love manual labour. This education was meant to prepare the new generation for the Ahimsic Samaj of his dreams. The work of Nai Talim is still in its inception the proposed institutes can produce the required literature for children for its advancement.

All the constructive workers know that just at present the country has gone down to low level of morality. Evils against which Gandhiji waged a war all his life are rampant, perhaps, in a greater measure than ever before, personal ambitions, nepotism, corruption, bribery, black marketing, pugree, etc. are today current coins.

A dynamic effort ought to be made to check this and if the proposed institutes are taken in the competent and influential hands, it is not any reason why these (institutes) should not succeed. After all communism, fascism and nazism could be made to live world forces in the course of one generation, there is no reason why if the same method of organization is adopted by us to canalize those forces of good which are latent in Gandhian philosophy, we do not succeed? We have the advantage that the principles and the ideology which we want to propagate are inherently good leading to Sarvodaya or the good of the whole people. We do not want to adopt means inconsistent with our ideology. Physical force may not be used, but co-ordination and organization consistent with our aims and objects is necessary and essential. The Sarvodaya Exhibition in Jaipur and the Gandhi Mandap Exhibition at Raj Ghat have shown what can be achieved through art, literature, picture, drarna and music.

There are such great personalities in India and abroad who have and had followed the Gandhian thoughts at national and global level. Vinoba Bhave was great follower of Gandhiji and latter has handed over the performance of Satyagrah to former. Later, Jai Praskash Narayana, Dr. Rajendra Prasad, Morarji Desai, Vallabh Bhai Patel, Pt. Jawahar Lal Nehru, Acharya Kriplani, Nirmala Desh Pandey and Rukmini Devi Arundel, etc. were the staunch followers of Gandhiji.

In addition to these personalities, Dr. Nelson Mandela, former President of South Africa who called as Gandhi of South Africa) made himself identified to be a true 'Satyagrahi' and got South Africa freed from White rule by dint of Gandhian non-violence (Ahimsa). Like Gandhi, Dr. Mandela identified his liberalism and greatness by forgetting prejudices towards white people whose rule had kept him in jail for 28 years. Yet, the white people were included too in the government of Dr. Mandela and P.K. Botha (White origin) became Vice president of South Africa. In the same way Martin Luther King (Junior) (of black origin) of U.S.A. was a staunch supporter of Gandhiji's non-violence and sacrificed his life on the alter of ahimsa like Gandhiji. The manner in which the Greens particularly in Germany adopted Gandhian techniques to arouse human consciousness and how they operationalized their strategy and the bold assertions made by Petra Kelly about the way they were influenced by Gandhi. Abdul Gaffar Khan (Frontier Gandhi) was also the devotee of Gandhi. He adopted Gandhian weapons like satyagraha throughout his life in his country (Pakistan). Wan Shan Suki is in Jail in Myamar struggling on the principle of satyagraha adopted by Gandhi.

Although Gandhiji's non-violence for bringing out peace in India and abroad has been overlooking by Indians and foreigners. But it realized that there is no alternative to Gandhian way at global level. From the local level to international one, non-violence is the only method to resolve the disputes and conflicts fully within the principle of non-violence. It, therefore, is essential for every one to contribute to world peace and non-violence.

Gandhi wanted to see every country to be organised in

accordance with the spirit of non-violence. It is vital to remember that Gandhi is still India and there is no future for us apart from the vision and values he has bequeathed. We have a hopeful feeling that the Gandhian ideal is global and the Gandhian process is pragmatic. In the eyes of India, Gandhi is above all else a rebel saint whose mystic voice foretells a free and creative universal order. His life, his martyrdom, his message, his word significance will for centuries become the themes of Gandhian scholarship. The very secret of the philosophy of Gandhi is its cosmic essence and pattern. The ruling idea in India today is fundamentally Gandhian but there is no corresponding deepening of moral and social discipline. This chasm between thought and action is edging Gandhism away from the stream of our historical life.

India has produced great thinkers, social leaders and social reformers who, by their revolutionary and path breaking thoughts and actions, have left a lasting impact on not only India, but in the abroad as a whole. They have developed indigenous ideas and have provided natural and ethical identity to India. There is a great need to acquaint the people, youths, women, teachers, students and different sections of society with their thinking and their work. In the present era we owe our duty to the nation to know and analyse the thoughts, which are pertinent and apply to their ideas in the construction of human society on moral, ethical and spiritual foundations for a non-violent society. In accordance with his rational approach to life Buddha emphasized on the age old concepts for the formation of an equalitarian society. Mahatma Gandhi gave a social dimension to the 'concept of non-violence' and demonstrated, both through his life and work, how it can be used as an instrument for fighting injustice at all levels. Our nation is known for the doctrines of 'truth' (Satya) and 'non-violence' (Ahimsa) in the world only due to Gandhi. Nehru, a great deal to the application of 'non-violence' for resolving conflicts at the national, and more so at the international level, as well as modernization of society with emphasis on science and rationality. Baba Saheb Ambedkar stressed on the empowerment of the oppressed as a means of their release from explosion and injustice, which are social forms of violence against oppressed. The idea of all those thinkers have a frame work of interrelated views which are mutually supportive to each other and yield profound insights into the conditions of the individual, his/her personal being, in socio-economic and political life.

Not only Budha, Gandhi, Ambedkar and Nehru, but there remained many great men and thinkers who contributed for the society as well as sacrificed their all on the alter of nation as Bhagat Singh, Raj Guru, Sukhdev, Chandreashekhar Azad, Netaji, Subhash Chandra Bose, Pandit Madan Mohan Malviya, Rahul Sankrityayan, Swami Sahajanand Sarswati, Dr. Radha Krishnan, Dr. Rajendra Prasad, Dr. Zakir Hussian, Swami Ram Krishna Paramahans, Swami Vivekanand, Raja Ram Mohan Roy, Swami Daya Nand Saraswati, Pandit Ishwar Chandra Vidya Sagar, Rabindra Nath Tagore, Shri Aurobindo, Sardar Vallabh Bhai Patel, Acharya Narendra Dev, Dr. Ram Manohar Lohia and others. It becomes essential to understand and disseminate the concepts relating to those philosophers and fundamental thinkers and the philosophies enunciated by them, related to social justice and equity, conflict resolution, non-violence and non-violent protest movements, empowerment of women, rural development and related ideas for the upliftment of the society. Mahatma Gandhi was a great philosopher, thinker and journalist. Gandhi made us emancipated from fear.

The masses cannot find their ideal outside the historical traditions. The martyrdom of Gandhi has given a jolt to their mind and they have begun to rethink their purposes. The crisis makes new outlook, new man. But contemporary speculative thought after widest roaming adopts the same idiom and pattern of Gandhi. The impulse of the Mahatma is not yet spent and the confection of his thought is rich with plums.

It must be admitted that we would be knocking beauty out of this concept if we fail to transvaluate it. For, as a nation evolves in its thought, its key concepts should also be given new meanings and aromas. Gandhism can absorb and surpass the sensations of the time. It is realistic, natural, evolving, free from cloudy jargon and shines the better for redefinition. Its pattern is ever on the loom and its texture is rich and stretches itself for greatness. The Indian grace and sense, its soul history and aspiration are symbolized in the evocative word.

Through the mists of the Gandhian dawn have hopped through scores of men of ascetic endeavour. Among them are seen intellectual swordsmen too. To gratify a more psychological age they should doubt their faith with a strong colour. Without injuring the delicate temperament and the classic fullness and purity of the Mahatma, his disciples should continue their quest under a new mental placard: neo-Gandhism.

We can through the heart of world's mystery when we are moved by the genuine literature of the Gandhian mood. Then we should shed out caste robes, turn power into service and face the ceaseless challenge of the enslaving lures. Unfortunately, Gandhism has attracted into its orbit many political advententures who lead a strange double life of ethical emotionalism and parasitic function. It is such types that stand between the soul of a free India and its programmed for the future.

Our struggle was started by Gandhi as peace, non-violence and other campaigns. He began struggle of independence. But that struggle is not over up to now. It will continue till the last person of the society is not fed and quenched his thirst. The corruption is great challenge for our system now. The cancer of corruption must be extinguished from the development and democracy. Let us think for millions of persons living below poverty line! Let us do something for down trodden people of nation!

By all means we can say that the study of peace and non-violence of Mahatma Gandhi is more relevant than other principles or theories in this environment of global unrest, i.e. terrorism, war, corruption, communal rift and for choosing the proper path for economic development of India. Use of power force and legal actions taken by the government are not proving adequate energy and power to end these evils. By those means both evil and evil doers will be ended. Here evils have to be abolished but not evil doers. In this case the peace and non-violence of Mahatma Gandhi only remain as final alternatives to abolish above evils all over the globe and, nothing else.

It will be advantage to study the ideas or these personalities as interrelated studies. Besides these centres, centres for comparative studies also had been established and should be opened for the study of specific areas of a thinker such as Netaji Subhash Chandra Bose, Pandit Madan Mohan Malviya, Dr. Radhakrishnan, Dr. Zakir Hussain, Swami Vivekananda, Rabindra Nath Tagore, Sri Aurobindo and Sardar vallabh Bhai Patel, etc.

References

Moorthy, P., "Value Crisis and the Way Out for World Peace", Journal of Gandhian Studies, 2003.

Kumar, Ravindra, Theory and Practice of Gandhian Non-violence (New Delhi: Mittal Publication), 2002, p. 177.

Nehru Rameshuri, Forward for 'Gandhism Will Survive', by U.G Krishnamurti, Pushtak Bhandar, Patna, 1949, pp. I-IV.

Murti, U.G. Krishna, Gandhism Will Survive (Patna: The Gandhi Institute, Pushtak Bhandar), pp. 24 32.

Kachru, J.L., Gandhi, Tagore, J.L. Nehru, Contribution and Thought (New Delhi: Book Hive Publication), 1982, pp. 41-44.

Chandra, Bipin, India's Struggle for Independence (1857-1947) (New Delhi: Penguin Books), 1988, pp. 172-78.

Roy, Surendra, 'The Half Clad Fakir Who Forced the British to Quit,' 'The Indian Nation', Patna, Oct. 2, 1999.

Grover, B.L., Modern Indian History (From 1707 to the Present Day) (New Delhi: S. Chand & Company Ltd.), 1993, p. 24

Maiduli, Ram Dayal, Bapu Ne Kaha Tha (New Delhi: Publication Division, Ministry of Information and Broadcasting, Government of India), 1991.

Jain, V., M.K. Gandhi, Leader of the Masses (New Delhi: Radha Publication), 2004.

Sharma, Jai Narain, "Gandhian Perspective of Rural Development," *Journal of Gandhian Studies*, 2004.

Sharma, Shri Ram, Gandhi, The Man Among Men (New Delhi: Radha Publications), 2004.

Kapoor, A.N. Gupta, V.P., Facts of Gandhian Life and Thought (New Delhi: Radha Publications), 2004.

Gandhi, M.K., 'The *Harijan*', Sarva Sewa Sangh Publication, Rajghat, Varanasi, June, 1937.

Gandhi, M.K., Constructive Programme, Sarva Sewa Sangh Publication, Rajghat, Varanasi, June, 1945.

Mishra, J.P., "Emergence of India", *Yojana* (English), 2007.

Parekh, Bhikhoo, 'Thoughts of Gandhi on Poverty Alleviation and Public Empowerment,' Political Analysis, International Conference on 'Peace, Non-Violence and Empowerment: Gandhian Philosophy in 21st Century', 2007

Thakur, R.N. and Roy, Surendra, 'Relevance of B.R. Ambedkar and Gandhi', 'Poltical Economy of B.R. Ambedkar', J.P. Gramin Shrama Adhyayan Sansthan,' New Colony, Gautam Nivas, Gannipur, Muzaffarpur (Bihar), 2007.

Thakur R.N., "Economics of Gandhi's Satyagraha and Development;"Indian Economic Association Journal, Srinagar, 2007.

Thakur, R.N. and Roy Surendra, "Mahatma Gandhi and Satyagraha," Indian Society of Gandhian Studies, Latoor Conference, 2007.

Roy, Surendra, 'Gandhi's Significant Role in the Freedom Movement', 'The Independent India: A Political Glimpse (1947- 2000),' Yuvak Sansthan Prakashan, Kishanpur, Samastipur, Bihar, pp. III-IV, 2004.

Non-Violence: The Key of Gandhian Studies

HIMANSHU SHEKHAR AND HEMLATA JHA

Mohandas Karamchand Gandhi is the foremost name in the small list of those illustrious and sensitive men of the twentieth century. Gandhi dreamed of a world without wars, a socieiy without caste or class, factories without forced labour. In fact a non-violent, non-exploiting social and economic order built on the foundations of universal education, basic morality and the principles of nature a society marked by plenty and prosperity.

Gandhi's revolutionary concept of satyagraha-based on the simple weapons of truth and non-violence unleashed an indomitable moral force should be the vital weapon by which the world can get rid of from all ills. Gandhi's mantra not only aroused Indian's to free themselves from colonial oppression and social injustice, but inspired millions of people all over the world in their quest for freedom, justice and a life of dignity we feel that this is the only weapon by which the world can get command over all the ills. In such circmustances Gandhian Studies becomes necessary.

The first and formost important principle of the

Gandhian economics was non-violence. He believed that true democracy and real growth of human personality are possible only in a non-violent community. Violence breed geater violence. Gandhi's idea of non-vioience was not based on any religious sedimentalism. This economics may be described as non-violent econornics. He was against exploration of the people.

Non-violence is a soul force of Gandhian study. Non-violence with Gandhi was not a mere concept but it was an article of faith, a condition of' existence, a cultural necessity. He has goodwill even for plants and animals and insects. He often said that non-violence is meant for the bold and the brave, not for the cowards and the meek. Non-violence is meant for the strong of mind and the soul of heart. Non-violence is neither passive nor passiveness, it is active, it is dynamic. It implies conscious suffering. Non-violence was mightier than violence, it was mightier than any sword. Violence is going to be the greatest challenge of the 21st century and therein lies the relevance of Gandhi.

In view of the growing violence in the coming years, Gandhi is most relevant in the words of Martin Luther King (Jr.) "If humanity is to progress, Gandhi is inescapable......we may ignore him at our own risk." Gandhi is relevant wherever there is struggle for freedom, wherever, there is struggle for justice, wherever there is oppression. The greatest tribute to Gandhi was paid by UNESCO when it adopted in its preamble the Gandhian thought that since wars begins in the mind's of men. It is in the mind of men that the defences of peace must be constructed. If the l9th century belonged to Carlyle and Ruskin and the twentieth to Russel and Huxley, the 21st century belongs to Gandhi alone, for he said that if there was choice between cowardice and violence he would choose the latter because non-violence is not for cowardly or the weak.

Mahatma Gandhi was the first world leader to condemn the Hiroshima and Nagasaki atomic holocaust on moral ground. The Third world war, if ever it takes place, would finish the world, it will be unwinable war. In the words of Gandhi: 'If there is a victor left the very victory would be a living death for the nation that emerges victorious'. He ridiculed the idea of war to end wars. Wars donot end anything except humanity. If, therefore, humanity is to survive, we must go back to Gandhi and bring peace to the 21st century. 'Disarmament', he said, 'war not a miracle. Even the hardest metal yield to sufficient heat, even so must the hardest that metal before the sufficiency of the heat of non-violence. And there is no limit to the capacity of non-violence to generate heat'.

Gandhi emphasized the importance of moral and human values as against the values of money and material wealth. He regarded economics and ethics inseparable like the French economist Biscamadi. The value of an industry should be judged less by the dividends it pays to shareholders than by its effect on the body and soul of the people employed by it. He preached the people to live simple life. Gandhi had been able to diagnose the malady of modern civilization which attaches the greatest importance to material welfare. The Indian ideal is against this. Gandhi said the founding father of Indian civilization and culture had warned us against excessive indulgences. Happiness was stated to be a mental condition. Gandhiji called both socialism and communalism as belonging to the same circle of ideas as acquisitive capitalism. He was therefore, in favour of simplicity. He wanted decentralization and localisation of industries.

Gandhiji's economic ideas are based on four cardinal principles Truth, Non-violence, Dignity of labour and Simplicity. In the words of Professor Huxley, Gandhiji's social and economic ideas are based upon a realistic appraisal of marks nature and nature of his position in the universe. He knew on the one hand, that the cumulative triumph of advancing organization and progressive technology cannot alter the basic fact that man is an animal of no great size and in most cases of very modest abilities. The mistake of most of Gandhi's contemporaries was to suppose that technology and organization could turn the petty human animal into a superhuman being and could provide a substitute for the infinities of a spiritual realization.

Gandhian economics is the economics of non-violence. He was opposed to materialism. His economic ideas like social and political ideas, was based on truth and non-violence. He extremely opposed to the accumulation of wealth earned by profits. Where as mercantalist and Adam Smith believed in wealth just reversed Gandhi believed in human values and welfare of the masses, he thought "Man is not for wealth rather wealth is for man." Wealth is not the means rather goal. Naturally, accumulation of wealth greeds immorality. The central point of Gandhian economics is equality among all irrespective of caste, creed, religion and wealth. He also believed in fraternity and liberty. This is not simply mere an economic ideas but we may say it Gandhian Philosophy.

To attain the goal of economic equality with a peaceful manners the Gandhian concept of "Trusteeship" is commendable. Gandhi advocated the trusteeship principle according to which the rich are to hold their wealth as trustees of society. They should not treat their accumulated wealth as their personal belonging but they should hold their wealth in trust for the benefit of the whole society.

Gandhiji's vision of "Swaraj" was not meerly an instrument of achieving political liberation from the British colonial rule but the symbol of achieving self-reliance and self-respect. For Gandhiji "Swaraj" was a means of achieving the welfare and dignity of teeming millions of villagers in India. Therefore, the Gandhian economic ideas are based on his vision of swaraj and the philosophy of non-violence.

Gandhi has advocated the principle of deliberate limitation of human wants, which according to him would help the individuals achieve happiness. Gandhiji accerts the Buddhist dictum that desire is the source of all sins and calls upon people to limit their desires. Concept of limiting of wants is a welfare economics. This states that an individuals welfare is best achieved not as economic theory suggests, by attempting to maximize the satisfaction of multiplicity of desire subject only to the prevailing budget constraint but rather by restricting or, his desires and trying to choose between them. The claim supported by arguments bearing on the relationships between desire, satisfaction, happiness and welfare.

Gandhiji articulated a moral vision of human life and

thought that the only thing that only ultimately mattered was the kind of life human beings lived. The quality of their soul and social relations. He also pointed out ·his disagreement about accumulation of material goods and endless multiplication of wants because these are the ways by which people become corrupt. He stressed his views to live a noble life through high tradition and moral value. Various writings of Gandhi was against indiscriminate industrialisation, which uprooted people from their true value-based happy lives. Gandhi stressed the need for building capabilities in the human resources and the approach of empowerment for taking advantage of the emerging opportunities in an equitable manner.

In the globalized and fast changing modern world equipped with scientific and tehnological advancements, we may find putting questionmark on the relevance of Gandhian thought in present context. Such questions point out to. the level of ignorance of the person otherwise well equipped with scientific and technical knowledge only. One may also ask how can a person who has not seen "Gandhiji's related oneself with the vision he nurtured, followed and envisaged as the guiding force of the people of India? Mahatma, as a moral being, may not be present among us, but he has been constantly guiding as an inspiration, an illuminated light on almost all the diversified issues that an individual, a society or the state may come across.

Mahatma Gandhi need not be seen as an individual, but as a movement, a phenomenon and light removing darkness from each and every walk of life. Wherever there is a struggle for survival, wherever there is injustice, poverty, hunger, literacy, inequality and darkness, Gandhiji showed a road to light. The greatest heritage he left is spiritual force that triumphed over the rear of guns and the might of the aggressors. His spirituality was based upon non-violence which promotes love and fearlessness. It seeks the divine in all living being irrespective of their caste, creed, gender or religion.

Mahatma Gandhi: Apostle of Peace

D. Nirmala Devi

From time immemorial Indian saints and seers have devoted themselves to the pursuit of peace. Moksha or liberation from birth, death and rebirth is the most desired goal of the past civilization of India. In the present day context, rationalism, secularism, democracy and scientific outlook are as important as the spiritual concepts. But the most desired goal of mankind is to have peace in every walk of life. Peace is a very precious commodity for all nation. Philosophers from ancient time till now are concerned with the problem of peace. They raise many important questions concerning the accomplishment of peace and progress. Perfect peace of mind, the peace of the soul was their goal in life and to achieve this they have striven hard and suffered hardships. 'Santhi' is an ancient word, meaning peace and Indian scriptures end with the benediction "Om Shanti" which means 'let there be peace'.

Gandhi was the latest link in the long chain of Indian saints and spiritual leaders. Gandhi was widely known among Indians as 'Mahatma' (Great Soul) for his courage, simplicity, penetrating insight and extraordinary impact of his teaching and his life. True to Indian adition, he had set his heart upon the goal perfect peace of mind and soul. To achieve this goal he was ready to face any hardship, bear any suffering, undertake any sadhana. The distinguishing aspect of Gandhiji's life and work was that he not only sought his personal liberation, but also sought the liberation of his fellow humans. He conducted his spiritual Sadhana in the social realm. He said, "I do not believe that an individual may gain spiritually and those that surround him suffer. I believe that if one man gains spiritually, the whole world gains with him and, if one man falls the whole world falls to that extent."[1] Gandhiji combined personal sadhana with social action. This was his new contribution to religion and spirituality.

EARLY YEARS

Gandhi was born in India, in 1869. His parents were merchant caste Hindus. He remained a devout Hindu through out his life. Gandhiji, as a student, was not brilliant but he had strong devotion to truth. He had in fact, more integrity and moral sense than even his teachers. During his boyhood the roots of spirituality were deeply laid in his mind and heart by the influence of his pious mother and religious minded father and his associates. He made room for numerous other religious and ethical traditions and was strongly influenced by pacifist, Christianity, as well as the writings of Thoreau and Tolstoy. He married very young and studied law in London. He practiced in Bombay. He had not any striking success at the bar. His conception of the role of the lawyer was unusual. He thought the lawyer should be more a helpful setter of disputer between the two parties than an exploiter of their differences for personal profit. The lawyer was a peace maker, according to Gandhi.

IN SOUTH AFRICA

After a brief time in India, the young barrister went to South Africa. Some Indian businessmen invited him to go there and work for them: There he found the Indians and the coloured people suffering under social injustice, all because of the pigment of their skin. Gandhi himself had to experience this injustice. He decided it should be resisted and rectified, but since he was a religious person, he could not think of adopting violent or destructive methods. So he discovered and developed novel method of non-violent resistance, resistance without hatred for the opponent, resistance which seeks to convert the opponent; which results in reconciliation and friendship. He remained there for 21 years, leading numerous campaigns for Indian rights, editing a newspaper and developing his philosophy of non-violent action as well as specific techniques for implementing it.

He gradually evolved and perfected the weapon of non-violent resistance, otherwise called 'Satyagraha', Gandhiji invented this new term to denote his new method of action. He was physically abused and arrested many times by British authorities, but he also served courageously in the British side.

He was participant in British Imperialistic war efforts both in South Africa and India. During the Boer war he organized a volunteer corps and during the Zulu Rebellion he raised an Indian Ambulance Corps of which he became Sergeant Major to the defense of Imperialistic war efforts. In defending his action he wrote later "I then believed that the British Empire existed for the welfare of the world. A genuine sense of loyalty prevented me for even wishing ill to the Empire."[2]

Gandhiji's Satyagraha campaign in South Africa were crowned with success. The unjust law against the coloured was repealed. Smuts and Gandhiji became friends. While Gandhiji was in jail, he made a pair of leather sandals and sent them to Smuts as gift. Many years later, Smuts said, "I am not worthy to walk in the shoes of so great man."

After achieving some notable reforms Gandhiji returned to India in 1913, and within a few years he became the leader of the Indian nationalist movement. Again he adopted the peaceful method of Satyagraha; the entire country became his laboratory for his "Experiments with Truth."

He was a freedom fighter, but of a new kind. He

evinced no ill will against the British. Many a Briton joined and helped him in his non-violent movement for independence. On many occasions Gandhiji decided to fast unto death for various causes. In 1940 he launched Satyagraha campaign. In 1942 he actively participated in the 'Quit India Movement'. Finally India became free. The British parted as friends without leaving behind any trace of bitterness. Dr. S. Radhakrishnan characterized the friendly parting of the British and the Indian people "as one of the greatest acts of reconciliation in human history." India voluntarily joined the commonwealth, a unique institution comprising many races and nationalities, a unique force for international co-operation and exchange of views. India continues to play a major role in the deliberations of the commonwealth.

After the advent of independence, in the last phase of his life, Gandhiji laboured more and more for peace and harmony between the Hindu and Muslims where communal riots broke out and innocent people suffered, there he was to quench the flames of violence, to bring solace and succour to those in distress, to draw the fanatics back to sanity. He walked barefoot in Naokhali on his, one man Peace Mission, while Delhi was celebrating the advent of independence. Lord Mount Baton wrote a famous letter to Gandhiji about his time, addressing him, "My Dear Mahatmaji." Mount Baton said that in Punjab, they had 40,000 soldiers and no peace. In Bihar they had Gandhiji and there was peace. Mount Baton called Gandhiji "our one man, boundary force." This was a handsome tribute from one distinguished soldier of war to great solider of peace.

Though the sub-continent was divided into India and Pakistan, Gandhiji worked for peace and amity between them. He undertook the last fast of his life for the sake of Pakistan. In India he continued to work for reduction of tension and promotion of amity between the Hindus and Muslims. Finally he fell a victim to the bullets of a fanatical Hindu offered the supreme sacrifice on the altar of communal harmony and human brotherhood. Thus he became a brilliant example of santi sainik, a peace solider for excellence.

SHATISENA

Mahatma Gandhi developed in South Africa the idea of Satyagraha which later on played an important part in the freedom struggle. He had talked first of a non-violent army in South Africa in 1913 and his first effort to organize a corps of peace volunteers was in 1922 in Bombay when he laid down five conditions for such a corps.

(1) Bear no arms, not sticks, (2) Receive no remuneration, (3) Wear Khadi Uniforms, (4) Accept voluntary self-discipline, yet be willing to take orders, (5) Practice non-violence in thought, word and deed.

In 1938 Gandhi wrote about peace keeping and 'Qualification of a Peace Brigade' through *'Harijan'*. A non-violent army (peace Brigade) is open only to those who strictly enforce in their lives all the implications of non-violence. It is open to all those who accept the implications and make an ever increasing endeavour to observe them."[3] The peace soldier intervenes in conflict situations, reduces tension and prevents outbreak of violence. When violence breaks out, he tries to extinguish it. He said, this brigade should substitute (for) the police and even the military. This sounds ambitious. Yet, if the congress is to succeed in its non-violent struggle; it must develop the power to deal peacefully with such situation."[4]

Gandhiji did not live long enough to develop the programmes of Shanti Sena in concrete terms. As a follower of Gandhian ideology Vinobhaji realised the importance of Shanti Sena. During his southern tour, he established the first unit of Shanti Sena on 27th August 1957. The idea was there but it lasted until 1957 when Vinoba Bhava in the context of the Bhoodan (land gift) Movement took up the new idea.

In 1971, during the Bangaldesh crisis young peace workers were active in the refugee camps, peace marches of refugees were organized, a large scale Freedom march was organized to enter East Pakistan. Santi Sena belongs to the group of Gandhian movement in India. Narayan Desai's 'Handbook for Satyagrahi' defined the objectives of the peace Army.

Gandhiji's great devotion to world peace, his method of

Satyagraha, his ardent advocacy of non-violence captured the imagination of the whole world.

Many eminent leaders saw in his non-violent method an alternative to war and violence "the moral equivalent to war in the words of the famous American Philosopher William James. The Great Russian writer and thinker Court Leo Tolstoy was attracted to Gandhiji's philosophy and work in South Africa. He wrote to Gandhi and said that his method of non-violence was what the world needed. The late Dr. Martin Luther King was very much attracted to Gandhiji and his non-violent method and his 'operational technique'. The late scientist Dr. Albert Einstein was a great admirer of Mahatma Gandhi. He said that "Mahatma Gandhi was the greatest political genius of our era. His influence is bound to increase in the years to come."

PEACEFUL SOCIETY

The present world is beset with problems like international terrorism, arms race, evil wars and ethnic and religious problems. Gandhiji had his own vision of an ideal peaceful society. He called it 'Sarvodaya'. The concept of Sarvodaya Society seems to be a direct outcome of Gandhiji's philosophy of Truth and Ahimsa by the establishment of Santi Sena. Gandhiji desired to establish a society dominated by peace characterised by Truth and non-violence. The idea of Santi Sena has not only a conflict resolving purpose but also it works as a constructive force for the all round development of society. In the Sarvodaya Society Gandhiji gave supreme importance to the individual. Peace is the highest principle of Sarvodaya ideology. For sarvodaya thinkers, peace is both a means to be adopted in solving different problems as well as an end to be sought to achieve in life. Only peaceful methods are morally acceptable and all systems political, social, economic and educational are desirable only when they promote peace in the individual and society.

It stands both for the peace of mind and soul on, the one hand, peace of society, and nation on the other, In both the case 'peace' stands for happiness either happiness of mind or soul or happiness of martial pleasure in individual and social life. Thus "welfare of all' means "peace of all kinds to all" it encompasses in itself peace to all nations, ie world peace. Sarvodaya, devoid of peace, is a selfvltradictory term. It is true that the spiritual peace is complete and internal and the material peace is partial and temporal. It can be achieved gradually by realizied peace in day to day's life. Like the ascetics sarvodaya thinkers do not reject the effort of worldly peace is in the hope of the spiritual, rather they seek spiritual peace through the material and social peace of life.

According to Gandhi, ultimate happiness lies in the peace of individual and society. He wanted to use the weapon of non-violence "to abolish all wars, destroy all conflicts, and settle all tensions."[5] He was of the firm view that a peaceful individual village, nation, alone can bring world peace.[6] He not only desired peace between Britain and India but "between warring nations of the earth."[7] As a matter of fact, he was the apostle of peace. Through out his life, he lived on the principle of peace and preached the gospel of peace in the hope that it must be realized, one day in the whole of the individuals, nations and the world. Vinoba launched a peaceful revolution of Bhodan gramdan movement to settle land and social problems in India. His slogan "let the world be happy is the symbol of his faith in world peace. J.P. up to his last breathing strove hard to bring socio-economic and political peace in the world.

The preamble of UNESCO says: "Since War begin in the minds of men, it is the minds of men the defence of peace must be constructed."[8] The creation of peaceful world society will be filling moment to the memory of Mahatma Gandhi.

In order to bringing about a state of International Peace and Co-operation Gandhi wanted India to take a leading role. For him, India is a land of duty (Karmabhumi).[8] India is an ancient land with moral weapons and has been a votary of non-violence and moral force in international relations. Therefore, it should remain a relevant force in international relations on the basis of its moral strength rather than its military strength. It is for the leaders and people of India to come up to such tasks by developing their moral qualities.

Notes and References

1. Bose, N.K., Selections from Gandhi (Calcutta: Indian Association Publishing Co.), p. 15.
2. Gandhi, M.K., An Autobiography or The Story of My Experiments with Truth (Ahmedabad: Navajivan Publishing House), p. 261.
3. *Harijan*, 21-7-40.
4. *Harijan* 18-6-38
5. Unnithan, T.N., Gandhi and Social Change (Jaipur: Rawat Publication), 1979, p. 106.
6. *Ibid.*, p. 112.
7. *Ibid.*
8. Gandhi, M.K., India of My Dreams (Bombay: Hind Kitab Limited), 1947, p. 9.

10

Models of Peace and Gandhi in Modern Democratic System

Shyam Chandra Gupta

"There has been no greater advocate of one humanity One World, and no stronger opponent of violence and war than Gandhi, for, his faith in non-violence was absolute and he believed that peaceful means alone could lead to peaceful ends."

The concept of world peace has been fascinating indeed. Behind every attempt at permanent world peace and even in the background of world organisations, snob as the League of Nations and the United Nations Organisation, there lurks the hope that one day there will be world peace.

Gandhi realised that if the embodied human spirit was to progress, muffled as it was by selfish desire, man must be free, full of dignity, and earnest about his own advance. Socially, all men and women, irrespective of caste, creed, or sex must be equal and be given equal opportunities. Thus he conceived a world in which all would be equal and all would uphold the dignity of each and help achieve spiritual progress.

While peace is undoubtedly one of the most universal and significant of human ideals, Raimon Panikkar describes it as "one of the few positive symbols having meaning for the whole of humanity" the ways that we think about peace are often diffuse and content-dependent. We profess to honour peace in the abstract-for example, within a framework of religious precepts and affirmations-while organizing our thoughts about life and politics around more mundane ends and objectives. Implicitly, we circumscribe the meaning of peace to accommodate a system of largely implicit beliefs about how the world works, about what power consists of, and about what is expedient. As a result, the peace ideal is either co-opted by competing value priorities or remains distant from our daily activities and experiences. The "ideal" becomes separated from the "real," and peace becomes a pious invocation, a means to an end, or an empty term of rhetorical self-justification.

It is precisely a desire to bridge this gap between the "ideal" and the "real" that attracts students to the M.A, programme in International Peace and Conflict Resolution of American University's School of International Service. Each year, our programme brings together several dozen more bright and highly motivated individuals, many from overseas, to pursue a course of studies dedicated to what Gandhi referred to as "practical idealism." During the spring 2002 semester, it was our pleasure to facilitate the entry of just over twenty new students into the programme, within the context of a core course called "Peace Paradigms." The purpose of this course is to provide an introduction to the theoretical foundations of peace studies, through an intellectually and personally challenging exploration of five "paradigms" of peace, considered as intellectual and practical models for peacemaking based on different sets of explicit as well as implicit beliefs and assumptions. The course begins with consideration of approaches to peace premised on the exercise of coercive power (power politics), and then proceeds to model for peace through international law and institutions (world order), peace through mutual understanding, Gandhian concept of peace and peace through meditation. By the end of a semester all have learned a great deal not only about the history and development of thinking about peace, but also about their own deeply internalized beliefs and existential commitments.

PEACE THROUGH COERCIVE POWER

The first peace paradigm, power politics or "realpolitik," is the traditionally dominant framework in the field of international relations. This paradigm, grounded in classic works such as Thucydides' History of the Peloponnesian War as well as in a more recent body of political theory that invokes Machiavelli, Hobbes, and Hans Morgenthau, promulgates a pessimistic reading of human nature and a competitive model of international politics. Advocates of this paradigm, who refer to it as "political realism," contend that there are no universal values that can be held by all actors in the international system. Furthermore, the absence of a world government or "higher power" to which states must submit themselves renders politics among nations anarchic and unpredictable, characterized by shifting alliances and the ever-present threat of violence. In the face of chronic insecurity and shifting balances of power, states must craft policies that serve the private good of their immediate "national interest" construed as the acquisition of material power and military capability to compel and deter others while steering clear of broader, humanistic ideas that depend on the trustworthiness or good will of others for their fulfilment. In other words, because there is no shared moral yardstick that can be used as a basis for stable co-operation among nations, states have no choice but to compete with one another for scarce resources and for the security that these resources are believed to provide.

Though not necessarily indifferent to global problems linked to widespread poverty and ecological deterioration, exponents of power politics argue for an outlook of moral minimalism, in which the world is construed as a "self-help" system, Justice is defined as an absence of gross abuses of human rights, such as genocide, and peace is conceptualized simply as an absence of war or, more precisely, as a temporary suspension of hostilities secured by military power. "If you want peace," argue proponents of the power politics paradigm, "prepare for war." Violence arises inevitably from human competitiveness and covetousness; peace is secured through the forceful imposition of order.

INTERNATIONAL PEACE THROUGH POWER OF LAW

The second approach to peace explored by the class is the world order paradigm. This paradigm, which views the "order" created by practices of power politics as a form of disorder, proposes that sustained co-operation among states and other significant actors, such as non-governmental (activist) organizations and intergovernmental organizations, is both possible and necessary. Co-operation is possible because human nature contains the potential for both selfishness and altruism; co-operation is necessary because the unmitigated competition favoured by the power politics paradigm cannot be sustained.

To affirm that principled co-operation is possible, the world order paradigm emphasizes human choice and intentionality while asserting that nation-states do not have a monopoly on power to shape global politics. The nation-state is not the only forum for political activity and accountability, and the national interest is not the exclusive criterion for desirable behaviour. In an age of globalization, politics involves a complex interplay of global and national as well as local loyalties, values, and interests. Modern communications and transportation technologies have empowered citizens to form transnational networks for advancing concerns linked to peace, human rights, ecology, and development. The concerns of these citizen networks have helped to define agendas both for national governments and for such institutions of global governance as the United Nations. Through conscious design, states and engaged word citizens can operate within the framework of these value-maximizing institutions to move beyond fearful and reactive behaviour, extend the rule of law into the international sphere, and provide global public goods.

It is precisely because of the failure of competitive, state-centered models of international relations to secure human interests that advocates of the world order paradigm argue that broader and more intense efforts to achieve international co-operation are necessary. In a shrinking and increasingly technological world, issues such as poverty (well over a billion of the world's people live in conditions of "absolute" poverty), environmental deterioration, infectious diseases, human rights abuses, and the spread of weapons of mass destruction are of concern to all. These problems cannot be addressed within the overwhelmingly competitive framework of the power politics paradigm, and require the articulation of new values, norms, and programmes for multilateral action through international dialogue and co-operation. When governments pool sovereignty in international institutions and collaborate with non-governmental organizations and social movements to provide global public goods, a more equitable and sustainable system can be realized.

The world order paradigm paints a different picture of the world than the power politics paradigm, a picture that foregrounds the roles of concerned citizens and ethical values in politics. Power is not only the ability to coerce others through the capacity to hurt or punish (destructive/threat power—"the power of the stick"), but also the ability to reach shared objectives through collaboration (productive/exchange power—"the power of the carrot") and solidarity (integrative/social power—"the power of the hug"). Whereas the "power politics" paradigm views peace as a temporary absence of war within a self-help system of sovereign states, the world order paradigm equates peace with presence of certain value conditions that are required for human flourishing and for long term survival within a global context: non-violent conflict resolution, human dignity, development, ecological balance, and political participation. "If you want peace," proposes the world order paradigm, "prepare for peace." Peace can be actively sought through policies and efforts that build consensus, reduce injustice, create opportunity, and provide multilateral frameworks for responding to common challenges.

PEACE THROUGH MUTUAL UNDERSTANDING

The third paradigm, conflict resolution, offers a highly pragmatic approach to peace through the development and refinement of skills for analyzing conflicts and responding to them with effective strategies of communication and negotiation. Where protagonists of world order concern themselves primarily with macro-level, structural issues such as distributive justice and the institutionalization of international co-operation, practitioners of conflict resolution focus more on processes of interaction among individuals and groups and on the relationships that characterize them.

According to the conflict resolution paradigm, conflict is natural at all levels of human interaction and organization, from the interpersonal to the inter-ethnic and international. Although it can cause estrangement and great human suffering, conflict does not inevitably lead to violence, and is often necessary for major changes in relationships and social systems (e.g., the American civil rights movement). Peace, then, is understood as a continuous process of skillfully dealing with and, whenever possible, preventing or transforming conflict. To manage and resolve conflicts effectively, we must become aware of our attitudes towards conflict and our habitual conflict management styles (competitive, collaborative, avoidant, submissive, etc.), so as to attain to greater freedom to define our own responses in a proactive and coordinated (as opposed to reactive and incoherent) way. Such awareness increases our chances of achieving "win-win" rather than "win-lose" or "lose-lose" solutions. We learn to understand and work with our own emotions, to generate openness to more authentic communication, and to control processes that might otherwise lead to escalation.

To respond effectively to conflict, conflict resolution theorists and practitioners underscore the importance of cooperative, non-adversarial processes for problem solving and relationship building, which are often conducted with the assistance of an external third party or mediator. These processes direct attention to underlying interests and human needs (e.g., security, identity, bonding, control, development) beneath superficial positions and demands, and highlight the significance of culture in human interactions. They affirm the importance of empathy, creativity, and "shared positive power" ("power with" rather than "power over") in all conflict resolution processes, whether between individuals, groups, or states. They also underscore the potentially positive role of non-official processes of dialogue and engagement in today's major international conflicts, most of which involve powerful feelings of ethnic and communal identity. Proponents of the conflict resolution paradigm, then, approach peace through direct interaction with the "other." "If you want peace," they suggest, "train for the processes of peace. Develop skills for communication and coexistence."

GANDHIAN CONCEPT OF PEACE

One of the most common misconceptions about the fourth approach to peace, non-violence, is that it is a 'paradigm that enjoins passivity. From the standpoint of non-violence activists, this assumption reflects the dominance of power politics assumptions, which equate power with the ability to hurt and therefore regard it as the exclusive possession of governments and armed militant groups. In response, the non-violence paradigm proposes that the power of any government derives primarily from the consent of the people, and only secondarily from coercion. By consenting to any given state of affairs and operating within the framework of norms that it offers, human beings empower that order and, if its norms are dehumanizing, disempower and dehumanize themselves. Alternatively, by defining their own behaviour as moral agents irrespective of external norms and pressures, they may become agents of change who can awaken others to new possibilities. Martin Luther King Jr. expressed his view—"Non-violence is a powerful and just weapon. It is weapon unique in history, which cuts without wounding, and ennobles the man who wields it. It is a sword that heals."

As Gandhi, Martin Luther King, Jr., and many others have underscored, non-violence is action animated by principle and informed by the proposition that means and ends are inseparable. Rhetoric about the ends of social change must always correspond with the actual effects of the means that have been chosen to advance these ends. Peace between human communities cannot be achieved through violence, nor can democracy be secured through armed insurrection within a society. Peace, then, cannot be disconnected from justice, and justice entails an absence of oppression, whether perpetrated indirectly by inequitable structures and institutions or directly through use of weapons. In other words, peace entails an absence of violence, broadly conceived as avoidable insult to human needs (and, we might add, to the balance of (nature). Genuine peace can only be attained through peaceful (and therefore just and non-violent) means of action-actions that seek to undo conditions that degrade human beings and to break cycles of retaliation that cheapen the value of human life.

The paradigm inspired by non-violence maintains that, in situations defined by unjust laws or oppression, change may be sought by steadfast, principled measures (Satyagraha--"clinging to truth") through which individuals with shared commitments refuse to participate in any actions that they deem unjust and immoral. These measures may take many forms, from symbolic protests to boycotts, parallel institutions, and direct non-violent intervention. Actions taken to promote non-violent change are intended both to initiate a process for realizing shared objectives and to invite a response; be it cooperative or repressive--from the society or governing authority. By refusing to dehumanize their adversary even in the face of repression or provocation, non-violent activists empower themselves to work in creative ways rather than enter into the destructive, "eye-for-an-eye" behaviours that, as Gandhi put it, "leave the whole world blind." Instead, by overcoming their own fear and anger, they offer to others a new way of seeing the reality around them, and deny legitimacy to institutions and actions that violate human community and the principle of ahimsa ('no harm').

According to the non-violence paradigm, genuine power derives from willpower and human solidarity rather than from violence, which undermines community and sows the seeds of its own destruction. Non-violence offers an approach to peacemaking that has been used not only to counteract forms of social discrimination and political repression but also to resist foreign imperialism or occupation. "If we want peace," assert non-violence activists, "work for justice—justly." This commitment to work for peace by peaceful means through training, strategic planning, Constructive Programmes, and personal discipline implies a revolution of the human spirit, and points to the possibility of a shift in human consciousness in which ahimsa becomes a way of life:

PEACE THROUGH MEDITATION

The final approach to peacemaking investigated in the peace paradigms course is the transformation paradigm, a paradigm that focuses on the centrality of education, cultural change, and spirituality in all genuine attempts to make peace a reality in daily life. From the standpoint of the transformation paradigm, peacemaking is not only an effort to end war, remove structural violence, or establish the presence of external value conditions. It is also a profoundly internal process, in which the transformation of the individual becomes a metaphor for and instrument of broader changes. Transformation, then, involves the cultivation of a peaceful consciousness and character, together with an affirmative belief system and skills through which the fruits of "internal disarmament" and personal integration may be expressed. Transformation unites doing with being, task with experience. Inner freedom is felt in the midst of action, and the individual personalizes sacred ideals for application. Peaceful behaviour is learned behaviour, and each individual is a potential and needed contributor to a culture of peace.

From the standpoint of the transformation paradigm, spirituality implies insight into the deep interconnectedness and sacredness of all levels and compartments of reality. It is innate to the person, and may be understood as a universal human "attempt to grow in sensitivity to self, to others, to non-human creations and to God" that recognizes and seeks to accommodate the presence of the divine in all actions and relations. Recognition of this divine presence and claim begets spontaneous loyalty, which cannot be restricted by boundaries of religion, race, class, or gender. This universal loyalty, in turn, inspires actions born of loving commitment to the wholeness and integrity of creation. The person has become the political in the most creative and inclusive sense possible, as we seek to make public life reflect non-partisan spiritual value. We become present in the moment, yet responsible for a shared and hopeful future inspired by the injunction, "If you want peace, be peace. Be an instrument of peace."

Taken together, these five paradigms Coercive power, International peace, Peace through mutual understanding, Gandhian concept of Peace and meditation attest that the paths to peace are many and that they are travelled not only by statesmen and diplomats, but also by advocates, educators, volunteers, and many other varieties of "ordinary" citizens. By exploring each paradigm, we learn to more actively wrestle with our assumptions and evaluate claims in the light of our full range of experiences. We exercise both our reasoning faculties and our intuitive sense of what is "right," "real," and "true." In such a manner, we make peace a more integral aspect of our lives, and become more aware of the homes we have built for our moral imaginations.

Mahatma Gandhi takes real democracy to be that admits governmental interference at the minimum, which has peace at the maximum and all progress on the basis of equality. It is possible only when non-violence is imparted the supreme status in practice as well as in principle and at social as well as individual plane. Only such a democracy can be successful in its real goal.

We could know the derivation pertaining to non-violence and also by perusing Gandhian point of view, its significance for human race. We could clearly know that it is so why should not the democratic countries make themselves prone to non-violence in the event that these countries with democratic governance system accept welfare of all citizens to be their ambition or goal? Mahatma Gandhi wants this very all out of the system of government and it is really a thing of significance. It is such a significant matter that this reality cannot be denied by me or by anyone amongst you. It is on this accord that Gandhian non-violence is immensely significant in system of today's governance, especially in a democratic system.

Presently, the democratic system in operation in worldly nations is not according to Gandhian principle. We are not getting what Mahatma Gandhi ultimately cherished from democracy. If it was so, these nations could be devoid of atmosphere of violence and presence of fear. There could not have been corruption and divided human society. It is already emphasized that there could not have been problems pertaining to terrorism, communalism, regionalism and problems relating to languages. More than this all, there could not have been observance of ethical and more degradation in public life. Such degradation is being observed constantly. The main cause after all these things remain that all activities of these nations are not non-violent. There cannot be any possibility of violence while there is Gandhism in democracy. Violence is not sacred, pure of welfaristic from any point of view. Whatever is gained on basis of it is impure and temporary. It is on this accord that it cannot pace with democracy even for a moment. Mahatma Gandhi says, "Democracy and violence can never be mutual."

MODERN SYSTEM OF GOVERNMENT AND GANDHIAN PEACE

The question arises before us as to how to guide modern system of government, especially democracy, towards Gandhian way, which undoubtedly has non-violence as its basic root. Then, it is to be made and quotable towards equal development of all citizens. This democracy must be such that "it should not warrant power of punishment."

- In it, "...people will certainly be conscious regarding their duties: they may sometimes, of course, be ignorant towards their rights."
- In case there is something anti-people in it, the people shall make it favourable to them through non-violent means.
- As we have analyzed, Mahatma Gandhi is in favour of spontaneous development of non-

violence. To make democracy ultimately in accordance with non-violence remains to be his goal. This is possible. He rightly said in this regard, ". . . Non-violence is not merely an individual concept. It is social conscept also. It must be developed in this form."

- Development is essential and it is insight. He again states in this regard along with citing a nice example, "Mutual practices in society are regulated by non-violence to a considerable extent. It should be development at largest scale."
- This should of course, be done in right direction and with truthful spirit.

It is the inference that the non-violence permanently present in human nature should be developed in practice from its present state towards progressive one in right direction per truthful spirit. A true and cherished democracy shall be established only in such a condition. A system shall be commendable in proportion to non-violence in it. This is important regarding every system, however, the government of the people-democracy-remains foremost in this chain. We have accordingly assigned it topmost place under our discourse.

Polity must be fearless, full of equality, providing protection to all eternal values and only then it can be pro-people. In can accord apt dimension to development. Man can contribute to world peace only in such a system of government along with gaining his goal. Government should be welfaristic to people and above being non-violent as enunciated by Mahatma Gandhi. Gandhian principle of non-violence is very much significant in modern system of government from this point of view. This significance is likely to be of permanent nature perpetually.

References

Diwakar, R.R.; 'One World and Mahatma Gandhi.

Nathan C. Funk; "Resolution", in M.A. Programme in International Peace and Conflict Resolution of American University's School of International Service.

Prabhu, R.K. and U.R. Rao, The Mind of Mahatma Gandhi, (Ahmedabad: Navajivan Publishing House), 1960.

Martin Luther King; The Meaning of Non-violence.

Captain (Retd.) Charles L. Alphin, Kingian Non-violence: A Practical Application in Policing.

Lafayette, Bernard, Jr., Jehnsen, David, C. and Alphin, Charles, Sr. The law of Enforcement.

Gregg, Richard; The Power of Non-violence (Revised ed.) New York, Schocken, 1966.

Introduction to Kingian Non-violence: the Philosophy and Methodology Galena, Ohio: The Institute for Human Rights and Responsibilities, 1995.

Ravindra Kumar; Relevance of Gandhism in the Modern Polity.

11

The Concept of Non-Violence in Indian Philosophies

KAMAL MANOHAR

The concept of non-violence assumes a peculiar character in the Gita. Non-violence and violence depends wholly upon the circumstances. The decision between the two, is a thorny problem, for, "kim karma kim akarme, ti kavavo, py atra mohitah"—sages too are perplexed as to what is action, what inaction.[1] Tilak has referred to the dilemma of Hamlet in arising at the decision.[2] Right sense of action is clouded with the conflicting duties raging in the mind of the doer. Non-violence has been accepted as a moral principle but moral principles are not an end in themselves. It is only through religious devotion to one's duty, that one can attain the highest bliss.

Websters English Dictionary has seven distinct meaning of violence. Basically, it refers to "roughness in action", a physical force used so as to injure or damage. Another meaning is "unjust use of force or power." Yet in another sense violence refers to "distortion of meaning." Oxford English Dictionary offers a more restrictive definition that it is the "exercise of physical force so as to inflict injury on or damage to persons or property." It is clear that there are several variables, some explicit and others not so explicit, that qualify violence and consequently what constitutes violence becomes a matter of considerable debate and a consensual definition more difficult to arrive at. If violence, as we find in another edition oxford English Dictionary, is "behaviour involving physical force intended to hurt, damage, or kill", then, how about psychological violence such as verbal assault or "tongue-lashing" that has unmistakable effect on the victims.

Jainism holds fast to the five moral principles for the achievement of the purification of soul. Ahimsa occupies the first place and the four other principles—satya, asteya, brahmacharya, aparigraha are subservient to it. They are only duties and could be adjusted in the interest of non-violence. Any of the four moral principles could be disregarded if such regard was necessitated by the principle of non-violence.[3]

In Buddhism non-violence has its positive counterpart. It demands not only abstention from injury but also the practice of loving kindness, "metta" to all.[4] In his sermon at Banaras, Buddha said, "By the practice of loving kindness I have attained liberation of heart."[5] In his sermon to Anathapindaka, Buddha, said, "We reach the immoral path only by continuous acts of kindness and we perfect our souls by compassion and charity.[6]

There are stories, fables and maxims in support of non-violence scattered through the Mahabharata, non-violence is extolled as the highest form of religion. Bhisma the old hero and the statesman, exalted non-violence in his consolatory preaching to Yuddhisthra. "Non-violence is the highest religion. It is the highest penance. It is also the highest truth from which all duty proceeds. Kapila also holds the moral principles of kindness, forgiveness, peacefulness, non-violence and truth, etc. as the road leading to Brahman (self-realization).

"Non-violence" wrote Mahatma Gandhi, is the first article of my faith. It is also the last article of my creed.[7] Non-violence is the greatest force at the disposal of mankind. It is mightier than the mightiest weapon of destruction devised by the ingenuity of man."[8] At another occasion, he said that non-violence has got to be all 'pervasive'. One cannot be non-violent about one of his activities and violent about others.[9] Indeed non-violence was a cardinal virtue around which the whole life and all the activities of the Mahatma revolved.

IMPACT OF NON-VIOLENCE OVER VIOLENCE

No one really disputes that non-violence resolution of conflict is preferable to violence (except perhaps those who see the evolutionary need for population control through violence and war). However, the question is whether non-violence can indeed be effective as a means of conflict resolution. Most people have reasonable doubts whether current terrorism or naxalism can be tackled by non-violent means. Therefore, it is felt, violence is indeed as a sort of necessary evil to maintain stability and order in society and that aggression and love would continue to necessarily co-exist. Gandhiji would of course challenge this on two grounds. First, the Mahatma strongly believe that non-violence is not only morally violence but that is also functioning more effective as a force and instrument of social action. He asserted that, "Violence cannot remain unaffected before non-violence."[10]

If we want to see non-violence, peace and development together, we have to understand that economics, social stability, personal well being-all of these must develop together and be developed in a constant consciousness of peace. Importantly, the answers to these questions can be found out primarily through dialogue and self-examination. There has to be a dialogue between those from different disciplines and professions, between people from different countries and regions, between the rich and the poor and between the oppressed and oppressors. A gathering of this kind, provides an appropriate form for initiating such dialogues.

"Satyagraha" literary means holding to truth. In practice, it is non-violent action to resolve social as well as individual conflicts. It may take a number of forms such as non-co-operation, civil disobedience and fasting, depending upon the nature of the conflict situation. Gandhiji has not prescribed a set theory to go by, and he has repeatedly emphasized that his techniques are essentially experimental in character. The basic assumption underlying satyagraha is that it is possible to generate extensive social action by non-violent means and that this action helps to transform the adversary non-violently when the cause is just. The social action engendered by non-violent techniques is far superior to the action involving violent means, because in the latter case the solution is attended with terrifying consequences that are often beyond the control of the acting agent. Gandhiji, doesn't, however, explicity state how non-violent action brings this miraculous transformation in the opponent, but the actual operation of satyagraha, whatever may be its mysterious force, would seem to involve delicate and human modes of communication.

The mission of non-violence can become successful only when it is imbued with consciousness of spirituality or consciousness of emotions. An integration of economic development, material development, moral development and spiritual development only can make us eligible to talk about human development. If only intellectual consciousness is developed and if only economic development takes place, then food cannot go together with non-violence and peace. If merely consciousness of spirituality is developed then both non-violence and food cannot go together. A happy blending of intellectual consciousness and spiritual consciousness is indispensable for a balanced, holistic and relative development. Non-violence, peace and food can co-exist only when intellectual consciousness, economic consciousness and spiritual consciousness are developed in a balanced manner.

Non-violence has come to be a creed, a matter of faith rather than simply an experimental instrument of social-action. Violence wrote Gandhiji, "Can be overcome by non-violence. This is clear to me as the proposition that two and two make four. But for this one must have faith. Even a weapon like atom bomb when used against non-violence will prove ineffective."[11] Responding to a reported statement of general Cariappa, Gandhiji remarked: It is his (Cariappa's) ignorance of this the greatest duty of the man in the world, which makes him say that in his age non-violence has little scope in the face of violence, whereas I make bold to say that in the age of the atom bomb, unadulterated non-violence is the only force that can confound all the tricks put together of violence.[12]

M.K. Gandhi began as an empiricist conducting a series of experiments for social and political change. However he ended up a thoroughbred moralist who trusted his intuition more than the facts around him. His thoughts on violence and non-violence seem to bear this out. Non-violence came to be the moral imperative, the supreme morality. He stretched the meaning of "violence" to a point that it came to be synonymous with everything that is undesirable and immoral. For the Mahatma, traveling in the train without a ticket is violence[13] and over work is violence. He wrote: "The work which becomes a burden or for which we have to overstrain ourselves at the cost of our health amounts to physical violence."

MAHATMA GANDHIJI AND NON-VIOLENCE

Sixty years ago, on December 3, 1947, general K.M. Cariappa met Mahatma Gandhi and told him that he would like to remind the army and the soldiers in his own way of the need for and value for non-violence. He then asked, "How I can put this over, i.e., the spirit of non-violence to the troops....without endangering their sense of duty to train themselves well professionally as soldiers", to which Gandhiji replied: "I am still groping in the dark for the answer. I will find it and I will give it to you someday.[14] That day never came as he himself was a victim of violence that snatched him away just a few days later. Yet the question, more relevant today than in 1947, remains unanswered. However what is significant in Mahatma's response is that there is indeed an answer and that we would find it sooner or later.

It was testimony of no less a person than Lord Lloyd, Governor General of Bombay, that in the opening months of his campaign, Gandhi came, "Within the breadth of an eyelash" of securing the emancipation of his people. Unconquerable is the non-violent resistant, so powerful the man or movement which wields not the sword of steel but the sword of the spirit. The British Empire, like the Roman empire before it, know exactly what to do with an enemy that comes armed against her. Every empire, every military power has long since learned the lesson of how to handle an attack of violence, whether it by a mob or any army. They have fought their foes through so many years, and under such varieties of circumstance, and to such ends of victory, that they have nothing now to learn. No effective instrument of force and violence is beyond their knowledge and expert use. But when a man, or rather a disciplined army of men, comes against an empire bare-handed and bare-footed, equipped not even with stones and staves, practicing not violence in any form but absolute non-violence, loving their enemies and seeking ways not of destroying but of serving them even as they love and their friends, the empire is helpless.[15] This was a great Gandhiji's training in non-violence.

How can the two opposite evolve together and co-exist in us? It would seem that aggression, selfishness and violence have a short term instrumental value where as love, compassion and non-violence are among the long-term strategic value defenses to secure survival, safety, cohabitation and co-existence. It would also appear that the latter, viz., love and altruism, have a control function to moderate and attenuate violence in human condition. The co-existence of the opposite appears to have the combined effect of enhancing human survival individually and collectively.

What Gandhi was doing in these creating actions was going to the Indian people the weapons where to carry on their fight against Britain—weapons of unimaginable power, guaranteed, if used patiently and bravely, to bring victory in conflict, ordinary weapons were of no use to India in her struggle against the greatest military empire since that of ancient Rome. Sword and spear were as useless to a disarmed and untrained people as they were spiritually wrong. If India was to win her fight for freedom, it must be on the higher level of human effort—in this case the weapon of non-violence. Once condemned and ridiculed, now regarded with awe and wonder.[16]

TRAINING IN NON-VIOLENCE

According to Acharya Mahapragya, "If we want to develop non-violence we have to pay attention to the right economics, morality and control over desires and emotions. Transformation of personality through meditational practices can alter the emotion of greed that would pave the gateway for safe and peaceful economic development." Acharya Mahapragya believes that unlimited personal wealth and unlimited consumption are the two great challenges of the present world. The two mantras of limited possession and limited consumption, as enunciated by Bhagvan Mahavir, can prove to be extremely effective in creating an egalitarian society.

Once British Empire decided to arrest Gandhi and his multitudinous followers and thrust them behind prison bars. But behind these bars Gandhi became more powerful than ever. In a moment of that charming humor which characterized his life, Gandhi said that he had early discovered that he could make the best bargains with British when he was in jail. Then the mind of the world was focused upon him, and by reason of sympathy demanded a justice which was beyond all reach when he was at large. So Gandhi in prison was a force more potent than "an army with banners." How to conquer this man and his followers clad only in the panoply of the loin cloth was a question never answered by the British Government.[17] This was Gandhiji's great training in non-violence.

The Journey of non-violence leads to greatness, rising to greater heights and there is an universal observation that it is difficult to soar high and here comes to fore the human exertion or purusharth as we may call it. An essential component of non-violence is austerity—the excitement to reach withering heights and embrace the cloud with a silver lining. Those who are addicted to an extravagant and a wanton lifestyle can never experiment with non-violence, because it takes courage to answer a call, it takes courage to give our all-it takes courage to be true. Acharya Mahapragya has embarked upon a journey attempting to create a bridge between economics and non-violence with the help of anekanta.[18] Therefore, Acharya Mahapragya proposes that a saint can forgo pleasures, it is expected from him, but spirituality must seep into a family and in a man's life too. He must learn and practice to forgo the worldly pleasures to some extent and embrace non-possession as a way of life. Non-violence is both a moral and spiritual value. In its micro form, non-violence is a determination of not retaliating even in the instance of another person attempting to inflict pain, harm and agony on us. It is this unconditional love which forms the spiritual premise of non-violence.

Acharya Mahpragya believes the physiology of human brain as having three layers. The superficial one that we use of reasoning and logicising is the neo-cortex. Beneath it lies the animal brain which when left untrained and untamed contaminates all our developmental efforts with corruption and other such banal tendencies. This require essential training and practice. The solution of this problem is training in non-violence.[19] More intellectual deliberation would not be enough to provide the solution. Without compassion, non-possessiveness is impossible and without non-possessiveness compassion is impossible.

CONCLUSION

As per Oxford English Dictionary meaning of violence is "exercise of physical force so as to inflict injury on or damage to person or property." According to Gita non-violence has been accepted as a moral principle but moral principles are not an end in themselves. It is only through religious devotion to one's duty that can attain highest bliss. Jainism holds fast to the five moral principles for the achievement of the purification of soul. Ahimsa occupies the first place and the four other principles-satya, asteya, brahmacharya and aparigraha are subservient to it. In Buddhism non-violence has its positive counterpart. It demands not only abstention from injury but also the practice of loving kindness, compassion and charity. As per Mahabharata, "Non-violence is the highest religion. It is the highest penance. It is also the highest truth from which all duty proceeds." Mahatma Gandhi wrote, "Non-violence is the greatest force at the disposal of mankind. It is mightier than the mightiest weapon of destruction devised by the ingenuity of man."

Mahatma Gandhi asserted that, "Violence cannot remain unaffected before non-violence." If we want to see non-violence, peace and development together, we have to understand that economics, social stability, personal well being-all of these must develop together and be developed in a constant consciousness of peace. The mission of non-violence can become successful only when it is imbude with consciousness of spirituality or consciousness of emotions. Non-violence peace and food can co-exist only when intellectual consciousness, economic consciousness and spiritual consciousness are developed in a balanced manner. Gandhiji wrote, "Violence can be overcome by non-violence. This is clear to me as the proposition that two and two make four. But for this one must have faith. Even a weapon like atom bomb when used against non-violence will prove ineffective." For the Mahatma, "Traveling in the train without a ticket is violence. Over work is violence. The work which becomes a burden or for which we have to overstrain ourselves at the cost of our health amounts to physical violence.

When a man or rather a disciplined army of men, comes against an empire bare-handed and bare-footed, equipped not even with stones and staves, practicing not violence in any form but absolute non-violence, loving their enemies and seeking ways not of destroying but of serving them even as they love and serve their friends, the empire is helpless. This was Mahatma's great training of non-violence. Gandhiji told, "Sword and spear were as useless to a disarmed and untrained people as they were spiritually wrong. If India was to win her fight for freedom, it must be on the higher level of human effort-in this case the weapon of non-violence."

According to Acharya Mahapragya, "If we want to develop non-violence we have to pay attention to the right economics, morality and control over desires and emotions.

Transformation of personality through meditational practices can alter the emotion of greed that would pave the gateway for safe and peaceful economic development." Acharya Mahapragya believes that unlimited personal wealth and unlimited consumption are the two great challenges of the present world. The two mantras of limited possession and limited consumption, as enunciated by Bhagvan Mahavir, can prove to be extremely effective in creating an egalitarian society. Acharya Mahapragya has embarked upon a journey attempting to create a bridge between economics and non-violence with the help of anekanta. Non-violence is both a moral and spiritual value. The solution of most of human problems lies in training in non-violence. Mere intellectual deliberation would not be enough to provide the solution. Without compassion, non-possessiveness is impossible and without non-possessiveness compassion is impossible.

Notes and References

1. The Bhagvad Gita, 4.16, p. 287.
2. B.G. Tilak, Gita Rahasya, Vol.-II, Poona, 1936, pp. 948-50.
3. M.K. Jain, Jain Darshan, Varanasi, 1966, pp. 48-67.
4. Dines Andersen edited, Suttanipata, Helmer Smith, Reprint, 1948, p. 394, cited in H. Sadhatissa, *op. cit.*, p. 90.
5. Paul Carus, The Gospel of Buddha (New Delhi: Publications Division, Ministry of Information and Broadcasting, Government of India), 1961, p. 45.
6. *Ibid.*, p. 62.
7. *Young India*, March 23, 1922.
8. *Harijan*, July 20, 1935.
9. *Ibid.*, October 12, 1935.
10. The Collected Works of Mahatma Gandhi (New Delhi: Publications Division, Ministry of Information and Broadcasting, Government of India), p. 192.
11. *Ibid.*, p. 453.
12. *Ibid.*, p. 249.
13. *Ibid.*, p. 173.
14. *Ibid.*, Vol. 97, p. 454.
15. Holmes, J.H., Gandhi and Non-violence, (Delhi: Akashdeep Publishing House), 1988, pp. 78-79.

16. *Ibid.*, p. 89.
17. *Ibid.*, p. 78-79.
18. Acharya Mahapragya's message in VIIth International Conference at Jaipur on subject: Peace and Non-violent Action, Nov. 11-14, 2008.
19. *Ibid.*

12

Truth and Non-Violence: Core Principles of Gandhi

Hossien Nemat Zadeh Gara

Mahatma Gandhi is an outstanding figure of the contemporary Indian Philosophy. Gandhiji has been called a "Moral revolutionary" and also a "moral genius." According to him, morality is the basic principle of life. Gandhiji wanted to establish "Ramarajya" or the Kingdom of God in our country through certain rigid moral disciplines. He also prescribes these moral principles for the development of man's ethical personality.

Truth was first and sovereign principle of Gandhiji's life. He thought that "devotion to this truth is the sole justification for our existence."[1] According to Gandhiji Truth has two categories, namely relative Truth as perceived by finite individuals in relation to a particular set of thoughts and circumstances and Absolute Truth which exists beyond and unconditioned by space and time.[2]

He believed that truth is not only truthfulness in word but also in thought and action.[3] Truth cannot be separated from Ahimsa and if one is to realize it one has to follow the path of Ahimsa. "I can with assurance, as a result of my experiments", he claimed, "that a perfect vision of Truth can only follow a complete realization of Ahimsa."[4] This truth is an impossibility for those who suffer from possession, anger, selfishness, hatred, etc.[5] Therefore, Gandhi advised to follow the path of Brahmacharya, Ahimsa, Aparigraha and Truth to reach the absolute Truth or God.[6] Therefore, also occupied a pivotal face in the philosophy of Mahatma Gandhi. It is practical application of the great truth, of spiritual unity and like truth, it is also potent, infinite and synonymous with God.[7] According to him it has two aspects in its negative aspect, it means refraining from causing injury or filing any creature out of anger or selfish motive.[8]

Secondly, in its positive aspect Ahimsa means the largest love, and greatest charity. It also includes Truth and fearlessness.[9] It involves goodwill towards whole creation and is not restricted to human being only, "It includes", remarks Dr. Abid Hussain. "the positive connotations of affection, sympathy, mercy, generosity, service and self-sacrifice, it also refers to God as the be—all and end—all of love."[10]

According to Gandhiji, Ahimsa and Truth are so intertwined that it is practically impossible for anyone to make them separate. They are like two sides of a coin or rather a smooth unstamped metallic disk.[11] But Ahimsa is simply a means, whereas truth is the end, Gandhiji was ready to sacrifice Ahimsa for Truth but never Truth at any cost.[12] Ahimsa is the virtue of the brave, not of cowards. Hence, Gandhiji referred violence to cowardiness.[13] But non-violence is certainly and infinitely superior to violence, as it is extreme limit of forgiveness.[14] According to Gandhiji, "Non-violence in its dynamic condition is conscious suffering. It does not mean meek submission to the will of the wrong-doer, it means the putting of one's whole soul against the will of the tyrang.[15]

The concept of "Non-violence" or 'Ahimsa' is one of the basic and important principle of Gandhian ethics. His concept of Non-violence is accepted as cardinal virtue in the individual as well as in social life. Gandhi was greatly influenced by Jainism as it is the Jaina religion which preached Ahimsa in the true sense of the term. He was also influenced by Hinduism and Buddhism, but Jainas contribution was somewhat greater. The Jaina Philosophy explains it as "Pranatipata-Viramana." Gandhi was also influenced by the ancient teaching "Ahimsa Paramo Dharma." Even our sastras seem to teach that a man who really practices Ahimsa in its fullness has everything at his command.

According to Gandhi Non-violence is the greatest and most active force in the world. He used the word 'Non-violence' in order to bring out the true meaning of Ahimsa. Literally Ahimsa means non-killing. But to Gandhi Ahimsa means more than that. Gandhiji clarifies that Ahimsa does not express a negative force, but a force superior to all the forces put together. A person who can express Ahimsa in life exercise a force superior to all the forces of brutality.

Gandhi accepts Non-violence in two aspects—positive and negative. Positively it is nothing but greatest charity and largest love. To Gandhi, Love is not of ordinary love. This love is idealistic quality where one loves without any expectation. It is the only realistic force in human life. Gandhi includes in love all that denotes inward refinement, compassion, charity, forgiveness, tolerance, sympathy to lift up mankind. He said, "The law of complete love is the law of my being" in *Young India,* 1922 March. Tolstoy's influence is seen in Gandhi's utterances about love.

Negatively, non-violence means not injuring anything in this world in thought, deed and action. A true follower of Ahimsa does not use such language in his relation with others as injuries their sentiments. Gandhi has conceived Ahimsa as the opposite of Himsa as such Ahimsa is conceived as non-injury. He also adds that Himsa or violence means causing pain or killing any life out of anger or from a selfish purpose or with the intention of injurying it. Refraining from doing all these is Ahimsa. But for Gandhi the positive aspects of Ahimsa are much more basic than its negative character.

Gandhi differentiated three levels of Non-violence. The highest of theses was the enlightenment Non-violence of the strong. It was the Non-violence of one-who adopted it not by necessity but by inner conviction emanating from moral consideration. Then came the Non-violence which is accepted as a sound policy and a measure of expedience in a certain sphere of life. Gandhiji called it the Non-vio!ence of the weak or passive resistance of the helpless.

The third type of Non-violence was the passive Non-violence of the coward and the effeminate. Fear and love contradict each other. So cowardice and Ahimsa do not go together any more than water and fire. According to Gandhi, it should not be thought that Ahimsa means cowardice. Because the practice of Ahimsa calls for the greatest courage and determination. Gandhi said clearly that when there is a choice between cowardice and violence, he would prescribe violence. Thus an individual or a nation could take resort to arms in order to define its honour rather than be a helpless witness in a cowardly manner. To Gandhi—Non-violence is an extremely active force. It has no room for cowardice or even weakness. Only a person who has conquered fear can be truly non-violent.

According to Gandhi, truth is God and Non-violence is the way of realizing him. Non-violence is the practical expression of truth. Gandhi says truth and Non-violence are so intertwined that it is not possible to separate them. They are like the two sides of a coin. To him, to practice Ahimsa would be to realize truth, to realize truth would be practice Ahimsa. In this connection Gandhi said, "Ahimsa is my God and Truth is my God. When I look for Ahimsa, Truth says, find it through me. When I look for Truth. Ahimsa says, find it through me."[16]

To attain the highest purpose of human being which is Truth one should follow the path of Non-violence. Truth is realized by actions of love or Non-violence. If one is Karmayogi and selfless seeker after truth, one has to practice Non-violence. Therefore, Ahimsa is the means and truth is the end. According to Gandhi, Truth is the highest law but Ahimsa is the highest duty. Without Ahimsa it is not possible to seek and find truth.

According to Gandhi, it was very difficult to define Ahimsa. To practice Non-violence was the only way to understand it. He said that Non-violence was the first article and it was also the last article of his creed. He said, "My life is dedicated to service of Indian through the religion of Non-violence."[17] He said that he was practicing Non-violence for a long period and applied it in every walk of life like domestic, economic, political and moral also.

Gandhi felt that Non-violence is the only means through which mankind and its civilization could be saved from destruction. With his faith on this method. Gandhi prescribed 'Satyagraha', the Non-violence technique as an effective substitute for the violent armed warfare to the world. Gandhiji believed that before this peaceful method of Non-violence the bayonet runs to rust and the gun powder turns to dust. Satyagraha utilizes non-violent methods of non-co-operation, civil disobedience, fasting, picketing and strike or temporary cessation of work as a protest.

Gandhi's life was a burning example of how people without arms could fight successfully against the injustice and armed men. To the nuclear age he is the only answer. By pursuing the path of violence, no-one will be able to continue his existence. All must come in the end to the path of Non-violence. Now, everyone feels that it should be better to take Non-violence for peace and stability to the world.

In the present day society, the principle of Non-violence is not very much realized and it is marked that violence is raising everywhere. So, there is no peace in the society. In this situation, we should apply this ethical principle to emancipate the society from all kinds of social evils. Because, Non-violence is the only way which can bring peace in society. According to Gandhi, Non-violence was the means to achieve truth and this would be brought about by the personal effort of the individual.

No doubt Gandhi was influenced by the ethical doctrines of Buddhism and Jainism. But he gave Ahimsa an active political context as an instrument for militant social action. He gave the doctrine of Non-violence a revolutionary intent and direction. He gave to the future generation a direction, an aim, a way of life; from political to personal conduct, from economics to ethics. Gandhi's moral force was Non-violence. And we have reasons to believe that Non-violence in spirit and action is the only solution to the ever conflicting and changing world order. Non-violence as a moral value is ever relevant for mankind for its expected survival in the future to come.

Notes and References

1. Gandhi, M.K., From Yervda Mandir (Ahmedabad: Navajivan Publishing House), 1940, p. 2.
2. Gandhi, M.K., An Autobiography or The Story of My Experiments With Truth (Ahmedabad: Navajivan Publishing House), 1940, p. XV.
3. *Ibid.*
4. *Ibid.*, p. 370.
5. *Ibid.*, p. 254.
6. *Young India*, December 31, 1931.
7. *Harijan*, May, 1, 1937.
8. *Young India*, November 4, 1926.
9. Speeches and Writings of Mahatma Gandhi (Madras: Natesan Publishers), 1964, p. 346.
10. Hussain, Abid, The Way of Gandhi and Nehru (Bombay: Asia Publishing House),1959, p. 13.
11. Gandhi, M.K., From Yervada Mandir, *op. cit.*, p. 13.
12. *Harijan*, March 28, 1936.
13. *Young India*, August 11, 1920.
14. *Ibid.*, November 4, 1926.
15. *Ibid.*, August 11, 1920.
16. Seshagiri K.L. Rao, Mahatma Gandhi and Comparative Religion, p.64.
17. Prabhu, R.K. and U.R. Rao, The Mind of Mahatma Gandhi, (Ahmedabad: Navajivan Publishing House), 1960, p. 49.

13

Training in Non-Violence

B.S. Bedi

Non-violence is not a mechanical performance. It is the finest quality of the heart and comes by training.[1] It takes a fairly strenuous course of training to attain to a mental state of non-violence. In daily life it has to be a course of discipline though one may not like it, like for instance, the life of a soldier. But I agree that unless there is hearty co-operation of the mind, the mere outward observance will be simply a mask, harmful both to the man himself and others. The perfect state is reached only when mind and body and speech are in proper co-ordination. But it is always a case of intense mental struggle.[2]

Gandhiji says, "I have nothing new to teach the world. Truth and Non-violence are as old as the hills. All I have done is to try experiments in both on as vast a scale as I could. In doing so I have sometimes erred and learnt by my errors. Life and its problems have thus become to me so many experiments in the practice of truth and non-violence. As a Jain muni once rightly said, I was not so much a votary of ahimsa as I was of truth, and I put the latter in the first place and the former in the second. For, as he put it, I was capable of sacrificing non-violence for the sake of Truth. In fact it was in the course of my pursuit of truth that I discovered non-violence."[3] Ahimsa and Truth are so intertwined that it is practically impossible to disentangle and separate them. They are like the two sides of a coin, or rather a smooth unstamped metallic disc. Who can say, which is the obverse, and which the reverse? Nevertheless, ahimsa is the means; Truth is the end. Means to be means must always be within our reach, and so ahimsa is our supreme duty. If we take care of the means, we are bound to reach the end sooner or later. When once we have grasped this point, final victory is beyond question. Whatever difficulties we encounter, whatever apparent reverses we sustain, we may not give up the quest for Truth which alone is, being God Himself.[4] The path of Truth is as narrow as it is straight. "Even so is that of ahimsa. It is like balancing oneself on the edge of a sword. By concentration an acrobat can walk on a rope. But the concentration required to tread the path of Truth and ahimsa is far greater. The slightest inattention brings one tumbling to the ground. One can realize Truth and ahimsa only by ceaseless striving."[5]

God travels at a snail's pace those who want to do good are not selfish, they are not in a hurry, they know that to impregnate people with good requires a long time.[6] Having flung aside the sword, there is nothing except the cup of love which I can offer to those who oppose me. It is by offering that cup that I expect to draw them close to me. I cannot think of permanent enmity between man and man and believing as I do in the theory of rebirth, I live in the hope that, if not in this birth, in some other birth, I shall be able to hug all humanity in friendly embrace.[7] This is the path of ahimsa. It may entail continuous suffering and the cultivating of endless patience. Thus step by step we learn how to make friends with the entire world; we realize the greatness of God-or Truth. Our peace of mind increases in spite of suffering; we become braver and more enterprising; we understand more clearly the difference between what is everlasting and what is not; we learn how to distinguish between what is our duty and what is not. Our pride melts away, and we become humble. Our worldly attachments diminish, and so does the evil within us diminish from day to day.[8]

Fearlessness connotes freedom from all external fear-fear of disease, bodily injury and death, of dispossession, of losing one's nearest and dearest, of losing reputation or giving offence, and so on.[9] We must give up all external fears. But the internal foes we must always fear. We are rightly afraid of animal passion, anger, and the like. External fears cease of their own accord, when once we have conquered these traitors within the camp. All such fears revolve round the body as the centre, and will, therefore, disappear as soon as one gets rid of attachment for the body. 'We thus find that all external fear is the baseless fabric of our own vision. Fear has no place in our hearts, when we have shaken off the attachment for wealth, for family and for the body. Nothing whatever in the world is ours. Even we ourselves are His. When we cease to be masters, and reduce ourselves to the rank of servants, humbler than the very dust under our feet, all fears will roll away like must; we shall attain ineffable peace, and see Satyanarayana (the God of Truth) face to face.[10] The pursuit of Truth is true bhakti (devotion). It is the path that leads to God, and, therefore, there is no place in it for cowardice, no place for defeat. It is the talisman by which death itself becomes the portal to life eternal.[11]

Just as one must learn the art of killing in the training for violence, so one must learn the art of dying in the training for non-violence. Violence does not mean emancipation from fear, but discovering the means of combating the cause of fear. Non-violence, on the other hand, has no cause for fear. The votary of non-violence has to cultivate the capacity for sacrifice of the highest type in order to be free from fear. He recks not if he should lose his land, his wealth, his life. He who has not overcome all fear cannot practice ahimsa to perfection. The votary of ahimsa has only one fear that is of God. He who seeks refuge in God ought to have a glimpse of the Atman that transcends the body; and the moment one has a glimpse of the imperishable Atman one sheds the love of the perishable body.

If we are to be non-violent, we must then not wish for anything on this earth which the meanest or the lowest of human beings cannot have.[12] Possession implies provision for the future. A seeker after Truth, a follower of the law of Love cannot hold anything against tomorrow. God never stores for the morrow; He never creates more than what is strictly needed for the moment. If, therefore, we repose faith in His providence, we should rest assured that He will give us every day our daily bread, meaning everything that we require. Perfect fulfilment of the ideal of Non-possession requires that man should, like the birds, have no roof over his head, no clothing and no stock of food for the morrow. He will indeed need his daily bread, but it will be God's business, and not his, to provide for it.[13] From the standpoint of pure Truth, the body too is a possession. It has been truly said, that desire for enjoyment creates bodies for the soul. When this desire vanishes, there remains no further need for the body, and man is free from the vicious cycle of births and deaths. The soul is omnipresent; why should she care to be confined within the cage-like body, or do evil and even kill for the sake of that cage? We thus arrive at the ideal of total renunciation, and learn to use the body for the purposes of service so long as it exists, so much so that service, and not bread, becomes with us the staff of life. We eat land drink, sleep and wake, for service alone. Such an attitude of mind brings us real happiness and the beatific vision in the fullness of time.[14] Love and exclusive possession can never go together. Theoretically when there is perfect love, there must be perfect non-possession. The body is our last possession. So a man can only exercise perfect love and be completely dispossessed, if he is prepared to embrace death and renounces his body for the sake of human service. But that is true in theory only. In actual life, we can hardly exercise perfect love, for the body as a possession, will always remain with us. Man will ever remain imperfect, and it will always be his part to try to be perfect. So that perfection in love or non-possession will remain an unattainable ideal as long as we are alive, but towards which we must ceaselessly strive.[15]

In the application of Satyagraha, I discovered in the earliest stages that pursuit of Truth did not admit of violence being inflicted on one's opponent but that he must be weaned from error by patience and sympathy. For what appears to be Truth to the one may appears to be error to another. And patience means self-suffering. So the doctrine came to mean vindication off Truth, not by infliction of suffering on the opponent, but on one's self.[16] The Satyagrahi seeks to convert his opponent by sheer force of character and suffering. The purer he is and the more he suffers the quicker the progress.[17] The religion of ahimsa consists in allowing others the maximum of convenience at the maximum of inconvenience to us, even at the risk of life.[18] It is no non-violence if we merely love those that love us. It is non-violence only when we love those that hate us. I know how difficult it is to follow this grand law of love. But are not all-great and good things difficult to do? Love of the hater is the most difficult of all. But by the grace of God even this most difficult thing becomes easy to accomplish if we want to do it.[19] I saw that nations like individuals could only be made through the agony of the Cross and in no other way. Joy comes not out of infliction of pain on others but out of pain voluntarily borne by oneself.[20] Suffering, cheerfully endured, ceases to be suffering and is transmuted into an ineffable joy.[21]

To see the universal and all-pervading spirit of Truth face to face one must be able to love the meanest of creation as oneself. Identification with everything that lives is impossible without self-purification. God can never be realized by one who is not pure in heart.[22]

CREATIVE NON-VIOLENCE

Creative non-violence is a force for truth, justice, and the well being of all that is neither violent nor passive. It challenges the power and belief system of violence, which is a destructive force designed to defeat and dominate others. It is a witness for justice and a method for helping to create it. It pursues this goal, not with passivity or retaliation, but with the third way of creative engagement and loving and determined resistance.

Creative Non-violence is organized love. It is an orientation, a set of principles, a method, and specific strategies that puts love into practice. In this context, love is the process of acknowledging, safeguarding and engaging with the humanness, woundedness, and sacredness of the other, while creatively challenging and resisting her or his violence and injustice. Creative Non-violence has "two hands" that are in creative tension: nonco-operation with injustice and steadfast regard for the opponent as a human being.

The Method of Creative Non-violence Includes

- Exposing and critiquing the reality of violence and injustice;
- Seeking to break the cycle of escalating and retaliatory violence;
- Withdrawing consent from it;
- Reaching out to opponents and potential allies;
- Unleashing people-power by alerting, winning and mobilizing the majority; and
- Supporting the long-term emergence of the larger truth: first it is ridiculed; second it is fiercely opposed; and finally it becomes self-evident.

Principles of Creative Non-violence

- Creative Non-violence acknowledges, repairs, and transforms the infinite relatedness and unity of all life.
- Injustice depends on either active or passive support (resulting from silence, indifference or fear) of the majority. Violence is any personal, interpersonal, institutional or systemic act, attitude or policy that dehumanizes, diminishes or destroys. It thrives by passive or active support. Creative non-violence is the process of transforming this support for injustice by mobilizing and unleashing non-violent people power.
- Each of us has a piece of the truth and the un-truth. Creative Non-violence is a process of acknowledging and revealing the pieces of truth and untruth on both sides in a conflict as the basis for a just and constructive solution. Creative Non-

violence seeks the truth rather than the conquest of one side over another.

- Creative Non-violence is the process of transforming us with thought and action.
- Creative non-violence unifies rather than threatens; integrates rather than fragments and destroys; draws us closer rather than excluding and separating; and challenges all double standards.
- Creative Non-violence recognizes that each of us has tendencies toward both violence and love. It maintains, as Alexander Solzhenitsyn put it, "The line dividing good and evil cuts through the heart of every human being." Each of us has only a piece of the truth, and therefore each of us possesses a piece of the un-truth. Creative non-violence fails when it is arrogant or self-righteous, especially when it claims to be free of violence, or when it asserts that only otherside violent.
- Creative Non-violence is stronger than the Power of Violence, which is a destructive force designed to defeat and dominate others and that oftenseeks to separate "us" from "them." Creative Non-violence, for this reason, disputes the claim that violence establishes peace, justice and order in any just and lasting way.
- Creative Non-violence pursues its goal, not with passivity or retaliation, but with creative engagement and loving resistance. It willingly faces the consequences of its engagement and resistance.
- Creative Non-violence is nurtured and strengthened by community, relationship-building, ongoing education, and practice. It requires training and experience in love, courage, creativity, and relentless persistence. This includes examining and transforming the ways that violence and injustice has been consciously or unconsciously internalized.
- Creative Non-violence is not a path toward an idealistic utopia but a process for envisioning,

weaving, mending, and honoring the web of personal, interpersonal, social, global and ecological relationships. The spirit and methods of Creative Non-violence are suited to this ongoing creation and re-creation of the world.

NON-VIOLENCE

There are a number of different ways to achieve peace and justice. We need to work to build a just world through sustainable development which involves ordinary people at the grassroots, we need to find creative ways of resolving conflict, and we need to build alternative structures and communities along sane and sustainable lines.

Some situations require us to engage in active non-violence. For instance, where there is a disparity in power between two sides in a conflict so that the powerless side has to take action so that negotiations can start. The need may be as basic as to demand recognition from the powerful that they are fellow human beings, or to get them to see that there is a problem. Or the situation may be one of such structural injustice that it cannot be improved or reformed, but has to be transformed.[23]

The aim of non-violence is both dialogue and resistance - dialogue with the people to persuade them, and resistance to the structures to compel change.

The Methods of Active Non-violence

Dramatizing actions, usually symbolic, can be used to reveal the truth of an issue and to draw attention to it. For example, homelessness campaigners in Washington claimed the body of a pauper who froze to death and carried it in a coffin to city hall, thus literally laying it at the door of those responsible. Faslane 365 will go a step further as we are actually shutting down the flow of traffic to the base and thus preventing workers from going in.

Characteristics of a Non-violent Campaign

- absolute respect for the opponent/everyone involved

- care for everyone involved
- refusal to harm, damage or degrade people
- if suffering is inevitable, willingness to take it on yourself rather than inflict it on others
- belief that everyone is capable of change
- appeal to the opponents' humanity
- recognition that no one has a monopoly of truth, so aims to bring together our 'truth' and 'the opponents' 'truth' understanding that the means are the ends in the making, so the means have to be consistent with the ends
- preparation and training, so that our behavior is non-violent.

WHY NON-VIOLENCE?

"Unarmed truth is the strongest power in the universe"- says, Martin Luther King. In all our direct action, trainings and workshops we emphasize that all our actions are totally non-violent. This paper explains briefly why this is so important.

Pragmatic Reasons

- The state or the power holders can always muster more force against protesters than we can. In the last resort, if violence is the tactic, they can always resort to greater violence and can always command more forces and resources.
- Violence used by protesters gives a negative image, and very often alienates the people we are trying to rally to our side. It plays into the hands of a negative press.
- Violence, while seeming to be effective in the short term, never produces long-term solutions. There is always a residue of hurt and pain that will erupt later.

Philosophical Reasons

- Bringing about peace by violent means is a real contradiction in terms. Peace can only come about by peaceful processes.
- Respect for others is at the heart of non-violence. By our actions we are seeking to win our opponents over to our way of thinking, and this involves a change of heart, which cannot be achieved by force.

Most important of all is the Non-violence works. Some examples where non-violence has worked. In all these examples non-violence has been part of a long and often costly struggle. Sometimes it has only achieved partial success, and often there are still issues to be resolved or carried further. However the important thing is that non-violent action has won results that have changed the course of history.

The students must be at the centre as the main actor in the establishment of a culture of peace and non-violence in schools. For this reason, the primary objective of the school must emphasize not only the traditional goals of the achievement of specific knowledge and skills, but also the development and practice of the social relations which characterize this culture. In fact, studies indicate that students learn best in a caring and cooperative environment. This requires that the education process involve not only students and teachers in an active teaching/learning relationship, but also the entire staff of the school, the parents and the surrounding community as a common and shared endeavor. This should be reinforced at all levels from the classroom to the national educational policy through a process of continuous critical reflection and reform. The principles and practices of peace and non-violence should be integrated into every aspect of curriculum, pedagogy and activities, including the very organizational and decision-making structure of the educational institution. These include cooperative learning, dialogue, intercultural understanding, and mediation and conflict-resolution strategies.[24]

The school is not an island but should be a centre of civic life in the community. It should nurture, through its organization and practice, citizens capable of democratic participation. Recognizing the interdependence of school and community, as part of its mission, the project will also help to address the major sources of structural and overt violence in the community which impact upon the students, such as ethnic or racial discrimination, drugs and unemployment.[25] Although recognizing that the world today is deeply scarred by the violence of wide disparities and structural inequalities between the North and South among nations and within nations and that this project by itself cannot resolve these issues, we believe that we can make a difference. We are challenged to contribute, by means of this project to action for global justice, reconciliation and international solidarity. As the Mozambican poet Jose Craverinha emphasized and wrote during the Sintra Forum, "it is not that we must be the same, but what is fundamental is that we are together, joined hand in hand."[26]

In addition, several groups in the United States are working on full-fledged alternatives to military action along the lines of Gandhi's Shanti Sena or Badshah Khan's Peace Army. The most ambitious is Non-violent Peace force, which is well along the way to fielding a force of several hundred people to be expanded to several thousand in a few years. They will be well trained in non-violent intervention, with full logistical support, able to intervene in conflicts anywhere in the world. If such efforts received even a tiny fraction of the funds allocated for military options, they would demonstrate what we've seen in virtually every part of the globe and in every historical era: that non-violent citizen movements can bring about lasting change, against even ruthless opposition, instead of just adding one more turn in the cycle of violence.[27]

Training in non-violence is thus diametrically opposed to training in violence. Violence is needed for the protection of things external where, non-violence is needed for the protection of the Atman for the protection of one's honour.[28]

Notes and References

1. *Young India*, 16-04-1931, p. 75.
2. *Ibid.*, 01-10-1931, p. 287.
3. *Ibid.*, p. 21.
4. *Ibid.*, 02-04-1931, p. 54.
5. George Lakey, Powerful Peacemaking: A Strategy for a Living Revolution (Philadelphia: New Society Publishers), 1987, p. 10.
6. *Ibid.*, p. 41.
7. *Ibid.*, p. 43.
8. Bondurant, Joan, Conquest of Violence: The Gandhian Philosophy of Conflict (Berkeley: University of California Press), 1971, p. 5.
9. *Ibid.*
10. *Ibid.*
11. Bondurant, Joan, Conquest of Violence: The Gandhian Philosophy of Conflict, *op. cit.*, 1971, p. 132.
12. *Ibid.*, p. 34.
13. *Ibid.*, p. 37.
14. *Ibid.*, p. 12.
15. *Ibid.*
16. *Young India*, November, p. 6.
17. *Ibid.*, 18-09-1924, p. 306.
18. *Ibid.*, 02-12-1926, p. 422.
19. From letter dated 3-12-1934.
20. *Young India*, 31-12-1931, p. 418.
21. *Ibid.*, 13-10-1921, p. 327.
22. *Harijan*, 28-03-1936, p. 53.
23. Bondurant, Joan, Conquest of Violence: The Gandhian Philosophy of Conflict, *op. cit.*
24. Bedau, Hugo (ed.), Civil Disobedience: Theory and Practice, *op. cit.*
25. Lakey, George, "Why Training for Non-violent Action?", International Journal of Non-violence, Vol. II.
26. George Lakey, Powerful Peacemaking: A Strategy for a Living Revolution, *op. cit.*
27. Cooney, Robert and Helen Michalowski, The Power of the People: Active Non-violence in the United States (Philadelphia: New Society Publishers), 1987.
28. *Harijan*, 01-01-1940, p. 268.

14

Role of Educational Institutions in Promotion of Peace and Non-Violence

DAYANIDHI PRASAD ROY AND REENA ROY

INTRODUCTION

The present world is beset with problems like international terrorism, arms race, civil wars and ethnic and religious problems. Though cold war is over, there are smaller conflicts between and among nations. These regional conflicts have disturbed international peace, attempts for disarmaments, confidence building measure, etc. The twentieth century was by far the bloodiest and most destructive century in the history of the human race. According to some UN Statistics, there were only twenty eight days in this entire century of genocide and destruction without a war of some kind, in some part of the globe. According to some other estimates, in the same period 231 million people were killed or allowed to die by human decisions. In this atmosphere of unrestrained violence and contempt for life, people the immediate goal in this type of situation must be to bring the warring side to the cessation of hostilities. Yet great peacemakers always look beyond the immediate goals and hope to establish the conditions of genuine and stable peace, even while the hostilities are still raging.[1]

Ahimsa is now widely recognized as the sure means to resolve conflicts within individuals, and among individuals, groups, communities, regions and nations. Gandhiji not only scripted his experiments with truth, but also launched the satyagraha movement. His experiments with truth will become a beacon of hope for generations to come. South Africa gave birth to the weapon of satyagraha, but it was in India that Gandhiji perfected it. Gandhiji did not enter a so called 'open field' but certainly brought new direction to the struggle. He introduced satyagraha, a non-violence resistance to oppression and, more importantly, a non-violent way of life. This mode of struggle influenced many struggles of independence throughout the world. In Gandhiji philosophy of life, there was place for love and not hate, respect and not anger, forgiveness and not revenge. He tried to transform people with love and respect, instead of defeating his opponents in battle. In the 21st century Gandhian voice of reconciliation that must be heard above the din of violence and war.

There is no denying the fact that in every society quality of life depends on the quality of education. Education is a continuous process of imparting knowledge, developing skills, inculcation of values and more importantly, promoting the overall personality development of human beings. Qualitative education helps in all round development of the young generation. Educational Institutions play very important role in shaping the personality of future generation.

Since times immemorial, the education has played a sublime role in child's education. During the Vedic period, aim of education in India was to train students in morality, mental growth, disciplined life and spiritual knowledge; to cultivate memorization of sacred texts and to enjoy academic freedom. During the Buddhist period, aim was to preach dharma and to train pupils in democratic attitudes and moral and mental discipline. The medieval education in India emphasized personal relationship between the teacher and the taught as in the ancient Hindu and Buddhist education. A teacher had a small group of students to whom he imparted instruction according to the level of intelligence of pupils. Teachers were held in high esteem and their pupils considered it a privilege to follow their example. During the Muslim period, the role of the teacher was to cultivate the fear of God, compliance with the Shariat, recitation and memorization of the Koran, friendliness with people and kindness to the poor.[2] Education in India during the British period was never seriously undertaken for the purpose of national development. Whenever it was pursued with some zeal, the basic principle enlightened colonialism, aimed to fulfil the immediate needs of British bureaucracy. Therefore, the role of teacher during the British period was to train and educate pupil to acquire modern skills and techniques, and to prepare pupils for various subordinate ranks in government service and to inculcate Western values and the spirit of Western Science.[3]

During the post-independence period, education to prepare minds for reconstruction of the nation, to develop scientific temper, to be the agents of national integration, change and modernization of society. It was expected to develop in students creative and independent thinking and to prepare them for a democratic socialist society.[4]

University system in India came into existence during the British rule, but seeds of higher learning in the form of Gurukul and Ashrams were already existed here. Individual Rishis headed their own Ashrams and Peeths. Prominent among those Rishis were Yagyawalka, Vashistha, Vishwamitra and Gargi. These rishis were just like the Vice-Chancellors of modern universities. The world's famous universities like Takshashila and Nalanda have laid the foundation of present university system. India build large institutions of higher learning form time to time to serve as the repositories of its spiritual, philosophical, scientific, artistic and literary achievements and as the media of transmission of this heritage to the future generations.[5]

Gandhi was critical of the existing system of education as he believed that to be wasteful and positively harmful. His ideas regarding education did not emerge all of a sudden, but were the outcome of long years of sustained thoughts and experiences in social, economic and political fields. His views on education have made a revolutionary contribution to the educational thought and entitles him to be termed as a great educationalist. Being a man of action rather than a theorist, his theory of education is also by and large objective and experimental rather than subjective and speculative. In fact there is no divergence in theory and practice.

The question that arises here is: what type of education is needed to empower citizens to become agents of change for better world societies? How can we prepare our future generations to cope with the challenges and fast changing realities of today and tomorrow? In a world struggling with the challenges posed by intolerance and fundamentalism, the perceptions about social cohesion forever, the meaning of the term "citizenship education" assumes particular importance. How can we develop citizens who can bring about the transformation of the culture of violence, intolerance and greed to one of peace, non-violence and respect for one another? These are not going to be achieved with the click of a finger. There is no readymade solution waiting to be adopted. In fact here must be a debate in the world over value education involving the best of the professional and academic intentions.

Today, globalisation is implying relentless advocacy and practice of freedom in the flows of capital, technology, information and resources for the benefit of a few powerful and vested interests. Gandhian Way, stressed the need for building capabilities in the human resources and the approach of empowerment for taking advantage of the emerging opportunities in an equitable manner. Today's world is obsessed with the approach of competition some times cutthroat (kill thy neighbor type) competitions, as a modality for improving efficiency. Gandhian Way advocates the virtues of co-operation and trusteeship, with a view to ensuring equitable distribution of the benefits of the emerging opportunities, for optimum welfare of many. Today's strategy of inclusiveness is some sort of afterthought, after varieties of rigid exclusivities are deliberately fostered and established in the system by the prevailing strategies and actions. Gandhian Way prescribes inclusiveness as an integral part of the growth and development processes. Gandhian talisman which advocates that we should look at the implications for the commonest of the common man, whenever we have to take some decisions, is worth noting here. Kenneth Kaunda, has rightly observed that "degrading poverty breeds fertile ground for instability, revolution and terrorism." This perceptive observation of and highly experienced statesman, like Kaunda, should provide the right signals for the choice of strategies best suited for the control of conflicts and terrorist tendencies in the world as a whole. Kenneth Kaunda also laments that "unprecedented advances in science and technology have not improved the devastating social and economic conditions of the world's poor."[6]

Mahatma Gandhi's ideas like truth and non-violence were based on external human values being practiced in society for times immemorial. His technique of conflict Resolutions viz., Satyagraha, ideas on social justice upliftment of women and amelioration of the condition of Dalits have permanent value as far as the establishment of an egalitarian social order remains a cherished dream. Similarly, his views on education which play a pivotal part in the reconstruction of any society are as valid today as they were in his life time and will continue to be so in the Twenty-First Century.[7] Of all the problems that the country is facing today, none is so pressing and urgent as the problem of educational reconstruction. The system of education introduced by the British served, their ends but is not relevant to the needs of the youths of free India. After independence, efforts have been made for evolving a new policy of education suiting to Indian genius and requirements, which may prove useful for national reconstruction.

Ahimsa in Buddhism, Jainism and Hinduism stood for non-injury to living being. It meant the attitude of the will not to injure any living being. Gandhi refined its meaning by stating that non-injury was the best expression or ahimsa. To his mind the principle of ahimsa was hurt by hatred, by wishing ill to anybody.[8] Gandhi's interpretation of ahimsa was that it was not merely a negative state of harmlessness, but a positive state of love, of doing good even to the evil doer. "But it does not mean helping the evil doer to continue the wrong or tolerating it by passive acquiescence. On the contrary, love, the active state of ahimsa, requires you to resist the wrongdoer by dissociating yourself from him even though it may offend him or injure him physically."[9]

Since the ideas of truth and ahimsa described above are likely to create the impression that Gandhi was an idealist floating in thin air rather than being down to-earth, we owe to his realism to correct that impression. We may best do so by citing some of his other experiential observations about the same subject. His personal advice in a specific context was of violence rather than cowardice, if the choice lay just between these two altematives.[10] His reasoning for it was that non-violent conduct was never demoralizing, while cowardice was demoralizing.[11] He gave yet another reason for it; "Non-violent conduct cannot be taught to a person who fears to die and has no power of resistance. He harbors violence and hatred in his heart and would kill his enemy if he could without hurting himself. He is a stranger to non-violence."[12] He added, "He who has not overcome all fear cannot practice ahimsa to perfection.[13]

The unity of life, truth and non-violence is the eternal value. It is not just immediate or relative. Truth and non-violence are the science and democracy. Science based on the primacy of truth and democracy on the primacy of individual are very near to truth and non-violence as moral value.

We can inculcate the qualities of good citizenship in young minds through education based on following things.

DEDICATED TEACHERS

Of all the different factors, which influence the quality of education and its contribution to the national development, the quality, competence and character of teachers are undoubtedly the most significant. Teachers are the role models for students and contribute to shaping the character and destinies of millions of our children. In that sense, they are the true nation builders since the children of today will be the leaders of tomorrow.[14] In most of our sacred scriptures, the guru is seen as the preceptor, the acharya and the teacher. They have always been hailed as pathfinders, who have generously shared their knowledge with their disciples. Sottoty, too, has always accorded the status of guide, guardian and mentor to teachers. Different scholars have glorified the role of teacher. Humayun, Kabir considers teachers literally as the arbiters of the nation's destiny. Dr. Zakir Hussain says that the teacher is indeed the architect of our future. Sir John Adam views the teacher as the real maker of man. Manu has glorified teacher as the image of Brahma. An Indian prayer says: the teacher is Brahma, the creator; he is God Vishnu; he is God Maheshwara. He is the entire universe. Salutations to him. "The true teacher", according to Swami Vivekananda, is he who can immediately come down to the level of the student, transfer his soul to the student's soul and see through and understand through his mind. Such a teacher can really teach and non-else." In Rabindra Nath Tagore's view "A teacher can never truly teach unless he is still learning himself. A lamp can never light another lamp unless it continues to burn its own flame. The teacher, who has come to the end of his subject, who has no living traffic with his knowledge, but merely repeats his lessons to his students, can only lead their minds. He can't quicken them." Eminents educationist and philosopher Dr. S. Radhakrishnan considers the teacher's place in society as of vital importance. He acts as the source of the transmission of intellectual traditions and technical skill from generation and helps to keep the lamp of civilization burning.[15]

It is often said that as is the teacher so is the child, and as the child, so is the nation. The influence of quality teacher is not confined to a particular time, region or state, but it extends to the whole world. Great teachers like Socrates, Plato, Aristotle in the West and Mahatma Gandhi, Swami Vivekanand and Sarvapalli Radhakrishnan in India have worldwide impact. These great teachers too had their gurus or teachers. Vashisht was the guru of Sri Rama and Sandipan was the guru of Sri Krishna, Dronacharya was the guru of Kauravas and Pandava. Gopal Krishan Gokhale was the guru of Mahatma Gandhi and Ram Krishna Paramhans was the guru of Swami Vivekanand. So in a way, history stands witness to the fact that great men had the impact of their teachers at some point of their lives.

In convocation address to the Punjab University. (19th December, 1953) Dr. Radhakrishanan aptly remarked, "We have to realize that the kind of education we provide for our children is determined overwhelmingly by the kind of men and women we secure as teachers. The low esteem in which teachers are held is the most eloquent evidence of the malady from which our society suffers." The sorry state of the teaching profession in India cannot but be a reflection of a grimmer reality. The society, (that is, all of us) is to be blamed for this state of affairs.

VALUE-BASED EDUCATION

It is a time for decision-makers and professionals in the field of education to lead in the total effort of designing and implementing new and more effective ways of preparing the future citizens and future leaders for the creation better societies. The priority should be to translate the valuable lessons from spiritual texts the Bible, Koran, and to transform the growing culture of violence, greed and intolerance into one of peaceful co existence. While there is general dissatisfaction with the fall in moral standards, there has been no concerted attempt on the part of society to address ...itself directly to the problem of value education. Unfortunately, education is becoming more or less materialistic and the value traditions are being slowly given up. The degeneration in the present day life, the demoralization of public and private life and the utter disregard for values, are all traceable to the fact that moral, religious and spiritual education has not been given due place in the educational system; religion is a great motivation force and is intimately bound up with the formation of character and the inculcation of ethical values. A national system of education that is related to life needs and inspiration of the people cannot afford to ignore this purposeful force. Value crisis of the present day life is mysterious to the minds of educators and education as well.

The effect of the value crisis in present day life is witnessed in many ways. The democratic ideology that has been accepted by the country is yet to be actualized in the form of social and economic democracy so as to realize democratic values guaranteed by the constitution. Also the present educational system is reflecting more or less borrowed ideologies and philosophies and the national values take the back seat. Apart from this, the teacher educators and teachers are not being clearly oriented to the national values, ideas, ideals and ideologies that they have to inculcate in the students. However, they are not in a position to play their role of values educators. The student community is drowned neck deep in poverty, ignorance and unhealthy surroundings. Hence, they are not in a position to understand the real values of contemporary India. The present curriculum to some extent reflects human values and the value system. Besides, the school and colleges have to promote the value based education.

Today even after about sixty-three years of India's independence, the country finds itself faced with serious tensions and challenges of casteism, lingualism, provincial ism, regionalism, etc. Value oriented education can go a long way in curbing these fissiparous tendencies and inculcate the sentiments of unity and solidarity amongst various sections of the Indian society.

Gandhi's value oriented education was based on the golden principle of simplicity. In fact, simplicity was not only the comer stone of this educational ideas but also of his life style. He wanted students to lead a simple life and do all their work by themselves viz., washing their clothes, cooking their food, etc. The thrust of his view's is simplicity in education by training the children in self-help and self-reliance.

He considers the life of students to be akin to that of a sanyasi student, according, to him, should follow the dictum of "Simple living in high thinking'. He should derive pleasure from his studies. For Gandhi there could not be a greater pleasure for a student than to march from knowledge to more knowledge.[16] Indian policy based on the principle of socialism, secularism, democracy, nationalism and internationalism requires an education based on the criterion of inculcating values in the youth for promoting equality, social justice, national cohesion and democratic citizenship.

NEED OF BASIC EDUCATION

According to Gandhi, education is an all round drawing out of the best in child and man body, mind and spirit, Gandhi's views on education were influenced by his general philosophy of life viz., belief in God, truth, ahimsa, dignity of labour, a new social order having justice and equality. According to him education should aim at developing an all round vigorous personality. He laid equal stress on education of heart, i.e., refinement of emotions and awakening of deepest feelings of love, sympathy, fellowship and right ordering of loyalities. It is a life long process and should help in cultivating the spirit of toleration, co-operation, public spirit and a sense, of responsibility.

Gandhi's concept of Basic Education has got the maximum attention. It aims at all round development of human personality. His primary emphasis is on the 3 H's viz., head, heart and hand rather than on 3R's, i.e., Reading, Writing and Arithmetic. For Gandhi the true development of head, heart and soul are necessary for a satisfactory system of education.[17] Gandhi further lays great emphasis on true non-violence in individuals life. Basic education also places truth on a high pedestal. It also aims at the establishment of an exploitation free society having a just social order wherein individual can develop himself without any hindrance.

To sum up it can be said that education is the foundation stone on which depends India's political salvation. Our country should be built not on bricks, but on brains, not by cement, but by enlightenment. World is changing very fast with the change of time, human beings change but no change of time urges the changes in humanism. Humanism distinguishes human beings from other species in creation.

Humanism comprises: truth, non-violence, strength in character, non-stealing, non-possession, purity, devoid of jealousy, penance, self-study, surrender to God, taking senses from external sphere to inner sphere, concentration on a point of conviction, meditation on Cosmic Energy absorption in the ultimate. On the wings of science, modern civilization has conquered Nature, has brought the human from Jungles and caves to towns and cities, has ensured security as against a precarious existence, and it promises abundance and amenities, mass education, better socio-political institutions, law, etc. apparently, it has paved the path to progress and welfare of man.

Yet, ours is a society of crime, violence and strife, predicting tension and lack of peace. The primitive society, marked with lack of education, had strife and other frailties of man, but not so ruinous and so regular as today. The modern society, boasting of prosperity, education and cultural flourishes seem unable to banish cruelty, strife and other frailties and rather witnesses them almost helplessly. The modern civilization has made the world a global village, only technologically and not psychologically. It has enough of elating rhetoric, more than any in the past that often overshadow the realities, no so elating.

CURRICULUM

The need for sound curricula, even though subsidiary, must be considered seriously by those earnest about blooming of decent qualities in man. We may only stress here that learning virtues begins the best in childhood. The child must be acquainted both at home and school with accounts of inspiring lives and humanities cultural achievements through ages. The history of wars, cruelties, etc., though taught, must not cloud a child's mind. He must know more of good things of life and must begin his onward journey with a robust optimist outlook and not with cynicism, Pessimism, fear, etc. shaking confidence, and course, ignorance, are the greatest enemies of progress. To a child, we must hold out alternative healthy models, ideas and programmes things that deepens and broadens the mind, facing caterers of, as Tolstoy said, "growing insane luxury of the rich" and such other vulgarities and cupidties.

Education can be both formal as well as informal. Formal education is deliberately and consciously planned and its curricula arc pre-designed and goals are pre-determined. It is imparted through educational institutions such as schools, colleges and universities. Informal educations are generally received by living and communicating with others. It may or may not be provided consciously or deliberately. This can be or is generally offered at the convenient place, time or level of understanding. It does not have fixed course of study. Now, that is hardly achieved without designing a concrete yet flexible programme or of course complete with activities of that each school can fulfil its mission of creating "civic capacities."

Education is the deliberate and systematic influence exerted by the mature person upon the immature, through instruction, discipline, and harmonious development of physical, intellectual, aesthetic, social and spiritual powers of the human beings. Therefore, to fortify the values in education, it can be suggested that to start a nationwide consultation process and has to involve eminent scholars from varied religious and institutional backgrounds. Their values inputs led to the decision to develop a Hand book for Schools on Strategies of Value Implementation which hopefully would keep those responsible for the selection and development of instructional material for inclusion in the schoolbooks they may think of developing. Simultaneously, National Curriculum Centre can start some projects for independent research and innovations in Value Education in collaboration with relevant institutions and organizations within and outside the country. The Curriculum should be also based on the need and demand of the Economy; Present century needs more scientific and technical knowledge to cope with the modern development strategies.

CONCLUSION

The present day approach to development consists of relentless pursuit of material progress. Gandhian Way, materialism and spiritualism and that True progress should cater to the materialistic and spiritualistic dimensions of human welfare, in a balanced manner. Satyagraha should be launched to bring about transformation in the understanding of what constitutes True Development.

"What shall it avail a man if he gains the whole world and lose the soul?" This is a question as old as the religions. But out civilizations fails as yet to offer a convincing answer, notwithstanding all its spectacular achievements. The failure lies in the fact that this materialist civilization, with all its achievements, is not in reality much worried with the question of the soul of man or his spiritual development. Ultimately, this is the most important thing in life to which everything else is subservient. But, there are scientists who would like to explain soul or mental qualities as epiphenomenon of matter.

It is high time, we move from just a knowledge Economy towards a Wisdom Economy. Processed information is knowledge, processed knowledge is wisdom. Economics audits obsession with money matters cannot solve most of the issues the world is facing today. It is Excenomics, the study of excellence that will furnish the solution to most of the problems mankind is facing, both collectively and individually.[18]

Today, excessive consumerism is ruining the world. Gandhian advocated the principle of sustainable consumption, by considering the basic needs of large masses of poverty stricken people in the world. It condemned the proliferation of green and asserted that there is enough on this planet, for the fulfilment of the needs of every one but not enough for the satisfaction of the ever growing greed of the people. Elimination of misery and destitution from this planet occupies the central place in the vision of Gandhian world order.

Notes and Reference

1. Journal of Gandhian Studies Vol V Nos I & 11 2007. Edited by Jai Narain Sharma page 17.
2. Edutracks (Hyderabad: Neel Kamal Publication Pvt. Ltd.), Vol. 07. No. 11, July, 2008, p. 14.
3. *Ibid.*
4. Indian Education Commission, 1964, p. 66.
5. Edutracks, *op. cit.*, p. 17.
6. The Indian Economic Journal (New Delhi: IEJ Academic Foundation), Vol. 55, No. 3, October 2007.

7. Pandey, Janardan (ed.), Gandhi and 21st Century (New Delhi: Concept Publishing Company), 1998, p. 218
8. Gandhi, M.K., From Yeravada Mandir: Ashrarn Observances (Ahmedabad: Navajivan Publishing House), 1975, p. 7.
9. *Young India,* Jan. 19, 1921.
10. *Ibid.,* Aug. IL 1920.
11. *Ibid.,* Oct. 31, 1929.
12. *Harijan,* July. 20, 1935.
13. *Ibid.,* Sep. 1, 1940.
14. Indian Education Commission, 1964, p. 66.
15. Edutracks, *op. cit.,* p. 13.
16. Pandey, Janardan (ed.), Gandhi and 21st Century, *op. cit.,* p. 218.
17. *Ibid.,* p. 223.
18. *University News,* Published by the Association of Indian Universities, Vol. 45, No. 28, 2007.

Gandhi's Education: Essence of the Complete Man

Ranjit Kaur

In India, Gandhi's View of education has not received as much attention as it deserves. In fact he and his ideas have always been in controversy because of one reason or the other. And so is the case with his thoughts on Education.

With the help of education, Gandhi wanted to evolve the complete man in us, which God has created in his own image. The educational system, with English as the medium of instruction introduced by Britishers, was to provide clerk for the company and not to stimulate initiative or skill in production. That education not only isolated educated from the masses but also made their bookish knowledge hardly of any practical use.

At that time Gandhiji thought that the only way of saving the nation was to revive village economic life and to relate education to it. This education was to be based c village occupations and young generation was to be traine to use their brain and brawn simultaneously, effectively ar efficiently.

According to Gandhiji, "true education means an a

round drawing out of the best in child and man-body, mind and spirit. Literacy is not the end of education nor even the beginning. It is one of the means whereby men and women can be educated." Gandhiji gave more importance to character than literacy in his scheme of education. In his views an unsophisticated shepherd who is possessed of character is a much better citizen of the world than one who has received the so called literacy training in a modern school.

In Gandhiji's philosophy of education the personality of the educand is of primary importance and not the tools and subjects. In fact personality constitutes the whole man and so education should bring about a harmonious development of all four aspects of human personality, i.e., body, heart, mind and spirit.

True education according to Gandhiji, "is that which draws out and stimulates the spiritual intellectual and physical faculties of the children."

Any educational system which stresses more on anyone aspect of the personality deteriorates the principle of basic education. But, contrary to this; our educational system right from the beginning to the present hour, militated against the basic principles of education and undue emphasis laid on one or more aspects of education and indifference to others.

Education must revolve around vocational and manual activity as centre and all syllabi should be woven round vocational training. Manual training should be the means of literary and intellectual training. And this will lead to self-supporting aspect of education. Gandhiji believes that handicrafts should make education self-supporting along with the development of the personality of the child. In Gandhiji's views this education will enable the energetic youth to take a suitable occupation after leaving the four walls of the educational institute. In his own words, "This education, ought to be for them a kind of insurance against unemployment."

Explaining the above idea he once elaborated: "The child at the age of 14, that is after finishing a seven year course, should be discharged as an earning unit. Even now the poor people's children automatically lend a helping hand to their parents - the feeling at the back of their mind being: What shall my parents eat and what shall they give me to eat, if I do not also work with them? That is an education in itself. .... you have to train the boys in one occupation or another. Round this special occupation you will train up his mind, his body, his hand writing, his artistic sense and so on. He will be the master of the craft, he learns."

In Gandhiji's views the present educational system does not provide any sense of responsibility in the students. Today's education lacks close relationship of education with life and there are no provision adjusting the child intelligently and actively to his environment.

Besides, these fundamental features of the Gandhian philosophy of education, some more secondary features, as mentioned by M.S. Patel are:

1. Free and compulsory education should be provided for seven years on a nation wide scale. The age limit of children under compulsion to be 7 to 14 years.
2. Emphasis on the mother-tongue: the mother-tongue not only to become the medium of instruction, but to occupy the first place among languages.
3. The scheme to include what we now understand by elementary and secondary education-matriculatonless English.
4. The state to take over the products of the children.

Gandhiji stressed on the use of hand along with heart and head. In his opinion the hand with its complex structure and its flexible fingers and opposable thumb has great use. In his educational philosophy he preferred three H—Hand, Heart and Head instead of prevalent R.W.A.—Reading, Writing and Arithmetic.

Since the antiquity the main aim of education has been reflection of ideal of life. Therefore, every national system of education is a reflection of the philosophy of the whole nation. Gandhiji does not set-forth only one-aim of education. He views education from different stand-points at different times and in different places. When we examine deeply his writings we find that all his different aims, deal with different aspects of life.

Food, clothes and shelter are our minimum needs and we are not able to satisfy them, all talks about higher ideals of life fall on deaf ears. What is the use of education if it does not help to provide the economic needs or basic necessities of our life? Yes, this was one of the opinion about education, which Gandhiji applied in his educational philosophy. Gandhiji arrived at his theory of self-supporting education independently without any authoritative book on education. Shri Mahadev Desai states that. "He has studied no educational theory; I do not think that he knows of the existence of a book called Emile."

Mr. C.J. Verkey points out that, "the term self-supporting is used, in connection with the Wardha Scheme, in two entirely different senses that will help one to be self-supporting in later life and education which in itself is self-supporting."

In fact Gandhiji wanted that a student should learn while he earns and earn while he learns. Use of hand and head is to be part of his study and is to fit him for the society in which he would be expected to live. Shri K.G. Mashruwala puts it, "The Segaon Method will aim at brining about in the child, at as early an age as possible, the determination of the future career it should expect to pursue, and will arm him a wage enough for a healthy subsistence."

'Bread-and-butter' was not the only aim of Gandhian philosophy of education, it also have cultural norm. No doubt knowledge and culture are two different things for most of the scholars. Dr. S. Radhakrishnan says, "mere knowledge which gratify curiosity is different from culture which refines personality."

But Gandhiji did not engage in academic discussion of knowledge and culture. His conception of culture was purely Gandhian and he would not care what others think of it. In his talks to the girls of the Kasturba Balikashram, New Delhi, on 22.4.1946 he said, "I attach far more importance to the cultural aspect of education than to the literary. Culture is the foundation the primary thing which the girls ought to get from here. It should show itself in the smallest detail of your conduct and personal behaviour, how you sit, how you talk, how you dress, etc., so that anybody might be able to see at a glance that you are the product of this institution. Inner culture must be reflected in your speech, the way in which you treat visitors and guests, and behaves towards one another and your teachers and elders."

Culture for Gandhiji was quality of mind rather than product of intellectual work. To Gandhiji's mind, this was an important aim of education. In his opinion education prepares us to see the things in improper perspective. The educand does not merely learn something, but becomes something by being exposed by constant clash of mind with mind, by the interchange of ideas, by the testing of opinions and the growth of knowledge of human nature.

Gandhiji regarded our educational system unbalanced as it emphasized only training of the mind. On one hand he will not minimize the importance of developing a sound vigorous intellect side by side with the heart and on the other he will not under estimate the need for developing a fine, healthy body. He firmly believed that the true education of heart and head can come through a proper exercise and training of the bodily organs. He said, "I would, therefore, give compulsory physical training through musical drill." It would be better to quote his words to know his views on the training of the body as part of education. He observed:

> "Nor I underrate the building up of the body. This they got in the course of either daily routine. For there were not servants on the farm, and all the work, from cooking down to scavenging was done by inmates. There were many trees to be looked after and enough gardening to be done as well. It was obligatory on all, young and old, who were not engaged in the kitchen, to give sometime to gardening. The children had the lions share of this work which included digging pits, felling timer and lifting loads. This give them ample exercise. They took delight in the work and so they did not generally need any other exercise or game."

Gandhiji had no doubt about what goes by name of education. In reality is only intellectual dissipation. The students' energy is largely wasted in acquiring the knowledge of mere facts. Memorising the facts, figures and latest who is who has become the 'be all and end all' of the education. But if we want to be profited by Gandhiji's educational philosophy, we should aim at a perfect, well balanced all-round education in which the head, the heart, the body and the spirit have all full play and develop together into a natural harmonious whole.

Herbart in his essay on the Aesthetic Revelation of the world puts morality as the chief aim of education. He writes, "The one and the whole aim of education may be summed up in the concept of morality." Gandhiji like many other educationists believed that character formation is one of the foremost aim of education. He stressed so much on the character building that he would relegate to a subordinate position or even sacrifice literacy training if the choice was to be made between the two. To a question "what is your goal in education when India obtain freedom," asked by Carlton Washburne he promptly replied: "Character-building", I would try to develop courage, strength, virtue, the ability to forget oneself in working towards good aims. This is more important than literary. Academic learning is only a means to this greater end. That is why India's great lack of literacy, deplorable as it is, does not appeal to me nor make me feel that India is unfit for self-rule."

In Gandhiji's opinion, "Schools and Colleges are factories for making of character. Parents send their boys and girls to them so that they may become good men and women." In 'To The Students', he puts, "The end of all knowledge must be the building up of character."

In his opinion righteousness or good life is that essential part of character, at which educations should aim. Addressing college students, he said, "Your education is absolutely worthless, if it is not built on a solid foundation of truth and purity. If you, boys, are not careful about the personal purity of your lives, and if you are not careful being pure in thought, speech and deeds then I tell you that you are lost, although you may become perfect finished scholars."

In Hind Swaraj he draws the vivid picture of a peasant who is rightly educated:

> "A peasant earns his bread honestly. He has ordinary knowledge of the world. He knows fairly well how he should behave towards his parents, his wife, his children and his fellow villagers. He understands and observes the rule of morality. But he cannot write his own name. What do you propose to do by giving him a knowledge of letters? Will you added an inch to his happiness? Do you wish to make him discontented with his cottage or his lot."

Gandhiji's new standard of education is not new for those who have some acquaintance with the history of Indian philosophy. His educational philosophy has its roots in Indian life and culture. Character building was the main aim of education in ancient times when young boys and girls studied at Gurukulas under the sleepless vigilance and control of gurus.

As Radhakurnud Mukerji puts it, "The growth of the whole nature of boys, and not the growth of his intellect merely, was the objective of this ancient pedagogy. The raw material is received into the workshop after due examination as to its soundness; it is then treated to different processes of manufacture; and finally sent out to the world as a finished product. The making of the country or the nation was in the charge of these schools. Their aim was to produce not mere recluses or scholars, but whole men, ideal house-holders who would perfect family, society and country."

Gandhiji was not a mere arm-chair dreamer. Had he not maintained unity between thought, speech and action, nobody would have followed him in his foot-steps. He practised what he preached and he preached what he thought, let heavens fall. He experimented his idea of education not only on the sons and daughters of the inmates of the Tolstoy Farm and Phoenix Settlement in South Africa, but also on his four sons, who were not fully satisfied with the type of education imparted to them in the Farm. He wrote to Manilal, his son: "Your duty is to learn whatever you can and serve your parents."

The atmosphere of Gandhiji's Farms whether it was Phoenix settlement or Tolstoy Farm or Sabarmati Ashram reminds us the atmosphere of our ancient Indian ashram's, young blood doing everything with their own hands and learning through work and experience.

No doubt Gandhiji regarded character building the supreme aim of education but he did not underrate the necessity of a literary training. He writes in his autobiography, "But I fully appreciated the necessity of a literary training in addition. I started some classes with the help of Mr. Kallenbach and Shri Pragji Desai, nor did I underrate the building up of the body."

'Sa vidya ya vimuktaye' (education is that which liberates) was one of the important aim of education for Gandhiji. Taking this freedom as political freedom is not the true interpretation and is too narrow to command universal acceptance. Gandhiji was of the opinion that spiritual freedom should be an important aim of education. He wrote in young vimuktye'. It means: that is knowledge which leads to salvation. On the principles that the greater includes the less, the national independence or material freedom is included in the spiritual. The knowledge gained in the educational institutions must, therefore, at least teach the way and lead to such freedom."

Gandhiji regarded every student a brahmachari or vidyarthi, because all his study and activity had as their objective the search of Brahman and he build his life on the foundation of stoic simplicity and self-realisation is the higher aim in Gandhiji's opinion and all other aims are subordinate to the supreme aim of life and education. Gandhiji divided educational aims in two broad categories, i.e. immediate and ultimate aims. Immediate aims are to be many because they touch life at different points and ultimate aim is one and only one, knowledge of God leading to self-realization or the merger of the finite being into the infinite.

Through his new model of education, Gandhiji wanted to achieve unity in diversity. He wanted to create a society in which all individuals have to play their part for the good of the whole without losing their individual character. He wished that the education should meet the requirements of the masses or the masses should meet their requirements through education.

Like his social and political ideas, Gandhiji had in mind while expounding his educational system; the development of all the people—rich and poor, rural and urban, men and women.

MYRIAD THOUGHTS OF GANDHI

1. The mass education should be made free, universal and compulsory.
2. This mass education should not be perfunctorily cut short when the children have barely achieved literacy.
3. The education should be given through mother tongue.
4. The mass education should be given through village crafts like spinning and weaving and (not primarily) through books. Children should actually produce articles education self-supporting.

On the last, i.e. to educate through crafts, Gandhiji put more emphasis because he warned the education to be self-dependent and self-supporting. It satisfied the most basic Gandhian principal of Bread Labour. Further through craft and labour, education provided a link with various human activities. Labour in Gandhian education is the unifying and integrating factor because its goals are to combine the intellectual, the scientific and the physical growth of students. The craft was not to be taken merely as part of curriculum but must reflect a change in educational methodology. It formed a kind of process known as 'learning by doing'. The type of education Gandhiji wanted would attempt to abolish the difference between education and industry. His education, being of universal nature, would remove the inequality between urban people and rural folk. It would provide a healthy and moral basis of relationship between the city and the village and eradicate some of the worst evils of the present social insecurity that has poisoned the relationship between the classes. It would check the progressive decay of our villages and lay the foundations of a just social order in which there is no unnatural division between the haves and have-nots and everybody is assured of a living wage and real freedom and about wage and real freedom. Thus through his ideas about education Gandhiji thought welfare of individual as well as welfare of all.

EPITOME OF THE THOUGHTS OF GANDHI ON EDUCATION

The important features of Gandhiji's basic Education philosophy are:

1. Basic craft as medium of instruction.
2. Cultivation of the ideal of the citizenship.
3. Self-supporting and self-dependent education.
4. Child as the centre of education.
5. More freedom to teacher and pupils without any rigid curriculum.

Evils of the present education system according to Gandhi:

1. It makes youth ashamed of their mother-tongues.
2. It makes youth assumed of their father's progressions.
3. It makes youth estranged from surroundings; ashamed of their own civilization.
4. It is based upon foreign culture to the almost entire exclusion of indigenous culture.
5. It ignores the culture of the heart and the hand and confines itself simply to the head.
6. It is imparted through a foreign medium.
7. The teachers of primary schools are not selected for their patriotism.
8. The higher education makes us foreigner in our own country and the primary education being practically of no use in after-life becomes almost useless.
9. The ideal of education is to bring out the best in

man to create a love for God and man. The present education falls far short of this ideal.

Gandhiji's Fundamental Belief on which His Educational Philosophy is Based:

1. Education is life itself and not a preparation for life. In other words, education is co-extensive with life itself. Education covers the whole life; there is nothing however small which is not the concern of education.
2. Man becomes great exactly in the degree in which he works for the welfare of his fellow men.
3. Willing submission to social restraint for the welfare of his fellow men.
4. True education does not consist in literacy training, but in character-building.
5. In India at any rate where majority of the population is agricultural and industrial, it is a crime to make education merely literacy and to unfit boys and girls for manuai work in after-life.
6. Education to be universal must be free. Therefore our children must be Blade to pay in labour partly or wholly for all the education they receive.
7. True education could be imparted only by the parents.
8. Culture of the heart and building up of character is to be given the first place in education.
9. The children of school should read more quickly than write.
10. True education of the intellect can only come through a proper exercise and training of the bodily organs in the hands, feet, eyes nose, etc. In other worlds, an intelligent use of the bodily organs in the child provides the best and quickest way of developing his intellect.
11. Of all the superstitions that affect India, none is so great as that a knowledge of English language is necessary for impending ideas of liberty and developing accuracy of thought.

12. For India a multiplicity of textbooks means deprivation of the vast majority of village children of the means of instruction. Textbooks in India, therefore, must means textbooks for teachers, not pupils.
13. I must cling to my mother-tongue as to my mother's breast, in spite of shortcoming. It alone can give me the life-giving milk.
14. Higher education should be left to private enterprise. It is not for a democratic State to find money for funding Universities. If the people want them, they will supply the funds.
15. There is nothing so ennobling or lasting as self-study. School and colleges have their use. But we are making altogether too much of them. They are but one of the many means of gaining knowledge.
16. God did not create us to eat, drink and be marry, but to earn our bread in the sear of our brow. Each of us must work eight hours a day. Nobody become slaves by working.
17. Manual training not only develops the intellect and trains the nervous system of the body but also creates self-confidence.

Gandhiji's Aims of Education

1. Character building must be the primary aim of education. Character building is independent of literacy training. The goal of education is not just that you get employment in Government Department or other depts.
2. Real education consists in drawing the best out of yourself. It is one realising the essential brotherhood of man.
3. The real education should make the students able to distinguish good from bad things.
4. Gandhiji aimed at education that will help one to be self-supporting in latter life and education which in itself is self-supporting. Gandhiji is not averse to the bread and butter aim of education.

The education ought to be kind of insurance against unemployment. Gandhiji wants the students to learn while he earns and to earn while he learns.

5. Gandhiji attached far more importance to the cultural aspect of education than to the literary. In his view, culture of education than to the literacy. In his view, culture is not the product of intellectual work, but the quality of the soul, permeating all aspects of human behavior. To Gandhiji, thus, soul culture is an important aim of education.
6. Perfection of our nature is an aim of education. According to Gandhiji, true education is that which draws out and stimulates the spiritual, intellectual and physical faculties of the children. He lays greater emphasis on the education of three H's (Hand, Heart and Head) than on that of the three R's (R)eading (W)riting and (A)rithmetic unless the development of the mind and body goes hand in hand, Gandhiji believes, with a corresponding, awakening of the soul, the former would prove to be a lopsided affair.
7. Gandhiji regards righteousness or good life as an essential part of character at which education ought to aim.
8. Besides character building Gandhiji made 'sa vidya ya vimuktaya' (education is that which liberates) one of the most important aims of education.

   The Hindu philosophers speak of bondage as due to maya and the Christians trace it to the fall. In fact, all religions refer to mans alienation from his deeper being. They teach that man is a dual being, participating in two worlds—the higher, the divine, the free world and the lower, the natural, task which man has to fulfil in life, says Gandhi, is to liberate his spirit from those shackles and to affirm spiritual purity. The aim of education should, therefore, be initiation into the higher life of the spirit.

9. An ideal society as visualized by Gandhiji is a harmonious community based not on cold and cruel competition but on co-operation and mutual aid. In it a spirit of service, sacrifice and love for labour will replace the mad rush for property and power. It should be a society based on equality and social justice, on love and amity, and one that will lead the individual to his divine destiny. Education is looked upon by Gandhiji as an instrument for the establishment of such an ideal society.
10. Gandhi's education aimed at forming a society of people who would be not only self-supporting, but who would not be a burden to the society, a society of people well behaved; respecting the rights of other around them and morally well advanced as to suffer no unwrought.
11. By education Gandhiji meant as all round drawing out of the best in the child and man—body, mind and education. It is one of the means whereby man or woman can be educated. Development of the whole personality is one of the aims of education. Gandhiji's educational ideal is to develop the man—body, mind and soul economically, mentally, socially and spiritually.
12. The object of education should be to produce good citizens, which is very important from the national point of view, as such education would enrich the democratic social, economic and cultural life of India. Gandhiji's scheme of education aimed at giving the citizens of the future a keen sense of personal worth, dignity and efficiency and will strengthen in them the desire for self-improvement and social service in a cooperative community.
13. The highest aim of education, according to Gandhiji is the knowledge of God and self-realization. All other aims are subordinate to this supreme aim of life and education. Gandhiji regards self-realization as the summum bonum of life and education. This is the ultimate goals after

which human beings ought to strive. All the apparently contradictory ideals of education in Gandhiji's education philosophy come together and show their interdependence with the ideal of self-realization forming the apex of the whole pyramided structure of his education philosophy.

GANDHIJI'S THOUGHTS ON RELIGIOUS EDUCATION, WOMEN'S' EDUCATION, HIGHER EDUCATION, UNIVERSITY EDUCATION AND ADULT EDUCATION

Religious Education

To Gandhiji religious means Truth and Ahimsa or rather Truth alone, because Truth includes Ahimsa, Ahimsa being the necessary and indispensable means for its discovery. Therefore, anything that promotes the practice of these virtues is a means for imparting religious education and the best way to do this, in his opinion, is for the teachers to practice these virtues rigorously in their own persons.

A curriculum of religious instruction should include a study of the tenets of faiths other than one's own. For this purpose the students should be trained to cultivate the habit of understanding and appreciating the doctrine of various great religions of the world in a spirit of reverence and broadminded tolerance. This if property done would help to give them a spirit assurance and a better appreciation of their own religion. There is one rule, however, which should always be kept in mind while studying all great religious and that is that one should study them only through the writing of known votaries of the respective religions.

This study of other religions besides one's will give one a grasp of the rock-bottom unity of all religions and afford a glimpse also of that universal and absolute Truth which lies beyond the "dust of creeds and faiths."

Let no one even for a moment, says Gandhi, entertain the fear that a reverent study of other religions is likely to weaken or shake one's faith in one's own.

Women's Education

Man and woman are of equal rank but they are not

identical. They are a peerless pair being supplementary to one anther; each helps the other, so that without the one the existence of the other cannot be conceived, and therefore it follows that anything that will impair the status of either of them equally runs for both. In framing any scheme of woman's education, according to Gandhiji this cardinal truth must be constantly kept in mind. Man is supreme in the outward activities of a married pair and therefore it is in the fitness of things that he should have greater knowledge thereof. On the other hand, home life is entirely the sphere of woman and therefore in domestic affairs, in the upbringing and education of children, women ought to have more knowledge. Not that the knowledge should be divided into watertight compartments, or that some branches of knowledge should be closed to anyone; but unless course of instruction are based on a discriminating appreciation of these basic principles, the fullest life of man and woman cannot be developed.

Higher Education

1. Gandhiji is not opposed to education even of the highest type attainable in the world.
2. The state must pay for it whether it has definite use for it.
3. Gandhiji is opposed to all higher education being paid for the general revenue.
4. It is Gandhiji's firm conviction that the vast amount of so-called education arts, given in our colleges, is sheet waste and has resulted in unemployment among the educated classes.
5. The medium of a foreign language through which higher education has been imparted in India has caused incalculable moral and intellectual injury to the nation.

Thus Gandhiji claims he is not an enemy of Higher Education. But he is enemy of Higher Education as it is given in this country.

University Education

What, according to Gandhiji's view, the State would not have is army of B.A.s and M.A.s with their brains sapped with too much cramming and minds almost paralyzed by the impossible attempt to speak and write English like Englishmen. And when they have the latter, it is usually clerkships at which most of the knowledge gained during their twelve year of High schools and colleges are of no use whatsoever.

University trading becomes self-supporting when it is utilized by the state. It is criminal to pay for training which benefit neither the nation nor the individual. In Gandhiji's opinion there is no such thing as individual benefit which cannot be proved to be also of national benefit.

University education must be originally related to the Indian scene. It must therefore be an extension and continuation of the Basic Education course.

Adult Education

Adult education, according to Gandhi should be much more than a mere knowledge of reading and writing as it is now. Literacy for Gandhiji was not the end of education, it was only means whereby man and woman could be educated. He wanted the adult education to be related to the real life needs of the benefactors emphasizing the need of craft centered education.

SALIENT FEATURES OF EDUCATIONAL PHILOSOPHY OF GANDHI, TO UNDERSTAND THE GREATEST MAN OF THE MILLENIUM:

1. The outstanding contribution of Gandhiji to the evolution of educational theory is his revolt against the existing content and methods of education which reduce the child to the position of a passive receiver the child to his rightful place in the class and make education pandocentric. In his view, education developing "the whole man thought craft"
2. The gospel of love had been stressed by the past

educationists, but Gandhiji makes love the sole compulsion and direction in the training of children since when love being to rule education, the problem of punishment vanishes, Gandihi thinks that children have finer sense of honour than adults.

3. Gandhiji is keen on finding the expenses of a teacher through the product of the manual work of his pupils, because he is convinced that there is no other way to crores of our semi-starved and half-naked children.
4. Such an integral, all sided education through remunerative labour would make children self-confident and brave by their paying for their own education by their own labour.
5. Gandhiji rescues education from the four walls of the classroom.
6. It is rooted in our culture and civilization and is eminently suited to genius of our people.
7. It is universal in application, because it is to be common to all-Hindus, Muslims, Parsees and Christians. It stresses practical religion of self-help.
8. The ideal of citizenship is implicit in Gandhiji's Education theory. It aims at seducing the minimum education of citizen for the intelligent exercise of their rights and duties in a democratic state.
9. It envisages the idea of co-operative community in which the motive of social service will dominate the activities of children.
10. Gandhiji through his philosophy of education has stressed that true education should result not in the lust for material power, but in spiritual force.
11. According to Gandhiji, every man is the real teacher of himself; experience is great schools; the knowledge acquired at schools is often superficial and a grown-up stands in need of development, perseverance and self-confidence than school education.
12. Regarding sex-education Gandhiji says that, such

education should automatically serve to bring home to children the essential distinction between man and best; to make pride to be gifted with facilities of head and heart both, that he is a thinking no less than a feeling animal.

13. Gandhiji's unique contribution to the education is of making manual training that means literacy training and not supplementing literacy with manual training.
14. Gandhiji's education system makes one physically and mentally strong, economically sound and beneficial to society.
15. The fundamental basis of religious education, according to Gandhiji, should be instruction in the universal essentials of religion and training in the fundamental virtues of Truth and Ahimsa, with make for purity of heart and purity of living.
16. According to Gandhiji, the education that children naturally imbibe in a well-ordered household is impossible to obtain in hostels. The young children thus, should not be separated from their parents. Under Ideal conditions, true education could be imparted only by the parents, and that there should be the minimum of outside help.
17. Gandhiji's educational concept involves (In order of preference)—
    1. Character building
    2. Body building (physical work)
    3. Literary training
18. Education, according to Gandhiji, means
    1. Physical training
    2. Mental training and
    3. Spiritual training-

       and to impart these in perfect manner, the teacher must himself be perfect in all these aspects.
19. Gandhiji's education system fulfils two basic condones namely—
    1. Education must be rooted in the culture and life of the people, and

2. Purity of personal life is the one indispensable condition for building a sound education

References

Jain, T.R. Elementary Statistics and Evolution of Indian Economics, Economic Survey, 1995.

Thomas, F.W., History and Prospects of British Education in India, 1891, p. 1.

Joshi, L.A., Foreward in Mitra, Ved, Education In India (New Delhi: Arya Book Depot, 1964), pp. VII-VIII.

Jaffar, S.M., Education in Muslim India (Delhi: Idarah-IAdabiyat-I-Delhi, 1972), p. 4.

Bhatnagar, Suresh, Indian Education: Today and Tomorrow (Meerut: International Publishing House Meerut, 1990), p. 42.

Competition Success Review Year Book, 2006, p. 640.

Yojana, January, 1997, p. 23.

Times of India, Sept. 25, 1996, p. 11 (Report by R.C. Srivastava).

Times of India, Sept. 27, 1996, p. 11 (Article by Ashok Celly).

Media in Gandhian Perspective

Manoj Rajan

Media as a backbone of the modern society, putting its inscription on every aspect of human being's life irrespective of place, religion, caste and creed to spread out the anonymity of the social order on such account without bothering whether such writings are acceptable in fashionable times or not. Mohandas Karamchand Gandhi, popularly known as Mahatma Gandhi, was one and the only who continues to evoke interest in every human beings mind and thought even several decades after his death in 1948. And to explore the journalist hidden in Gandhi is no easy exercise, as he was versatile, meticulous and authentic in his writings as in his speeches and actions. No wonder he produced about two million English words alone, the estimate for Hindi and Gujarati being not known. Initially in South Africa as a free-lance Journalist, Gandhi went on to become one of the finest journalists, producing some of the best journals in the history of Indian journalism. Indian Opinion, Young India, Harijan and Navajivan were the important journals that were edited by Gandhi. Further, he was associated with a lot of other publications during the peak of India's freedom struggle.

Gandhi always set high standards for printing words and was of the view that it is the only platform where you can address the mass society in one go and educate them for their legal rights. The most potent weapon to revolutionize the society, Gandhi visualized its importance in early stage of his life and makes it a part and parcel of his plan of action. Journalism, which is a discipline of gathering, writing and reporting news, and more broadly it includes the process of editing and presenting the news articles, fascinated everyone and the man of the millennium Mohandas Karamchand Gandhi was not an exception. The power of his communication was so forceful that whatever he said and wrote made an everlasting mark on reader's mind and his approach to journalism was totally devoid of any self-interest. None of his contemporary or afterwards ever used the media so forcefully to ponder over the general issues that concerned the society. He knows the importance of communication and used it to shape the opinions and mobilzing the people.

Mass communication means transfer of information from sender to the receiver, with the information being understood by the receiver in the same sense in which the sender wants is to be understood.[1] In the overall process of communication feedback, the sender can know whether his communication has been rightly understood or not. Since communication means reaching out to the other person or persons, the process can be verbal or non-verbal, intentional or unintentional, provided the goal is achieved and one man who can fit in this communication theory exactly is none other than Mahatma Gandhi. Taking the center stage after returning from South Africa, he led from front and put forward his own opinion. Gandhi always set high standards for printing words and was of the view that it is the only platform where you can address the mass society in one go and educate them for their legal rights. In his autobiography, he wrote, "The sole aim of journalism should be the service of nation and people. The newspapers are a great power, but just as unchained torrent of water submerges whole countryside and devastated crops, even so an uncontrolled pen serves to destroy. If the control is from without, it proves more poisonous than want of control. It can be profitable only when experienced from within."[2]

Bhikhu Parekh has beautifully summed up this aspect of Gandhi's communication skills in the following words: After a long reflection and experimentation he evolved a distinct mode of discourse that was also a form of praxis. Convinced that human actions derived their emotional energy from heart which could only be addressed and activated by a judiciously selected language of symbols, and recognizing that Hindu culture was deeply symbolic, he evolved a powerful cluster of culturally evocative symbols including such things as the spinning wheel, the khadi, the cow and the Gandhi cap...... partly by conscious design and partly as spontaneous expressions of his own way of life his dress, language, mode of speaking, food, bodily gestures, ways of sitting, walking and talking, humour and staff, became a symbol of a specific way of life. Each evoked deep cultural memories, spoke volumes and conveyed highly complex messages.[3] Communication happens at many levels (even for one single action), in many different ways, and for most beings, as well as certain machines. Several, if not all, fields of study dedicate a portion of attention to communication, so when speaking about communication it is very important to be sure about what aspects of communication one is speaking about.

Definitions of communication range widely, some recognizing that animals can communicate with each other as well as human beings, and some are narrower, only including human beings within the parameters of human symbolic interaction. "What is really needed to make democracy to function is not the knowledge of facts, but right education. And the true function of journalism is to educate the public mind, not to stock the public mind with wanted and unwanted impressions. A journalist has, therefore, to use his discretion as to what to report and when. As it is, journalists are not content to stick to the facts alone. Journalism has become the art of intelligent anticipation of events."[4] The renowned personality of mass media and was probably the greatest journalist of all time Mahatma Gandhi reached out to millions of people across the world through his communication skills and journalistic approach, put an ever lasting impact on Indian National Movement's and wage a battle single handily against mighty Britishers. He took journalism as a medium to educate the common masses as well as to install patriotic feeling in their hearts for the cause of others. In his journalistic career, which roughly spanned four decades, he wrote articles on various topics, simple and clear with passion and burning indignation. Gandhi was not a journalist in the popular sense of the term. His life and writing had a symbiotic relationship with each other. Gandhi wrote with a purpose. Writing for him, was not a writer's pursuit for creativity for a role, it was a duty bound to perform. Neither was writing a proselytizing mission with him. Writing satisfied his need to share his ideas with others, a two-way dialogue, between him and his readers on a joint journey on the path leading to the truth.[5]

Newspapers were not only informative and entertaining to Gandhi but also made him ambitious and he started thinking to write for them. The desire latent in a human beings everyone want to see his name and article in print and it was that temptation which could not be resisted. His friendship with the members of London Vegetarian Society provided him a necessary launching pad to write for its organ the Vegetarian and that were his earliest writing on the record. A struggling barrister of Bombay that he was at that time, he had to do something more tangible than indulging in non-remunerative journalism. South Africa not only shaped many of his ideas and traits of Gandhiji, but made him an out and out journalist as well. If London Vegetarian Society afforded him a forum to write and speak, the political situation in South Africa chiseled him into a conscientious journalist. While fighting incessantly against all disabilities imposed on Indians, through representation, petition, memorandum etc, he did not, for a moment, minimize the great role of newspapers. He would scan through all local papers and reply suitably to any queries or distortion of facts. In a letter to the editor of *The Times of India,* he wrote, "Publicity is our best and perhaps the only weapon of defense."[6] Gandhi considered journalism as a selfless service to the society. He advocated that journalism should never be prostituted for selfish ends for amassing money. As an operation in ideas, journalism should be as free as possible from the limitations of industrialism. Using print media for the dissemination of his ideas was part of a clear strategy with Gandhi. Gandhi was a prolific writer who has left behind a vast body of articles and books.

Gandhi's first major essay in journalism was the 'Green Pamphlet', describing the conditions of Indians in South Africa. Gandhi wrote the piece while he had come home to Rajkot on a brief visit from South Africa (1901). The success of the pamphlet made Gandhi more confident of the efficacy and publicity value of print media. The Hindu, The Statesman, *The Times of India* and The Englishman vied with each other in publishing Gandhi. By that time, Gandhi had made name for himself in the arena of Journalism. By 1903, Gandhi had realized that occasional writing and open letters or articles in newspapers were inadequate to meet the great campaign strategy he had in his mind. This realization led to Gandhi taking over the editorship of the Indian Opinion, a weekly that published from South Africa, which established Gandhi as a journalist. On the one hand, they were given lessons in hygiene and sanitation, and, on the other, they were reminded of their rich culture and civilization. In short, the journal addressed itself to the whole gamut of Gandhi concerns that was communicated in the most straightforward and lucid manner. Care was taken to make the whole exercise of communication come to the level of the dialogue between the readers and the writers. Through judicious use of print media, Gandhi was abele to highlight the light of Indians in South Africa, publicize the discriminatory laws and actions they were subjected to, and finally, to organize Satyagraha to streamline the things. Another great quality of Gandhi, the editor, was his direct and forthright manner in conveying the things. Direct presentation was the beauty of all his writings. He had a clear thinking and knew well what he was going to say. He would put forth his ideas and arguments in crisp short sentences.

Gandhi attempted to realize his dream through effective use of his writings and was fairly hopeful of doing so. Gandhi used the print media actively during his stay in South Africa and highlights the plight of Indians in his columns. He continued to follow the standards of journalism even later part of his life that he set for himself and his staff during the initial struggle in South Africa. Similarly his ornamental style of writing and his restraint were emulated by the upcoming journalist of the contemporary times. About impact of his writing during that period one can safely said that he was at least able to make the Indian community aware of their rights in the colony. Gandhi used very dignified language to put across his ideas, which were in the nature of educating the Indians and others. His attitude, as revealed from his writings, never had a tune of confrontation or challenge; rather Gandhi was developing a new technique and style of appealing to the fairness for which the British were known. Mahatma Gandhi's life, attitude and political action were informed by the highest moral principles and compassion. Uniquely among public men, he sought to analyze and explain events and his own reaction in terms of these principles through his talks, statements, writing and interviews. The moral force that he brought to bear on the political discourse was compelling and inspired large section to take up the cause of the freedom.

Gandhi in fact, brought in many new elements, which introduced fresh life in the field of journalism. "As a result of his wide interest, his genius for simplification, his eagerness to reach the largest number of people and startling nature of his activities, there was a quickening of life in journalism. Many of his followers were moved to write and publish in the Indian languages and in imitation of his own direct style, they wrote a simple prose. Regional journalism began to acquire an importance and there was hardly an area of the county which did not have its newspapers."[7] Undoubtedly, Gandhi introduced a new and a noble element in the field of journalism. It was his approach his human approach which gave his writings a character. He never looked upon the reading public as target for propaganda. He belonged to the people by identifying himself with them and wrote about their feelings and aspirations. For Gandhi, neither subject was too big nor was too small. Louis Fisher once said that Gandhi would attach equal importance to a letter written to President Roosevelt as much to an article on the subject of individual rights. Gandhi was very much laconic in speech. He seldom used a superfluous word. Each coma or colon conveyed something or the other. Moreover his expression was much less than his profound thinking on the subject. He had suggestions to give on each item published in the journal.

Gandhi as an editor would correct himself publicly if he found that some untruth had crept in his writings. To cite an example, he compared the Jalianwala Bagh massacre to that of Glenco. A correspondent drew his attention saying that the latter was more horrible. In the next issue of the *Young India*, Gandhi corrected his statement. Newspapers or view papers is a social institution. Its success depends on how they produce materials in their columns. It also judged by the readers whom they are going to address through their writings. Unfortunately papers mostly cater to the lower taste of the readers, through sensation mongering rather than educating him for better citizenship. Some times the monetary benefits pushed back the ethics in journalism and yellow journalism and page 3 stories occupied the main attention. To whom the journalist is loyal? To the proprietor, to one's own self-or to the particular class, he belongs to? As per Gandhiji, readers were the most important. A journalist may be a patriot, a party member or a faithful employee but his loyalty primarily associated with his readers. Public has the right to know the truth. He must be informed objectively as to what is happening. His stories neither are hampered by partiality nor by loose connectivity. If the paper looses confidence of its readers, it has lost all that is worth in journalism. Gandhi interpreted that the writer alone is in a position to link up with the very sources of life on important event, be it political, social or economic and bring it into the strictly human domain that is accessible to all.

Personally, Gandhiji did not like to write much in English though he loved the language and developed a style of his own. He knew English could not be the national language of India. But as long as the national language, Hindustani, was not developed, he had to choose a medium through which his message could be reached to the four corners of the country. As a nationalist, he wanted a common language for the country and though aware of the richness of the Gujarati literature, did not hesitate to support and foster the claim of Hindustani for this honor. He made all efforts to make the language acceptable in all over India. On his writing skills, J.H. Holmes wrote, "Gandhi's literary achievement is the more remarkable in view of the fact that he was never, in any sense of the phrase, a literary man. Unlike his great contemporary, Ravinder Nath Tagore and his accomplished successor Pandit Nehru, the Mahatma had no special grace of style. Seldom, in his writings, did he rise to heights of eloquence and beauty. Gandhiji interests were never aesthetic but rather pragmatic. He had no desire or ambition, no time to be an artist. His own thought was of his own people and his struggle to make them free. So he wrote with disciplined simplicity, seeking only to make himself clearly understood. The result was the one most important quality of literary art namely clarity. I doubt if, in all his works, Gandhi ever wrote a sentence, which failed to express with utter precision the thought he had in mind to convey. He wrote a style that was perfect for his purpose of communication. To read his writings is to think of the contents and not of the style which means a triumph in the adoption of means to ends."[8]

His articulation is not only clear and simple but also meaningful taken in the contest of his leadership of the most gigantic nationalist struggle of the twentieth century. He wrote extensively in *Young India* and *Harijan,* the leading voice of the era presenting various contemporary issues and forces readers to give it a thought. Writing for ordinary folk, he usually employed various metaphors to realize Indians about their abilities and rich traditions. Gandhi was not merely a leader; he has also become a part of the masses. His simple attire, use of colloquial Hindi reference to the popular allegory of Ramrajya had made him comprehensible to the common people. Gandhiji introduced a new lively tone in his correspondence. Unlike the formal artificial letters in and average newspaper office, his was couched in simple and direct language. It was fashioned to suit the needs of the occasion. When he was away from the scene of action, he would make sure, through letters, etc. to keep in constant touch with them. Gandhi was very methodical in whatever subject he laid his hands on. He knew that mere good writing was not enough. He must see that the paper was published and dispatched in time and that proper account was maintained. He used to take the best out of his associates in running the paper. In his first meeting with Gandhi, Lord Reading, the Viceroy expressed surprise at his growing popularity among the Indians by saying, "There is nothing striking about his appearance. He came to visit me in a dhoti and cap, woven on a spinning wheel, with bare feet and legs and my first impression on seeing him ushered into my room was that there was nothing to arrest attention in his appearance and that I should passed him by in the street without a second look at him. When he talks, the impression is different."[9]

When Gandhiji arrived in India on January 9, 1915, journalism did not establish itself as a profession, excepting in case of Anglo Indian press. Advertisement did not play that important role as it plays today. By and large, people had to depend on sales promotion and more important, on monetary help from individuals. More over, advertisement was meant for the capture of a section of the society whereas in modern times it's catering to influence all strata of life. Gandhiji's objection to advertisement was more on moral and ethical grounds. It becomes difficult to draw a line between what is bad and beneficial advertisement. Once a newspaper agreed to take advertisement there was no limit to that. In their quest for money, they published indecent and harmful advertisement. This was, according to him, not the objective of journalism. Rather than serving the community, such action would run to the detriment of its interest. Gandhi commenting on Hind Swaraj in 1921 elaborated the purpose behind the book, he says, "It was written in answer to the Indian school of violence and its prototype in South Africa. I came in contrast with every known Indian anarchist in London. Their bravery impressed me, but I feel that their zeal was misguided. I felt that violence was no remedy for India's ills and that her civilization required the use of a different and higher weapon for self-protection. The Satyagraha of South Africa was still on infant hardly two years old. But it had developed sufficiently to permit me to write of it with some degree of confidence. Hind Swaraj teaches the gospel of love in the place of that of hate. It replaces violence with self-sacrifice. It pits soul force against brute force."[10]

Gandhiji was great advocated for the freedom of press. In the *Young India* of January 12, 1922, he wrote on the liberty of press, "Liberty of speech means that it is not gagged even when the speech hurts, liberty of the press can be said to be truly respected only when the press can comment in the severest terms upon and even misrepresent matters, broken against misrepresentation or violençe being secured not by and administrative gagging order, not by closing down the press but punishing the real offender, leaving the press itself unrestricted. Freedom of association is truly respected when assemblies of people can discuss even revolutionary projects, the state relying upon the force of public opinion and the civil policy, not the savage military at its disposal, to crush any actual outbreak of revolution that is designed to confound public opinion and the state representing it."[11] Gandhi further put forward his views on nation, nationalism and national identity in *Harijan*. He rarely used the term nation except when forced to do so under circumstances in which Jinnah defended the two nation theory. In opposition to Jinnah, he argued that the language of nationalism was both incompatible with the Indian situation and inherently absurd. India was not a nation but a civilization, which had benefited from the contribution of different races and religions over the centuries. Challenging the basis of two nation theory, Gandhi therefore asked, "Is India composed of two nations? Are not Christians a third, Parsis a fourth and so on? How are the Muslims of Punjab different from the Hindus and Sikhs? Are they not all Punjabis drinking the same water, breathing the same air and deriving the sustenance from the same soul?"[12]

Although Gandhi's responses in *Harijan* were issue based, they largely followed the theoretical conceptualizations that he articulated in the Hind Swaraj, one of the most important treatises that he wrote to clarify his views to readers. While writing in Hind Swaraj, Gandhi was influenced by leading western thinkers of the contemporary times. As he himself admitted, "Whilst the views expressed in Hind Swaraj are held by me, I have but endeavored humbly to follow Tolstoy, Ruskin, Thoreau, Emerson and other writers besides the master of the Indian philosophy."[13]

The Mahatma was perhaps the first to have realized the political inadequacies of the urban centric national movement in a diverse society like India. In addition to article written by Gandhi, a regular section in *Harijan* was the 'Question Box', where Gandhi responded to questions on various issues of contemporary relevance. Questions generally structured around what the Mahatma had written in weekly and elsewhere. Since the question box ensured a dialogue with those seeking to grapple with his views, the Gandhi always favorable disposed towards the section. *Harijan* was important in another aspect, as the forum where Gandhi generally dealt with the criticism of his published views. Gandhi differentiated between news and journalists impression of coming events. He would not like interpretative news, which to him, was journalistic kite flying. He would advice journalists to print authentic news with no fear of contradiction. He would ask them to withhold news as long as it could not be verified. The readers in the west were not only getting the news but speculative news with particular slant or with different interpretations so as to create a public opinion the paper desired.

The tendency of the journalists to pick up the bits from here and there and dish them up for the purpose of creating sensation was, according to him, back door journalism. Such type of journalism misled the public and harmed the genuine cause. Calling them bad examples of foreign journalists, he requested his Indian counterparts to desist from such cheap performance. The main aim of the journalist would be to strengthen the society along with unbiased reporting. During the Quit India movement, he appealed to Princes, to Government servants, to soldiers and to students with the request to help the struggle. But Hiren Mukherjee, Deputy leader of the Communist Party in the parliament criticizes, "No particular role was allotted to the workers and peasants and though they formed the overwhelming majority of the people, they were expected simply to line up in the manner directed by their superiors. The priorities given to journalists in Gandhi's order of appeal, it perhaps not entirely accidental, the Mahatma, with all its great coverage and occasional sublimity, had throughout his life, had a shrewd eye to publicity whatever he thought and did."[14]

Gandhi had of late, been greatly distressed at the general fall in the standard of the press. He hated speculation. This was sometimes mischievous and often misleading. He hated fabrication on facts and news. He did not believe in so called journalistic 'scoop'. As one who believed in the service to the community, he would advise against publication of doubtful news. Due to the charismatic personality and his journalistic qualities, the journalist of contemporary times began to imitate him. They went to the field and collected stories about the common man his thought and feeling, his desire and ambition. Whether it was a political, economic or social article, it invariably moves around the masses. The modern media still taking a leaf out of the books of Mahatma Gandhi regarding moral and ethics in journalism but due to the cutthroat competition in this field, few are the buyers of Gandhi's journalism. Media, in contemporary times has become so powerful that it can mould the society and change the viewpoint of common masses towards any general issues that come across its way. Thus he was a man of thought and action, a rare combination. As a man of thought, he was highly critical of the madness of modernity and articulated an alternative vision, the best insights of both, the pre-modern and modern worldviews while avoiding the naive individualism and moral vacuum of the currently fashionable post-modernism.[15] As a man of action, he led from the front the nationalist struggle of freedom on the basis of what he thought was morally acceptable. Without compromising one's integrity, he also demonstrated how to build a strong political platform drawing upon the moral strength of Satyagrahis.[15]

Notes and References

1. Harold Koontz, and Heinz Weihrich, Essentials of Management (Singapore: McGraw Hill Book Co.), 1990.
2. Gandhi, M.K., An Autobiography or The Story of My Experiments with Truth (Ahmedabad: Navajivan Publishing House), 1956.
3. Parekh, Bhiku, Gandhi (Oxford: Oxford University Press), 1997.
4. Tendulkar, D.G., Mahatma Gandhi: Life of Mohandas Karamachand Gandhi, Eight Volumes (New Delhi: The Publications Division, Ministry of Information and Broadcasting, Government of India) 1953.

5. Mehta, D.S., Mass Communication and Journalism in India (Bombay: Allied Publishers Private Limited), 1979.
6. *The Times of India*, Bombay, October 20, 1896.
7. Natarajan, S.A., History of the Press in India (Bombay: Asia Publishing House), 1962.
8. Homer, A Jack (ed.), The Wit and Wisdom of Gandhi (Boston: Beacon Press), 1951.
9. Oriental and India Office Collections, London, Mss Eur F 238/3, Reading papers, Reading, the Viceroy to Montague, the Secretary of state, 19 May 1920.
10. The Collected Works of Mahatma Gandhi (New Delhi: The Publications Division, Ministry of Information and Broadcasting, Government of India), Vol. 19, p. 277.
11. Sitaramayya, B. Pattabhi, The History of Indian National Congress (Bombay: Padma Publications), 1946, Vol. 1.
12. *Harijan*, 28-10-1939, p. 283.
13. Gandhi's Preface to the English Edition of Hind Swaraj in Parel's Hind Swaraj and Other Writings (Cambridge: Cambridge University Press), 1997.
14. Mukherjee, Hiren, Gandhi: A Study (Calcutta: National Book Agency Pvt. Ltd.), 1958.
15. Parekh, Bhiku, Gandhi, *op. cit.*, p 42.

17

Gandhi's Socialism for Peace

RAMESH KUMAR

The history of politics in India during last three decades has been profoundly influenced by the three forces of nationalism, socialism and Gandhism. Mahatma Gandhi began his political career in India in the early thirties dedicated to the realization of certain well defined political goals comprehensively described as purna svaraj. He started his leadership as a nationalist, though as time passed he constantly enlarged the scope of his nationalist philosophy. This finally emerged as sarvodaya and acquired the official sanction of the Indian National Congress as its philosophy of political action and corporate life. Gandhi transformed nationalism from being a mere politics of protest to a consistent philosophy of life.

The four dominant influences on Gandhi's thought have been those of Ruskin, Tolstoy, the Bhagavad Gita and the 'Sermon on the Mount'. From Ruskin Gandhi learnt, if we may so put it, the doctrine that the good of the individual is contained in the good of all; that all labour, whether performed by a stonemason or a philosopher, is of equal value, being equally 'socially significant'; and that each individual, in order, to claim the privileges of membership of the social group, must perform some physical labour which he termed 'bread labour'. With Ruskin Gandhi firmly believed in the supremacy of spiritual values, the essential goodness of human nature, that character was a much more significant achievement than anything else and that the machine degrades, rather than ennobles, humanity. From Tolstoy: Gandhi acquired his deep admiration for Christian ethics as expressed through the 'Sermon on the Mount'. Charity, compassion, love, these formed the core of his philosophy of life, and this love meant the love of God. As he said: 'I have been' a willing slave to this most exacting Master for more than half a century. His voice has been increasingly audible as the years have rolled by. He has never forsaken me even in my darkest hour. He has saved me often against myself and left me not a vestige of independence. The greater the surrender to Him, the greater has been my joy.'[1] This attitude of love for God and, as its corollary, love for man, became the law of his being.[2] All other ideas flowed logically from this central concept. For him the ethical consideration was supreme, equally valid in religion and social and economic life. He said: 'True economics never militates against the highest ethical standards, just as all true ethics worth its name must at the same time be also good economics. An economics that inculcates Mammon worship and enables the strong to amass wealth at the expense of the weak is a false and dismal science. For Gandhi, then, economic relations, as all other human relations, are ethical relations. He always insisted on ethical means and for him means and ends were mutually convertible terms. He spoke of life in a series of dichotomous terms, like truth and untruth, non-violence and violence, nonpossession and possessiveness.

Gandhihji's socialism was not "to rise on the ashes of the blind, the deaf and the dumb."[3] He wanted full freedom of the development of human personality, which western democracies lacked in practice. There was no place to authoritarianism in the envisioned socialism of Gandhiji.[4]

Gandhiji had perfect faith in democratic socialism. The spirit of democratic socialism is evidently clear from his following two statements that he made while explaining the term Swaraj.

"By Swaraj", I mean "the government of India by the consent of the people as ascertained by the largest number of the adult population. Real Swaraj will come not by the acquisition of authority by a few but by the acquisition of the capacity by all to resist authority when it is abused."[5] And explaining the economic aspect of Swaraj, he said: "The Swaraj of my dream is the poor men's Swaraj. The necessaries of life should be enjoyed by you in common with those enjoyed by the princes and the moneyed men.... You ought to get all the ordinary amenities of life that a rich man enjoys have not the slightest doubt that Swaraj is not poorna Swarja until these amenities are guaranteed to you under it."[6]

He wanted Swaraj for all, men and women, rich and poor, Hindu, Muslim, Sikh and Christian and emphatically including the maimed, the blind, 'the starving, toiling millions.'[7] So, he declared, "I shall work for India in which the poorest shall feel that it is their country in whose making they have an effective voice."[8]

The socialism of Gandhiji was humanitarian in its approach and not mechanical. To him, socialism stood for love, mutual trust and good will. He wanted to build a new social order but not through coercive power of the state machinery but by changing the heart of the rich. He was conscious that "grinding pauperism can lead to anything else than moral degradation. Every human has a right to live and therefore, to find the wherewithal to feed himself and where necessary, to clothe and house himself."[9] Hence, economic equality was necessary which "means the leveling down of the few rich in whose hands concentrated in the bulk of the nations wealth, on the one hand, and a leveling up of the semi starved naked millions of the other."[10] He appealed to upper classes on the ground of humanity to give up their superfluous property for the common good of the society.[11]

He wanted to bring socialism by preaching the gospel of love. According to Gandhiji love was non-possession, and therefore, love and possession could not co-exist.[12]

According to Gandhiji the real meaning of socialism was services to the people, addressing a conference on July 2, 1947 he said: "Nearly fifty years ago, when I was practicing law in South Africa, many used to call themselves socialists.

But they were less of socialists than I was. I used to work among the labourers. I have made this part of my life's work. This is true socialism. I have always considered myself a true servant of the peasant and the workers.[13] In this socialistic pattern of society, his ideal was equal wages for all ... doctor, engineer, lawyer, teacher and even bhangi, but for the present he had "to see that every labourer get enough to feed and clothe himself and his family. A government that does not ensure this much is no government."[14] Besides, he had also realized that the concept of high and low had done harm to society, hence, he issualised to bring about an equalization to status. "The working classes", he said, "have all these centuries been isolated and relegated to a lower status. They have been shoodras, and the world has been interpreted to mean an inferior status, I want to allow no differentiation between the son of a weaver, of an agriculturist and of a schoolmaster."[15]

In this insistence on ethics Gandhi differs markedly from Marxism. Marxian thought, as it has developed, always speaks of capitalist morality and proletarian morality, while for Gandhi morality was a single and indivisible corpus of principles applicable to all human beings regardless of class affiliations. Property and labour he viewed from, this central points of ethics and stressed the primacy of the individual. On the basis of this he attempted an essay in the reconstruction of society.

But if Gandhi was uncompromisingly clear about his faith he could be perplexingly vague in the use of some of the terms. For instance, on several occasions he declared that he was a socialist.[16] 'Socialism', he said, 'is a beautiful word' and, so far as I am aware, in socialism all the members of society are equal none low, none high. In the individual body, the head is not high because it is the top of the body nor are the soles of the feet low because they touch the earth. Even as members of the individual body are equal so are the members of society. This is socialism.

In it, the prince and the peasant, the wealthy and the poor, the employer and the employee, are all on the same level. In terms of religion, there is no duality in socialism. It is all unity. . . . Socialism begins with the first convert. If there is one such, you can add zeros to the one, and the first zero will account for ten and every addition will account for ten times the previous number. If however the beginner is a zero, in other words no one makes the beginning, multiplicity of zeros will also produce 'zero value.'

But Gandhi insisted that he was a socialist of a different genre. 'The socialism and communism of the west', he said, 'are based on certain conceptions which are fundamentally different from ours. One such conception is their belief in the essential selfishness of human nature. I do not subscribe to it, for I know that the essential difference between man and brute is that the former can respond to the call of the spirit in him, can rise superior to the passions that he owns in common with the brute and, therefore, superior to selfishness and violence, which belong to the brute nature and not to the immortal spirit of man.[17] Gandhi further declared: 'My fundamental difference with the socialists is well known. I believe in conversion of human nature and in striving for it. They do not believe in this.'[18] Jawaharlal Nehru says that when Gandhi calls himself a 'socialist', he uses the word in a sense peculiar to himself which has little or nothing to do with the economic framework of society which goes by the name of socialist. For Gandhi points out that 'socialism, and more particularly Marxism, because of their association with violence' are such as to go counter to his creed. The very words 'class war' breathe conflict and violence and are thus repugnant to him. He has also no desire to raise the standards of the masses beyond a certain very modest competence, for higher standards and leisure may lead to self-indulgence and sin. It is bad enough that the handful of the well to do are self-indulgent, it would be much worse if their numbers were added to.

That outlook is as far removed from the socialistic, or for that matter the capitalistic, as anything can be.... The promise of socialism, therefore, holds no attraction for him, and capitalism is only partly tolerable becaase it circumscribes the evil. He dislikes both, but puts up with the latter for the present as a lesser evil and as something which exists and of which he has to take cognizance.[19]

Thus, while Gandhi shares the socialist abhorrence of

exploitation and social injustice, his differences with socialism are equally profound. While Marxism views history in terms of classes in conflict Gandhi views it as a ceaseless growth, an 'unfoldment in terms of spirituality'.[20] This poles apart from the Marxist dialectic. If the Marxist accepts violence as a part of revolution ary changes, to Gandhi nothing is worth while, not even socialism, if it is based on violence. Where the Marxist says that class war is not only inevitable but desirable in certain contexts, Gandhi declares that 'class war is foreign to the essential genius of India, which is capable of evolving communism on the fundamental rights of all, on equal justice.' The Ramarajya of my dreams ensures the rights alike of prince and pauper.[21] Gandhi accused the conventional revoluntionary, parties and trade unions of 'trying to become capitalists themselves by destroying the capitalists rather than sterilizing capital'.[22] He never subscribed to the Marxist contention that capitalists and land lords were 'exploiters by an inherent necessity, or that there is a basic or irreconcilable antagonism between their interests and those of the masses'.[23] In his view the setting up of one class against another was not only unnecessary but also immoral. He supported the plea for equal distribution of wealth but added that if this was not possible then there should be at least equitable distribution. In his opinion capital as such is not evil; it is its wrong use that is evil. 'Capital in some form or other will always be needed.'[24] He argued that 'all men do not have the same ability but a just social order should ensure that there is equal opportunity for all'.[25]

Gandhi's theory of trusteeship is the most significant departure from Marxian economic thinking. Gandhi exhorted the owners of capital to look upon themselves as trustees of the people for the property in their care. They must not think in terms of rights of absolute ownership over the instruments of production and should draw from them only as much as was needed for their living, returning the rest to society. In this way he sought not to destroy the capitalist but to destroy capitalism. He held that the production of wealth is a cooperative process involving the contribution of labour, capital and management, and all these, according to him, stand in relation to one another on the basis of an equality of status. If the capitalist uses the power of his wealth for social control, labour may also use its own power, that of saying 'No' in unity and strength to the capitalist who is out to exploit. In place of vertical class divisions Gandhi argued in favour of horizontal groupings, as implied in his interpretation of the theory of varna, or occupational divisions, without any hierarchy of power or prestige associated with them.

Gandhi also significantly differed from the socialist in his view of the state and its role in social and economic change. While the Marxists argue that the working class should capture the levers of state power to turn the apparatus against the capital owning classes. Gandhi turns away from the state. Philosophically he calls himself an enlightened anarchist. He favours the maximum decentralization of power through a plurality of institutions effectively sharing power with the state. He says: 'The end to be sought is human happiness combined with full mental and moral growth. I use the adjective "moral" as synonymous with spiritual. This end can be achieved under decentralization. Centralization as a system is, inconsistent with the non-violent structure of society.'[26] He amplified this by saying: 'What I would personally prefer would be not a centralization of power in the hands of the state but an extension of the sense of trusteeship; as, in my opinion, the violence of private ownership is less injurious than the violence of the state. However, if it is unavoidable I would support a minimum of state ownership."[27] For Gandhi the state represents violence in a concentrated and organized form. The individual, has a soul and a concience, but the state is a soulless machine which can never be weaned from the violence to which it owes; its very existence.[28] And consequently he looks upon any 'increase in the power of the State with the greatest fear because although apparently doing good by minimizing exploitation, it does the greatest harm to mankind by destroying individuality which lies; at the root of all progress.'[29] And therefore, if the state is used as an instrument for the ending of capitalism through organized violence it is bound to perpetuate this violence in new forms. For Gandhi self-government meant a 'continuous effort to be independent of governmental control'[30] leading to the establishment of the 'sovereignty of the people based on pure morat authority'.[31] Real freedom, then, means 'not the acquisition of authority by a few but the acquisition of the capacity by all to resist authority when abused'.[32] Gandhi admits that the ideal state of his conception is well nigh an impossibility and quotes; with obvious approval Thoreau's dictum that 'that government is best which governs the least'.[33]

Gandhi envisages, as an ideal State, a 'stateless' democracy which works through small autonomous village republics. He argued against large scale industrialization and decried the crazer for machinery. He recommended as an ideal an economy of subsistence based on the spinning wheel under which the instruments of production would be universally owned.[34] According to, him the 'economic constitution of India and, for the matter of than the world, should be such that no one under it should suffer from want of food and clothing. In other words everybody, should be able to get sufficient work to enable him to make the two ends meet. And this ideal can be universally realized only and the means of prduction of the elementary necessaries of, like remain in the control of the masses. These should be freely, available to all, as God's air and water are, or ought to be; they not be made a vehicle of traffic for the exploitation of others. Their monopolization by any country, nation or group of persons would be unjust.[35] His socialism, he asserts is that which is handed down by the ancients when they said: 'All land belongs to God, where then is the boundary line? Man is, the maker of that line and he can, therefore, unmake it'.[36] This socialism, therefore, is something quite different from the socio economic theory propounded by Marx. Gandhi equates his socialism with truth, non-violence, bread labour, voluntary co-operation and an agricultural rural civilization based on handicrafts. He points out that he is not against the machine as such, as he says, that, he does 'visualize electricity, ship building, iron works machine-making and the like existing side by side with village handicrafts. But the order of dependence will be reversed. Hitherto, industialization has been so planned as to destroy the villages and village crafts.' And finally he declares: 'I do not share the socialist belief that centralization of the necessaries of life conduce to the common welfare, when the centralized industries are planned and owned by the state.'[37]

Notes and References

1. *Harijan*, 5 June 1933.
2. *Young India*, 3 September 1922.
3. *Harijan*, August 4, 1946 (Interview with Louis Fischer).
4. *Ibid.*
5. *Young India*, January 29, 1925.
6. *Ibid.*
7. *Ibid.*
8. *Ibid.*, September 10, 1920.
9. Kumarappa, Bharatan, Gandhism, Socilaism or Villagism (Varanasi: sarv Seva Sang Prakashan), 1966, p. 115.
10. Speeches and Wrtings of Mahatma Gndhi, (Delhi: S. Chand & Co.), 1980, p. 350.
11. Gandhi, M. K., Constructive Programme, Its Meaning and Place (Ahmedabad: Navajivan Publishing House), 1944, p. 180.
12. *Ibid.*
13. *Harijan*, 10 September 1937.
14. Tendulkar, Mahatma, (Delhi: The Publications Division, Ministry of Information and Broadcasting, Government of India), Vol. VIII, p. 40.
15. *Ibid.*, p. 45.
16. *Amrit Bazar Patrika*, 8 February 1934.
17. Tendulkar, Mahatma, *op. cit.*, Vol. V, p. 114.
18. Nehru on Gandhi, pp. 94-96,
19. *Young India*, 16 September 1926.
20. *Amrit Bazar Patrika*, 8 February 1934.
21. Bose, N.K., Selections from Gandhi, (Ahmedabad: Navajivan Publishing House), 1978, p. 87.
22. *Amrit Bazar Patrika*, 8 March 1934.
23. *Harijan*, 28 July 1949.
24. *Young India*, 28 November 1911.
25. *Ibid.*, 26 November 1931.
26. *Harijan*, 18 January 1942.
27. Bose, N.K., Selections from Gandhi, *op. cit.*, p. 42.

28. *Ibid.*, p. 159.
29. *Ibid.*, p. 42.
30. *Young India*, 8 June 1925.
31. *Harijan*, 1 February 1937.
32. *Young India*, 29 January 1925.
33. *Young India*, 2 July 1931.
34. *Harijan*, 10 December 1938.
35. *Young India*, 15 November 1928.
36. Tendulkar, Mahatma, *op. cit.*, Vol. IV, p. 140.
37. *Ibid.*, Vol. V, p. 277.

18

Economic Ideas of Gandhi

TAWINDER KAUR

Gandhi never claimed to be an economist. On the contrary, admitting his limitations he declared before the Economic Society of Muir Collet Allahabad: "Frankly and truly I know little of economics as you natural understand it ......"[1] It is of course, an understatement. Commenting this confession of nescience of the science of economics two famous economists wrote: "an examination of his above mentioned lecture clearly points to what he knew rather than what he did not know. He was not interested in the scope and method of economic science as we economists 'naturally understand it'. Rather, he worked for a whole life time on articulating the principles of an alternative and 'more real' human economy, centring on the very themes outlined in his lecture: the lack of correlation between material expansion and genuine progress, the need for an economic-*cum*-ethics that will enable moral growth and dignity for all, the fallacy of seeking happiness in individual acquisitive behaviour, and the need for encouraging people to seek a life rich in self-esteem and genuine meaning."[2] This alternative economic paradigm, according to the renowned economists, is rich in insight and relevance for the developed and develop economies, as well as for contemporary economic theory.

Three points which are basic to the understanding of Gandhi's approach to economics need to be emphasised at the outset itself in order to put the survey of Gandhi's views on economics in perspective. First, as J.B. Kripalani had rightly pointed out, Gandhi's economics has to be studied from the view point of his moral and spiritual principles and ideals and also from the conditions that existed and still exist in India. Second, Gandhi did not recognise the separation of economics from ethics and what he wanted to achieve in the economic field was the ethical ordering of the economic life of society and, therefore, his approach to economic problems and the language he used in the discussion of economic questions were not that of a specialist but of a moralist and a reformer. It was the language of the common man.[3] Third, Gandhi considered economics as the constituent of a larger indivisible whole, and not an independent human activity having its own exclusive operative laws. In the light of these, let us proceed to examine the economic ideas of Gandhi.

ECONOMICS AND ETHICS

Any economic system is concerned with the production, exchange, distribution and consumption of material goods and personal services which are necessary to satisfy human wants. As the science of economics attempts to determine what is valuable at a given time by studying the relative exchange values of goods and services, it is the most clearly value, dependent and normative among the social sciences. Therefore, "its models and theories will always be based on a certain value system and on a certain view of human nature; on a body of assumptions that E.F. Schumacher calls 'meta-economics' because it is rarely included explicitly in contemporary economic thought."[4] The science of economics as Gandhi found it in the beginning of the twentieth century was "free from all values except those of the market"; it was viewed as "an autonomous logical system unconcerned with human beings except as workers and capitalists."[5] The divorce of economics from moral values which set in right from the inception of economics as a science nearly two centuries ago had reached a critical point when Gandhi examined the working of this 'dismal science'. Why did this divorce take place? The economists, in their misguided attempt to make economics as exact science like the physical sciences, consistently avoided non-economic factors and the issues of unstated values, because values always disproved theories.

Whenever the question of values was brought in economists rejected the challenge and pushed out values as belonging to some other field of analysis. Even earlier, Adam Smith, the father of modern economics, desperately tried to deal with both (facts and values) but could not link the two. The questions that he asked in his Moral Sentiments were left out in his Wealth of Nations despite the fact that he waited for years to publish the latter, in order to find in it a place for ethical issues.[6]

Commenting on the shedding of the non-economic contents from economics, especially by Adam Smith, Gandhi wrote: "You know how Adam Smith in his Wealth of Nations after laying down certain principles according to which economic phenomena are governed, went on to describe certain other things which constitute the 'disturbing factor' and prevented economic laws from having free play. Chief among these was the 'human element'. Now it is this human element on which the entire economics of KWi rests; and human selfishness, Adam Smith's 'pure economic motive' constitutes 'the disturbing factor' that has got to overcome."[7]

Thus it becomes evident that Gandhi wanted to reinstate the human element and the value factor into economics and there through achieve the integration of moral sentiments and the science of economics which is considered to be a felt need of the times. The economic philosophy that has been gaining ascendancy not only in the West but throughout the world may be called 'economism' which is based on value premises of which the central core is materialism defined in terms of raising the standard of living or maximising consumption and thereby optimising the pattern of production.[8] In other words, with its basic focus on material wealth and physical comfort it is upholding sensate values and attempting to legitimise unlimited consumption and greed. Gandhi had no difficulty in identifying this divorce of economics from ethics as the root cause of the general degradation to Western civilisation. So, naturally he emphasised the ethical content of the economic activities as the foundational principle of his economics. "I must confess that I do not draw a sharp or any distinction between economics and ethics. Economics that hurts moral well-being of any individual or nation is immoral and therefore, sinful", averred Gandhi and he went on to add: "true economics never militates against the highest ethical standard, just a true ethics to be worth its name must at the same time be also good economics. An economics that inculcates Mammon worship, and enables the strong to amass wealth at the expense of the weak is a false and dismal science. It spells death. True economics, on the other hand, stands for social justice, it promotes the good of all equally including the weakest and is indispensable for a decent life."[9]

Gandhi questioned the basic premise of mainstream economics that fully articulated and formal systems of economic theory are possible only on the basis of an assumption that the economic aspects of human life are completely separable and distinct from such values and emotions as love, altruism, hope, creativity, piety and anything else that is not an expression of the acquisitive spirit. Gandhi rejected the assumption that economic values could be considered apart from moral values and in effect denied not merely that economic man was as he had been described by economists but the very ideas that there was any such thing as economic man.[10]

It is clear, thus, that the main reason why Gandhi denounced modern economics was the fact that it ignored and disregarded moral values and promoted instead acquisitiveness and vulgar consumerism. "The first principle of economics", according to Edgeworth, one of the founders of modern economics, "is that every agent is actuated only by self-interest."[11] This dogma, technically known as the principle of maximising behaviour has been adhered to by all modern economists of the conventional school. This view based on the perception that 'the unlimited character of human want is the sole determinant of economic activity and its unrestricted satisfaction is the index of human progress' was totally unacceptable to Gandhi. It will not be an exaggeration to say that the root cause of the crisis in which humanity finds itself today is this perverted notion of human nature and progress. Gandhi foresaw this and denounced this view of economic progress in unequivocal terms. "I do not believe that multiplication of wants and machinery contrived to supply them is taking the world a single step nearer its goal ... I whole-heartedly detest this mad desire to destroy distance and time, to increase animal appetites and to go to the ends of the earth in search of their satisfaction."[12]

The consequences of following the modern path of economic progress is as clear as day light today. It has created problems like acute resource depletion, energy crisis, environmental hazards and eco-degradation, cutthroat competition for appropriation of scarce resources and raw materials and also for gaining monopoly over market, all leading to conflicts at regional and international levels which, in turn, result in arms-race and war. Gandhi, with his 'acute understanding' of the problems confronting mankind and with his capacity for intuitive perception, could foresee the likely turn of events and therefore, as early as 1909 warned humanity: "the mind is a restless bird, the more it gets the more it wants and still remains unsatisfied. Therefore, the ideal of creating an unlimited number of wants and satisfying them seems to be a delusion and a snare."[13] Gandhi dis-illudes those who conceive of modernity and progress in terms of high standard of living measured by conspicuous consumption, by defining true civilisation as follows: "Civilisation, in the real sense of the term, consists not in the multiplication but in the deliberate and voluntary reduction of wants."[14]

LIMITATION OF WANTS

This brings us to one of the major tenets of Gandhian economics, viz., the limitation of wants. This is, understandably, one of the most grossly misunderstood principles of Gandhi's economic thought. Gandhi was severely lambasted by thinkers and quacks in and outside India for placing the principle of voluntary simplicity or limitation of wants at the top of his economic philosophy. Nehru, for example, found in Gandhi's idealisation of simple, peasant life an opposition to modernisation and wrote reprovingly: "I have almost a horror of it and instead of submitting to it myself I want to drag out even the peasantry from it not to urbanisation but to the spread of urban facilities to rural areas. Far from this life giving me true happiness it would be almost as bad as imprisonment for me. What is there in the 'Man with the Hoe' to idealise over? Crushed and exploited for innumerable generations, he is only little removed from the animals who keep him company."[15]

In one of 'the most unkindest cut of all', Nehru derides Gandhi': simplicity verging on asceticism: "Gandhi has been compared to the medieval Christian saints and much that he says seems to fit in with this. It does not fit in at all with modern psychological experience and methods."[16] Believing that Gandhi, by advocating the limitation of wants, was glorifying poverty Arther Lewis observed: "not all nationalist politician favour economic development. Some like Gandhi resisted Westernise and desire on the contrary, to return to old ways."[17] The basic mistake of these unfounded criticisms lies in the fallacious belief that progress and development consist in the ever growing multiplication of wants and the production of more and more goods to satisfy them. But Gandhian emphasis lay elsewhere. As K.J. Charles commented: "Gandhi believed in the total development of the human being in his physical, mental, moral and spiritual dimensions. He believed that poverty was degrading and that adequate economic progress was essential to satisfy the economic needs of man. Once this was achieved, instead of continuing to aspire for higher standards of living man must attempt to develop his mental, moral and spiritual qualities."[18]

Gandhi's objection to the idea of the multiplication of wants and his insistence on their limitation were based on his conviction that the former obstructed while the latter facilitated the moral and spiritual development of the individuals which was the highest Gandhian criterion for the acceptability of any human activity, Gandhi said: "A certain degree of physical harmony and comfort is necessary, but above a certain level it becomes a hindrance instead of help. Therefore, the ideal of creating unlimited number of wants and satisfying them seems to be a delusion and a snare. The satisfaction of one's physical needs, even the intellectual needs of one's narrow self, must meet at a certain point a dead stop, before it degenerates into physical and intellectual voluptuousness. A man must arrange his physical and cultural circumstances so that they do not hinder him in his service of humanity, on which all his energies should be concentrated."[19]

Emphasising the message, he wrote again: "The less you possess, the less you want, the better you are. The better for what? Not for the enjoyment of this life, but for enjoyment of personal service to the fellow-beings; service which you dedicate yourself, body, soul and mind."[20] One is likely to misunderstand a statement like this unless he is familiar with the total body of Gandhi's economic thought. One may even mistake him to be preaching a pie-in-the-sky sermon and extolling poverty. But it is far from the truth. To those who are advocating material abundance Gandhi said: "If by abundance you mean every one having plenty to eat and drink and to clothe himself with, enough to keep his mind trained and educated, I should be satisfied. But I should not like to pack more stuffs in my belly than I can digest and more things than I can usefully use. But neither do I want poverty, penury, misery, dirt and dust in India."[21]

Vehemently opposed as Gandhi was to artificial multiplication of wants, equally strong was his repugnance to the grinding poverty of the masses. According to him, the economic constitution of India and the world, "should be such that no one under it should suffer from want of food and clothing. In other words, everybody should be able to get sufficient work to enable him to make the two ends meet." Gandhi had said more than once that "to a people famishing and idle, the only acceptable form in which God can dare appear is work and promise of food as wages." He also added: "I dare not take before them (starving masses) the message of God. I may well place before the dog over there the message of God as before those hungry million's who have no lustre in their eyes and whose only God is bread.[22] Any number of such telling passages can be cited to substantiate Gandhi's consistent and committed opposition to poverty. He considered poverty to be materially harmful and morally degrading. That was why he said, "No one has ever suggested that grinding pauperism can lead to anything else than moral degradation."[23]

Thus, it is evident that what Gandhi idealised was simplicity and not poverty. Poverty, he detested with all his heart and fought it with all the might at his command. And the removal of poverty was the first item on his economic agenda. It is clear, therefore, that what Gandhi aimed at was the total eradication of poverty. He believed that limitation of wants was an indispensable condition for the realisation of his objective. As a true socialist, Gandhi also advocated a simultaneous levelling up of the poor and a levelling down of the rich, for the Gandhian economic goal of the welfare of all could not be achieved either in a Western model affluent society or in a society groaning under the burden of abject and grinding poverty as seen in the Indian villages.

That multiplication of wants was inconsistent with high thinking and the total development of individuals and was obstructive to self-realisation was not the only reason why Gandhi opposed it and advocated simplicity instead. Gandhi with his deep insight into human nature and with the evidence collected from the study of human history saw that material abundance did not lead to contentment and happiness. It had been claimed by the science of economics that wants were multiplied and production optimised thereto in order to provide satisfaction to the human individuals and thus to keep them happy. But Gandhi argued that, "even if the paradise of material satisfactions which they envisage as their final goal were realised on earth, it would not bring mankind either contentment or peace."[24] In the Hind Swaraj Gandhi had made this point explicitly clear: "The more we indulge in our passions the more unbridled they become. Our ancestors therefore, set a limit to indulgences. They saw that happiness was largely a mental condition. A man is not necessarily happy because he is rich or unhappy because he is poor. The rich are often seen to be unhappy, the poor to be happy."[25]

In Gandhi's view man could attain real happiness only through the limitation of wants and the acceptance of voluntary simplicity. That was why he said: "Man falls from the pursuit of the ideal of plain living and high thinking the moment he wants to multiply his daily wants. History gives ample proof of this. Man's happiness really lies in contentment. He who is dis.contented, however much he possesses, becomes a slave to his desires. And there is no slavery equal to that of the desires."[26]

Gandhi advocated simplicity and limitation of wants not only for individuals but also for society as a whole. He believed that what was true for the individual was true for society also. Just as Gandhi visualised for the individual a simple but ennobled life that lent contentment and happiness, in the case of society he visualised not an affluent society wading and wallowing in material abundance like the Western industrial-urban society, but a self-sufficient, no-poverty, prosperous society based on non-violence and voluntary co-operation ensuring a dignified and peaceful existence for all. That the pursuit of the higher goals of life is possible only in such a society was the reason why Gandhi set it as a social ideal.

BASIC NEEDS STRATEGY

Another reason why Gandhi insisted on the limitation of wants was that it was inseparably related to the achievement of the goal of sarvodaya, the welfare of all. Though in the paradigm of the multiplication of wants, the greatest good of the greatest number is promised, what has been really fulfilled at best is 'the greatest good' of the blessed and crafty few. While a few become fabulously rich, the vast majority are doomed to perish in abject poverty. While, on the one side, the gap between the rich and the poor in a particular country widens, on the other side, the gulf that separates the rich nations and the poor nations becomes menacingly unbridgeable.

The rosy promises of the escalation of affluence either through trickle down effect or through percolation are totally belied and falsified; centres of affluence appear as patches of riches in the vast and almost endless deserts of poverty—a ridiculous caricature indeed! The greatest good or welfare visualised in sarvodaya is not the material abundance or affluence as promised in other economic ideologies. Gandhi steered clear of both affluence and poverty. He knew only too well that it was impossible to raise the standard of living of the rest of the world population to the level of affluence of an average European or American simply because the earth did not have enough natural resources to achieve this. As Gandhi said, "earth has enough to satisfy everyone's legitimate needs but not anyone's greed'. Given the finite nature of earth's resources, any attempt to go on artificially multiplying human wants is doomed to failure. Thus the limitation of wants becomes a sine qua non for sustaining the earth's ecosystem.

Moreover, as we have already pointed out, undifferentiated and exponential economic growth, according to Gandhi, was undesirable as it was bound to be exploitative and violent and therefore, could not lead to the establishment of a classless, egalitarian social order. In short, in order to realise the goal of sarvodaya the emphasis must be on (a) the basic needs of the people and not on conspicuous consumption, and (b) all people especially the weaker and deprived sections of the population and not the elite who occupy the higher rungs of the social hierarchy.

Thus, although in the Gandhian paradigm the supreme consideration is man, it is important to note that it is the last man (unto this last) that Gandhi cared most and by the last man Gandhi meant the Indian villager who is the true representative of the people in India. This naturally leads us to what Amritananda Das called "the central problem" of Gandhian economic analysis, viz., the problem of rural-urban conflict and village decay in underdeveloped economies.

VILLAGISM

As pointed out at the outset of this article Gandhi's economic ideas can be best understood in the light of the socio - economic conditions that existed in India during his times and that still exist in most of the under-developed countries of the world. Gandhi's opposition to the multiplication of wants and the creation of an urban-industrial society was linked to his 'love of the Indian village and its traditional way of life which he was felt was near an approximation as possible that could be found in history for the functioning of a non-violent society.' A glance through his writings is enough to convince anyone that "Gandhi was drawn by his vision of a rural civilisation where men and women in small groups would, by their activity, be self-sufficient in meeting their elemental needs and yet inter-dependent for many others in which dependence is necessary."[27] Gandhi wanted independent India to be a union of such self-sufficient but inter-dependent village republics.

Time there was, when, known to the outside world as 'the Golden Ind', India through a proper integration of agriculture and industry achieved very high levels of material well-being. The 'hoary civilisation' that the foreigners found on the Indian soil furnished the country not only with a sound political system, but with social and domestic institutions of the most ramified description.[28] It was, in fact, the unique institution of the Indian village that served as the bulwark against all disorders and held the torch of this universal civilisation high.

The ancient Indian villages were self-sufficient, prosperous and autonomous. The integration between agriculture, village handicrafts and industries provided full employment to almost the entire population. Agriculture was not oriented towards making profits. The production of food materials for the local people and raw-materials for the local industries was the sole objective of agriculture. Farming was not a business but a way of life. The type of farming in vogue was subsistence or conservation farming and not intensive and large scale farming (known today as scientific agriculture) which amounts to a virtual rape of the soil. Village handicrafts, cottage and other small scale industries depended mainly on locally available raw materials. Production was need-based and not on a mass scale as in the mechanised industrial sector.

There was a studied attempt at all levels to make life as simple as possible. As Gandhi said, our ancestors had set a limit to indulgence. People were not fond of luxuries and pleasures. Co-operation was emphasised and life-corroding competition scrupulously avoided. The kings and their swords were considered to be inferior to the sword of ethics and the rulers were considered to be inferior to Rishis and Fakirs.[29] The testimony of Sir William Wedderburn, Bart, is worth quoting here: "The Indian villages has, thus, for centuries remained a bulwark against public disorder and the home of simple domestic and social virtues. No wonder, therefore, that philosophers and historians have always dwelt lovingly on this ancient institution which is the natural social unit and the best type of rural life: self-contained, industrious, peace loving, conservative in the best sense of the word ... I think you will agree with me that there is much that is picturesque and attractive in the glimpse of social and domestic life in an Indian village. It is a harmless and happy form of human existence. Moreover, it is not without good practical outcome."[30]

It was this rural civilisation whose economic organisation was a happy and balanced blend of subsistence farming and sustainable industries that Gandhi admired and projected as a model. It was not difficult for Gandhi to see that the only way to save the impoverished rural people who constituted more than eighty percent of the total population was to refurbish and regenerate the system of village economy in a large way. It must be made clear that what Gandhi visualised was not a revival of the ancient village system as such but a modified, purified and modernised form of it that will serve the needs and aspirations of the rural people of India. Gandhi wrote: "I would say that if the village perishes India will perish too. India will no more be India. Her own mission in the world will get lost. The revival of the village is possible only when it is no more exploited. Industrialisation on a mass scale will necessarily lead to passive or active exploitation of the villagers as the problems of competition and marketing come in. Therefore, we have to concentrate on the village being self-contained, manufacturing mainly for use. Provided this character of the village industry is maintained, there would be no objection to villagers using even the modern machines and tools that they can make and can afford to use. Only they should not be used as a means of exploitation of others."[31]

The Indian village system depicted above was battered down by "the working of English steam and English Free Trade ... by blowing up their economic basis."[32] British domination of India meant economic exploitation of the worst kind, especially of the village through industrialization and urbanisation. On the British exploitation of India Gandhi wrote: "When I read Dutt's Economic History of India, I wept, and as I think of it again my heart sickens. It is machinery that has impoverished India. It is difficult to measure the harm that Manchester has done to us. It is due to Manchester that Indian handicraft has all but disappeared."[33]

Industrialisation naturally led to the pauperisation of the villages, mass unemployment, and exploitation of villages by towns and cities. It has therefore, been rightly pointed out that in his very strong reaction against modern industrial civilisation and in his idealisation of the village as the basis of a non-violent social order Gandhi was greatly influenced by the distress and pauperisation he had seen in the Indian villages and the desperate exodus to urban areas that this brought about, all largely as a result of the impact of modern industry brought into India under British rule.[34] So Gandhi was highly critical of industrialism and rejected it saying that it could create more problems than it could solve. He enumerated the evils of industrialisation with scientific precision and advanced his arguments for its rejection quite forcefully at a time when the entire world was caught in its magic spell. And the reasons Gandhi adduced for the rejection of industrialisation are noteworthy.

LIMITS TO INDUSTRIALISATION

First and foremost, the very philosophy underlying industrialisation was unacceptable to Gandhi as it ignored the moral and spiritual aspects of the human individual. Secondly, industrialisation owed its very existence to exploitation (which for Gandhi was another name for violence). It involved exploitation of the underdeveloped countries by the industrialised countries, of the rural areas by the urban areas, of the weak by the strong, of the underprivileged by the privileged and of Nature by man. The end result would be, as pointed out earlier, economic rat-race and unhealthy competition for raw materials and market leading to eco-destruction, conflicts and war. Thirdly, as industrialisation had to depend upon large scale and highly sophisticated technology it would throw a large number people out of job for the sake of or in the name of efficiency, leading to mass unemployment. The consequences of this backwash effect are too plain to require further elucidation. In underdeveloped countries like India, this has generated not only economic, but also socio-political and Psychic problems that have become almost chronic. Citing the Puerto Rico experience where the economic development programme had been unusually vigorous and successful but which threw a progressively larger number of people out of employment every succeeding year, Schumacher pointed out that India was an equally powerful illustration "where highly ambitious five year plans regularly show a greater volume of unemployment at the end of the five year period than at the beginning ...."[35] Fourthly, as large-scale industries require heavy capital investment, it would be far beyond the capacities of the third-world countries to follow this path of industrialisation without bartering away their economic and political independence to foreign capitalists and/or multi-national corporations.

In short, according to Gandhi, industrialisation of the Western model, (which at present has turned out to be the industrial-military complex) was least suited to the socio-economic conditions of India and hence unacceptable. Moreover, it didn't fit in either with the ideal social order that Gandhi visualised or with the final goal that he had set for mankind to strive after. That was why he proposed a new economic organization of society which could fulfil the economic aspirations of the people and at the same time lead to their moral and spiritual development.

INDUSTRY AND TECHNOLOGY

The chief concern behind Gandhi's economic programme was to device a method for mitigating the grinding poverty of the Indian masses. The typical condition of the poor in India was that they were under-employed or totally unemployed. Therefore, Gandhi felt that the first thing to do for them was to provide them with employment and the only way to do this was to bring into existence millions of new work places in rural areas and small towns. As Schumacher pointed out: "That modern industry, as it has arisen in the developed countries, cannot possibly fulil this task, should be perfectly obvious. It has arisen in societies which are rich in capital and short of labour and, therefore, cannot possibly be appropriate for societies short of capital and rich in labour."[36] Gandhi did not accept modern industrial method as the best way to provide people with employment. So he said: "mechanisation is good when hands are too few for the work intended to be accomplished. It is an evil when there are more hands than required for the work, as is the case in India... The way to take work to the village, is not through mechanisation but that it lies through revival of the industries they have hither to followed."[37]

In other words, Gandhi wanted to substitute mass production with production by the masses. For him mass production was a technical term for production by the fewest possible number through the aid of the complicated machinery. "I have said to myself that that is wrong. My machinery must be of the most elementary type which I can put in the homes of the millions."[38] It was with the intention of solving the twin problems of poverty and unemployment by putting the most elementary type of machinery in the homes of the millions that Gandhi tried to revive the swadeshi movement and launched khadi in a big way.

As cloth is next only to food (which of course, is universally accepted as the most basic of human needs) Gandhi took up production of cloth as the first industry in his Constructive Programme. He had another reason for doing so. He knew that before the introduction of the power mills every home in India produced its own yarn to make cloth and thus, serving as auxiliary to agriculture, provided full employment to all. "At one time our national economics was this", Gandhi pointed out, "that just as we produced our own corn and consumed it, so did we produce our own cotton, spin it in our own homes and wear the clothes woven by our weavers from our own yarn...."[39] According to Gandhi the best way to provide work to the masses in the Indian situation was the revival of khadi (hand spinning and hand weaving) and other cottage and village industries which would cater to the basic needs of the masses. It is important to note that Gandhi always emphasised the complementary roles of khadi and other village industries such as hand-grinding, hand-pounding, soap making, paper making, match making, tanning, oil pressing, etc. Gandhi explained: "Khadi is the sun of the village solar system. The planets are the various industries which can support khadi in turn for the heat and the sustenance they derive from it."[40] Underscoring the main thrust of his argument in favour of khadi and village industries Gandhi went on: "the sole claim advanced on its (hand-spinning and hand-weaving) behalf is that it alone offers an immediate, practicable, and permanent solution of that problem that confronts India, viz., the enforced idleness for nearly six months in the year of an overwhelming majority of India's population, owing to lack of supplementary occupation to agriculture and the chronic starvation of the masses that result therefrom."[41]

Gandhi had other reasons also for advocating khadi and village industries and handicrafts for the solution of the economic problems of India. The most notable of them is the significance of the charkha. For Gandhi the charkha was the symbol of a technology that was simple, comprehensible even to the illiterate villagers and environment-friendly. As is well-known, Gandhi was against the craze for labour saving machines and giant technology, not only because they displaced labour and created more unemployment but also because they enslaved, dehumanised and alienated the workers as well as the consumers, creating serious psychic moral problems. So he stood for what is called appropriate technolog in Schumacher's words 'technology with a human face', which is free from the above evils. Enumerating the various advantages of khadi and charkha Gandhi said: "Khaddar does not seek to destroy all machinery but it does regulate its use and check its weedy growth. It uses machinery for the service of the poorest in their own cottages. The wheel is itself an exquisite piece of machinery."[42]

In the Gandhian system of production technology must satisfy three major conditions. (1) Technology must increase the productivity of the worker. (2) Technology must not replace the worker. (3) The worker must have complete control of the technology.[43] These stringent conditions are elegantly fulfilled by the charkha. This exquisite piece of machiner, as Gandhi called it, created co-operation and eliminated competition; it would breed love and humility and eliminate greed and self-aggrandisement. "The message of the spinning wheel is much wider than its circumference", said Gandhi, "its message is one of simplicity, service of mankind, living as not to hurt others, creating an indissoluble bond between the rich and the poor, capital and labour, the prince and the peasant."[44]

DECENTRALISATION

Khadi and village industries stand for a decentralised economic system that can promote the economic and moral regeneration of the masses of India. Centralised industry, besides the other evils it generates, leads to the concentration of economic power in the hands of a few which in turn will result in the concentration of political power and its consequent abuses. As a result of the concentration of the economic and political power the people will lose control over the means and modes of production as well as on the manner of distribution and thus they will be reduced to a state of utter dependency. This is incompatible with non-violence and hence cannot find a place in a non-violent social order. So, Gandhi advocated decentralisation as a remedy for the evils of industrialism. "Moreover, Khadi mentality means decentralisation of the production and distribution of the necessaries of life. Therefore, the formula so far evolved is, every village to produce all its necessaries and a certain percentage in addition for the requirements of the cities."[45]

Hinting at the implications of insisting on decentralisation, Gandhi went on to add subsequently: "I suggest that, if India is to evolve along non-violent lines, it will have to decentralise many things. Concentration cannot be sustained and defended without adequate force. Simple homes from which there is nothing to take away require no policing; the palaces of the rich must have strong guards to protect them against dacoity. So must huge factories. Rurally organised India will run less risk of foreign invasion than urbanised India, well equipped with military, naval and air forces."[46]

The advantages of decentralised production are many and varied. It is based on locally available resources and is intended to satisfy the basic needs of the local population. It uses appropriate technology and depends chiefly on renewable sources of energy. It reduces the exploitation of men and nature to the minimum. Thus it is free from most of the evils associated with the neo-classical mode of production and distribution and promotes the economic and moral growth of the individuals.

Gandhi knew that the goal of sarvodaya could be achieved only if the economic system was decentralised, organised on small scale and on local basis and individuals were made the essential ingredient of the economic process. That was why he stressed the role of khadi, cottage industries and other handicrafts as they would satisfy the conditions necessary for the realisation of his economic goals. It is important to note here that the need for a decentralised order has been subsequently emphasised by such eminent economists and thinkers as Gunnar Myrdal, E.F. Schumacher, Wilfred Wellock, Bertrand Russell, Aldous Huxley, Herbert Marcuse et. al., and that decentralisation has been included in the manifestos of such groups belonging to the New Age movement as the German Greens.

INTEGRATION OF SMALL AND LARGE SCALE INDUSTRIES

The depiction of Gandhi's ideas on decentralisation would be incomplete if it is not mentioned that Gandhian economics is not based entirely on handicrafts and cottage industries. Gandhi was not against large scale industries *per se*. On the other hand, he admitted its due role and significance. He visualised a balanced and organic relationship between the two sectors. In the Gandhian scheme: "Cottage and large scale industries were not competing alternatives but complementary and helpful to each other. Gandhi wanted small scale production and large industries to be developed in such a way that each sector will provide those supplies which cannot be produced by the other."[47]

Hitesranjan Sanyal's exposition of the complementary role of small and large industries as envisaged by Gandhi, deserves to be cited: "Gandhi was ready to accept modern machinery and heavy industry in a situation as obtaining in India provided this would serve the needs of small units in the villages by supplying infrastructural facilities and essential machines and tools. But heavy industry would not be allowed under any circumstances to produce the elementary requirements of man and replace bread-labour. These are the essential conditions for ensuring the economic freedom of the village community. If machinery could be employed without jeopardising the freedom and dignity of man and the self-reliance of the villages, Gandhi had no objection to mechanisation of production even at the level of the villages."[48]

In short, Gandhi wanted industrialisation to be so well planned as not to destroy but to subserve village and village crafts. It is in this perspective that we must situate such statements of Gandhi as "I do visualise electricity, ship building, iron works, machine-making and the like existing side by side with village handicrafts."[49] But Gandhi wanted such industries of public utility to be owned by the state and used entirely for the benefit of the people and not of the profiteers. To sum up, Gandhi would accept large scale industries against the following severe condition: "They must not deprive people of employment, they must not exploit the villages or compete with village crafts, they must help the village artisan to reduce his drudgery and improve his efficiency. They should not tend to make atrophied the limbs of man. They must not lead to monopoly or concentration of wealth power in a few hands and they must not lead to exploitation, national or international. And when involving large capital or large number of employees they must be owned by the state and administered wholly for public good."[50]

In order to grasp the full significance of Gandhi's idea of decentralisation we must also consider it in the light of his total philosophy. As Gandhi explained: "The end to be sought is human happiness combined with full mental and moral growth. I use the adjective moral as synonymous with spiritual. This end can be achieved under decentralisation. Centralisation as a system is inconsistent with non-violent structure of society."[51]

Another notable feature of this system is the importance given to manual labour. Although in large scale industries labour saving device, are used the workers in them are put to heavy physiological and psychological strain resulting in serious personality disorders which can be summed up by the word "alienation." In industrial societies the transformation from work-orientation to consumption-orientation has brought about the loss of autonomy of the individual, so much so that it often degenerates into psychopathic delinquency or disorientation or psychosis bordering on paranoia. Gandhi viewed manual labour as having a vital role to play in order to get over the tide of alienation."[52] According to Gandhi labour had four components, (a) bread-labour which is a kind of minimum physical labour which must be performed by everybody from philosopher to ordinary labourers; (b) earning labour for a living as is normally understood in economics; (c) as an instrument of self-actualisation; (d) as a method of service to others. Once this four-fold view of labour is accepted no degree of division of labour can really dehumanise man totally.[53]

DOCTRINE OF TRUSTEESHIP

The question of the ownership of the means of production has been a bone of contention ever since the inception of the principle of private ownership of property. In fact, the chief, if not only, difference between the two major contending economic systems—capitalist and Marxian socialist—is that of ownership. While capitalism upholds private ownership, Marxian socialism rejects it and advocates state ownership. What is unique about Gandhian economic theory is that Gandhi did not accept the concept of ownership as such whether it be private or state. He considered both as equally exploitative and hence inconsistent with non-violence. So, in tune with his basic tenets of. non-possession and non-stealing, Gandhi formulated the theory of Trusteeship in order to save society "from the Scylla and Charybdis of rampant capitalism and bureaucratic socialism."[54] Gandhi claimed that Trusteeship would, perhaps, be his most lasting contribution.

Granted that private ownership is to be abolished in order to realise the goal of sarvodaya, the question arises: how do we achieve it? As Gandhi did not believe in the use of force or violence for achieving any noble objective; he did not advocate the expropriation of property through violent means as advocated by the other opponents of private ownership. On the contrary, Gandhi prescribed Trusteeship which combined the positive elements of both private enterprise and social ownership. As V.K.R.V. Rao pointed out: "Gandhi evolved his theory of Trusteeship not only on his deep religious conviction that everything belongs to God and therefore, a human being can hold either his property or his talents only as a trustee, but also on a number of practical considerations. He knew that to dispossess the men of property or of talent by force was bound to involve class war, hatred, proletarian dictatorship, an all powerful and coercive state, and the consequent elimination of all hope of creating a non-violent society. He also felt that many men who had acquired property had some special abilities for increasing production and many men of talent had exceptional contributions to make and, therefore, to destroy them by force may lead to much less of production and would be like killing the goose that lays the golden eggs. Hence his emphasis on persuading them to function as trustees rather than dispossessing them by force, of their income or wealth."[55]

So Gandhi advised the owners of property to consider themselves as trustees of the property which really belonged to the whole society anc manage it accordingly, taking only what they needed for their own up keep but using the rest for the welfare of society.

Gandhi knew that just by giving an opportunity to the capitalists, the might not relinquish voluntarily their property rights and act as trustees He, therefore, wanted the power of satyagraha and state legislative action to be used for getting the rich to change their attitude. Gandhi wanted the tenants and the workers to know that without their active co-operation the rich will not be able either to accumulate or retain their wealth. So he strongly recommended the use of non-violent non-co-operation and civil disobedience, i.e., Satyagraha, as the infallible means for persuing and pressurising the rich to accept trusteeship in public interest. He also warned the rich that if they did not become trustees of their own accord, they would court destruction. "The present power of zamindar, the capitalists and rajas can hold sway only so long as the common people do not realise their strength. If the people non-co-operate with the evil of zamindari or capitalism, it must die of inaniation."[56]

In order to remove all doubts and speculations that hovered over the concept of trusteeship, the Trusteeship Formula was drawn up and published.

It reads :

1. Trusteeship provides a means of transforming the present capitalist order of society into an egalitarian one. It gives no quarter to capitalism, but gives the present owning class a chance of reforming itself. It is based on the faith that human nature is never beyond redemption.
2. It does not recognise any right of private ownership of property except so far as it may be permitted by society for its own welfare.
3. It does not exclude legislative regulation of the ownership and use of wealth.
4. Thus, under State-regulated trusteeship, an individual will not be free to hold or use his

wealth for selfish satisfaction or in disregard of the interest of society.

5. Just as it is proposed to fix a decent minimum living wage, even so limit should be fixed for the maximum income that could be allowed to any person in society. The difference between such minimum and maximum incomes should be reasonable and equitable and variable from time to time so much so that the tendency would be towards the obliteration of the difference.
6. Under the Gandhian economic order the character of production will be determined by social necessity and not by personal whim or greed."[57]

A diligent perusal of the above formula will convince anyone about the validity of Gandhi's claim that Trusteeship theory was likely to be his most lasting contribution to posterity. Although Gandhi did not leave us an elaborately worked out model of trusteeship, in the light of the above formula and the numerous other clarifications he made, a model can be constructed. Gandhi was prepared to concede the legal ownership of the trusteeship concern to the erstwhile owner and also the right to propose the name of the successor. But he laid down the condition that the choice must be finalised by the state. "The choice", said Gandhi, "should be given to the original owner, who becomes the first trustee, but it must be finalised by the state. Such arrangement puts a check on the state as well as on the individual."[58] But at a later stage he wanted the erstwhile owner and the workers of a concern to jointly hold trusteeship over it. The series of measures that Gandhi contemplated as his programme for achieving trusteeship in property relations and the use of personal talents in public interest is summarised thus: Appeal to the better instincts in the rich, persuasion, education regarding the inevitability of change and the greater unattractiveness of the alternative of change by violence, non-violent non-co-operation by the exploited that would make the exploiter's functioning impossible, and finally legislative action ...."[59]

As is clear from the preceding discussion Gandhi's

economic ideas are perfectly consistent with his metaphysical and ethical presuppositions. According to him the whole gamut of man's activities constituted an indivisible whole and therefore, he did not draw any distinction between economics and ethics and considered that economics as untrue which ignored or disregarded moral values. It was this insistence of Gandhi on the indivisibility of economics and morality that prompted some economists to consider his economic system to be a path that leads to non-economic goals. Gandhi considered the introduction of moral values as a regulating factor in economic matters an extension of the law of non-violence in the domain of economics. "True economics", wrote Gandhi, "never militates against the highest ethical standard, just as all true ethics to be worth its name must at the same time be also good economics... true economic...stands for social justice, it promotes the good of all equally including the weakest and is indispensable for a decent life."[60] The end sought in a non-violent economic order is happiness combined with full mental, moral and spiritual growth.

Notes and References

1. Murti, V.V. Raman (ed.), Gandhi: Essential Writings (New Delhi: G.P.F.), 1970, p. 292.
2. Diwan, Romesh and Mark Lutz (ed.), Essays in Gandhian Economics (New Delhi: G.P.F.), 1978, p. 56.
3. Kripalani, J.B., Gandhian Thought (New Delhi: Gnadh, Samark Nidhi), 1961, p. 366.
4. Capra, Fritjof, The Turning Point (London: Fontana), 1984, p. 197.
5. Diwan, Romesh and Mark Lutz (ed.), Essays in Gandhian Economics, *op. cit.*, p. XIII.
6. *Ibid.*, p. XII.
7. *Harijan*, September 21, 1934, p. 322.
8. Diwan, Romesh and Mark Lutz (ed.), Essays in Gandhian Economics, *op. cit.*, p. XVII.
9. *Harijan*, October 9, 1937, p. 292.
10. Ross, David, F. and Mahendra S. Kanthi, Gandhian Economics (Bangalore: Prasad Publications), 1983, p. 89.
11. Diwan, Romesh and Mark Lutz (ed.), Essays in Gandhian Economics, *op. cit.*, p. 13.
12. *Young India*, March 17, 1927

13. Gandhi, M.K., Hind Swaraj (Ahmedabad: Navajivan Publishing House), 1962, pp. 44-45.
14. *Ibid.*
15. Nehu, Jawaharlal, An Autobiography (New Delhi: Jawaharlal Nehru memoral Fund), 1989, p. 511.
16. *Ibid.*, p. 509.
17. Lewis, W. Arthur, Theory of Economic Growth (London: William Collins and Sons), 1987, p. 153.
18. Charles, K.J., Total Development: Essays Towards Perspectives (New Delhi: Vikas Publishing House), 1983, p. 94.
19. *Harijan*, September 29, 1936, p. 226.
20. Tendulkar, D.G., Mahatma (New Delhi: Publications Division, Ministry of Information and Broadcasting, Government of India), Vol. III, 1952, p. 157.
21. *Harijan*, Feburary 12, 1938, p. 2.
22. *Young India*, November 15, 1928, p. 381.
23. Kripalani, J.B., Gandhian Thought, *op. cit.*, p. 369.
24. Pyarelal, Mahatma Gandhi: The Last Phase, Vol. II (Ahmedabad: Navajivan Publishing House), 1958, p. 139.
25. Gandhi, M.K., Hind Swaraj, *op. cit.*, p. 61.
26. *Harijan*, Feburary 1, 1942, p. 27.
27. Rao, V.K.R.V., The Gandhian Alternative to Western Socialism (Bombay: Asia Publishing House), 1970, pp. 7-8.
28. Gandhi, M.K., Hind Swaraj, *op. cit.*, Appendecies, p. 106.
29. *Ibid.*, pp. 61-62.
30. *Ibid.*, p. 110.
31. *Harijan*, August 29, 1936, p. 226.
32. Dutt, R.C., The Economic History of India (New Delhi: Publications Division, Government of India), 1963.
33. Gandhi, M.K., Hind Swaraj, *op. cit.*, p. 93.
34. Rao, V.K.R.V., The Gandhian Alternative to Western Socialism, *op. cit.*, p. 8.
35. Schumacher, E.F., Small is Beautiful, p. 146.
36. *Ibid.*
37. *Harijan*, November, 16, 1934, p. 316.
38. *Ibid.*, Novemebr 2, 1934, p. 301.
39. *Young India*, January 8, 1925, p. 11.
40. *Harijan*, Novemeber 16, 1934, p. 317.
41. *Young India*, October 21, 1926, p. 368.
42. *Ibid.*, March 17, 1927, p. 85.
43. Diwan, Romesh and Mark Lutz (ed.), Essays in Gandhian Economics, *op. cit.*, p. 61.
44. *Young India*, September 17, 1925, p. 321.
45. Gandhi, M.K., Constuctive Programme (Ahmedabad: Navajivan Publishing House), 1981, p. 15.

46. *Harijan*, Decemeber 30, 1939, p. 400.
47. Prasad, Nageshwar (ed.), Hind Swaraj A Fresh Look (New Delhi: Gandhi Peace Foundation), 1985, p. 176.
48. *Ibid.*, pp. 177-178.
49. *Harijan*, January 27, 1940, p. 317.
50. Rao, V.K.R.V., The Gandhian Alternative to Western Socialism, *op. cit.*, pp. 21-22.
51. *Harijan*, January 18, 1942, p. 5.
52. Sethi, J.D., "Poverty Alienation and The Gandhian Way Out", Gandhi Marg, Vol. 1, No. 4, July 1979, p. 186.
53. *Ibid.*, p. 189.
54. Choudhary, Manmohan, Exploring Gandhi (New Delhi: Gandhi Peace Foundation), 1989, p. 210.
55. Rao, V.K.R.V., The Gandhian Alternative to Western Socialism, *op. cit.*, pp. 38-39.
56. Sharma, Jai Narain, An Alternative Economic (New Delhi: Deep and Deep Publications), 2002, p. 28.
57. Pyarelal, Mahatma Gandhi: The Last Phase, Vol. II, *op. cit.*, p. 92.
58. *Ibid.*, p. 85.
59. *Ibid.*, p. 45.
60. *Harijan*, October 9, 1937, p. 292.

19

Relevance of Gandhian Humanistic Concepts in Modern World

SHEEJA O.K.

The modern man is living in a world which is advancing with an unprecedented growth of industrialization and technological progress in all spheres. The dynamics of heavy industrialization and technological progress have far-reaching effects on the modern society. There are some major issues in the modern world, such as ecological imbalance, terrorism, crisis caused by violence and wars, communal riots and so forth.

Through this paper I aim to make a humble effort to examine the humanistic approaches in Gandhian thought. Gandhiji discussed nothing under the title of humanism. But his whole thinking-political, ethical, economical, sociological—is humanitarian in nature. The two pillars of Gandhian thinking are Truth and Non-Violence. He had developed his whole thinking on the basis of these two cardinal virtues.

Gandhi demonstrated the practical applicability of Non-Violence in all spheres of human endeavor and its usefulness to the whole world. The concept of Non-Violence as interpreted by Gandhi assumed ecological significance for its sustainability and enables people to live in harmony with nature without exploitation and stands as a solution and an alternative to violence and terrorism.

HUMANISM—GENERAL VIEWPOINTS

Each and every discipline starts its enquiry by asking question concerning various aspects of human being. Man and his nature are the main topics of almost all subjects, especially social sciences. They begin this discussion with the questions such as what is man. What is human nature? What is his role in the world process?, etc.

Discussions regarding human nature and humanism have a long historical background. From the historical stand point the philosophic image of the word humanism is of very recent origin. F.C.S. Schiller[1] and Marvin Fabiner,[2] two great thinkers treat humanism from a positivistic angle of vision which is partial and incomprehensive. Erich Fromm defines humanism as "belief in the unity of human race and man's potential to perfect himself by his own efforts."[3] According to Paul Kurtz, "Humanism is an ethical philosophy in which man is central."[4]

Humanistic thinking after Schiller can be summarized as follows. Humanism is conferred by relativism. It is the denial of all sorts of transcendentalism and absolutism which ignore their relation to man. Humanism and pragmatism are closely related to each other. Also humanism is primarily the name for a method, and not for a system of Philosophy. It provides grand scope for toleration and other virtues. It establishes common truth on the basis of social agreement which undergoes continuous modification, elaboration and improvement.

In the West, humanism has its root in Hellenic thought. Sophists have argued for the importance of man in every sphere of life. Protogoras' dictum "Man is the measure of all things; of those that are that they are, of those that are not that they are not", shows the magnificent role of man. For Socrates, man's fundamental reality and central place among the existents are quite harmonious with their objectivity. The theocentric humanism linked man with the transcendental. We can see humanistic background in the works of Plato, especially in Ethics and Politics. Aristotle treated man as man and not as angel or devil. Man who is by nature a political animal attains highest fulfilment in communal life. Opposed to theocentric humanism of his predecessors, Aristotle constructed anthropocentric kind of humanistic approach.

Another important humanist is Jesus Christ according to whom all human institution social, political and religious are meant for service to human beings. Theoretically, Christianity is theocentric, but in practice it is anthropocentric. Gandhian humanism consists of these two aspects of humanism.

The Renaissance movement was anthropocentric. The man was considered as an end in himself, the centre and creator of all values. The great humanistic revival during the European renaissance may be taken to be the foundation of modern culture, and civilization in the world. In modern times the humanistic tradition was carried on by various thinkers.

The main contemporary humanists include Existentialists and Marxian humanist accounts. The existentialist humanists lay emphasis on truth and action. An individual should seek truth and final fulfilment through action since he is nothing else but the sum of his action.[5] Existentialist humanism presents man as a solitary, abandoned creative; and brings his complex psyche to light. It separates man from his self-and from everything else. The existentialist's contribution is not at all positive. Its pessimist fragmentary outlook leads to the denial of ideal, scope and possibility.

Marxian effort to set-up a social society throws light on humanism from different angles. Marx writes "that would criticize all human acts, movements, relation, etc. by the principles of utility must first deal with human nature is general and then with human nature as modified in each historical expoch."[6] Man is the first and foremost concern of his thought.

While western thinkers lay emphasis on anthropocentric

trend, Indian thinkers give importance to theocentric trend. The earliest record for the humanistic ideal in Indian thought is found in the Rigvedic hymns which centre round man as an earthly being. Indian humanistic aspects can be seen in Upanisadic thought. The Upanisads proclaim the existence of spiritual unity behind all physical existents. The atman is the fundamental and single active principle that steers the sense-organs. The humanistic element of Mahabharata is brought forth in the saying, "I tell you this, the secret of the Brahman there is nothing superior to man." Here the focus of attention is the earthly man that is put at the zenith of creation. Opposed to this spiritualistic trend the Carvaka adopted an atheistic and materialistic outlook.

Both Buddhism and Jainism arose as a reaction to Vedic authority. They preached the message of liberation from bondage and sufferings. Buddha advised his disciples to go to the people and work tirelessly for their welfare, since nothing higher and nobler than man. Both these traditions give importance to human personality as well as human body because it is through this physical body that an individual performs penance, and thereby attains liberation from suffering. They share the anthropocentric tradition of humanistic thought.

For Sankhya, Purusa the human personality is eternally free. An individual can get rid of the life cycle by realizing his true self-through self-knowledge and self-development. Yoga prescribes eightfold discipline to get rid of the pollution, both mental and physical Nyaya-Vaisesika and Mimamsa followed the humanist trend of the Upanisad.

Indian thinkers though differ in their scholastic views, agree on the primary and practical importance of human personality. The history and development of Indian humanistic tradition exhibit a leaning towards spiritualism.

HUMAN NATURE: GANDHIAN CONCEPT

"An individual's inherent nature is distinct and different from his deeds, creation and institution. Irrespective of merits and demerits of creation his times being deserves respect."[7] Man is divine in nature. "Man is also a brute, an irrational, sensual, crude, passionate animal. Brutality and divinity go together in human being."[8] Man's mission on earth is to overcome the brutal force.

Gandhi believes in the infinite possibilities and goodness of man. He also recognizes imperfection in human nature. "No one can attain perfection while he is in the body.[9] In his view, human nature is elastic and hence can be changed. "We can mend or mar the present and on that will depend the future." The concept of human nature is concrete, not abstract in Gandhian thought. To him, an individual is an end in himself, the roots of human motivation are embedded in human nature itself. But according to him, environment like heredity also plays an important role in the formation of human personality. Since environment contributes to the growth of human nature, change of environmental factors is necessary for an effective change of human nature. Thus, Gandhi laid much emphasis on the inner being, and thereby on the spiritual, non-sensuous aspects of human nature.

HUMANISM: GANDHIAN PERSPECTIVE

Gandhi's concept of human nature is real, concrete and deeply rooted in the soul of the empirical world. His whole life was dedicated to bring down the kingdom of God on earth, and thereby elevate the human beings to the level of celestial ones. Gandhi anthropomorphized God and divinized man. He never used the term humanism, but he spoke of human fraternity.

Gandhi conducted a life-long experiment in Truth and Non-violence. He identified them with God whose being constantly he felt, breathed, and lived for. Gandhi's concept of history is quite humanistic in nature. Truth and Non-violence are the ceaseless growth of the human race. Non-violence does not mean cowardice. Gandhian philosophy is based on the concepts of Truth, Non-violence and self-restraint. "The role of the individual was central to Gandhi's view of history."[10]

We can see humanistic elements in Gandhi's religious ideas. Gandhi was a theist, an ethico-religious personality. But his was not a transcendent God, rather an immanent

God. "Man's ultimate aim is the realization of God... if I could persuade myself that I should find Him in a Himalayan cave. I would proceed there immediately. But I know that I cannot find Him apart from humanity.[11] "My creed is service of God and therefore of humanity."[12] Gandhi's religion leads to humanism and presuppose it.

His political ideas follow from humanism. Rene Fulpo-Milles observes,".....all the ideas which Gandhi made the basis of his political system are rooted in his humanity."[13] The motto of service to humanity inspired him to enter into politics. In his words, "Hence my passion for the service of the suppressed classes and as I cannot render this service without entering politics, I find myself in them."[14] For Gandhi, politics is not a lip service, rather a weapon to fight against evils of the suffering humanity.

Gandhi's aesthetic opinions on art, music, literature, beauty, etc. arose out of his deep concern for mankind. His economic policy arose from his naïve mind, his innate feelings; that is from humanistic urge. To him human beings are the most valuable wealth of a country; and hence upon them the property of country depends. He preached economic programmes for the best utilization of man power. His concepts of Khadi, Swadeshi, bread-labour, small scale and cottage industries; apathy for large-scale and mechanically industries, etc. do enhance the significance of his humanistic outlook."[15] According to him "The Supreme consideration is man. The machine should not tend to make atrophied the limbs of man."[16] He considers the individual as the prime mover of all social changes. His humanistic mind did not submit the individual to any institution or organization like society. His theory of education also has humanistic elements. The object of Nai Talim (Vocational Training) was to give light and food to the starving millions. His antipathy to modern civilization is also the result of his humanism. He condemns it as irreligious immoral, etc. M.D. Jouvenal points out that "his was essentially a humanistic critique of industrial civilization."[17] Impressed by some Marxian principles, he constructed the socio-economic structure of society in his own, the non-violent way. Most of his concepts such as non-possession, abolition of private property emancipation of women, etc. arose from his ardent humanism to free mankind from exploitation in any form.

The whole work and life of Gandhi is based on the fundamental assumption that man is inherently moral and spiritual in nature. Gandhi emphasized the point of moral recovery in every sphere. The virtues and vows that he prescribed were directed towards one goal—the removal of dehumanization, elimination of alienation, recovery of the true moral self.

The method which Gandhi adopted towards the world lies embedded in the matrix of humanism. His method was an experiment with truth through the service of humanity. He writes "I will give you a talisman. Whenever you are in doubt or when the self-becomes too much with you, try the following expedient. Recall the face of the poorest and the most helpless man whom you may have seen and ask yourself: if the step you contemplate is going to be of any use to him. Will he be able to gain anything by it? Will it restore him to control over his own life and destiny?"[18] Gandhi puts men as the centre of his study in every step of interpenetration. Throughout his life he applied pragmatic measures on numerous occasions. But he disliked utilitarianism or the principle of utility from the core of heart. Being a characteristic of humanism, dynamism enriches Gandhian thought. He was an ever-growing, ever-making, ever-developing personality.

Gandhi was both an idealist and a realist. He used to call himself a practical idealist. His eager search for truth and non-violence in every sphere of life in the highest degree led him to a great extent to transcend his realistic surroundings. Gandhi was a Utopian, a dreamer who strove to set-up the Kingdom of God on earth, to establish a new social order, Ramrajya where truth and non-violence would be the guiding stars, and people would enjoy freedom in every sense of the term. His Utopianism arose out of his love for humanity.

Gandhi innovated the traditional idioms like Ahimsa, Satya, Brahmacharya, Charka, Hartal, Harijan, Karma, Maya, Swaraj, Swadesi, etc. in the modern perspective. He infused life into the traditional ideas, idioms and concepts, and adopted them as a technique of human communication only to identify himself with the masses, to be one of them. This identification with the people is a salient feature of humanism. Gandhi was also an anti-communalist, and thus a humanist. "I am striving to become the best cement between the two communities. My longing is to be able to cement the two with my blood, if necessary.[19] He became symbol of human brother hood among people of all religions. He wandered from one corner of the country for the restoration of communal peace and harmony. His was not a lip-service but demonstration in his life and work. He offered blood as living ablation to the abolition of communalism in India.

We can see his conception of humanism in his approaches to nationalism and internationalism. He got the inspiration of nationalism from western ideology during his stay in London. We can see metaphysical outlook dominates in Gandhi's accounts of nationalism. In his view all men are sparks of truth, and all land belongs to God. Thus our nationalism should transcend all barriers, geographical, religious, social and political. "God never made those frontiers."[20] He says "Indian nationalism is not exclusive, nor aggressive, nor destructive. It is health giving religious and therefore humanitarian."[21]

Gandhi created a mass basis for the Indian independence movement. He was the author of the first mass struggle of the Indian people. Gandhi's nationalism is conterminous with humanity. In Gandhi's words "For me patriotism is the same as humanity. I am patriotic because I am human and humane."[22] "My patriotism includes...the service of humanity."[23] His nationalism is continuous with his notion of internationalism. These concepts are two faces of the same reality like other concepts such as ends-means, rights-action, truth-non-violence, etc. his conception of internationalism is not an abstract one. He found it in nationalism. D.M. Dutta observes "Love of man impelled Gandhi to be both nationalist and internationalist."[24] These conceptions are rooted in his humanitarian approaches. Humanism transcends all national and provisional limitations.

Gandhi is a proponent of human freedom too. He treated human being as the crown of creation; and hence fought for human freedom in every walk of life. G.

Ramachandran observes, "The first element in the humanism of Gandhi is the freedom of man. No man unfree was part of the great humanity of his dream. Freedom and free men alone can make a just human society."[25]

Gandhi's humanistic concept can be seen through his work for Indian independence movement. As he knows the human psychology, he inspired the semi-comatic people and turned them into morally strong beings. With magic spell of humanism he instilled life, self-confidence, dignity and patriotism in them. With the touch stone of humanism he awakened them from the age-old slumber. He was a man of speech, deed and thoughts. What he practiced, he practiced. He represented not only the peasants, the outcastes, the untouchables, the weavers, the workers, but the oppressed or suffering humanity in general. "Humanism was inherent in every spoken word and thought of Gandhi."[26]

Gandhi's integral humanism is indicated by his enumerated seven social sins:

- Politics without principles
- Wealth without work
- Commerce without morality
- Knowledge without character
- Pleasure without conscience
- Science without morality
- Worship without sacrifice

The eleven vows recited in his Asrama prayer began with Truth and Non-Violence as foundational for the integration of moral, social, political and economic values. Non-Violence should be a creed rather than a policy. Gandhi's Truth meant freedom of self-actualization for societal development. He fulfilled these two principal themes of humanism in the civic function of religion and religious tolerance which aimed at evolving moral individual in moral societies. Gandhi described 'Ahimsa' to be the law of life. He identified Ahimsa with Universal Love. To him, all well constructed societies are based on the law of Non-Violence that the families are bound together by ties of love and so are groups in the so called civilized society. Gandhi transformed

Ahimsa from a passive attitude to an active and dynamic factor by welding renunciation and action in to one force.

CONCLUSION

Gandhi's whole thinking, i.e. political, social, economic is rooted in the two cardinal virtues, Truth and Non-violence. What he preached, he practiced throughout his life. According to him, "if there is sufficient Non-Violence developed in any single person, he should be able to discover the means of combating violence, no matter how wide-spread or severe within his jurisdiction." He also says "non-violent action without co-operation of the heart and the head cannot produce the intended result."[27] Gandhian principles are so relevant in the contemporary developing world, especially to the present situation of India.[28]

The modern youths are misguided and have no respect for human values. The discontented and frustrated youths resort to evils, they resort to crimes for their sustenance. In modern times terrorism increases much large scales. Because of the latest modern communication network, the terrorist ideas spread immediately. The terrorists have been indoctrinated with a type of ideology supporting violence and terrorism.

To prevent terrorism, Gandhi aimed a non-violent society and a non-violent state. He advocated the doctrine of trusteeship of realize the ideal of economic equality for the emergence of an egalitarian society basing on non-stealing and non-possession to avoid exploitation. He held that to avert the violence, the gulf between the rich and the poor should be bridged. He advocates a non-violent decentralized democracy to promote the full growth of all the individuals. When the government is non-violent and all the people are involved in the affairs of state, it results in a healthy and dignified independence. In such a liberal decentralized democracy terrorism would not be flourished.

Gandhi also discussed the necessity of peace which has greater significance in modern times. Peace is not only a state of absence of war, stress, strain, conflict and disturbance, but also a positive state of contentment, blissfulness and love.

According to Gandhi, Non-Violence is applicable to resole the national and international problems. He demonstrated that Non-Violence is the only indisputable way to attain peace and tranquility. The concept of Non-Violence as interpreted by Gandhi is a way of life and conduct to sustain order.

Non-Violence plays an important role in the tensed and disturbed world. The modern world has been dominated by the politics of power, balance of power, diplomatic relations and other constraints. So non-violence and love have to be brought about in the place of violence and hatred for the establishment of a new peaceful world.

The modern world confronts with so many issues such as nuclear arms race, civil wars, ethnic and religious conflicts etc, which leads to internal insecurity, international armament and mutual disbelief. In accordance with Gandhian Principles, all deeds should be based on Non-Violence that provides a peaceful environment in society.

The modern world is going with poverty, oppression and sufferings. Rich have become richer and poor have become poorer. Wars are everywhere killing thousands of humans. We inhale dirty air and there are diseases and epidemics. We are not secured in the present situation. Each individual is in direct competition with everyone else for jobs, raw materials, oil and food. In such a condition, the Gandhian concepts are more relevant. Each individual has to be familiar with Gandhian thought. We should learn and practice Gandhian principles.

Each individual and each country should behave in accordance with Gandhian principles. Conflicts among countries still go on and there are so many sufferings till embedded today. We need to reflect on Gandhi's principles for a better condition in this world.

Notes and References

1. Schiller, F.C.S., 'Humanism', in James Hastings (ed.), Encyclopaedia of Religion and Ethics, Vol. VI, p. 830.
2. Marvin Fabiner, 'Humanistic Ethics and the Conflict of Interests', in Paul Kurtz (ed.), Moral Problems in Contemporary Society, p. 255.
3. Erich Fromm, 'Introduction', in Erich Fromm (ed.), Socialist Humanism, p. ix.

4. Paul Kurtz, 'What is Humanism'? in Paul Kurtz (ed.), *op. cit.*, p. 2.
5. F. Copleston, A History of Philosophy, Vol. I, p. 87.
6. Amiya Chakravarty, Humanism and Indian Thought, p. 5.
7. Marx, Karl, *Capital*, Vol. I., p. 688.
8. Gandhi, M.K., An Autobiography or The Story of My Experiments With Truth, p. 203.
9. *Harijan*, 2 April 1938, p. 65.
10. *Young India*, 20 September 1928, p. 319.
11. Buddhadeva Bhattacharya, Evolution of the Political Philosophy of Gandhi, p. 120.
12. *Harijan*, 29 August 1936, p. 226.
13. *Young India*, 23, October, 1924, p. 350.
14. Rene Fulop-Miller, Gandhi: The Holy Man, p. 57.
15. *Young India*, 11 September 1924, p. 298. also see *Harijan*, 2 March 1934, p. 24; F.R. Movaes, *op. cit.*, p. 23, S. Chakravarthi, 'Truth and Non-violence in Gandhi's Humanism', in T.K. Mahadevan (ed.) *op. cit.* p.40; Supra (ch. v, sec. from Morality to Politics).
16. For details, see *Supra* (ch.VII, sec. Bread Labour, Swadeshi, etc.).
17. *Young India*, 13 November 1924, p. 378.
18. Cited in Buddhadeva Bhattacharya, *op. cit.*, p. 172.
19. Mulk Raj Anand, The Humanism of M.K. Gandhi, p. 30.
20. *Young India*, 25 September 1924, in *Young India*, 1924-26, p. 83.
21. *Ibid.*, 31 December, 1931, p. 427.
22. *Ibid.*, 13 October 1921, in *Young India*, 1919-22, p. 673.
23. *Ibid.*, 16 March 1921, in *Young India*, 1919-22, pp. 646-47.
24. *Ibid.*, 17 September 1925, p. 320.
25. D.M. Datta, The Philosophy of Mahtma Gandhi, p. 159.
26. G. Ramachandran, 'The Relations of Truth and Non-Violence in Gandhi's Thinking, in T.K. Mahadevan (ed.), *op. cit.*, p. 71.
27. *Ibid.*, p. 83.
28. Bidyut Chakrabarty, Social and Political Thought of Mahatma Gandhi, 2006, pp. 56-71.

Relevance of Mahatma Gandhi's Philosophy Today

Amit Narula and Kusum Narula

In. this age of crisis we have to remember Mahatma Gandhi. His philosophy is relevant today amidst privatization, globalization and marginalization. He was symbol of selfless service, sacrifice, compassion and of Indian culture. His weapon was spiritual force as attained through Satyagrah. Albert Einstein stated that Mahatma Gandhi's work and philosophy are relevant in modern times and will be remembered for ever. His position in world history is unique.

The thought, philosophy and the message of Gandhi are very much relevant to-day. We must say they alone constitute the only positive factor which can save the modern civilization which is heading for a disaster. We witness a sure and certain dilution of higher values of life in the scheme of our lives. Permanent values of service before self-sacrifice before hoarding and concern for others are fast dwindling and their place is being taken by selfishness, greed, opportunism, deceit, cunning and falsehood. Gross materialism is eating into the vitals of society and a certain agnostic attitude is in evidence almost everywhere. Even family ties are being broken, love is losing ground to hatred, distrust and suspicion. The present civilization is growing more and more mechanized and materialized and the old innocence born of simplicity stands at bay. All human values are being sacrificed at the altar of Mammon. All this has given birth to conflicts and confrontations and has led to the erosion of the noble standards of tolerance and fellow-feeling. To complete this grim picture has come the unending race for armaments. Destructive weapons of war are waiting in the nuclear arsenals of the superpowers to be delivered one day on the innocent humanity. They menace the very existence of mankind. Efforts for bringing about disarmament have never succeeded; on the contrary, they have always led to further and more and more armament. The dropping of two atom bombs on Hiroshima and Nagasaki and the total devastation of these cities thereby should serve a constant reminder to everybody that a nuclear war whenever fought would bring about the extinction of mankind.

Even nearly six decades after Gandhi's death, opinions about his achievements remain deeply divided. For some he was too implacably hostile to modernity to offer an adequate understanding of its nature, let alone provide answers to its malaise. He was basically a man of action whose major contribution consisted in leading his country's struggle for independence. Some of his critics regard even this as a mixed legacy. In their view his basically conservative, puritanical, pro-bourgeois, and pacifist thought hindered the development of radical political movements, harmed the long-term interests of the dalits (formerly untouchables), burdened the Indian psyche with a paralyzing sense of guilt about economic development, hampered the emergence of a strong and powerful state and perpetuated unrealistic and confused ideas about human sexuality. His introduction of religious language into politics alienated the Muslims and rendered the partition of the country unavoidable. And his flawed strategy of national regeneration failed to develop the conventional forms of institutional politics and political parties that independent India badly needed and in whose absence its political life suffered grave damage.

Gandhi's admirers take a radically different view. For them he was a man of both thought and action, a rare combination. As a man of thought, he saw through the madness of modernity and offered an alternative vision that combined the best insights of both the pre-modern and modern world-views while avoiding the naive individualism and moral vacuum of the currently fashionable post-modernism. He also discovered a uniquely moral method of political change in the form of satyagraha and provided an effective alternative to violence. As a man of action he led the greatest anti-colonial struggle in history, developed a humane and liberal form of patriotism, showed how to lead a successful political life without compromising one's integrity and offered a rare example of morally responsible leadership. Christian commentators, who suggestively have long compared him to and even seen him as the twentieth-century version of Jesus Christ, argue that he was the first man in history to show how to relate religion and politics without corrupting either and to give political life a much-needed spiritual basis. Some of Gandhi's admirers go even further and contend that we should not be surprised if one day he were to prove as influential and be placed on the same footing as Jesus Christ and the Buddha.

All his adult life Gandhi sought to articulate and live out an original and powerful vision of human existence. As we have seen, he was deeply troubled by violence in all its crude and subtle forms and passionately yearned to lead a life of true non-violence. He wondered if and how it was possible to be profoundly at peace with oneself, other human beings, and one's natural and social environment, to hurt and harm no living being, to delight in their existence and do all one could to help them flourish. He relentlessly explored the logic of that vision, asking what stood in its way and if and how it could be overcome. For him the question was not merely of theoretical but also of existential importance and the answer had to be not only theoretically satisfactory but capable of forming the basis of personal and collective life.

Since mankind had long accepted violence as the inescapable basis of life and organized its affairs on the opposite vision to his, Gandhi was led to ask the deepest and most searching questions. He asked why a civilization should be based on the technological mastery and exploitation of nature and the untenable attitude of anthropocentric hubris and how it could be designed differently. He asked why there should be such a coercive institution as the state, indeed why human beings should be subjected to coercion at all when it so clearly violated their dignity and what kind of society would eliminate the need for it. He felt deeply troubled about the armed forces, the police, the prisons and the wars, all of which seemed to him an affront to human dignity and indicative of a profound failure of moral and political imagination. He felt no less troubled by the violence and dehumanization of both capitalism and communism and asked if there was a more moral way of organizing the economy.

For Gandhi non-violence implied inner peace, being profoundly at ease with oneself and required a sense of stability and rooted-ness, a home, a boundary. However it also required that rootedness should not become imprisonment, the home a fortress, the boundary a barrier, for it then excluded others, feared their closeness, saw them as a threat to one's security and identity. Even when they were not treated in a hostile manner, they were perceived as outsiders, not part of us, an object of mild or strong indifference. Gandhi thought that all such exclusions were not only potential sources of, but themselves constituted a subtle form of, psychological violence. Non-violence required a secure but non-exclusive identity, firm but open.

Accordingly, Gandhi challenged religious, gender-based, national, racial and other divisions. He could not see why religions should see themselves as closed worlds, open only to their adherents and hostile to mutual influence. We have seen what this entailed. Gandhi felt the same way about the gender-based division which stereotyped and trapped each sex within its narrow and exclusive confines. Accordingly he proposed and sought to live up to the ideal of an androgynous person who was both a man and a woman, and freely combined the psychological characteristics and moral virtues conventionally associated with each other. Gandhi's challenge to national, racial, civilizational and other boundaries was equally probing, striving in each case to integrate rootedness and openness.

Gandhi carried his search for non-violence into the realm of the human mind itself and asked how one should relate to one's thoughts, beliefs, and feelings in a truly non-violent manner. It was important to co-ordinate and harmonize one's ideas but to systematize them into a neat and logically coherent theory was to do violence both to the inherently fluid world of experience and to the inescapably tentative process of thinking itself. It was necessary to hold firm beliefs and pass judgements on individuals and situations but one needed to ensure that these did not do violence to the ambiguities of the subject matter or to other ways of looking at it. Gandhi thought that the spirit of violence in modern and indeed many a pre-modern society had deeply penetrated our attitudes to the mental processes and their products, including feelings, sentiments, emotions, judgements, convictions, knowledge and the very activity of thinking itself. Violence thus had struck deep roots into and distorted the human psyche itself and Gandhi's lifelong concern was patiently to expose them and explore what it meant to think, judge, feel, believe, hold convictions and maintain religious faith in a genuinely non-violent manner.

Gandhi's vision was intensely moralistic and yet it remained remarkably free from the utopianism, romanticism, fanaticism, and despair that have often shadowed moralism. This was so because he took great care to ensure that his vision was not itself pervaded by the spirit of violence. He did not think of it as an ideal to realize but as a moral compass with which to navigate one's way through life. This not only left room for but required a firm grip on reality. It also made ample allowance for the fact that different individuals were bound to interpret and articulate the vision differently and thus avoided dogmatism and fanaticism. Gandhi's vision was also sensitive to the limitations of the human condition and encouraged compromise and accommodation. It was striking that when his countrymen disappointed him, as they did during the intercommunal violence, he did not become bitter, condemn them for not being worthy of him and his ideals, despair of them, or withdraw from the scene. He persisted in his task, patiently appealed to them, rebuked but rarely blamed them, never flew into a rage or felt self-righteous and superior and generally succeeded in evoking the desired response.

As for the content of Gandhi's vision, it had its strengths and limitations. He rightly argued that human beings were interdependent in ways they did not often appreciate, that in brutalizing and degrading others they brutalized and degraded themselves as well. This led to a fascinating theory of social criticism and change. He showed that it was far more coherent and effective to criticize an unjust system from the standpoint of not merely its victims but all involved, to appeal to their common humanity and interests and to show that it diminished and damaged them all. Rather than polarize the battle against injustice and place the onus of struggle on its victims, Gandhi's view turned it into a shared moral task to which all alike had a duty to contribute.

In such a climate Gandhism alone provides a ray of hope. The values and principles, ideals and precepts which Gandhi stood for, propagated and preached can give a right direction to humanity to reach a destination of perpetual peace both internal and external. In this connection it needs to be stressed that what Gandhi stood for was not simply an exercise in idealistic, impracticable thinking, Gandhi preached what he practised and said that what he practised was capable of being practised by everyone if only one cared to practise his precepts. Gandhiji's experiments with truth had convinced him beyond doubt that truth always triumphs and the only right path is the path of truth. Truth may be suppressed by adverse forces, but it can never be put down. In Gandhi's own life occasions came when it appeared that falsehood and tyranny based on it would triumph, but to his great bliss, the tables were turned and truth ultimately became victorious. The deliverance of humanity to-day lies through the pursuit of the path of truth. Gandhi identified Truth with God. He had an unshakable faith in God whom he described as an unseen power that exists. Faith in God and pursuit of truth can save humanity from disaster. Closely allied to his conceptions of God and truth is his faith in non-violence. Non-violence in fact is the sheer anchor of Gandhi's philosophy. Non-violence is very much related to truth. Violence is untruth, for it offends against the unity of life and the path of violence is always fraught with serious dangers. Peace in the world can be established if we follow the path of non-violence. Violence for violence's sake will create a vicious circle from which we cannot get out save at the cost of the extinction of humanity. Gandhiji would reply violence with non-violent resistance. In Satyagraha principle Gandhi has bequeathed to us a weapon of unfailing power for the solution of individual and social problems.

Gandhi's faith in religion and morality was deep. By religion he did not mean the observance of rituals and religious ceremony. His religion was synonymous with morality. He preached the path of religion not only for individuals but also for nations, not only in individual life but also in politics. He introduced religion into politics and in this way spiritualized politics. He never agreed with those who said that religion had nothing to do with politics. For Gandhi, politics bereft of religion are a death trap that kill the soul. So much tyranny and blood-shed. that politics has witnessed from time immemorial have drawn strength from the separation of religion from politics. Activities that draw no sustenance from the spiritual nature of man, but derive all their energy and motive power from the non-spiritual side of man's composition, are bound after running their allotted course, to end in disaster and ruin.

Gandhi preached simplicity of life. He was at one with Gautam, the Buddha that multiplication of desires leads to suffering. Our real good lies in the progressive reduction of wants. Cessation of desire leads to the cessation of suffering and hence to salvation. Gandhi himself practised utmost simplicity in life. True culture or civilization consists in the reduction of wants and leading a simple life. All the hurry and worry and mad rush for wealth will never give us peace. According to Gandhi, simplicity of life, leads to purity of life. He gave the idea of bread labour which indeed is based on his notion of simplicity. According to this idea, man must earn his own bread by manual labour. This will be beneficial in two ways. First it will generate a climate of equality between man and man. Second, it will end exploitation of the manual workers by those who earn their living by intellectual labour. Let those who possess superior intellect use that intellect for the welfare of the society rather than for exploitation. Manual labour will also exercise healthy influence on our capacity of intellectual exercise improving it and refining it.

Gandhi advocated decentralization, both political and economic. Gandhi's faith in non-violence made him conscious of the violence inherent in centralization. Centralization leads to the suppression of initiative and enterprise. It blunts innovativeness and inventiveness. It strengthens exploitative tendencies. The way out of the evils of centralization lies through decentralization which can liberate the inherent capacity and talent of a large mass of humanity both for the good of the individual and the good of the society. Gandhi was in favour of the establishment of self-sufficient and autonomous panchayats. The problems of the villagers should be solved by the villagers themselves through the medium of an organization which they themselves help create. The central authority should play only a supportive and sustaining role. In the economic sphere too, Gandhi was against centralized industry. He stressed the need for the improvement and establishment of cottage industries. Simple crafts of the villagers must be to invent new tools and instruments which may eliminate the boredom. This decentralized economy will be free from the problem of unemployment, exploitation of labour by capital and the dehumanization of humanity. Today, when we are painfully suffering from the evils of centralized industry, Gandhi's conception of decentralization provides a ray of hope. Hence, Gandhism in this sphere is not only relevant to-day but is the crying need of the hour if we have to prevent ourselves from sliding further into the abyss of the evils of centralization.

Gandhi's unique contribution lies in his harmonizing and reconciling Capitalism and socialism. His principle of trusteeship achieves this objective. Gandhi did not believe in dispossessing the rich of their riches, nor would he distribute the hard-earned income of the rich among the poor, for that would promote idleness on the part of the poor. He favoured the excess wealth of the rich to be held in trust by the rich themselves for the betterment of the society. This idea of Gandhi is very much relevant to-day for it is not possible either to establish pure socialism of the Marxian type or to ensure annihilation of capitalism. By his principle of trusteeship Gandhi struck a mean between capitalism and socialism, advocating a structure which would promote the good points of both.

Gandhi's ideas on nationalism and internationalism are very much valid and relevant to day. In the world of today we cannot afford to be nationalist at the cost of internationalism. The nationalism of the nazist and fascist type is out of order today, nay, it is fraught with terrible dangers. What is necessary today is the adoption of an enlightened brand of nationalism. We should be nationalists so that we may do the duty of internationalism. In other words, our road to internationalism should be constructed through nationalism. Nehru wrote in his book "The Discovery of India', "Gandhi was an intense nationalist: he was also, at the same time, a man who had message not only for India, but for the world, and he ardently desired world-peace. His nationalism, therefore, had a certain world outlook and was entirely free from any aggressive intent." Indeed there is need to establish a happy synthesis between nationalism and internationalism as Gandhi brought it about in the scheme of his ideas and practice. He wanted the freedom of India so that India could develop its resources for the good of the entire mankind.

Thus, we find that Gandhi has much relevance today. Rather we have to accept the fact that the propagation and practice of Gandhism alone may rid our present civilization of so many blemishes and negative points which forebode to crush humanity and the sound values, it may survive on, under their steel heels. It is good that we have been able to enshrine a number of Gandhian principles and ideas in the 'Constitution' of free India and must endeavour to see them installed on the rightful place. We should aim at material prosperity and equality so as to 'wipe tears from every eye' but should not imitate the foreign models. Communism of the Soviet type and Capitalism of the Western type, neither of them finds a congenial soil in India. Both in their extreme form are bad for India. India requires its own brand of communism and its own brand of capitalism, an order which may accord well with our national genius and our glorious past traditions. Gandhism provides the best anwer.

"Gandhi is relevant for the building up of a peaceful society."[1] A thing or thought is considered as relevant if it is deemed as feasible and practicable. Feasibility indicates logical possibility and freedom from contradiction. So far Gandhian as a socio-economic political ideology is concerned, it is neither self-contradictory nor inconceivable.[2] To attain Ram Rajya or Kingdom of God on earth or Gram Swaraj, Gandhian thought is inevitable. Gandhiji Hind Swaraj or Indian Home Rule is a manifesto of counter civilization, where there will be no rule of the brute force. Man is going to be master of machines rather than its slave. If one gets rid of seven sins, i.e. politics without principles, wealth without work, pleasure without conscience, commerce without morality, science without humanity, education without character and last but not the least worship without sacrifice. Then one can achieve ideals and as consequence a better society will emerge. The present socio-economic political scenario has been deteriorating day by day. Where no man's life is safe, no man's wife is safe, life has become most insecured due to the fact that is governed by money and power and so there is need to change way of life.

Relevance also refers to its being practicable. His principles are not beyond practice. He was considered as "Practical idealist."[3] Who tried his level best to resolve national issues in a realistic and down to earth manner. He himself showed through experiments the great qualities like truth, non-violence or celibacy. He was an ordinary man and became great due to the practice of the above principles in life. His concept of Satyagraha is no Utopia, it is a reality. His complete life is an experiment with truth. His whole autobiography is model before us. He says "Truths and non-violence are cloistered virtues but applicable as much in the forum and the legislatures as in the market place."[4] He wanted to spiritualize politics and worldly affairs. "Truth and non-violence can be practiced by individual group, communities and nations."[5] To him an absence of action is better than tons of words. One has to understand his relevance Judiciously for example he was pledged believer in protection of cows but when a calf was undergoing an unbearable pain and doctors declared it as incurable. Gandhi permitted mercy killing to the great charge of fundamentalist Hindus. In the same where there was widespread plague in Borsad Taluka (Gujarat) he allowed Dr. Bhaskar and his party to carry on wholesale destruction of rats and flies. Where people did not ever think of killing a single rat or flies. If one finds contradiction in his teaching because life itself is full of contradictions. The relevance is to reach perfections. A non-violent person lessens the circle of destruction.

In the field of economic ideal we see that the good of the individual is contained in the good of all. To meet the ends everybody must be given sufficient work. This is only possible if the means of production remains under the thumb of the masses, monopolization would be unfair. "The neglect of this simple principle is the cause of the destitution."[6] Gandhi introduced the doctrine of trusteeship which avoids demerits of capitalism and communism. The good of society is the main aim. He believed in liquidating class-interests by conversion. If it fails non-violent, non-co-operation and civil disobedience are there. To him moral values play major role particularly in economics. True economics never militates against the highest ethical standard. He spoke of "Gospel of Work" or "Bread labour" to provide large number of jobs to the large population. He started Swadeshi or non-exploitative economy. "He wanted not mass production but production by the masses."[7] "Gandhi was not against machinery."[8] He wanted sustainable development. Many advanced countries like Rome, USA, suffered due to material progress. He stressed the value of voluntary poverty and limitation of wants. He favoured equality of income so as to avoid the gap between hard labourer and the intellectual laborers.

In the field of politics he was in favour of decentralization. He agrees with Thoreau who says "that Government is best which governs the least."[9] In the words of Lord Eton "power corrupts and absolute power corrupts absolutely." Apparently it seems that it minimizes exploitation on the contrary it destroys individuality which is the core of progress. He says "State represents violence in concentrated and organized form. The individual has a soul but the state is soulless machine."[10] He believed in democracy and individual freedom which is the core of democracy. In his opinion "true democracy can only be outcome of non-violence."[11] He was in favour of a grassroot participatory democracy one must start from bottom and not from the top. It is necessary that the bottom should control the top. Isolated independence is not the goal of the world. Man made barriers must be wiped out which are based on power politics. Tagore said, "O father let my country away where freedom of heaven exists."[12] There is no limit in extending services to the neighbours.

In the social field he knew very well that India is multi-religious, multilingual and multi racial country. He started the work of nation building through the constructive programmes of communal harmony, abolition of untouchability, propagation of rural industries, literacy, regard for women and the poor. He started a slogan of treating all religions with the same amount of respect. "Sarva Dharma Sambhav." He was a crusader against the manifold evils like evil system, child marriage, compulsory widowhood, dowry system, prostitution, prohibition is one of the major element by which millions suffer. He says "India's salvation depends on the sacrifice and enlightenment of her women."[13] According to him woman is incarnation of non-violence. Many women took active part in his non-violent struggle. He was not only against untouchability but also against caste system. His Phoenix Ashram, Tolstoy Farm, Sabarmati Ashram, Seva Gram Ashram are best examples to illustrate. He practised all his principles irrespective of sex, creed, religion, caste and language.

He knew that the destiny of the nation shapes in her class room as he enunciated the most scientific and integral system of education known as Basic education. Mere literacy has no attraction to him. Development of hand, heart and head is important. Education forms the common mind. As Woodrow Wilson says that Education is the only hope. It draws the best out of the pupils. He was against British system of education which helps to build a castle in air and is based on foreign culture. The best education system deals with learning by doing. There must be scope to the development of soul and mind. "His aim of education was character building."[14] Gandhi combines science and spirituality. As Einstein said "Science without spirituality is blind and spirituality without science is lame." Khan Abdul Gaffar Khan said in the year 1969 "In India Gandhism is dead. It is a story of Buddha over again." Acharya J.B. Kriplani lamented. There is yet nothing like Gandhism. According to him "The real India is not military but peace loving."[15] He prayed "God forbid that India should ever become a military nation."[16] He taught us to accept simple living and high thinking which has gone to dogs now. There has been grave erosion of moral and spiritual values, in all walks of life, due to drink and drugs. According to Narayan Bai Desai the so called Disciples of Gandhi have accepted the technique but not the principles. The real trouble lies in this. Dalit leaders accused and abused Gandhi for the sorry state of their affairs. While Gandhi in the heart of heart favoured Dalits unto the last. He identified with their miseries and their humiliation and harassment. He said "I do not want to be reborn. But if I have to be reborn, I should be born as an untouchable."[17] There is need of Gandhi's rebirth like phoenix bird which rises out of the ashes to eradicate impact of western civilization in order to bring peace and prosperity. Gandhi's life in toto is to be understood if we want to get into the not-so-simple world view he envisioned. He was no doubt, simple in dress, food habits and in the language he used for communication. What followed from the life he lived and propagated and around which what is known today as Gandhian Philosophy is built constitute the core of human striving.

Have we tried to understand the revolutionary nature of his philosophy? In fact he was one of the greatest revolutionaries of all times. The language and methods he used did not encourage spilling of blood; on the contrary persuasion, non-violent suffering to convince the opponent—or the oppressor were the hallmarks of his approach. In understanding Gandhi what is required is a revolutionary, rather unconventional approach and not the off beaten traditional approach. An academic approach will not also help anyone to understand Gandhi. Unless we understand the revolutionary Gandhi and the evolutionary nature of his views and philosophy.

The message from his martyrdom is loud and clear: should we hate each other, kill and get killed in the name of what we very often do not know? As Mathew Arnold described in his poem "Dover Beach", we are like the ignorant army clashing in the night. Gandhi showed a lamp so that we might recognize such other and behave like civilized human beings. Let it not be forgotten that Gandhi too was a human being. To deify him and to see in him answers and solutions to all our problems will be an attempt which Gandhi himself would not approve of much of what Gandhi did and said was on the basis of his own understanding of the situation that existed at that time. During the last many years since his death, humanity has witnessed breath taking developments. The relevance of Gandhi is that despite all this, his striving for alternatives don't make his theory and practice irrelevant; on the contrary, they superimpose.

Notes and References

1. Rai, Chhaya, Relevance of Gandhian Thought, p. 3.
2. *Ibid.*, p. 3.
3. Shriman Narayan, "Towards the Gandhian Plan", p. 91.
4. *Harijan*, 8.5.1937.
5. *Ibid.*, 8.5.1937.
6. *Young India*, 15.11.1928.
7. *Harijan*, 2.11-1934.
8. *Young India*, 13.11.1924.
9. *Harijan*, 2.7.1931.
10. Modern Review (Monthly magazine) Calcutta 1935, p. 412.
11. Gandhi, M.K., Gandhi's Correspondence with Govt. 1942-44 (Ahmedabad: Navajivan Publishing House), 1945, p. 175.
12. Tagore "Where the Mind is Without Fear" A Poem from Gitanjali.
13. *Harijan*, 27.6.1936.
14. Wash Burne Callton, Remarks of Mankind 1932, pp. 104-05.

15. Tendulkar, D.G., Mahatma (New Delhi: Publications Division, Ministry of Information, Government of India), Vol. 5, p. 17.
16. *Ibid.*, Vol. 11, p. 387.
17. *Young India*, 4.5.1921.

Relevance of Gandhi in the Modern Societies

PARMOD CHAUHAN

"The opinions I have formed and the conclusions I have arrived at are not final. I may change tomorrow; I have nothing new to teach to the world. Truth and non-violence are as old as the hills. All I have done is to try experiments in both on as vast a scale as I could do. In doing so, I have sometimes erred and leant by my errors. Life and its problems have thus become to me so many experiments in the practice of truth and non-violence."[1]

On its face, Western democratic societies have seldom been stronger. Their dangerous totalitarian opponents have been vanquished; their technology continues to move at a dizzying pace; their citizens are living longer, are more literate, and generally enjoying a higher standard of living than earlier generations; their models of the economy and polity have been one dominant, and their culture is becoming globalized. The West has put its stamp on the world: modernity and modernization provide the standards by which we understand success and failure.

But there are signs of trouble and discontent in the

West. Political participation is declining while cynicism is increasing; hard choices assert themselves between full employment and a generous state; drugs and crime climb to troubling levels; the family is under siege; people live longer but many seem neither secure nor satisfied; and the environment is degraded while the world's population increases.

Spacial problems await the two largest groups in the world, the young and the poor. The young are likely to have some education, live in urban areas, move away from the traditions of their parents, accept cosmopolitan norms of identity and of the good, be less deferential to authority, and be part of a changing, mobile environment At the same time, very large numbers will be underemployed or unemployed, finding that the promises of modern culture have been broken and that they have no worth in their own society.

Where this lead is uncertain. Strong, disciplinary governments may check unrest with harsh police measures that are not respecters of basic rights; political leaders may manipulate loneliness and frustration into ugly, violent, nativist movements; crime and social disorganization may intensify; internal civil strife may explode; or the poor may be intimidated and humiliated in the harsh realities of their urban slums. From a Gandhian perspective, such outcomes are neither imaginary nor inevitable. They are not imaginary because severe dislocations, the intense demands of individualism, a decayed tradition, a continued devaluation of persons in the economy, and a host of other dislocating moves are bound to have an effect, sometimes leading to violence, always involving some measure of domination, and invariably sacrificing autonomy. However, Gandhi thinks this state of affairs can be challenged in two different but related ways. In the first place, he wants to show that injustice can be confronted non-violently. Secondly, he insists that a different imperative one that emphasizes the cosmological interdependence of everyone and different institutional arrangements can foster (though not guarantee) a society that resists these assaults on autonomy. In this way he speaks to those at the margin, admonishing them to discard their lethargy, reject fatalism, and claim their own dignity through public, non-violent assertion.

One of Gandhi's great contributions as a political theorist of the twentieth century comes with his invitation to think freshly about the future, and he does this by reaching for both the past and present. If the future is as menacing as Gandhi fears it can become, then his importance increases with his reminders of what we risk losing and his claim that people can non-violently challenge modern version of fatalism.

His sweeping challenge to modern expressions of fatalism makes Gandhi distinctive in the late modern by questioning the inevitability and intractability of modernity, he wants to expose it as a construction that can be resisted. He is not interested in replacing everything that is modern, but in contextualizing the modern temper within a cosmological framework that guards autonomy. Moreover, he sets out to defend and nourish local traditions where individuals live and work and which, Gandhi believes, provide them with purpose and dignity. To do this, he confronts modern versions of fatalism; some hold that we cannot escape complexity, that we cannot avoid centralization, that we cannot resist the globalization of modern culture, that we cannot repeal the inevitability of violent conflict, or that we cannot challenge the growing impersonality of a world that judges the good in terms of its economic contribution.

Although it is impossible to return to an earlier cosmos, Gandhi means to fill in some of the blank spaces left by modernity. He does this by continually applying ethical standards to contemporary practices and institutions. For him, the earlier cosmic harmony promised that the autonomy of everyone would be assured, and he wants to make this the ultimate standard for judgment in the modern world. Therefore, he constantly asks about the status of autonomy and all that he thinks autonomy requires.

Gandhi challenges the contemporary tendency to see modernity embodying progress, reason, and liberation and to believe that alternative standards and practices that stand in its way can be eliminated without costly consequences. Should this attitude prevail, Gandhi fears that an increasing number of persons will become obsolescent, seen as having no worth and nothing to contribute in the modern world. For him the modern tendency to make economic criteria the standard for judging persons and institutions reduces human beings to means; with such an outlook, talk about their dignity is beside the point.

As society becomes increasingly complex, there is an accelerating tendency for greater centralization, coordination, and hierarchy and the increasing dominance of the specialist. Deeply troubled by these encroachments on autonomy, Gandhi is especially armed at the prospect of the centralized state. His specific proposals for the panchayat raj may not offer much guidance in the crowded polity of the late modern world, but is political critique signals what has traditionally been at the heart of the democratic project, namely that people ought to govern themselves. Accordingly, he wants to show the dangers of concentrated power and the need to disperse power and encourage participation throughout society.

Gandhi warns about the globalization of the modernized economy, not only because of its economic effects but also because it is accompanied with the globalization of culture. He continually celebrates the diversity he sees in India and fears that such globalization is reducing what is distinctive and fostering what is uniform. Local cultures are critical to Gandhi's project because he sees each providing a concrete, not abstract sense of identity and meaning apart from productivity and consumption. To defend autonomy and resist domination, Gandhi argues that persons must be equipped with a standard and that standard typically comes from tradition. However, one cannot rely on a tradition that has grown, tired and corrupt, and so Gandhi continually revisits tradition and, where he finds it necessary, challenges it. For him, a revitalized and reformed tradition represents the best moral resource to question the efficiencies of the age.

GANDHI'S POLITICAL REALISM

Although it seems strange to think of Gandhi as a political realist, much of his work is infused with a rich understanding of power and he shares much with conventional political realists, such as Machiavelli[2] in the West and Kautilya in India. On the realist account, power is unavoidable, seductive, and important. Whether we like it or not power surrounds us; for realists, including Gandhi, the issue is not whether we can avoid power by ignoring it but how we understand and respond to its nature and uses. Realists share the views that power cannot be completely tamed, that it frequently carries dangerous consequences, and that it can never be fully exonerated by a comprehensive morality.

To the realist, power itself is ubiquitous, unpredictable, and often hazardous. It provides us with the means to achieve some goal or overcome obstacles, but our quest for power often blinds us to its dangers. Realists see us frequently inflating our capacity to direct and control power and failing to appreciate its limits. Entering the fluid, unpredictable world of power, we frequently harm others and unintentionally injure ourselves. For all of the problems associated with it, realists find people continually searching for more power, often to keep pace with their competitors.[3]

For someone such as Machiavelli, the power of any person or state is always problematic. Even though one actor has greater power than its opponents at any given moment it can be undermined by unexpected changes or unconventional power.[4] One reason is that power takes many forms, and what seems to be an overwhelming expression of power in a particular setting can be undermined by alternative modes of power.[5]

Gandhi's realism follows from his reading of power as unavoidable, dangerous, and coveted. For him, power needs to be understood more expansively than it generally is, not to repackage in new containers that deny its hazards or inevitability, but to show people its many locations and forms. Although Gandhi does not hold the bleak view of conventional realists that people are constantly driven by ambition and ready to dominate others, he finds that any society is open to this possibility. For this reason, Gandhi wants to domesticate power by dispersing it throughout society to avoid monopolistic concentrations.

Gandhi's civic realism departs from conventional

realism in several important ways. One reflects his argument that politics is about more than power and must address the purposes for which it is employed and how it is used. He intends to direct it in ways that speak to the dignity, freedom, and equality of persons. For him, the way power is applied has profound effects, and often unintended ones. In arguing that violent applications of power undermine even generous principles, Gandhi insists that people pay attention to the kind of power they employ and the means they use to mobilize it. If the purpose of power is to foster mutuality and autonomy, he means to show that violence only subverts these goals.

Gandhi's civic realism is also reflected in the attention he gives to the institutions of civil society which are critical to his understanding of power. The ways they organize and distribute power serve to facilitate or diminish individual self-governance, and he calls attention to the ways that institutions reward, ignore, and penalize particular forms of behavior. Some arrangements signal to people that they can protect their own economic well being and security only by transferring their self-governance elsewhere. For these reasons, Gandhi leaves a conventional political realism that is preoccupied with state power and moves to a wider understanding of power which pays attention to how civil society is organized and what happens there.

The very features of politics that Gandhi makes a central part of his understanding of power and politics, namely love and conversion, seems to disqualify Gandhi as a realist, but I think not. He finds that lasting change does not come through coercion; that support born of good economic times often falters when the economy grows sour; that appeals to conscience often have a profound effect if not immediately, then over time; and that some of the most intractable issues are not settled by violence but require dialogue and understanding. He takes his readers beyond conventional meanings of power to show what an expanded version can accomplish. Gandhi's civic realism, for all of its emphasis on love, speaks more directly to power than a political realism purporting to be scientific, a realism trying to mimic economic markets, or a realism that makes efficient management its center. In presenting a multidimensional understanding of power and its effects on individuals, Gandhi leaves a crude realism and attempts to teach a civic realism in order to reach ethical conclusions about political life.

Notes and References

1. *Harijan*, March 28, 1936.
2. Parel, Anthony, "Gandhian Satyagraga and Machiavellian Virtu" in The Meanings of Gandhi (ed.) Paul Powers (Honolulu: University Press of Hawaii), 1971.
3. Bloom, Alan, The Closing of the American Mind (New York: Simon and Schuster), 1987.
4. Bondurant, V. Joan, Conquest of Violence (Berkeley: University of California Press), 1967, p. 194.
5. *Ibid*.

Buddhist Perspectives of Non-Violence

RANJANA BHARDWAJ

Non-violence is directly related to the Mahatama Buddha's life, He is the founder and propounder of Non-violence in the world in a true sence. He was thoughtful from his childhood. He was sad due the sufferings of the people in the world. He often thought about the principles of life and death, pain and pleasure, etc. He saw some very heart rending sights of sufferings of the world such as old age, death and disease, which turned away his mind from the Luxurious life. These sights made him realize that this world was full of misery and distress. His mind was ever busy as to how the people can get rid of misery and sufferings in this world. Buddha left his home and sat in meditation for a long time and ultimately he got enlightenment and true path that would save mankind from sufferings and the world would be a happy place. He began to preach the tenets of his new religion. He taught that all people would be happy in this world by leading a life of good conduct, with purity of heart and by showing kindness to all living beings. His main emphasize was on the Non-violence and brotherhood. He founded an organization 'Buddhist Sangha' or an order of Bhikshus who spread his religion inside and outside the country. The main essesence of his religion was Non-violence. Non-violence was the teaching of Lord Buddha or main principle of Buddhism. Non-violence or Ahimsa is very essential for peace and calm in the society. The Buddha laid great stress on Ahimsa, or doing no harm to living beings. He firmly believed that one should neither take meat, nor kill and injure the animals in any way. He taught that man should foster the feelings of love for all living beings. Buddha wanted that love and amity should prevail among all living beings and there should be no violence amidst them. Animal sacrifice was the main feature of Hinduism during the Vedic period. It disturbed Buddha a lot. Innumerable animals were sacrificed in the yajnas and sometimes even human sacrifice was offered. This kind of practice of animal sacrifice was becoming common, yet a large number of people rose against it. Buddha began to preach that God was not pleased with the sacrifice of speechless animals and helpless human beings. People were, therefore, in quest of living a non-violence, simple, pure and peaceful life. Buddha favoured the idea of Brotherhood in the society and peace among the people of the world. The greatest evil of the society was that it was based on discrimination and distinction. People from higher classes hated the people of the lower strata. In The Vedic times society was based on the system of varnas, which later developed into an ugly picture of castism. Higher caste people treated the lower caste ones like an animal. They were not allowed to enter the temple, not to draw water out of the wells. Sometime low caste people were punished by the higher caste people for breaking the rules against the inequality. It ultimately created unrest and violence which was resisted by the Buddha with the weapons of non-violence and equality, kindness for all the living ones. Principle of non-violence influenced the Indian society and the world in a deep sense. It had great impact on the society in various ways. It changed the thinking and eating habits of people. It established brotherhood among the people of the world and emphasized the need of leading a pure and moral life and following the principle of Ahimsa or Non-violence. It helped the world to get back peace and discourage the cruel actions.

Buddhism put up strong opposition against caste system and accepted the principle of equality. Buddhism favoured equal opportunities for all in the society without any discrimination of caste and creed. Caste system was very rigid in Hinduism. The people of higher classes treated Sudras very disgracefully. Buddhism was against such type of discrimination and bad treatments committed by higher classes, which became the reasons for violence in the society.

So Buddhism denounced all claims to superiority on the ground of birth as the higher classes claimed. It opened the door for the people of lower classes. Even the untouchables could attain salvation by following the path of Dharma. The people of lower classes embraced this new faith in large number. So Buddhism appealed to the hearts of people. They accepted Buddhism as the best religion. Thus the caste system began to lose its significance which contributed to the Non-violence principle of Buddha.

Buddhism influenced the eating habits of the people. So the animal killing began to be disliked and the use of meat as an article of food was being discouraged day by day. Kindness is the main principle of Buddhism, so it preached against the killing of animals for food. In fact, Hindus were meat eaters. But under the influence of Buddhism they decreased the use of meat in their diet. It popularized the idea of vegetarianism instead of flesh eating. This change in the society inspire the people for non-violence and gave strength to the principle of equality and kindness in the society to all the living ones.

Buddhism was the great defender of principle of Non-violence and kindness. It was the result of Buddhist influence that people daringly rejected the idea and practice of slaughtering of animals for sacrifices and religious ceremonies. Even it was the result of Buddhism that from that time Brahamans stopped the practice of killing of animals for religious ceremonies. They adopted the substitute for live animals, that were the images made of corn flour. So, Buddhism influenced Indian society to a great extent. Ideas of equality, kindness and humanity became the moral principles of Indian people. These principles had brought the atmosphere of brotherhood and peace. To some extent, caste system, idea of superiority, discrimination, such types of evils in Indian society reached their end. In Buddhism, we find references of life of Gautama Buddha that during his lifetime, he taught lesson of Non-violence by virtue of that many ruthless persons amend themselves to a kind hearted human being. Example of Harriti who originally was a demoness at Rajagriha. She had the habit of eating up the human flesh. She killed children's of many families. Buddha taught her lesson of Non-violence by virtue of which she stopped this bad habit and became a protector of the children. Buddha transformed another cruel person whose name was Angulimala. He left his evil nature to harm the other people by cutting their limbs or fingures. Buddha also transformed him by teaching Non-violence or Ahimsa and inspired to shed off his bad nature of crime. During his life Buddha was opposed by his enemies who wanted violence in the society and to gain their selfish motives by doing any type of inhuman activities. Cinca and Sundari were two females who charged Buddha with false alligations. They were hired by the mischievous persons to defame Buddha, but their plot was disclosed in the public. People wanted to give harsh punishment to them, but Buddha by stopping them gave a message of Kindness and Non-violence. He even forgave the bad elements of the society who wanted to harm and defame him. It was the unique feature of Buddhism that Buddha did not hate the person or criminal, but to despise the crime. The rulers of that time too could not escape the touch of this tenet, so due to Buddhist influence kings of that time did many welfare works for animals and their people. Spirit of peace and Ahimsa was propagated by them. On account of this theory and principle of Buddha, many kings like Bimbisara, Asoka, Kanishka, Harsha, became peace loving and began to oppose war. When most of the kings became the followers of Buddhism, they had to act upon the principle of Ahimsa themselves before preaching it to others. 'An example is better than a precept' was their guiding rule. In this way, it helped a good deal in the maintenance of peace in this subcontinent of India for a long time. When many rulers became followers of Buddhism, it gave rise to the spirit of social service also. Hospitals for men and animals as well as roads for travellers were built. Shady trees were planted on the boths sides of roads, wells were dug up. Kindness to living beings began to be considered as an important human duty. Thus Non-violence in the life of human being improved a lot in general. Gradually teaching of Non-violence broke down the racial barriers among the people and Buddhism spread kindness, equality, peace into all provinces and kingdoms of India and abroad.

Even now a days many people believe in Ahimsa. They are of the view that we should not harass or harm anyone for selfish motive. According to Buddhism in every human being Non-violence should be incorporated in word, thought and action. So Buddhism influenced Indian society to a great extent. Ideas of equality, kindness and humanity became the moral principles of Indian people. These principles had brought the atmosphere of brotherhood and peace. To some extent caste system, idea of superiority, discrimination, such types of evils in Indian society reached an end. Animal sacrifice and cruelty were stopped. Non-violence principle came as fresh air to the violent cruel social atmosphere, which eventually came to a fatal blow for the cruelness. Buddhism too influenced China, Tibet, Ceylon, and the whole world with the idea of Non-violence.

Mahatama Gandhi also followed the principle of Non-violence. Consequently if could be possible to keep the country integrated. He gave the message of peace, amity, brotherhood, equality, untouchability to the world. He was also against the ethnic discrimination in some parts of the world. So Mahatma Gandhi adopted this teaching of Non-violence and gave us fruits of his legacy of principle of Non-violence.

References

Odenberg, H., Vinaya Pitaka, Vol. I (London: Pali Text Society), 1904.

Bapat, P.V., 250 Years of Budhism (New Delhi: Manoha Publishers), 1956.

Pande, G.C., Studies in the Origins of Budhism (Allahabad: University of Allahabad), 1957.

Basham, A.L., The Wonder That was India (London: London Press), 1969.

Gandhi's Concept of Humanism: An Overview

Suresh Kumar Soni

Humanism is a philosophy, which has immensely attracted the attention of human beings all across the world. The first conscious emergence of human existence is the real origin of the notion of humanism. It is an integral consciousness of humanity. The conception is as old as man itself. Humanism exerted profound faith in the ability and capacity of man to solve his problems at his own and consequently exalted the position of man. This man centered or an anthropomorphic philosophy, however, attained vitality and vibrancy during the Renaissance period, and got culminated into a movement in the Western World. Indian philosophy is proficiently abound with humanistic utterances, seeks to attain an all round and holistic fulfilment of human being. Indian thinkers may differ in their approaches but all are unanimous to work for human advancement. Mahatma Gandhi is one of the foremost persons who launched numerous movements for the cause and well being of man. His entire life is an earnest endeavour impelled to seek and realize truth through the service of humanity. Gandhi lived a life of engagement, enunciated various ideals, and practiced all those in his life. In his action and thought, man was at the center-stage and human advancement occupied highest place. He adroitly synchronizes his thought and action with humanism. Therefore, it is necessary to examine the various. humanistic orientations and manifestations enshrined in Gandhi's ideas.

According to Gandhi, "Man is not all body but he is something infinitely higher of all the animal creation of God. Man is the only animal who has been created in order that he may know his Maker."[1] He further writes, "Man is higher than the brute and has a divine mission to fulfil."[2] He believes that man is not only a physical entity but also an intellectual and spiritual being. Thus Gandhi presents a spiritual concept of man. This stance of Mahatma Gandhi seems to be influenced by the Upanisadic doctrine, which believes in divinity of man. In this context, he resembles the modern Indian thinkers such as Vivekananda, Radhakrishnan, Shri Aurobindo, Deendayal Upadhyaya, etc. For Vivekananda, man is a conglomeration of body, mind and soul. Body is the name of a stream of matter continuously changing. Soul is unchangeable, eternal and all comprehensive.[3] For Radhakrishnan, man is more than matter, life or mind or all these put together.[4] According to Shri Aurobindo, man is a "complex being"[5] comprising of three elements viz., infrarational, rational and superarational. To him the infrarational element in man is "a human enlargement of the little animal sector"[6] and concerned with satisfaction of physical and vital life. The rational differentiated man from animals and is concerned with the development of mental faculty. The superarational element is turned towards the self, or the Absolute "its special power is to realize the infinite in the finite, the enternal unity in all divisions and differences."[7] Deendayal Upadhyaya is of the view that man is a complex of (tatvas) elements. He says, "Body, mind, intelligence and the soul, these four make up the individual."[8] it is worthwhile to refer here the western thinker, St. Thomas also who postulates," man possesses not only a bodily nature but also a rational and spiritual soul."[9]

Man can not live in isolation. Being a social animal,

man has to coexist with other members of society. Gandhi attaches great importance to individual. He declares, "The individual is the one supreme consideration."[10] According to him, "The first step to Swaraj lies in the individual. The Truth: 'As with the individual, so with the universe', is applicable here as elsewhere."[11] He insists that "Swaraj of a people means the some total of the Swaraj of individuals."[12] Like the Western Liberals, he argued that the progress of any society depends upon the extent of freedom that it allows to individuals since liberty, according to him, is the first condition of the growth. He said, "If the individual ceases to count what is left of society? Individual freedom alone can make a man voluntarily surrender himself completely to the service of society. If it is wrested from him, he becomes and automation and society is ruined. No society can possibly be built on a denial of individual freedom. It is contrary to the very nature of man."[13]

However, Gandhi is opposed to degenerating individual freedom into license. He justified willing submission of the individual to social restraint for the welfare of the society. He says, "I value individual freedom but you must not forget that man is essentially a social being. He has risen to his present status by learning to adjust his individualism to the requirements of social progress. Unrestricted individualism is the law of the beast of the jungle. We have learnt to strike a mean between individual freedom and social restraint. Willing submission to social restraint for the sake of the well- being of the whole society enriches both the individual and society of which one is a member."[14] Thus by his own value commitment the individual is required to fulfil his responsibility toward society and also not to interfere as well with other individuals while seeking his enrichment. The individual and society are closely related. In this context, Gandhi remarks, "There is not a single virtue which aims at, or is consistent with the welfare of the individual alone. Conversely, there is not a single offence which does not directly or indirectly affect many others besides the actual offender. Hence, whether an individual is good or bad is not merely his own concern, but really the concern of the whole community, nay, of the whole world."[15]

It is worthwhile to mention here that man realize is potentialities and attain advancement only in free, fair and just society. In order to realize the objective of human fulfilment, Gandhi vehemently opposed imperialism of any kind and emphatically, stressed for national independence. He strived hard to attain Indian independence from the iron cage of British Imperialism because according to him the alien government imposed from outside will not deliver the goods to the people at large. On the contrary such a government will prove disastrous for the development of society. He says, "I cannot conceive a people governing them selves rightly through a government imposed from without, even as the fabled jackdaw could not walk like a peacock with feathers borrowed from his elegant companion."[16] In his historic speech at the all India congress committee in August 1942, Gandhi thundered," I want freedom immediately, this very night before down .... Today they (the masses) have no touch of life left. It has been crushed out of them. If lustre is to be put into their eyes, freedom has to come not tomorrow but today."[17]

In the struggle for India's independence Gandhi evolved a way of resisting evil through the organization of Satyagraha. Satyagraha is the technique of resisting all that is evil, unjust impure and untrue and resolving all maladjustment in human relations by love, voluntary suffering and self-purification by appeal to the divine speak in the opponents soul. It is an expression of a purest Ahimsa or non-violence and it precludes hatred, deception or untruth. To Gandhi, "Ahimsa is the supreme law of Dharma."[18] While explaining is principle of Ahimsa he says, "Ahimsa is a comprehensive principle. We are helpless mortals caught in the conflagration of himsa. The saying that life lives on life has a deep meaning in it. Man cannot for a movement live without consciously for unconsciously committing outward himsa. The very fact of his living—eating, drinking and moving about necessarily involves some himsa, destruction of life, be it ever so minute. A votary of Ahimsa therefore remains true to his faith if the spring of all his actins is compassion, if he shuns to the best of his ability the destruction of tiniest creature, tries to save it, and thus incessantly strives to be free from the deadly coil of himsa. He will be constantly growing in self-restraint and compassion, but he can never become entirely free from outward himsa."[19] Gandhi achieved his objective of Indian independence from alien rule on the basis of moral force-ahimsa. Although Gandhi's immediate objective was the end of British rule in India, but he regarded independence from foreign rule as a mare prelude to the establishment of self-rule. He was apprehensive of indigenous government became oppressive and denying freedom to its people. Gandhi saw a basic contradiction between the freedom of individual and authority of the state. Therefore, Gandhi, envisaged an ideal of ramrajya- an ideal society which does not have any room for state since life therein becomes so perfect as to become self-regulated. It is a state of enlightened anarchy in which every one in his own ruler and rules himself in such a manner that he is never a hindrance to his neighbor. But since the ideal, according to Gandhi, cannot be attained fully, the existence of state, he holds, can be tolerated for a limited purpose. In this regard, Gandhi adopts the formula of Thoreau that government is best which governs the least.[20] He says," Self-government means continuous efforts to be independent of government control weather it is foreign government or whether it is national Swaraj Government will be a sorry affair if people took up to it for the regulation of every detail of life."[21] Gandhi stressed the need of a little role of state in regulating social life. In this context he writes, "To me political power is not an and but one of the means of enabling peoples to better their condition in every department of life. Political power means capacity to regulate national life through national representatives. If national life becomes so perfect as to become self-regulated, no representation is necessary. There is then a state of enlightened anarchy. In such a state everyone is his own ruler. He rules himself in such manner that he is never a hindrance to his neighbour. In the ideal state, therefore, there is no political power because there is no state. But the ideal is never fully realized in life. Hence the classical statement of Thoreau that Government is best which governs the least."[22]

Gandhi was of the opinion that the centralization of

power is inconsistent with non-violence. Gandhi asserts," The end to be achieved is human happiness combined with full mental and moral growth. I use the adjective moral as synonymous with spiritual. This end can be achieved under decentralization. Centralization as a system is inconsistent with a non-violent structure of society."[23] Gandhi was quite convinced that India reflected a rural society consisting of villages. He wanted to build up self-sufficient village units in order to seek the growth of the village folk. He says," My idea of village Swaraj is that it is a complete republic, independent of its neighbours for its vital wants, and yet interdependent for many others in which independence is a necessity. Thus every village's first concern will be grow its own food, crops and cotton for its cloth. It should have a reserve for its cattle recreation and playground for adults and children. Then if there is more land available, it will grow useful money crops thus excluding ganja, tobacco, opium and the like. The village will maintain a village theatre, school and public hall. It will have its own waterworks ensuring clean supply. This can be done through controlled wells and tanks. Education will be compulsory up to final basic course. As far as possible every activity will be counted on the cooperative basis. There will be no casts such as we have today with their graded untouchability. Non-violence with its technique of Satyagraha and non-co-operation will be the sanction of the village community. There will be a compulsory service of village guards who will be selected by rotation from the register maintained by the village. The government of the village will be conducted by the Panchayat of five persons, annually elected by the adult villagers, male and female, processing minimum prescribed qualification. These will have all the authority and jurisdiction required. Since there will be no system of punishment in the accepted sense, this Panchayat will be the legislature, judiciary and executive combined to operate for its year of office."[24]

It may be noted that Gandhi's aim was than political emancipation. He fought against social injustices, tyrannies and oppressions too. His noble crusade for the liberation of suppressed and depressed in India shows his earnest concern and deep attachment for the problems and causes of the downtrodden. Gandhi tirelessly worked to emancipate the degraded section of the society from unjust discriminations and bondages.

He vehemently opposed untouchability. He exhorts," untouchability at as present practiced is the greatest blot on Hinduism. It is against the shastras, it is against the shastras, it is against the dictates of reason that a man should, by mere reason of birth, be forever regarded as an untouchable, even unapproachable and unseenable. These adjectives do not convey the full meaning of the thing itself. It is crime for certain men and women and their children to touch, or to approach with in stated distance, or to be seen by those who are called cast Hindu."[25]

Gandhi wanted to end this discrimination and social injustice, therefore, he argued, "We should reach their hearts and understand their feeling. If we had gone through the experiences that Harijans have gone through, there is no telling how embittered we might not have become and how little our ahimsa would have endured. Therefore, on such occasions we should look inward and if there is the slightest vestige of untouchability felt we should purge ourselves, of it. It is my firm belief that if Hinduism to survive, untouchability must go ...... The removal of untouchability root and branch thus becomes a religious duty for me and for other Hindus like me. If we want to achieve Swaraj through non-violence then untouchability will have to be eradicated. We can not attain Swaraj without that."[26] He added "Under Swaraj public temples, public schools, and public wells will be used equally by Brahmins and Bhangis. If this does not happen it can not be regarded as Swaraj."[27] Justifying the reason for removing the ills of untouchability, Gandhi refers to the inseparable relationship between man and God that reflect the great essence of Humanism. Gandhi says, "If we believe that we are all children of one and the same God, and God is Truth and justice, how can there be untouchability amongst us, His children? God of truth and justice can never create distinction of high and low among His own children."[28]

Women is an integral part of society however, one can witness wide spread discrimination against women all around. Gandhi was opposed to any kind of discrimination on the basis of sex. He considered both men and women equal in status and laid stress upon treating women equally in all the spheres of life. In this context he emphasizes, "Women is the companion of man gifted with metal capacities. She has the right to participate in the minutest detail of the entitled to a supreme place in her own sphere of activity as man is in his. This ought to be the natural condition of things, and not a result only of learning to read and write. By sheer force of a vicious custom, even the most ignorant and worthless men have been enjoying a superiority over women they do not deserve and ought not to have."[29]

Gandhi was of the opinion that women is not the weaker sex but on the contrary superior to man. While asserting such a feeling he says, "to call woman the weaker sex is a libel, it is man's injustice to woman less brute than man. If by strength is meant moral power, then woman is immeasurably man's superior. Has she not greater institution, is she more self-sacrificing, has she not greater powers of endurance, has she not greater courage? Without her man could not be. If non-violence is the law of our being, the further is with woman....... Who can make more effective appeal to the heart than woman?"[30] there are other categorical statements, which regard woman superior sex. For example: Woman, the noblest of God's creation"; "woman, an incarnation of ahimsa".[31]

Gandhi also pleaded for equalization of status in economic terms in a sense that he wanted to eliminate unreasonable economic differences between man and man. He states, "I want to bring about an equalization of status. The working classes have all these centuries been isolated and relegated to a lower class. They have been Shoodras, and the word has been interpreted to mean inferior status. I want to allow no differentiation between the son of a weaver, of an agriculturist and of a schoolmaster."[32]

Gandhi favored leveling down of the a few rich who are semi-starved naked millions.[33] Gandhi evolved the principle of trusteeship in both land and industry, compatible with non-violence for narrowing down the gulf between the rich and the poor. He suggested that "The rich man will be left in possession of his wealth, of which he will use what he reasonably requires for this personal needs and will act of the utmost effort, the rich do not become guardians of the poor in the true sense of the term and the latter are more and more crushed and die of hunger, what is to be done? In trying to find out the solution to this riddle, Gandhi has talked of non-violent, non-co-operation and civil disobedience as the right and infallible means.[34] He argued, "The rich cannot accumulate wealth the co-operation of the poor in society. If this knowledge were to penetrate to and spread among the poor, they would become strong and would learn how to free them selves by means of non-violence from the crushing inequalities which have brought them to the verge of starvation."[35]

Gandhi favoured a society in which, "Everyone must have a balanced diet, a decent house to live in, facilities for the education of one's children and adequate medical relief."[36] As a humanist visionary, Gandhi hopes to eliminate economic disparities and foresee India where people live together sharing mutual weal and woe. In order to realize the objective he says, the economic constitution of India and for that matter of the world, should be such that no one under it should suffer from want of food and clothing. In other words everyone should be able to get sufficient work to enables him to make the two ends meet. And this ideal can be universally realized only if the means of production of the elementary necessaries of life remain in the control of the masses. These should be freely available to all as God's air and water are or ought to be, they should be made a vehicle of traffic for the exploitation of others. Their monopolization by any country, nation or group of persons would be unjust. The neglect of this simple principle is the cause of the destitution that we witness today not only in this unhappy land but in other parts of the world too."[37]

Anxious to make Indian society economically viable for all, he put the spinning wheel at the center if his constructive economic plan. He was of the opinion that the Charkha or the spinning-wheel will certainly help redeem the common man from the problems of poverty, ignorance, diseases and squalor. In a country where, "Eighty per cent of the Indian population are compulsorily unemployed for half the year; they can only be helped by reviving a trade that has fallen into oblivion and making it a source of new income. He stressed the use of the spinning-wheel as an occupation supplementary to agriculture."[38]

Gandhi was against the labour-saving machinery because according to him such machinery leaves thousands without work and throws them on the open streets to die of starvation. Therefore, he said, "it is criminal to displace hand-labour by the introduction of power-driven spindles unless one is at the same time ready to give millions of formers some other occupation in their homes."[39]

Gandhi favoured hand-spinning in the then prevailing circumstances because it "does not, it is not intended that it should complete with, in order to displace, any existing type of industry; it does not aim at withdrawing a single able-bodied person, who can otherwise find a remunerative occupation from his work. The sole claim advanced on its behalf is that it alone offers an immediate, practicable, and permanent solution of that problem of problems that confronts India, viz., the enforced idealness for nearly six months in the year of an overwhelming majority of India's population, owing to lack of suitable supplementary occupation agriculture and the chronic starvation of the masses that result there from."[40] Emphasising the importance of spinning-wheel he further says, "I can not be satisfied, not till every man and woman in India is working at his or at her wheel. Burn that wheel if you find a better substitute. This is the one and only work which can supply the needs of the millions without disturbing them from their homes."[41] Gandhi's heart bled to see the disintegrated Indian economy, which had its basis in the villages. Gandhi gave a slogan 'Back to the villages' to strengthen rural economy and generate employment through the promotion of small-scale industries and use of swadeshi-indigenous things. He asserted, "The revival of the village is possible only when it is no more exploitation of the villagers as the problems of competition and marketing come in. therefore we have to concentrate on the village being self-contained, manufacturing mainly for use."[42]

Gandhi craves to attain the development of both the individual as well as society. He is prompted by his philosophy of Sarvodaya, which tended to seek the good of one for the good of all and vice-versa. This notion of Sarvodaya seems to be remodeled by Gandhi on the principle of great Indian sarve sukhina bhavantu all should be happy. According to D.M. Praharaj, Gandhi's concept of Sarvodaya "aims at the upliftment of everyone" and "put maximum emphasis on man as a whole."[43] The essence and the spirit of Gandhian thinking which fosters a concern for the development of every man and the poor in particular represents his abounding humanism. Gandhi was not merely interested in freeing India from the British yoke but he was also bent up on freeing India from any yoke whatsoever.[44] He assertively says that I shall work for an India in which the poorest shall feel that it is there country in whose making they have an effective voice; an India in which there shall be no high class and low class of people; an India in which all communities shall live in perfect harmony. There can be no room in such an India for the curse of untouchability or the curse of intoxicating drinks and drugs. Woman will enjoy the same right as men. Since we shall be at peace with all the rest of the world, neither exploiting nor being exploited, we shall have the smallest army imaginable. All interests not in conflict with the interest of the dumb millions will be scrupulously respected. Personally, I hate the distinction between foreign and indigenous. This is the India of my dreams.[45]

The proceeding discussion reveals that Gandhi wanted to build and erect all those conditions, which are conducive for man to harness various opportunities for his development. Gandhi, however, is not contended to seek empirical development of man but aspires high to seek inner development, awaking, purification and realization too. It is worthwhile to mention here that Gandhi has deep faith in the goodness man's nature and needed in man's divine potentialities. Gandhi says, "I am a humble seeker after truth." I am impatient to realize myself, to attain moksha in this very existence...... I have no desire for the perishable kingdom of earth. I am striving for the kingdom of heaven which is Moksha."[46] Gandhi is a humble seeker of truth or God he states that "what I want to achieve-what I have been striving and pining to achieve these thirty years-is self-realization, to see God face to face, to attain moksha."[47] However, one can only realize God by identifying one self-with the service of humanity, for I know that God is neither in heaven, nor down below, but in everyone."[48] To Gandhi service to humanity is a service to God. He observe, "The immediate service of all human beings becomes a necessary part of the endeavour, simply because the only way to find God is to see Him in His creation and be one with it. This can only be done by service of all. I am a part and parcel of the whole, and I cannot find Him apart from the rest of humanity."[49] while seeking the realization of God through the service of humanity· Gandhi shows his sincere concern also for those who fail to express themselves. He says, "I recognize no God except the God that is to be found in the hearts of the dumb millions. They do not recognize His presence; I do. And I worship the God that is Truth, or Truth which is God, through the Service of these millions."[50]

Gandhi wants to enkindle the spirit of humanism in everyone by realizing God through the service of man-God and humanity. His humanism is not circumscribed and confined to boundaries but transcends all across the world and encompasses the entire humanity in its fold. All persons are children of same God, 'tarred with the same brush'[51] reflects the comprehensive and all embracing thinking of M.K. Gandhi. Thus Abdul Sattar is of the view that Gandhian humanism embraces the whole mankind as it reaffirms the spirit of cosmopolitanism and brotherhood of man.[52]

Gandhi lays a stress to identify oneself with humanity. Therefore, all the actions of man should be guided to seek the benefit of entire humanity. However, according to him, "Identification with everything that lives is impossible without self-purification."[53] Gandhi stresses the need for self-purification in life. To him, "life is an aspiration. Its mission to strive after perfection, which is self-realization."[54] Self-purification helps to observe law of ahimsa and also to realize God as well. Gandhi asserts, "without self-purification the observance of the law of ahimsa must remain an empty dream; God can never be realized by one who is not pure of heart. Self-purification therefore must mean purification in all the walks of life. And purification being highly infectious, purification of oneself necessarily leads to the purification of one's surrounding."[55] But according to him the path of self-purification is hard and steep. To attain to perfect purity one has to become absolutely passion-free in though, speech and action; to rise above the opposing currents of love and hatred, attachment and repulsion."[56] He added, "You will wish to know what the marks of a man are who wants to realize Truth which is God. He must be completely free from anger and lust, greed and attachment, pride and fear. He must reduce himself to zero and have perfect control over his senses—beginning with the plate or tongue. Tongue is the organ of speech as well as of taste. It is with the tongue that we indulge in exaggeration, untruth and speech that hurts... But with proper discipline, we can make ourselves into being only a 'little below the angles'. He who has mastered his senses is first and foremost among men. All virtues reside in him. God manifests. Himself through him."[57]

The forgoing discussion reveals that Gandhi actively fought against odds and evils, which hampered the growth, well-being and advancement of man. He relentlessly worked to establish a just and equitable socio-political and economic environment for the fulfilment of man and mankind. He believed in complete and comprehensive development of human being. His concern was not merely to seek material development of man but also to attain his moral and spiritual perfection. From the above, it is clear that the various tenets of Gandhian thought signify the spirit of humanism, which has its basis in reason, self-purification, morality, ethics and love for humanity, and truth that is God.

Notes and References

1. Gandhi, M.K. quoted in N.B. Sen, Wit and Wisdom of Mahatma Gandhi (New Delhi: New Book Society of India), 1995, p. 178.
2. Verma, Visvanath Prasad, The Political Philosophy of Mahatma Gandhi and Sarvodaya (Agra: Lakshmi Narain Agarwal), 1959, p. 49.
3. Swami Vivekananda, "Real and Apparent Man", in Swami

Vivekananda: A Biography of His Vision and Ideals, ed., Verinder Grover, *op. cit.*, pp. 172-74.

4. Schilpp, Paul Arthur, The Philosophy of Radhakrishnan (New York: Tudor Publishing Co., 1952), p. 531.
5. Shri Aurbindo, The Human Cycle, in the Human Cycle, The Ideal of Human Unity, War and Self-Determination (Pondichery: Shri Aurobindo Ashram), 1977, p. 174.
6. *Ibid.*, p. 75.
7. *Ibid.*, p. 118.
8. Upadhyaya, Deendayal, Integral Humanism (New Delhi: Bhartiya Jan Sangh, 1965), p. 24.
9. Sabine, Georg H., A History of Political Theory (New Delhi: Oxford & IBH Publishing Co.), 1973, p. 237.
10. Bandyopadhyaya, Jayantanuja Social and Political Thought of Mahatma Gandhi (Bombay: Allied Publishers), 1969, p. 72.
11. Speeches and Writings of Mahatma Gandhi (Madras: G. Natesan & Co.), 1938, p. 409.
12. Gandhi, M.K., Socialism of My Conception (Bombay: Bhartiya Vidya Bhavan), 1957, p. 143.
13. Gandhi, M.K., Democracy: Real and Deceptive (Ahmedabad: Navajivan Publishing House), 1961, p. 190.
14. Nirmal Kumar Bose, Selections from Gandhi (Ahmedabad: Navajivan Publishing House), 1948, p. 190.
15. Gandhi, M.K., Truth is God (Ahmedabad: Navajivan Publishing House), 1959, p. 135.
16. Verma, V.P., Modern Indian Political Thought (Agra: Lahshmi Narain Agarwal), 1961, p. 286.
17. *Ibid.*, p. 230.
18. Chakrabati, Mohit, Gandhian Humanism (New Delhi: Concept Publishing Company), 1992, p. 39.
19. M.K. Gandhi quoted in *Ibid.*, pp. 37-38.
20. Bose, Nirmal Kumar, Selections from Gandhi (Ahmedabad: Navajivan Publishing House), 1948, p. 41.
21. *Ibid.*, p. 109.
22. Bose, Nirmal Kumar, Studies in Gandhism (Ahmedabad: Navajivan Publishing House), 1972, p. 41.
23. Bandyapadhyaya, J., Social and Political Thought of Gandhi (Bombay: Allied Publishers), 1969, p. 117.
24. Prabhu, R.K. and U.R. Rao, The Mind of Mahatma Gandhi (London: Oxford University Press), 1945, p. 269.
25. Ramana Murti, V.V. (ed.), Gandhi: Essential Writings (New Delhi: Gandhi Peace Foundation), 1970, pp. 335-56.
26. The Collected Works of Mahatma Gandhi, Vol. XLVI, 1945, p. 298.
27. *Ibid.*, p. 327.
28. M.K. Gandhi quoted in Mohit Chakrabati, Gandhian Humanism, *op. cit.*, p. 87.

29. Gandhi, M.K., Woman and Social Injustice (Ahmedabad: Navajivan Publishing House), 1954, pp. 4-5.
30. Prabhu, R.K. and U.R. Rao, The Mind of Mahatma Gandhi, *op. cit.*, p. 112.
31. Bose, Anima, Mahatma Gandhi: A Contemporary Perspective (Delhi: B.R. Publishing Corporation), 1977, p. 91.
32. Gandhi quoted in Mohit Chkrabati, Gandhian Humanism, *op. cit.*, p. 83.
33. Bose, Nirmal Kumar, Selections from Gandhi, *op. cit.*, p. 77.
34. *Ibid.*, pp. 78-79.
35. *Ibid.*
36. Bandopahyaya, J., School and Political Thought of Gandhi, *op. cit.*, p. 89.
37. Bose, Nirmal Kumar Bose, Selection from Gandhi, *op. cit.*, p. 40.
38. Mcdermott, A., Basic Writing of S. Radhakrishnan (Bombay: Jaico Publishing House), 1970, p. 265.
39. Bose, Nirmal Kumar Bose, Selections from Gandhi, *op. cit.*, p. 66.
40. *Ibid.*, p. 58.
41. Mohit Chakrabati, Gandhian Humanism, *op. cit.*, p. 17.
42. Bose, Nirmal Kumar, Selections from Gandhi, *op. cit.*, p. 71.
43. Praharaj, D.M., Humanism in Contemporary Indian Philosophical Perspective (Meerut: Anu Books), 1995, p. 37.
44. Gandhi, M.K., The Selected Works of Mahatma Gandhi, Vol. VI, *op. cit.*, p. 442.
45. McDermott, A., Basic Writing of S. Radhakrishnan, *op. cit.*, 1970, p. 265.
46. Prabhu, R.K. and U.R. Rao, The Mind of Mahatma Gandhi, *op. cit.*, p. 13.
47. Gandhi, M.K., An Autobiography or the Story of My Experiments with Truth (Ahmedabad: Navajiven Publishing House), 1927, p. 4.
48. Prabhu, R.K. and U.R. Rao, The Mind of Mahatma Gandhi, *op. cit.*, p. 24.
49. Mohit Chakrabati, Gandhian Humanism, *op. cit.*, p. 57.
50. Radhakrishnan, S., The Great Indians (New Delhi: Kalyani Publishers), 1973, p. 46.
51. Verma, Vshwanath Prasad, The Political Philosophy of Mahatma Gandhi and Sarvodaya, *op. cit.*, p. 61.
52. Sattar, Abdul, "Gandhi's Humanism: And Contemporary Society", Gandhi Marg, 12, No. 4 (Jan-Mar., 1991), pp. 444-53.
53. Mohit Chakrabati, Gandhian Humanism, *op. cit.*, p. 19.
54. *Ibid.*, p. 20.
55. Gandhi, M.K., An Autobiography or The Story of My Experiments with Truth, *op, cit.*, p. 371.
56. *Ibid.*, p. 616.
57. Pyare Lal, Mahatma Gandhi: The Last Phase II (Ahmedabad: Navajiven Publishing House), 1956, p. 233.

24

Gandhian Philosophy of Political Change

SEEMA PASRICHA

There is a proverb in Political Science that "Political cultures are changed and maintained in the family." If the family of a child belongs to one particular party, there is every likelihood that their children will become the members of the same political party when they grow up for the time being the ideology of that particular party will have far reaching effects on the minds of their children. If family changes its political ideology its effects can be traced on the mind of the children.

Gandhi, the philosopher, has always been underestimated. He was not a theorists; he was primarily an actionist - a Karmayogi. This lop-sided estimate of him is due to a conspiracy of circumstances. Historically, he was too near for us to take a balanced and just view of him, i.e., a photographic view of his contribution to the general fund of thought as well as his contribution to the winning of Independence for India. He lived and moved and had his being amidst us and his close associates and admirers preferred to eulogise him more as the Father of the Nation or to take a mystical view of him as the Mahatma. Some who were impressed with his profound thinking were emotionally overwhelmed into linking him with the philosophical traditions of the Gita, the Buddha, and the Christ. He was credited only for having rediscovered the wisdom of the ancients or for reinterpreting and practising the age-old truths in modern circumstances.

All these have landed Gandhian scholars in a difficult predicament, Gandhi either became narrowly local and narrowly dated or the problem of proving him relevant to the times was posed and discussed or as is the want in India, he has been converted into concrete statue for worship or an abstract myth for adulation or a slogan for chanting by the uncritical mass of people. The pendulum sometimes swings to the other extreme and people are accused of forgetting the teachings of Gandhi and of paying a lip-service, to his ideals acting all the time to the contrary, and proving unworthy of Gandhi. Some lament saying, '`Gandhism is dead, long live Gandhi'. The fact of the matter is that the Gandhian philosophy has not been clearly and cogently formulated, though such ideas are there lying dispersed in his writings and speeches. Ideas, seemingly unrelated and widely apart to be written into a system of philosophy. Gandhi denied that he was a system builder but it is the responsibility of scholars to place his ideas in a wider frame of reference.

NATURE OF CHANGE

One of the cornerstones of political philosophy is the understanding of the nature of change, explanation of the process of change, charting the direction of change, and measuring the rate and speed of change. The contributions of Gandhi to the understanding of the phenomenon of change in general and political change in particular, stand as monumental contributions in the history of political philosophy, specially when we study it in the light of the contributions made by other philosophers and thinkers. One conspicuous thing about Gandhi's profound conception of political change is his tremendous effort to apply his philosophy for the realisation of the political change in

India's status, i.e., the struggle for the Independence of the country. Karl Marx had criticised philosophers who wrote before him saying, 'Hitherto, the philosophers have only thought about the World; the problem, however, was how to change it'. In Gandhi, there is a perfect unity of thought and action. The one does not overwhelm the other and tilt the balance this side or that. The same cannot, in all fairness, be said even about Karl Marx himself.

Change is movement of time. Therefore, time may also be described as the impression we get of changes that are taking place around us. No change of impressions, no conception of time, i.e., time will be standstill.[1]

SOURCES OF CHANGE

Generally there are two sources or dimensions of change. One source is non-systematic change, such as climate change, some kind of technology innovation from the outside, or changes forced by foreign countries.

The other source is a systems change: Eisenstadt argued that modernisation required a basic level of free resources and the development of standardised and predictable institutions, such as a stable but flexible market system and political process. An additional requirement was that governing institutions be flexible enough to adapt to the changes that come up. Most of the time, changes to society come about through some combination of both systematic and non-systematic processes.[2]

The time frame of change also plays a significant role, and the distinction between long-term and short-term change is important. According to Harper, short-term changes, as in family developmental stages, may be obvious and easy to comprehend, but they may not actually constitute changes at all in the long run.[3]

DIFFERENT SCHOLARS VIEWS ON NATURE OF CHANGE

Zeno, the Greek philosopher,[4] betrayed his sensitiveness of the nature of change, when in his epigrams he said that the arrow cannot overtake the kill or one cannot cross the same river twice. Everything at every moment was in a state of flux.

.The classic Hegalian dialectic model of change is based on the interaction of opposing forces. Starting from a point of momentary stasis, Thesis countered by Antithesis first yields conflict, then it subsequently results in a new Synthesis.[5] Thomas Kuhnian[6] argued with respect to the Copernican Revolution that people are unlikey to jettison an unworkable paradigm, despite many indications that the paradigm is not functioning properly, until a better paradigm can be presented.

The Chinese philosophical work Dao De Jing,[7] I.8 and II.78 uses the metaphor of water as the ideal agent of change. Water, although soft and yielding, will eventually wear away stone. Change in this model is to be natural, harmonious and steady, albeit imperceptible.

The Greek philosopher Heraclitus used the metaphor of a river to speak of change thus, "On those stepping into rivers staying the same other and other waters flow".[8] What Heraclitus seems to be suggesting here, later interpretations notwithstanding, is that, in order for the river to remain the river, change must constantly be taking place. Thus one may think of the Heraclitan model as parallel to that of a living organism, which, in order to remain alive, must constantly be changing. He had a different conception of change and therefore, he was for stability and democracy. Socrates believed in Dialectic, the confrontation of good and bad in which the good always won. This is the straight line theory of change. Plato wanted time to be frozen into a perpetual Republic of Virtue. He did not like political change but all the same it had to be faced as a fact of life. His classification of governments, however, makes it clear that he was conscious of change and anxious to avoid political change.[9] It is Aristotle who presents the Greek theory of change in his Theory of Cycle of governments. Political changes are in a perpetual circular motion, from Monarchy to Aristocracy and Polity and after short intervals of their perversion, back again Monarchy. That is how the cycle of change moves in the natural fashion. Abrupt change, that is, revolution, has to be forestalled by suitable measures. A revolution (from the Latin revolutio, "a turn around") is a fundamental change in power or organizational structures that takes place in a relatively short period of time. Aristotle described two types of political revolution: Complete change from one constitution to another; Modification of an existing constitution.[10]

Another point in the theory of change of Aristotle is political relativism. Governments suit people not vice-versa. It is relativism of political change as also his methodology that have earned Aristotle the title of the Father of Political Science.

TYPES OF CHANGE

Change occurs in many ways, but it may be categorized into three types:

Reform is a type of change that does not advocate the overthrow of basic institutions. Instead, reformers want to change some of the methods that political and economic leaders use to reach goals that the society generally accepts. For example, reformers may want to change business practices in order to preserve real competition in a capitalist country, or they may want the government to become more proactive in preserving the natural environment. In neither case do the reformers advocate the overthrow of basic economic or political institutions.

Revolution, in contrast to reform, implies change at a more basic level, and does involve either a major revision or an overthrow of existing institutions. A revolution usually impacts more than one area of life. For example, the Industrial Revolution first altered the economies of Europe from feudalism to capitalism, but eventually changed their political systems, transportation, communication, literature, and social classes. Likewise, the French and American Revolutions were directed at the political systems, but they significantly changed the economies and societal practices of both countries, and spread their influence throughout the globe.

Coup d'etats generally represent the most limited of the three types of change. Literally "blows to the state," they replace the leadership of a country with new leaders.[11] Typically coups occur in countries where government institutions are weak and leaders have taken control by force. The leaders are challenged by others who use force to depose them. Often coups are carried out by the military, but the new leaders are always vulnerable to being overthrown by yet another coup.

ATTITUDES TOWARD CHANGE

The types of change that take place are usually strongly influenced by the attitudes of those that promote them. Attitudes toward change include:[12]

Radicalism is a belief that rapid, dramatic changes need to be made in the existing society, often including the political system. Radicals usually think that the current system cannot be saved and must be overturned and replaced with something better. For example, radicalism prevailed in Russia in 1917 when the old tsarist regime was replaced by the communist U.S.S.R. Radicals are often the leaders of revolutions.

Liberalism supports reform and gradual change rather than revolution. Do not confuse a liberal attitude toward change with liberalism as a political ideology. The two may or may not accompany one another. Liberals generally do not believe that the political and/or economic systems are broken, but they do believe that they need to be repaired or improved. They may support the notion that eventual transformation needs to take place, but they almost always believe that gradual change is the best.

Conservatism is much less supportive of change in general than are radicalism and liberalism. Conservatives tend to see change as disruptive, and they emphasize the fact that it sometimes brings unforeseen outcomes. They consider the state and the regime to be very important sources of law and order that might be threatened by making significant changes in the way that they operate. Legitimacy itself might be undermined, as well as the basic values and beliefs of the society.

Reactionary beliefs go further to protect against change than do conservative beliefs. Reactionaries are similar to conservatives in that they oppose both revolution and reform, but they differ in that they also find the status quo unacceptable. Instead, they want to turn back the clock to an earlier era, and reinstate political, social, and economic institutions that once existed. Reactionaries have one thing in common with radicals: both groups are more willing to use violence to reach their goals than are liberals or conservatives.

TRENDS

In comparing political systems, it is important to take notice of overall patterns of development that affect everyone in the contemporary world.

DEMOCRATIZATION

Even though democracy takes many different forms, more and more nations are turning toward some form of popular government. One broad, essential requirement for democracy is the existence of competitive elections that are regular, free, and fair. In other words, the election offers a real possibility that the incumbent government may be defeated. By this standard, a number of modern states that call themselves "democracies" fall into a gray area that is neither clearly democratic nor clearly undemocratic. Examples are Russia, Nigeria, and Indonesia. In contrast, liberal democracies display other democratic characteristics beyond having competitive elections:

- ¢ Civil liberties, such as freedom of belief, speech, and assembly
- ¢ Rule of law that provides for equal treatment of citizens and due process
- ¢ Neutrality of the judiciary and other checks on the abuse of power
- ¢ Open civil society that allows citizens to lead private lives and mass media to operate independently from government
- ¢ Civilian control of the military that restricts the likelihood of the military seizing control of the government

Countries that have regular, free, and fair competitive elections, but are missing these other qualities (civil liberties, rule of law, neutrality of the judiciary, open civil society, and civilian control of the military) are referred to as illiberal democracies.

According to political scientist Samuel Huntington, the modern world is now in a "third wave" of democratization that began during the 1970s. The "first wave" developed gradually over time; the "second wave" occurred after the Allied victory in World War II, and continued until the early 1960s. This second wave was characterized by de-colonization around the globe. The third wave is characterized by the defeat of dictatorial or totalitarian rulers from South America to Eastern Europe to some parts of Africa. The political turnover in Mexico may be interpreted as part of this "third wave" of democratization.[13]

- ¢ Why has democratization occurred? According to Huntington, some factors are:
- ¢ The loss of legitimacy by both right and left wing authoritarian regimes
- ¢ The expansion of an urban middle class in developing countries
- ¢ A new emphasis on "human rights" by the United States and the European Union
- ¢ The "snowball" effect has been important: when one country in a region becomes democratic, it influences others to do so. An example is Poland's influence on other nations of Eastern Europe during the 1980s.

One of the greatest obstacles to democratization is poverty because it blocks citizen participation in government. Huntington gauges democratic stability by this standard: democracy may be declared when a country has had at least two successive peaceful turnovers of power.

CHANGE IN ANCIENT TIMES

Change is not necessarily bad; and good and bad

changes alternate-these are some of the ideas concerning change that we find in Aristotle. The Hindu theory of change broadly resembles the Greek one except in details. The ancient Hindu believed in the circular theory of change -from Satyuga to Treta, Divapar, and Kalyug and back again to Satyug. There is nothing like progress, as one age is inevitably followed by another till the starting point is reached once again and the wheels of time are set in motion anew.

With the advent of Christianity, the theory was popularised that the change in the condition of man was due to the Original Sin committed by the Original Man. Change was a decline from heaven to earth. No wonder Christianity became a State religion of Rome, where rulers wanted perpetuity in the name of political stability, the Divine Right of Kings came to be justified as a divine dispensation to last for ever and ever.

In the Middle Ages, the feudal society came to be organised on the basis of ownership of land. Status denoted status quo. Feudalism took a long time to die because it was averse to all kinds of change. It was another frozen political system on this earth. Change was a taboo and privileges were well-preserved with all their inequities. This was one of the reasons why the Middle Ages were politically barren and unproductive of worth while ideas. The Renaissance and the Reformation in Europe prepared the background for a theory of change which the Social Contract thinkers produced. Change from State of Nature to Civil Society and Political Society was good. Change was not to be a bugbear and people were not to be afraid of it when it came. The Utilitarians believed in the calculus of Pleasure and Pain and they even tried to measure change in the subjective terms. So on, till we come to Hegel, who explained change by his idealistic dynamic dialectics, change through conflict of existing ideas with a new idea, culminating in a synthesis or some sort of compromise between the old idea and the new one. This triadic formula of thesis, anti-thesis, and synthesis moving adinfinitum without any finality or end charted the course of change. Karl Marx applied this Dialectic to material circumstances which brought about changes in the superstructure.[14] Dialectical Materialism was opposite of Dialectical Idealism of Hegel.[15] However, it may be said that the Dialectical methods of studying change were not to be applied to the individuals. They were to be applied to the systems of ideas or to systems of production. Marxian theory of change can be more simply put as Conflict-Change-Progress adinfinitum. Force was the midwife of change. Violence bred change which was progress for the Marxists. Change was always for the better.

However, this kind of change stopped or was simply not required after the classless and stateless society was established. Change according to Marxism was more or less confined to the organisational set-up. If the organisation was strictly on Marxian lines, the individuals and groups of individuals could be reformed automatically. The falsity of this claim was exposed by movements, like, Cultural Revolution which became necessary to deepen and to widen the changes. A political revolution was not enough because it brought about changes only at the top levels of organisation. This spiral theory of change could not be called satisfactory.[16]

GANDHI'S CONCEPTION OF POLITICAL CHANGE

Gandhi's conception of political change has to be studied in the light of the history of the theories of change given here. Put negatively, it does not simply mean making the individual, the paragon of virtue. It is not simply the conversion but the individual from a Satan to an Angel, something depending on a miracle or divine grace. Change to be real must be in the very nature of man, a realisation on the part of the individual to follow his Swadharma-his basic nature-the will to develop in him the desire to be a human being first and last, to imbibe non-violence in thought, deed, and word. It is not a change in the ordinary sense of the word, it is transformation by purification of the soul. This theory of change is quite different from the change envisaged in ancient Greece by Sophists who used the Dialectical method to bring back the youngmen of Athens to the right track of conduct by debate and discussion by rational conversion, change after being convinced of a particular point of view, not after being purged of all grossness and instincts of animality. It may be recalled here that Greek Dialectic was a static Dialectic. It brought more information not knowledge, much less wisdom. It simply believed in pacing light by the side of darkness and thinking that automatically the darkness would vanish. Dialectic may bring about change to some extent but it cannot bring about progress. It may dispel the darkness but it cannot bring about enlightenment. Gandhi's conception of change in the individual is, therefore, much abiding and much sure and effective. It is not superficial. It is not temporary. It is deep, enduring, and effective too, because it is a change of heart, purification of soul, and cleansing of mind of animality.

But since saints and prophets all through the ages have been advocating that with very little results so far, Gandhi did not consider the problem of change only from the side of the individual. Change is a multi-dimensional phenomenon. Therefore, the state at the other end has also to be changed radically by transforming its nature from a power Organisation, to a Sarvodaya organisation-an organisation which is, shades better than the party state or the welfare state. Its organisation is to be decentralised to such an extent that the individuals are physically and emotionally so involved in state affairs that they do not remain mere passive citizens. In this process there will remain the 'minimum' of state.[17]

Gandhi believed in change not for the sake of change but change for the sake of Sarvodaya. It is not senseless change. It is change in accordance with Swadharma, beneficient change, change for happiness and welfare of all without any injury to anyone. Change is neither superficial, nor partial. It is change in accordance with the laws of life, aiding man in the future course of evolution towards a more human and a more humane existence. Change prepares the path to march onward and higher in the steps of the ladder of civilisation.[18]

Gandhi had no faith in the straightline theory of change also called the Dialectic theory of change, no faith in the circular theory of change, positive hatred for Dialectical, Idealistic and spiral theory of change. According to him, remove the impediments and hurdles and the natural goodness of man would assert itself in a congenial organisational set-up with pure motivations in accordance with the laws of evolution of life. Change at one point in life, should correspond with changes elsewhere also. Unbalanced superficial or partial change is the source of all other troubles. Gandhi's theory of change could be but illustrated by the symbol of Charkha, the spinning wheel, which is such a balanced thing that imbalance anywhere would affect all points. This Charkha theory of change recognises all the complexities and delicacies, takes care of the different aspects of life and is a very sound theory of change.

The direction of change is neither arbitrary nor senseless. It is change in the right direction and where it is needed most. As the state becomes the framework within which life must be lived any change in the organisation, structure, functions, and working of the state must fulfil the supreme test of its possible effect on life and the course of its higher evolution.

Gandhi's main difference with his contemporaries lay in the choice of methods. He thought that the new society that he was to bring in would be qualitatively so different from all existing social orders that a completely new approach was required for its establishment. To use a traditional weapon for the fruition of so modern a concept was indeed ethically untenable. Gandhi therefore did not consider it appropriate, nor necessary to use hate to end all hatred, to use conflict to end all conflicts or, for that matter, to use force to reckon with the doctrine of force. Gandhi did not, in other words, decide to fight violence by new violence. He however knew full well, and had given vent to his feeling on several occasions, that any surrender to violence, social or individual, would be disastrous to the society. He had accordingly preferred even to use 'violence' to counteract violence, if no other means of protest or struggle was available at hand. Yet, Gandhi had no manner of doubt in his mind that a new technique of revolution was not far from sight. This, his new method of change, was non-violence: one that still provides the central dictum of 'the Gandhian thesis of social revolution.

The new meaning of violence the old term-has been discussed earlier. If violence thus meant hatred, exploitation, over-organization and use of force; non-violence provided the very antithesis of all these. It had however a positive as well as a. negative connotation; both dynamic as well as a clinical meaning. In its positive and ethical forms non-violence refers to the type of society that Gandhi was seeking for; one that has been described earlier in some details. In its 'negative' or dynamic context non-violence however meant some thing very different. It provided a new method of change -the much sought for know-how for the great social revolution of his dreams.

Non-violence as a movement, thus, meant a democratic manoeuvre; one that inspires a whole people to move on, as against a limited coterie to launch struggle in the name of the people. Non-violence is thus a people oriented rather than a `coterie' oriented strategy for political upheavel. It is a stimuli for total social change initiated by a whole nation or people all by themselves.

Since such a revolution leads to total transformation of institutional and value systems, it helps not only those who spearhead the revolution or the victims of the existing order. But the process of transformation is so sweeping that it helps both, the victim and the victor alike to tide over the fetters that hold them down. A non-violent movement thus aims to change social systems and revolutionise motivations, making it evident to the victor and the victim that they were in the final analysis the co-sharers of a common destiny of exploitation. A non-violent struggle that succeeds thus leads to a change of heart of both the parties. The victor now sees that the enemy also was a victim of its own fraility and the latter, although defeated, realises the great values of the defeat. The victory now leads to a new bold set-up, where not only the victor but the vanquished too, can live with honour. The primary motivation for struggle stems here from societal considerations. It begins by strengthening the weak and ends up by helping the aggressor as well. It inspires the latter to give up his rights so called, through a process of self-abrogation and to realise the limitations of his strength. The dynamics of change thus arise in this context, from a spirit of brotherhood and harmony, from the prospects of resolution of conflict and peace, rather than from the horrors of war and hatred. Non-violence, however, does not mean surrender to the evil. Nor, does a non-violent struggle mean compromise with violence. It means a total victory instead, one that helps the oppressor to realise his follies and seek rehabilitation in a spirit of equality with those who were one—their enemy.

The change must be peaceful, natural, and self-adjusting, opposed to violent and unsettling change. Gandhi's theory of Ends and Means has to be interpreted as laying down a sound and safe rule for bringing about a natural change in the natural manner. The means should be in keeping with the end in view. Purity of means is as much important in the Gandhian theory of political change as the purity of ends. The speed of change, therefore, cannot be at a running speed, it should be an effortless change at natural pace, not a forced change at furious speed.[19]

Thus, the Gandhian Philosophy of political change on all counts, emerges as the most satisfactory and flawless theory or change. It encompasses the ages but does not let even a split-second escape out of its ambit. It aims at the transformation of the individual with the simplification and purification of the state apparatus. It is neither uncontrolled change nor selective change. It is neither change at whirlwind speed nor mere reformism at sluggish snail's pace speed. It is the Charkha theory of change, requiring patience and perseverence, deft touch and delicate handling. It touches all points and covers entire life. It is because of this life theory of change with its non-violence, Satyagraha and truth that Gandhi's deep political philosophy with its deeper implications has to be universally realised. Wherever the Gandhian laws of life are contravened in individual, national or international life, man has to pay very dearly for his transgressions.

Notes and References

1. Gene, Shackman, Liu, Wang, The Global Social Change Research Report, 2002.
http://gscociology.icaap.org/report/summary2.html.

2. Eisenstadr, S.N., Tradition, Change and Modernity (London: Krieger Publishing Company), 1973, pp. 25-30.
3. Harper, C.L., Exploring Social Change (New Jersey: Engelwood Cliffs), 1993, p. 7.
4. Wesley, C. Salmon, Zeno's Paradoxes (New York: Hackett Publishing Company), 1970.
5. Plant, Raymond, Hegel: An Introduction (Oxford: Blackwell Publishers), 1983.
6. Kuhnia, Thomas, The Structure of Scientific Revolution (Chicago: University of Chicago), 1962.
7. Laozi, Roger, T., Ames, David L. Hal, Dao De Jing: A Philosophical Translation (China: Ballantine Books), 2004.
8. Kahn, Charles, The Art and Thought of Heraclitus: Fragments with Translation and Commentary (London: Cambridge University Press), 1979, pp. 1-23.
9. Plato, The Republic transl. by R. E. Allen (Yale: Yale University Press), 2008.
10. Aristotle, The Politics V, tr. T.A. Sinclair (Baltimore: Penguin Books), 1964, p. 190.
11. Edward Luttwak, Coup d'état: A Practical Handbook (Harvard: Harvard University Press), 1969.
12. Jeff Goodwin, No Other Way Out: States and Revolutionary Movements, 1945-1991 (Cambridge: Cambridge University Press), 2001, p. 5.
13. Huntington, Samuel, The Third Wave: Democratization in the Late Twentieth Century (London: University of Oklahoma Press), 1991.
14. Fundamentals of Marxism and Leninism (Moscow: F.L.P.M.), 1975.
15. Frederick Beiser, Hegel (New York: Routledge), 2005.
16. Jack Goldstone, "Towards a Fourth Generation of Revolutionary Theory", Annual Review of Political Science, Vol. 4, 2001, pp. 139-87.
17. Bhattacharyya, Buddhadeva, Evolution of Political Philosophy of Gandhi (Calcutta: Calcutta Book House), 1969.
18. Sharma, Jai Narain, Alternative Economics (New Delhi: Deep and Deep), 2003.
19. Iyer, Raghavan, N., The Moral and Political Thought of Mahatma Gandhi (Delhi: Oxford University Press), 1973.

Gandhi's Views on Women

Kusum Solanky

Women, who roughly constitute half of the population of a country, play very significant role in the development of a nation. In fact, National Development is linked with women's development. The importance of role of women in society has changed from time to time. Their position in it has been variously estimated and dramatically opposite views are current regarding her place in different stages of civilization. It is no longer a question of what women are physically and mentally capable of doing. The long controversy about feminine abilities has been settled by the recent experience. Women are not considered fit for a much wide range of activities than the traditional familial roles of wife, mother, daughter or those roles which are compatible with the idea of the weaker sex.

Gandhi exposed the cause of women with great concern. He had advocated the abolition of all economic and legal disabilities from which women in India suffer today.

He is opposed to the suppression of women, whether by law or by custom. He had almost dramatically, in an unprecedented manner, brought our women to the forefront and converted them into an important functional group of our population. If today women in India are enjoying so many facilities, particularly some equality with men, it is because of the sudden and spectacular call from Gandhi to join his world renowned political struggle for freedom for India. He had seriously taken up the unfinished task of the early reformers and began to work earnestly for its completion. Gandhi did not differentiate between man and woman. He wants women to take part in social and political activities. They should not consider themselves inferior to man. He advised women to resist to civil rebellion against all un-desirable and unworthy restraints. On the other hand, man should learn to give place to woman. Woman is the personification of self-sacrifice. Woman endures several sufferings during child birth and child reusing. She suffer daily so that her baby may wax from day to day.[1]

Society has not been static through the ages. In vedic period women had a high status in the society. No distinction was made between the men and women in the field of education and she had equal social rights. She had freedom in choosing her life partner. There was equality between the sexes in the field of religion. The Rigvedic woman was not considered a chattel. Though polygamy was practiced in rich families, monogamy was the social rule. The custom of sati was unknown and a widow had full liberty to conduct another marriage. According to Tara Ali Baig, howevere, women of the vedic era, were comparable to modern Indian women of the upper strata or the very gifted, who were permitted every advantage of education with the capacity to rise to the highest status and authority, while injustice and impediments hampered the life of women at lower levels. It is generally believed that the women in vedic period, on the whole, enjoyed a better status and occupied a respectable position.[2]

From 500 B.C. onwards, women not only lost their position had freedom but were also reduced to a state of subservience. They ceased to be considered as useful members of society as were thought to be incompetent for vedic studies and for performing religious duties.

During the Mughal rule, their position deteriorated further imparting of education to women became an exception rather than a rule. Purdah system was strictly enforced. Child marriage became a general practice sati had its raying effect on Hindu widows. Women became victim of various other social evils like enforced widowhood, etc.

During the early period of British rule, literacy among women had almost become non-existent. The inexperienced and uneducated child wife ceased to inspire respect and her position vis-à-vis the husband and the family declined further. She had already become a victim of various bad practices like illiteracy, child marriage, Purdah system, institution of sati, devdass, etc. She occupied a very low place in the feudal and rigid caste ridden society.

19th century witnessed a radical change and various social and religious reformers like Raja Ram Mohan Ray, Dayanand Saraswati, Ishwar Chandra Vidyasagar, Swami Vivekanand, etc. pledged to ameliorating the condition of women. Their work was further assisted by the emergence of some institutions like national social conference and women Indian Associations. Mrs. Annie Besant who made relentless efforts for improving the condition of women had already prepared the ground for Gandhi to Champion the cause of women. He attitude towards position of women was unique as she laid stress on the fact that progress of India depended on the emancipation of her women. She gave a call to them to participate in the freedom movement. She was mainly responsible for putting the demand for political rights for them in 1917. She was the first woman to become the President of the Indian National Congress.[3]

Gnadhi, the implacable for of injustice in all walks of life was instrumental for bringing a new dimension in the debate on women's question. He tried to improve their position not only by preaching for the abolition of the social evils but also by introducing a revolutionary note-of treating them on a footing of perfect equality with men. Starting with the premise that they were suffering because of man's interested teaching and women's acceptance of them, he supported their cause for being considered as individuals in their own person. He also tried to remove injustice under the pre-text of religion, custom and law. He also invited them to participate in the freedom movement which was in turn responsible for resolving many of shackles women were fettered with. He treated women at an equal footing with men, Gandhi said, "Women is the companion of man fitted with equal mental capacities. She has the right to participate in the very importance detail in the activities of man and she has an equal right of freedom and liberty with him". In spite of their fundamental equality, he opined that both were equal but not identical. They are different in nature and aptitude and have varied interests and functions Man is supreme in outward activities of a married couple and he should have a greater knowledge there of "woman", he said, "is essentially the mistress of the house, while man is the breadwinner, the woman is the distributor and keeper of bread-she is the care-taker in every sense of the term".[4]

In a well ordered society the additional burden of maintaining the family should to be entrusted to the women. He wanted this work to be done by men. Equality of sexes did not imply equality of occupation. There may be no legal bar against a woman but she should instinctively recoil from a function that belongs to man. Simultaneously Gandhi considered certain roles to be essentially important for women. Motherhood, the art of bringing up the infant of the race, without which the race may become extinct, is her special prerogative. It also enjoins upon women special qualities like patience, sympathy, toleration and sacrifice. The fact perhaps was mainly responsible for Gandhi's objection to women's working outside home as he believed in her special function of transmission of moral values to children. He thought that if they get involved in the try of war for jobs with men, the care and upbringing of child will suffer greatly.[5]

All these ideas were a natural corollary of the living faith in God, belief in Hindu and a teleological conception of life. The living faith in God made him believe in self-realization, morality and spiritual pursuits of life as compared to materialist approach. His critique of western civilization is also based on the same view of precedence of spiritualism over materialism. He asked them to apply indigenous methods suited to the Indian genius and Indian environment and conserve what is best in our culture, and reject what was base and degrading. He did not like hankering after the western materialistic pursuits which under the impact of consumerism was pushing increasing number of women to seek lucrative jobs at the cost of their household responsibilities and feminine qualities. Infact, he wanted women to have strong, purifying and controlling influence on family and society. His ideal woman was Sita or Draupadi having all the traits of morality. He said to women, "The economic and moral salvation of India rests mainly with you. The future of India lies on your knees for you will nurture the future generation. You can bring the children of India to become simple, God fearing and brave men and women". Similarly Gandhi attached great importance to their participation in public affairs. This call to invite women to participate in the freedom movement was mainly responsible for removing many shackles. He said, "The women in India should have as much share in winning Swaraj as men. Probably, in this peaceful struggle, women can outdistance man by many a mile. Responding to his call women from different communities and all walked of life came forward to join the struggle as political campaigners, joining protest, marches and demonstration as constructive workers, participating in and taking charge of the village reconstruction programs as workers in the cause of social and economic justice working for the removal of untouchable and other forms of social oppression. They joined hand to spread literacy and develop self-reliance among the people. Women who had spend their lives behind Purdah came out to fight orthodoxy, superstition and communal separatism. Gandhi proved right in thinking about the importance of women in the struggle for Swaraj Civil Disobedience and Salt Satyagraha Movement saw scores of women in the forefront. Breaking of forest laws, boycott of foreign cloth and liquor shops, resulted in women suffering police repression, incarceration in prisons and other indignities Gandhi believed that induction of women in public life would result in its purification and in restricting unbridled ambitions and accumulation of property as woman was incarnation of sacrifice and self-suffering. He also envisaged the tremendous potentiality of women inculcating peace awareness, a role, which has acquired immense importance in the modern world confronted with the challenges of Nuclear and Chemical warfare, which can bring the doomsday in a split second. Gandhi was conscious of this role of women when he told the women of Italy that they can do infinitely more than men against war. He told your great soldiers and generals would do if their wives, daughters and mothers refused to countenance their participation in any shape or form in militarism. Similarly he told women at Lausanne that if ...will drink in the lesson of non-violence it will do so through its women. He regretted that unfortunately women did not realize the advantage they have over men in this regard. He was firm in the belief that it was given to her to teach the art of peace to the warring world thirsty for that nector.[6] Thus one finds in Gandhi's views a unique blend of modernity and tradition about the role of women in Indian society. He was modern in so far as he considered women as an individual human being in he own right and sough a new social and moral role for them outside sex relationship and propagated for equality of opportunity, equal rights to property and economic freedom for women. But his opposition to women's forsaking the heart to become breadwinner and his glorification of the role of motherhood with qualities of suffering and sacrifice reflect that he was guided by traditional Indian ethos. Surprisingly, some of the ideas of women were remarkably similar to those of the leading feminist movement carried on the later half of the 20th century in developed and developing countries. They were quite close to the 'feminist paradigm' implying that women should be 'equal to men'. Rights and opportunities open to men should also be available to women. They should receive equal pay for equal work, universities, banks, hospitals, offices and other government and private organizations and agencies should not discriminate against women.[7].

Gandhi condemned dowry and considered it as 'the sale of girls. He said that marriage must cease to be a matter of arrangement made by parents for money. The custom of giving dowry in the marriage of a daughter was generally unknown in ancient India. The system is based on the concept of marriage as a Daan. It used to be nominal in almost all cases with time it has increased to an unbelievable extent. The affluent strata of Indian society give so much in dowry hat the financially weak people find it difficult to marry their daughters. It has become a social custom rather a social evil. The custom is not uniform in Hindu society as it varies from community to community. The Anti Dowry League was started in the 1st session of the Madras students' convention. All unmarried member's had to pledge that they would not accept dowry. Similar leagues were started in North India (1914). The government of India passed an Anti Dowry Act in 1961 to check this evil. It is sad that young men and their parents are as much interested in accepting dowry as they were before this law was passed. Parents of girls are pressed hard to give dowry and clothes for the parents of the boy along with many other things most parents provide it with great difficulty. But what happens when the greedy in-laws are not satisfied? The increase in education has completely failed to liberalise the minds of people regarding dowry. It has in reality increased the evil. The parents of educated girls have to spend first on their education and then on their marriage.[8]

Gandhiji was against child marriage. The custom of child marriage is both a moral as well as a physical evil for it undermines our morals and induces physical degeneration. When people suggested legislation to raise the age consent to eradicate the obnoxious custom, Gandhi had said that it might be good for brining a minority to book, but then it is not legislation that will cure a popular evil. It is an enlightened public opinion that can do it. He said that a father has not right to arrange early marriage of his children. It was observed that weak and sickly parents produced only similar children. Early indulgence, which was forced on boy-husband and girl wife by early marriage, obviously resulted in premature fatherhood and premature motherhood. Because of this fully developed manhood and womanhood was very rare among Hindus child marriage was directly responsible for the increasing number of widows among Hindus. Because of early marriage the death rate of children was very high. The custom of early marriage had its beginning in medieval

India. It was performed at the prenkile age of three or four. Hence no minimum age for marriage was fixed and a girl was married when she should have been playing with her dolls. She was asked to look after her husband when she did not understand the difference in relationship with a husband and a brother. This also resulted in the deaths of large number of child wives. Gandhi has worked against this social evil. It was felt that a law should be passed to prevent child marriage and the widow remarriage. Act of 1856 came into existence. The marriageable age for a girl under Brahma Samaj riles was 14 early marriage, however, remained unchecked despite the sincere and earnest effort of the reformers who continued to oppose it. The reformer were successful only when the government of India Passed the Child Marriage Restraint Act, popularly known as the Sarda Act of 1929. But this act was not every effective as dwellers in villages were not aware of it. The evil of child marriage is at least as extensive in the villages as in the cities. It is pre-eminently woman's work man no doubt have to do their share but when a man turns into a beast he is not likely to listen. In the 1930 with the increase of education and also because of some impact of Sarda act, the number of child marriage had been reduced this opposition to Purdah system.

Gandhi was also against the Purdah system or Purdah Partha. 'Purdah' which literally means a woman's covering her face was primarily responsible for the seclusion of Hindu women. It is a curtain especially one serving to screen women from the eyes of strangers. In ancient India, Purdah was not observed. It was rarely in Soth India. Like many other social evils it was the direct result of the Muslim invasions. Husbands thought it would protect their women from evil eyes and it was better if their women covered their faces with a veil 'purdah' which became a status symbol for the aristocracy denied women of all opportunity for normal personal relations in every day living Purdah was very strictly followed in North India. The system had strong roots where Muslims predominated. Hindu asked their women to observe it because of fear of Muslims. It was common among the Rajputs, but not among the women of the lower classes as they had to work with their men in the fields. It is strange to observe that Hindu women observe Purdah ever from their own male relatives for them it is Purdah with in Purdah. It was because of this custom that Hindu women were completely secluded from the outside world and from mixing with men of their families. If a woman ever tried to do away with it, she was said, to be a bad character. Purdah does not have religious sanction. It began among the Hindu women with the coming of the Muslims, and it persists because it gradually received the sanction of Hindu traditions and customs, which developed and ultimately became a status symbol. It was first observed among the upper classes. It was observed by the ruling class and their officers, and the middle class and the lower class followed them. Gandhi worked to create public opinion against this evil practice.[9]

Now women are beginning to understand that strict Purdah will lead them nowhere, when women can work like men why should they not be given an opportunity to do so? Since 1947 most women have moved out of their homes to work as will be seen in the fields. It is because our good women are kept secluded that the level of morality among our men in public as well as in Private like has sunk so low.

Gandhi advised women to reawaken the old spirit of self-sacrifice, love and inner strength in themselves we will have to produce women, pure, firm and self-controlled as Sita, Draupadi and Damayanti. If we produce them, such modern sisters will receive the same homage from Hindu society as is being paid to their prototypes of ..... He wanted women to be atleast aware of their position and the actual hardships that they had been undergoing. Gandhi's view, however, did not completely favour the women liberation paradigm in which mainly across rape and antagonism against men and the perception that men have oppressed women as a class, which is a pattern of women-over-against men, in which new forms will come from women. Similarly he might not have completely endorsed the 'androgynous' position postulated by Graham Yates Gayle, which supports sharing of power by women and men in private as well as public spheres. In India, too it may find many advocates working for women's liberation, because woman at the end of 20th century is required to fulfil the two roles as housewife and as career woman.

An analysis of Gandhi's fundamental ideas further reveals that in Gandhi's social order based on justice and equality, there was no place for competitor and confrontation between man and woman and he did want women to ignore their duty as housekeepers, mothers, moulders of future generation and builders of the nation. But at the same time he did not put any limit on their role in practice. They very fact that he invited woman to take part in public and political life of the country even in 1920s and 1930s postulates that he believed in complete gender equality and considered women fit for all types of activities outside home. His call to parents not to kept their daughters utterly ignorant and illiterate and bring them up only for purpose of marriage, to girls to get education and to remain unmarried and to be economically independent provide ample evidence of his belief in equality of the sexes. In his Ashram he treated men and women as equals.[10]

Notes and References

1. Gandhi, M.K., Bunch of Old Letters (Ahmedabad: Navajivan Publishing House), 1958.
2. Gandhi, M.K., Constructive Programme: Its Meaning and Place (Ahmedabad: Navajivan Publishing House), 1981.
3. Gandhi, M.K., Women (Ahmedabad: Navajivan Publishing House), 1958.
4. Gandhi, M.K., Women Role in Society (Ahmedabad: Navajivan Publishing House), 1959.
5. Gandhi, M.K., An Autobiography or The Story of My Experiments With Truth (Ahmedabad: Navajivan Publishing House), 1938.
6. Agnes, Flavia, Law and Gender Inequality: The Politics of Women's Rights in India (New Delhi: Oxford University Press), 1999.
7. Ghadially, Rehana (ed.), Women in Indian Society (New Delhi: Sage Publications),1990.
8. Gopalan, Sarla, Towards Equality: The Unfinished Agenda-Status of Women in India (New Delhi: National Commission for Women), 2002.
9. Pal, B.K., Problems and Concerns of Indian Women (New Delhi: ABC Publishing House), 1987.
10. Klein, Uta, "Returning to Work: A Challenge for Women", World of Work, I.L.O., No. 12, May/June 1995.

26

Women Education in Punjab: A Case Study of Kanya Maha Vidyalaya, Jalandhar

MONICA SHARMA

The Kanya Maha Vidyalya was set-up in 1886 to impart to women a special kind of education which would enable them to adapt themselves to the new demands made by the educated men of the family without losing the moorings. The Vidyalaya soon crossed these restricted parameters bringing out a class of woman who not only fulfilled the above objective but also were among the most successful experiments of its kinds which was both daring and radical in its innovativeness. Lala Devraj the founder and his supporters most of whom were faced criticism and attack conservative opinion both inside and out side the Samaj. The success story of KMV strikes out the condition of women education in our country.

The history of women education in India can be divided into three different epochs, the Vedic times women enjoyed an equal status in the society with no child marriages, sati, prohibition on remarriage of widows and seclusion in the Zennana. The Vedic text mention learned women like Gargi and Maitreyie repeatedly an indication of the position of women during the period in the educational system evolved by the Vedic Aryans, a fairly long period education was prescribed for all children. The education began with the Upanayana ceremony performed the eight year that introduced them into the house of the Guru. This system of education disappeared almost completely due to the social changes that took place which led to the gradual marginalisation of women. They were first denied the right to study scared texts later the Upanayana ceremony was limited to the boys and finally right to all education was denied to them. The situation worsened with the Muslims conquests and the Purdah system which came along with its withering influence. The child marriage gave the final blow among the scope of women education.

The East India Company was first compelled to accept responsibility for the education of the Indian people under the Charter Act of 1813. But while the officials of the company took up the cause of education of women, refusing to even grant any financial assistance to the special private school established for girls. They argued that the policy of the company was one of strict social and religious neutrality. The strong prejudices against the education of woman which prevailed among the people were so deeply rooted was sure to create a very great commotion.[1] Under such circumstances it was the missionaries what took the issue of women education. The Danish missionaries in the 18th century included girls in their schools. From 1819 when the Baptist mission in Calcutta started its first school till 1854, the missionaries were the sole crusaders of women education in India. This was in part linked the ordinary mission work of the churches and in part carried on through separate women societies founded for the purpose in Scotland and Germany. The pioneering efforts of some Englishmen were also of great help in the progress of women education. In this context the names of Mr David Hare who in 1820 established a school for girls in Calcutta, Prof. Patton of Elphinstone college Bombay, J.E.D. Bethune, member of the council Governor General and president of the council of education. Bengal and

Mary Carpenter stand out.[2] Inspired by these efforts of Philanthropic Englishmen and women several Indians began to lend their support to the organization of special schools for girls. Among them Raja Ram Mohan Roy and Pundit Ishwar Chandra Vidyasagar played a prominent role of school in Bengal.

The efforts of all these agencies helped in the progress of women education in India. In 1854 while considerable progress was being made in Bengal, Madras and Calcutta, the condition was not as good in Punjab. The figures available for the year's 1865 to 1882 clearly show the steady decline in the girl's school in the girl's school in Punjab.[3]

Year	*Number of Schools*	*Number of Scholars*
1865-66	1,029	19,561
1871-72	455	11,819
1882	311	9,353

While earlier the casual attitude of the Government was compensated by the missionaries during the later half of the 19th century this work was taken up in some Provinces by associations such as the Seva Sadan, the Arya Samaj, the Dev Samaj and the Khalsa Diwan. In Punjab the efforts of Swami Dayanand Saraswati to reform the Hindu religion by resorting was fast catch in the imagination of the educated and the business class. The most commendable work in the field of women education was done by the Arya Samaj. The educational activities of the Arya Samaj, illustrate how social reform movements within Hinduism used education to express their cultural norms and identity.[4] Both the College and the Gurukul played significant role in establishing educational institutions, though there was a difference both in their orientation to modern values and life styles.

The Arya Samaj became the torch bearer of women education in Punjab. Swami Dayanand rejected the common notion, Street Shudhro Nadhityam (teach not women and sudras) as the creation so selfish pundits citing from the Vedas, he tried to impress upon the people that no society could progress culturally materially or spiritually unless its womenfolk were enlighten. This enlightenment he believed could be achieved by imparting education which was to be based on moral training and religion.[5] Inspired by the educated men of the family. A section of the Samajists was in favour of promoting women as this would produce educated wives for the newly educated young men. Education was to fill the mental gap between the two and also an educated generation, it was under these circumstances the Kanya Maha Vidyalaya came into existence in 1886.

Lala Munshi Ram and Lala Devraj the forces behind the establishment of the Vidyalya were prominent members of the Jalandhar Arya Samaj. There is a very interesting story behind the establishment of the Vidyalaya, one day on returning home, Lala Munshi Ram heard his daughter Ved Kumar, a student in the mission school recite the following lines:

Ek bar Isa Isa bol.
Tera Kya Lagega mol?
Isa mera Ram Ramayya,
Isa mera Kaneyha.

He was horrified at the proselytizng activities of the missionaries. He decided that Hindus would have to make women education priority if they wanted to preserve their culture and religion from the influence of Christianity. Due to the combined efforts of Lala Devraj and Lala Munshi Ram the Antrang Sabha of the Jalandhar Samaj passed a resolution on 26th December 1886 for opening a Zannana school for which they sanctioned an expenditure of one rupee per month.[6]

As during this period Lala Munshi Ram became busy with the Samaj activities. In other places it was Lala Devraj who took charge of the girls school. The school started with six girls but no teacher could be arranged and even the one rupee assistance was stopped by the Samaj. At this point Lala Devraj's mother came forward, she appointed a woman on a monthly salary of one rupee to teach two to three girls at their house.[7] In 1890, Lala Devraj made another unsuccessful attempt to the question of the girls school. Lala Mushi Ram started a series "Adhura Insaaf" in the second volume of Sadharm Pracharak to address the issues of equality and women education. Due to their combined efforts the school finally took off in 1890 with eight girls and a male teacher pundit Shripathi. The number rose to 55 in 1892.[8]

In 1893 the proposal to expand the school into a high school sparked off a debate between the two wings of the Arya Samaj. The Mahatma of the Gurukul section and the college section to which Lala Munshi Ram belonged was promoting High Education for women. The differences were chiefly over funds, as both sections depended on charity. It was believed by the college section that if appeal was made from the same platform for the girl's school, the much needed funds and resources for men's education would be diverted.[9] Unmoved Lala Devraj carried on his efforts and in 1896, the Kanya Maha Vidyalya, Mukhya Sabha was registered.

Once the Vidyalaya was established Lala Devraj had other obstacles to overcome. Some of the difficulties in the progress of female education in India as listed by the education commission were:

- There was no demand for education as a means of livelihood in case of women.
- Child marriage, which was responsible for secluding the girls at an early age.
- Lack of qualified female teachers.
- Absence of text books to meet for girls as the system of instruction and textbooks were framed keeping in mind the requirement of boys.[10]

Regarding the first problem, the Samajists were of the view that even though there was no demand on upper caste women to earn their livelihood, the instruction, which would help them in becoming good housewives. The growing contradiction between the kind of education provided by government schools and this purported intention to produce educated housewives was time and again pointed out in the course of the debate on whether women education should be secular education or religious. The upper castes were averse to giving their daughters the same education as their sons. To avoid controversy, Lala Devraj proceeded with the moral and religious education in the formative years. Even the History consisted of the religious past of the country, the college magazine. Panchal Pandita was also full of stories, which conveyed some moral message.

The movement of the Arya Samaj against child marriage helped in clearing the second hurdle to some extent. Swami Dayanand called upon people not to marry their daughters before the age of sixteen.[11] Responding to the call, the Jalandhar Arya Samajists took a pledge not to marry their daughters before 15.[12] This gave the girls more time in school. KMV took another significant step in this field by opening its door to young widows, whose condition was most pathetic. Though this was restricted to certain upper castes and classes, their number was considerable in 1881, it was 24.8% for women over 15 years in all communities. There was ever lurking danger of these women taking top prostitution. Trained only for a lifetime of dependence both mental enclosed in a world whose limits were exceedingly narrow the upper caste widow of deserted wife was helpless if maltreated. The only option available were prostitution conversion to Christianity or going to a pilgrimage center to survive.[13] KMV provided an opportunity to such girls. Acharya Swami Devi, a child widow at an age of 10, entered the institution in 1890 and went on to become the Principal. The manner in which she addressed various social particularly her 5000 miles long journey across the country to collect funds for the Vidyalaya is an indication enough to show the confidence KMV was building in these young widows.

A general and comprehensive literature for girls was necessary to disseminate true education among women. A separate curriculum became essential as they could not spare as much time for school as boys. Moreover in their case the study of Sanskrit became more important as it would enable them to understand the philosophy of religion and morality better. Swami Dayanand had advocated the use of Sanskrit and Arya Bhasha of Hindi, though his objective was different. He was of the view that while knowledge should be gathered from all corners and sources. A sound system of education was one which made a student proud of his language, his country proud of his nation's past and product of her glory. This could never be achieved if Hindi and Sanskrit were relegated to the background. But as the women education was in its formative years, there were no books that could fulfil these objectives an obstacle acknowledged by Lala Devraj. Taking up the challenge he began to write text books which were more suited to the Punjabi and Sanskritised Hindi.[14]

The contribution of KMV in the field of education in North India is nowhere more evident than in this contribution of Lala Devraj, who was even honoured for this work. He not only wrote most of the books himself but also arranged for their publication and distribution. Some of these books were later translated into Marathi, Telugu and Gujarati. In 1904, the Punjab and Central Provinces recommended some of these texts for their schools. This was a triumph for their schools. This was a triumph for the KMV concept of women education.

Lala Devraj introduced a novel concept of education through stories in the Vidalaya. He was of the opinion that while the children did not remember lecturer they never forgot the stories. By this method it also became easier for the uneducated mothers to teach their children at home. Stories preached with moral, religious, and patriotic spirit became a part of the curriculum. Thus stories like "Desh Bhakta Kanya,"[15] "Shurvira Stiriyan,"[16] and "Janani Janam Bhumi", "Swadeshi Preet",[17] were written to invoke the feeling of patriotism among them. The Pahili Pathyavali included lessons on the moral science and discipline.[18] The Pathshala Ki Kanya also carried lessons on morality, punctuality, hygiene, and benefits of going to school lessons on conduct towards teachers and fellow students was also included. History was given importance as in Lala Devrajs words: it gave examples and one could learn from the blunders of others.[19] But he felt sad that people were not interested in the subject. Women had not even heard the word History as a subject was introduced to the girls though in the early years religion formed a major part of it with emphasis on stories from the lives of the celebrated women of the ancient period like Gargi, Gandhari, Sharmistha, Mandodari, and Sita.

Besides the texts, Panchal Pandit the KMV magazine started in 1897 became the mouth piece of women issues in Punjab. The Panchal Pandit propagated the view that women's education was not a charitable wok but a vital nation building task, part of the regeneration of enslaved India Biographies and achievements of successful western women were published with hope that Vidyalaya girls would prove as illustrious intelligent and scholarly. The writer of these biographies began with an appeal to the reader not to read further unless she was making an effort to become like the women depicted. Gradually Annie Besant, Florence Nithtingale, Sarojini Naidu emerged as new role models for the girls. Panchal Pandita also cultivated the habit of writing among the young girls as a number of articles in the magazine were contributed by them. To cultivate a habit of reading newspapers the girls wee invited to write essays critically analyzing the contemporary social and political events.

Through Panchal Pandita KMV took up the cause of social reform, articles against Purdah system wee published time and again. The arguments advanced were that it had no Vedic sanction, examples from the Vedic texts were cited to impress upon the people that it was not a part of Indian tradition. Gargi's challenge to Yagvalkya, Gandhari's presence in the court, Sanghmitra's journey to Lanka for the cause of Buddhism were cited to show the freedom enjoyed by the women in the ancient period. The educated women asked for initiative, they were told, "if you want your welfare, then remove Purdah and educate women.[20] A very significant step towards social reform was the performance of the Upanayana ceremony of five girls of the ashram.[21] This was significant as this ceremony traditionally of marked the beginning of education and had been stopped in case of girls. The simplicity and contents of the books and this magazine made them immensely popular. By 1918 there were more than 104 schools included Panchal Pandita in their syllabus.[22]

KMV was the last moving beyond the restricted parameters of providing educated wives. The wide range of activities of the Vidalaya was building new confidence and outlook among the young girls. As the college had to depend on public charity it faced a lot of financial problems in the initial years. Lala Devraj devised new schemes to overcome such constraints; the most of the popular of these were the Raddi and Atta funds.[23] A normal educated house generally has used papers (Raddi) which was not required. Lala Devraj planned to collect this Raddi from such houses and use the money obtained for the Vidyalaya expenses. In Punjab, there was a custom in most of the houses to give Atta to the needy. Devraj ji placed containers in such houses in which everyday the family put some Atta which was later sold in the market. This Raddi and the Atta funds were of considerable financial help to the Vidyalaya in the early years.

In addition to these novel schemes Lala Devraj under took a number of journeys distant places to collect funds. It was in these fund activities the transition in the girls is clearly visible. In 1905 Acharya Savitri Devi undertook a journey of 4799 miles visiting places like Pune, Bombay, Hyderabad and a very courageous attempt to raise funds for the college and promote women education. During the four of three and half months she addressed twenty three meetings. Her oratory skills won her admirers everywhere. The KMV experiment was catching the imagination or the people wherever she went in Hyderabad impressed by the institution and many families were ready to send their daughters with her.[24] In 1917, Acharya Lajwanti went to the Frontier Provinces, Uttar Pradesh and Calcutta in a similar fund raising campaign and returned with Rs 25.000.[25] A number of girls followed her example Bhiksha Mandli's consisting of the Vidyalaya girls toured different parts of the country to collect funds.

This confidence was later evident in the various meeting of the congress, where the KMV girls participated in considerable numbers. The spirit of Nationalism was deeply rooted in the Lala Devraj, the founder of this institution. It is of great significance that while the Gurukul wing had sponsored the founding of KMV increasingly reactionary in politics and loyalist to the British Raj. Lala Devraj and the

KMV defined an independent commitment to the cause of national independence. He left no stone unturned to infuse the spirit of patriotism among the girls. Stories of Rana Pratap and Shiva Ji along with Laxami Bai and Durga Walia were published time and again in Panchal Pandita. Patriotic songs were composed for the girls. It was this spirit of nationalism, which made Acharya Lajawati refuse the government aid by saying ; " At least in our sheds, we are free to sing patriotic songs." Thus, the founders ensured that KMV enjoyed much greater freedom and opportunity for innovation. This spirit of nationalism was reflected in various activities of the Vidyalay. The prospectus from very beginning had made it clear that only Khadi was to be worn at the school and no foreign manufactured goods were to be used by the hostel inmates. As early as Nov. 1901 Panchal Pandita carried a note on Swadeshi Vastu Prachar. There was a Charkha Mandir of the premises where the girls learnt to spin as an integral part of their curriculum. In 1905 during the Swadeshi Movement, Panchal Pandita was in the forefront of propaganda urging women to remember that with their involvement, Swadeshi would spread faster. In Nov 1905 issue, there was an article on how the echoes of Swadeshi and Vande Mataram in Bengal had brought down the consumption of foreign goods in the state and hoped the same would be witnessed in Punjab. The Jan 1906 issue carried a lengthy article on how imported goods had destroyed local industry and drained the country of its wealth. During this period the earlier Ved Prachar in the magazine gave way to the nationalist propaganda. In 1905 Vande Mataram replaced the prayer on the first page of the Panchal Pandita.

The gradual transition from the older role of woman as supportive home makers to the newer one of women as participants in the struggle that was being witnessed in the country was quite marked in the case of the Vidyalaya girls. This wave of nationalism brought a sense of pride and a new confidence among the girls. This transition was reflected in the annual sessions of the Indian National Congress and the National Social Conference. On several occasions the Vidyalya girls were called to sing Vande Mataram and patriotic songs.[26] Many of them used the platform of the social conferences to spread the message of women education and once related social issues. As early as 1906 Lala Devraj and Acharya Saviti Devi took some girls of the Vidyalaya to attend the Kashi Banarasi session of the Congress. Here Acharya Savitri Devi was given the change of the woman conference, she also translated the presidential speech in the national social conference. The girls again participated in the 1919 Congress session in Amritsar along with Lala Devraj and Acharya Lajawati. Here too the girls sang Vande Mataram and patriotic songs, which later became a regular feature in all the Congress meetings in the city.[27] The girls responded to Gandhiji's call for Non-Co-operation. Khadi already a part of KMV became more popular. In fact the Vidyalya girls were the first participants in the National movement in Jalandhar. The first woman Satyagrahi, Parvati was a student of KMV. In the historic congress session of 1929 at Lahore more than half of the woman volunteers working with Acharya Lajawati were from the Vidyalya. The activities of the students Sushila Devi and Leela Wati were involved in the revolutionary activities of Sardar Bhagat Singh.[28]

Sushila Devi came in contact with Satyadev Vidyalankar a well-known journalist in Calcutta, with whose assistance was instrumental in establishing the Bhagat Singh who had reached the city after the Saunders killing. She arranged for his stay in the city. Later when Bhagat Singh and Batukeshwar Dutt were arrested after the central assembly bomb case, she arranged Rs 12.000 for his defense by staging the famous play "Mewar Patan" (decline of Mewar). For the next three years she worked enclose association with Chandershekhar Azad and Bhagawaticharan. In 1942 she actively participated in the Quit India movement and after partition worked for the safety of Muslims in Delhi.[29]

For an institution which had started with a very noble objective in the most adverse conditions, the progress was quite remarkable. At the time when the question of women education was over looked if not out rightly rejected this institution through its magazine made an appeal to the girls in the form of a poem. The poem was published way back in 1878, a stanza from the poem will show the sincerity of the founders of KMV to the cause to women education:

Women! Who too long have lain,
Bound by tyrant customs chain,
Forward now and boldly gain,
Knowledge and be free.[30]

Once the institution was established there was no looking back in the formative years. Lala Devraj had to go to every house to convince the parents to send their daughters to the school. At times he would leave early in the morning with sweets in his pockets to get the girls to school. Over the years it became a matter of prestige for the parents to send their daughters to KMV. The seeds of patriotism, which were sown by Lala Devraj were nurtured by the illustrious students like Acharya Sartiri Devi and Acharya Lajawati who took charge of the college.

It was this spirit which took Lala Devraj and Acharya Lajawati to Haldi Ghati, The Karam Bhoomi of one the most courageous and patriotic Rajput ruler Maharana Pratap. The soil brought from this battlefield was added to the foundations of the Krishna Bhavan which was under construction at the time. Inspired by such patriotic personalities Acharya Lajawati got a huge pole erected in the premises where every week the National Flag was hoisted. This was a very bold step considering the political circumstances in the country with the British Government adopting strict policy against the nationalists.

It is this rich tradition of KMV, which is being carried on till date. There the blend of modernism and traditionalism is quite evident moving with the times. On one hand the girls are given computer education while on the other hand the use of Khadi, the Monday prayer meetings and the Amarjoyti ceremonies keep them close to the rich tradition of this country.

Notes and References:

1. Indian Education Commission Report, 1959, p. 14.
2. *Ibid.*, p. 17.

3. *Ibid.*, pp. 287-88.
4. Hoeber, Susane, Rudolf and Lloyd, I. Rudolf (eds.), Education and Politics in India, Studies in Society and Policy (Delhi: OUP), 1972, p. 21.
5. Sidharta, N. K., Swami Dayanad as an Educationist, pp. 129-33.
6. Vidyalankar, Satydev, Lala Devraj (Jalandhar: KNV Prabandh Kritre Sabah), n.d., pp. 1-2.
7. Vidyalankar, Bhinsen, Arya Pratinidhi Sabha Punjab Ka Sachitra Itihaas, Lahore, 1992, p. 14.
8. Vidyalankar, Satya Ketu and Haridult Vedalankar, Arya Samaj Ka Itihas, Bhag-3, Shiksha Ke Shetra Mein Arya Samaj Ka Karya Kalap, New Delhi, 1983, p. 237.
9. *Ibid.*, p. 239.
10. Sir Alferd Craft, "Review of Education in India in 1886", Report of the Education Commission, 1888, p. 278.
11. Fardooni, Rustomji, Swami Dayanad and The Position of the Women, pp. 291-92.
12. Vidyalankar, Bhinsen, Arya Pratinidhi Sabha Punjab Ka Sachitra Itihaas, *op. cit.*, p. 208.
13. Kishwar, Madhu, The Daughters of the Arya Vrata (New Delhi: IESHR), 1986, p. 23.
14. Panchal Pandita, 15 June, 1899, p. 20.
15. Kathavidhi, Lala Devraj (Lahore: Punjab Economical Press), n.d.
16. *Ibid.*, p. 31.
17. Pathavali, Doosri, Lala Devraj (Kanpur: Merchant Press), 1975.
18. Pathavali, Paheli, Lala Devraj (Lahore: Punjab Economical Press), 1903.
19. Senaremis, Lala Devraj, Jalandhar, 1906.
20. Panchal Pandita, February 1906, p. 15.
21. *Ibid.*, September 1901, p. 13.
22. *Ibid.*, November 1905, p. 4.
23. Joshi, Shadi Ram, Uttar Paschimi Bharat Mein Stri Shakti Jagran Murtroop (Jalandhar: Kanya Maha Vidyala), p. 144.
24. Panchal Pandita, January 1906, p. 145.
25. Joshi, Shadi Ram, Uttar Paschimi Bharat Mein Stri Shakti Jagran Murtroop, *op. cit.*, p. 145.
26. Panchal Pandita, January 1906, p. 22.
27. Vidyalankar, Satydev, Lala Devraj, *op. cit.*, p. 129.
28. *Ibid.*
29. *Ibid.*, p. 267.
30. Poem Composed by Warner Snoad on request of KMV, Panchal Pandita, February 1898, p. 19.

27

Gandhian Approach to Tribal Issue

RANJU DEVI

The Mahatma's preoccupation was with the development of a technique of social action based on non-violence. He took up a few major issues, such as; national freedom, communal unity, and rural reconstruction and sought to develop through the implementation of the programmes revolving around them the people's collective will, the Lok shakti, as the solvent of social ills. The Adivasi problem, as such, did not claim his attention until the early 1940s, but he exercised the imagination of the tribal people as of other segments of the rural community, and his life and mission became known through the Adivasi welfare programmes implemented by number of organizations. A good many social movements among the tribes were influenced by him. Two key figures, Amritlal Thakkar, popularly known as Thakkar Bappa, and Verrier Elwin, who shaped free India's tribal policy, came into close contact with him; Thakkar Bappa was a life long collaborator, and he, in a way, influenced the Mahatma's interest in the tribal problem. When Gandhi saw the condition of Adivasi he was very hurt. Commanding the programme to Nation and worker in the cruse of Independence Gandhiji wrote, the term Adivasi like Raniparaja is a coined word. Raniparaja stands for Kaliparaja (meaning that there skin is more black than that of any other) was coined by Shri Jagatram.

The term Adivasi (for Bhils, Gonds or other variously described as Hill Tribes or aboriginals) means literally original inhabitants and was coined by Thakkar Bappa. Upajati is an umbrella term for a heterogeneous set of ethnic and tribal groups believed to be the aboriginal population of India.[1] They comprise a substantial indigenous minority of the population of India.

Upajati societies are particularly present in the Indian stares of Kerela, Orissa, Madhya Pradesh, Chattisgarh, Rajasthan, Gujarat, Maharashtra, Andhra Pradesh, Bihar, Jharkhand, West Bengal, Mizoram, and other northeastern states, and the Andaman and Nicobar Islands. Many smaller tribal groups are quite sensitive to ecological degradation caused by modernization. Both commercial forestry and intensive agriculture have proved destructive to the forests that had endured swidden agriculture for many centuries.[2] Officially recognized by the Indian government as "Scheduled Tribes" in the Fifth Schedule of the Constitution of India, they are often grouped together with scheduled castes in the category "Scheduled Castes and Tribes", which is eligible for certain affirmative action measures.[3]

It must be noted that the correct translation of the term "tribe" is "upajati" and not "adivasi", and the latter term does not appear anywhere in primary Sanskrit literary sources or in regional literature.[4] Although terms such as atavika (Sanskrit for forest dwellers), vanvasi or girijan (hill people)[5] are also used for the tribes of India, adivasi carries the specific meaning of being the original and autochthonous inhabitants of a given region, and was specifically coined for that purpose in the 1930s.[6] Over a period of time, unlike the terms "aborigines" or "tribes", the word "adivasi" has also developed a connotation of past autonomy which was disrupted during the British Colonial period in India and has not been restored.[7] Opposition to usage of the term is varied, and it has been argued that the "original inhabitant" contention is based on dubious claims and that the adivasi - non-adivasi divide that is created is artificial.[8] It should also be noted that in Northeast India, the term Adivasi applies only to the tea-tribes imported from Central India during colonial times, while all tribal groups refer collectively to themselves by using the English word "tribes".

There are more than 400 groups in Indian society which are officially designated as scheduled tribes (STs). Scheduled Tribes are the disadvantaged groups than rest of the Indian population. The term "tribe" is nowhere defined in the Constitution and in fact the definition of this word given by sociologist and anthropologist still leave scope for definition. To the ordinary man the word suggests simple folk living in forests and hills; to an administrator it means a group of citizens who are the special responsibility of the President of India, to a social worker it means traditionally isolated population which needs help themselves for their development.

The term Scheduled Tribes is of recent origin, which came in to being with the birth of the Republican Constitution of India on January 26, 1950. Upto 1919, they were included along with other categories of backward classes under the head "depressed classes". Under the present constitution the tribals are Scheduled and are popularly termed "Scheduled Tribes".

The Constitution of India, Article 366 (25) defines Scheduled Tribes as "such tribes or tribal communities or part of or groups within such tribes or tribal communities as are deemed under Article 342 to the scheduled Tribes (STs) for the purposes of this Constitution". In Article 342, the procedure to be followed for specification of a scheduled tribe is prescribed. However, it does not contain the criterion for the specification of any community as scheduled tribe. An often used criterion is based on attributes such as:

- Geographical isolation - they live in cloistered, exclusive, remote and inhospitable areas such as hills and forests.
- Backwardness - their livelihood is based on primitive agriculture, a low-value closed economy

with a low level of technology that leads to their poverty. They have low levels of literacy and health.

- Distinctive Culture, language and religion - communities have developed their own distinctive culture, language and religion.
- Shyness of contact - they have a marginal degree of contact with other cultures and people.[9]

The Scheduled Tribe groups who were identified as more backward communities among the tribal population groups have been categorised as 'Primitive Tribal Groups' (PTGs) by the Government at the Centre in 1975. So far seventy-five tribal communities have been identified as 'primitive tribal groups' in different States of India. These hunting, food-gathering, and some agricultural communities, who have been identified as more backward communities among the tribal population groups need special programmes for their sustainable development. The primitive tribes are awakening and demanding their rights for special reservation quota for them.[10]

The report of the Scheduled areas and Scheduled Tribes commission (1960-61) observes the "largest concentration of tribal people anywhere in the world except in Africa and in India". Prior to the Constitution, the term "Scheduled Tribes" was not in existence, but the tribes were variously called as aboriginals, adivasi, forest dwellers, hill tribes, primitives tribes, adimjati, etc. Upto 1919, the tribes were included under the head of "Depressed Classes". The Indian Franchise Committee in 1919,accorded a separate nomenclature for the Census Reports.

The term Scheduled area is a successor. The term Scheduled tracts, backward tracts, backward areas, excluded and partially excluded areas were usual in the pre-Constitution era in the Government of India Acts 1919 and 1935. Thus the adivasis or the aboriginal population of our country are considered as early settlers. They are generally found to live in unhealthy jungle-covered regions, mostly remote and inaccessible to other people. In the Constitution of India, they have been described as weaker sections because they are not in position to compete with their stronger brethren in socio-economic sphere.

There are three important tribal concentrated zones in India where most of the tribals inhabit. These are (1) North-eastern zones of India comprising the sub-Himalayan mountainous region with dominating tribes. (2) The central or middle zone comprising the state of West Bengal, Bihar, Orisssa, Southern Uttar Pradesh, Northern Maharashtra, Madhya Pradesh, Northern Rajasthan, in which a good number of tribal communities live. (3) The southern zone consisting of Kerala, Tamilnadu, Andhra Pradesh, where the important tribal communities live.

Tribal communities are also found in some other pockets like Andaman and Nikobar Islands, Laccadive, etc. The hostile Jarwa, Nicobarese Onge, etc. are notable for their primitive style of life in these areas.

Due to various factors and impact of historical forces some tribal communities have been pushed back into their first dwellings, whereas some other groups have come into closer interaction with other non-tribal communities. This process of interaction, however, has brought about some changes from tribe to tribe in various areas of life. Based on Hunters definition of tribe acceptable in many ways we can have the following main characteristics features of the tribe,(1) a tribe descends from a common biological mythical ancestors (2) it occupies a defined territory (3) it has a common history (4) the tribe speaks a common dialect, and (5) it is invariably endogamous in nature.

The states where in primitivism and tribalism yet prevail to a large extent are Assam, Orissa, Madhya Pradesh and Bihar. All tribals shared and are sharing the history of India. This is called uniting force of entire Indian population, the bulk of whom has been known traditionally and universally as Hindus. There is a socio-cultural gulf between tribals and neighbouring plain people.

Problems of these people are complex in nature. As much as the means of communication are developing, the impact of extraneous influences is also increasing unfavourably on the part of tribal population. Due to this impact we find cultural disintegration and disorganization in them. Besides these, various other factors are also responsible for their problems. They are

(1) Exploitation by outsiders
(2) Unapproachable habitation
(3) Policy of the then British India
(4) Approach of Christian missionaries and so on

The existing problems may be summarised as (1) land problem (2) problem of education (3) cultural problems (4) problem of religion (5) economic problems (6) health problems.

The Constitution of India contains an impressive array of provisions for removal of disabilities and discrimination against Scheduled Castes and Scheduled Tribes. They are buttressed with by the protection of civil Rights Acts,1955 and Scheduled Castes and Scheduled Tribes Acts,1989.

Article 46 of the Constitution requires that the states shall promote with special care the education and economic interests of the weaker sections of the people in general and the Scheduled Castes and Scheduled Tribes in particular.

The Constitution prescribed protections and safeguards for Scheduled tribes and other weaker sections either specially or by way of insisting on their general rights as citizens with the object of promoting their educational and economic interests and removing social disabilities they are subjected to. Main safeguards are:

(1) promotion of their education and economic interests and their protection from social injustice and all forms of exploitation (Article 46);
(2) throwing open by law of Hindu religious institutions of public character to all classes and sections of Hindu (Article 25);
(3) curtailment by law in the interest of any Scheduled Tribes of general rights of all citizens to move freely, settle in and acquire property (Article 19(5));
(4) forbidding or any denial of admission to educational institutions maintained by the state or

receiving grant out of state funds (Article 29 (2));
(5) permitting the state to make reservation for backward classes in public services in case of inadequate representation and requiring the state to consider claims of the Scheduled Castes and Scheduled Tribes in the making of appointments to public services (Articles 16 and 335);
(6) special representation in the Lok Sabha and State Legislative assemblies to Scheduled Castes and Tribes till 25 January 2000 (Articles 330, 332 and 334);
(7) setting up of tribal advisory councils and separate departments in states and appointment of a special officer at the centre to promote their welfare and safeguard their interests (Articles164 and 338 and fifth Schedule);
(8) special provision for administration and control of Scheduled and Ttribal areas (Article 244 and fifth and sixth schedules);
(9) prohibition of traffic in human beings and forced labour (Article 23).

With a view to effectively deal with crimes against Scheduled tribes and to tone up administrative machinery to tackle this vital issue, comprehensive guidelines containing precautionary, preventive punitive and rehabilitative measures exist, which states/UTs have to follow. Still these communities continue to be vulnerable and atrocities are committed against them in one form or other. Government enacted the Scheduled Castes and the Scheduled Tribes (Prevention of Atrocities) Act, 1989. It came into force from 30 January 1990. It specifies offences which are considered as atrocities and provides for deterrent punishments for commission of the same. It also envisages preventive measures and states have to evolve schemes, among other things, for economic and social rehabilitation of such victims. All States and UTs except Arunachal Pradesh, Mizoram and Nagaland have specialized courts for trial of offences under this Act.

By virtue of the constitution (sixty-fifth Amendment)

Act 1990, the 'Special Officers' post under Article 338 of the Constitution has been substituted by the National Commission for Scheduled Castes and Scheduled Tribes. It consists of a chairperson, vice-chairperson and five other members to be appointed by the President, under his hand and seal. It shall be the duty of Commission: (a) to investigate and monitor all matters relating to the safeguard provided for the Scheduled castes and Scheduled tribes under the Constitution or under any other law; (b) to enquire into specific complaints with respect to the deprivation of rights and safeguards of the Scheduled Castes and Tribes; (c) to participate and advise on the planning process of socio-economic development of the Scheduled Tribes and Scheduled Castes and to evaluate the progress of their development under the Union and State; (d) to present to the President annually and at such other times as the Commission may deem fit, reports upon the working of these safeguards; (e) to make in such reports recommendations as to the measures that should be taken by the Union or any State for the effective implementation of those safeguards and other measures for the protection, welfare and socio-economic development of the Scheduled Castes and Scheduled Tribes and (f) to discharge such other functions in relation to the protection, welfare and development and advancement of the Scheduled Tribes and Scheduled Castes as the President may, subject to the provisions of any law made by Parliament, by rule specify.

The President shall cause all such reports to be laid before each House of Parliament along with a memorandom explaining the action taken or proposed to be taken on the recommendations relating to the Union and the reasons for the non-acceptance, if any, of any of such recommendations. Where any such report or any part thereof relates to any matter with which any State Government is concerned, a copy of such report shall be forwarded to the Governor of the state who shall cause it to be laid before the legislature of the state.

Government had set-up three Parliamentary Committees, first in 1966, second in 1971 and the third in1973 to examine the implementation of the Constitutional safeguards for welfare of Scheduled Castes and Scheduled Tribes. The Committee has since been constituted as a Standing Committee of Parliament, the tenure of its members being one year.

State and UTs have separate departments to look after the welfare of Scheduled Castes and Scheduled Tribes and Other Backward Classes. Administrative set-up varies from state to state. In Bihar, Madhya Pradesh and Orissa, separate ministers have been appointed to look after tribal welfare as prescribed in Article 164 of the constitution. Some other states have set-up Committee of members of state legislatures on the pattern of Parliamentary Committee at the centre. All the states having Scheduled areas including Tamil Nadu and West Bengal have constituted Tribal Advisory Councils as per the provision in the fifth Scheduled to the Constitution to advise on matters pertaining to welfare and advancement of Scheduled Tribes.

National Scheduled Castes and Scheduled Tribes Finance and Development Corporation has been set-up by the Government of India under section 25 of the Companies Act, 1956 and is functioning with effect from 8 February 1989. The objective of the corporation is to stimulate economic development of Scheduled castes and Scheduled tribes and also identify and fill in the critical gaps in the programmes of state level Scheduled castes development corporations and other agencies. It is also to function as an apex institution for the agencies engaged in the economic development of Scheduled Castes and Scheduled Tribes. The corporation also plays a catalystic role in developing the 50:50 matching basis for construction of hostel buildings with a view to providing hostel facilities to Scheduled tribes girls studying in middle and higher level of education. The schemes of post-matric scholarships to Scheduled Castes and Scheduled Tribes was introduced in 1944-45 with the objective of providing financial assistance to students studying at post-matriculation stages in different schools and colleges so as to enable them to complete their education.

Article 335 of the constitution provides that claims of the members of the Scheduled Castes and Scheduled Tribes shall be taken in to consideration consistently with the maintenance of efficiency of administration making of appointment in services and posts in connection with affairs of the union or of a state. Article 16 (4) permits reservation in favour of any backward class of citizens which in the opinion of the state is not adequately represented in services under the state. In pursuance of these provisions, the Government has made reservations for Scheduled Castes and Scheduled Tribes in services under its control in proportion to their population. For Scheduled Tribes, reservation is 7.5 percent on all India basis otherwise open competition to facilitate their adequate

(1) Relaxation of five years in upper age limit
(2) Relaxation in the standards of suitability, for selection provided they are not unfit for the posts
(3) Relaxation of qualification regarding experience in the case of direct recruitment wherever necessary
(4) Exemption from the payment of application fee
(5) Inclusion of scientific and technical posts upto the lowest range of Group 'A' posts required for guiding and conducting research in the scheme of reservations have been provided for
(6) If sufficient number of suitable SC/ST candidates are not available against the share of vacancies reserved for them, the shortfall will not be filled up by general category candidates and such vacancies will be kept unfilled till SC/ST candidates become available. This scheme of reservation is also being followed by public sector undertakings including nationalized public sector banks.

State Government have also framed rules under the powers given to them by item 41 of the state list of the seventh Schedule to the Constitution for reservation of posts for these classes and have taken steps to increase their representation in state services. Reservation in state government services, however, is under the exclusive jurisdiction of state government.

In order to save tribals from exploitation by private

traders and to offer them remunerative prices for their produce and surplus agriculture products Government has set-up Tribal Cooperative Marketing Development Federation of India Ltd, (TRIFED) in August 1987 which is registered under the multi state Co-operative Society Act 1984. It start functioning effectively from April 1988. TRIFED handled about 12 items in 1988-89. In almost all the items, the price offered to tribals by TRIFED was higher than the price given to them in the previous years. During 1989-90, it expanded its activities to cover a number of new items. It has been appointed as a canalizing agency for export of gum keraya and other seeds of tribal area, and has also been declared as the nodal agency for collection, processing, storage and development of oilseeds of tree and forest origin. TRIFED is also acting as Food Corporation of India (FCI) for procuring wheat and paddy as an agent of department of Agriculture and Corporation (DAC) for coarse grains, pulses and oilseeds. The tribal sub-plan (TSP) strategy which was evolved during the fifth five year plan for protection of interests of tribals through legal and administrative support and promotion of developmental efforts through plan schemes to raise their level of living. There are many Tribal Development Projects (ITDPs) which stands in the way of effective implementation of various schemes and projects for development of tribals.

Gandhiji felt that India is a one Nation and every unit must have this realization. He, therefore, believed that whatever difference exist should be obliterated and every unit should feel one with the other. In fact, on the demand of the nation all must appear with the one voice. For this the atmosphere of oneness has to be created. This cannot be achieved unless: (1) the inequality existing in the society is obliterated; (2) violence is eschewed; and (3) the foreign power is removed.[11]

He felt very deeply the inequality existing in the society then. It was not inequality of wealth that hurt Gandhiji, there was inequality in every sphere of life . Vast inequality in education, vast inequqality in receiving medical treatment, and vast inequality in living conditions. On the one side there were persons who could compete in their intellectual attainment with anybody in the world, like; Shri

Ravindra Nath Tagore, Shri Jagdish Chandra Bose, and others, and on the other there was vast army of completely illiterate of Adivasis, Harijans and others. The persons in urban areas were fortunate in having all medical facilities available on the earth whereas millions of people living in rural areas died like mosquitoes for want of a pill of quinine. Similarly, some have the fortunate to live in most sanitary conditions while others in millions lived in hoods surrounded by water, logged around them.[12] The disparity was vast and bewildering, and distorted with that disparity India could never dream of attaining nationhood. Not only that the British could always exploit this but that it was repugnant to the building of an Independent nation based on non-violent society. Gandhiji believed that the disparity could only be maintained in a society based on violence. Once violence is eschewed and universal franchise is accepted people would not accept the disparity even for a day.

Gandhiji, therefore, said that the prime condition of building a non-violent society is to remove all inequalities. There should be equilibrium in wealth, education should be universal, illiteracy should be banished, medicine should be available to everybody, food should be available to everybody. Everybody should have place for shelter. This would need leveling down and raising up. Society must not grudge this operation. Nationhood can only thrive in this atmosphere of equality of opportunity and service. Where many people are forced to live under circumstances of privation, no nationhood can be built up. This was the approach of Gandhiji to tribes.[13]

It was this approach that Gandhiji inspired hundreds of workers to go to Adivasi, embrace them, and serve them. The Adivasi responded to this attitude of Gandhiji. Thousands of Tana Bhagats in Ranchi district and Sapa Hores in Santal Paraganas joined Gandhiji's non-co-operation movement and the sacrifice which they made as a group is unique in the history of the fight for freedom. The Tana Bhagats did not join the movement as individual but as a group and every man, woman or child of the group was a Satyagrahi. They suffered jail and more than that they lost their property which has not been yet returned to them in many cases.

Hundreds of them met Gandhiji in Gaya, Kokananda Coronpor and Belagaon Congress by travelling on foot. They suffered untold miseries at the hands of the Britishers and yet undaunted they marched with Gandhiji till last.

When Swaraj was achieved the Adivasis were not forgotten. Once Shri Ambedkar suggested that Adivasi should have no representation in the legislature, and as they were simple and uneducated their representative would be exploited. Gandhiji opposed this as he had seen the devoted Tana Bhagats and demanded that their representation should be in proportion to their proportion. Gandhiji prevailed, Indian Constitution provided for the representation of the tribes in proportion to their population.14 Then in the Constitution a dignitary in shape of Commissioner for Scheduled Castes and Scheduled Tribes was safeguards provided in the Constitution. The safeguards went as far as to give representation to the tribes in service as well. Circular were issued by the Home Department. The provisions of our Constitution regarding the Scheduled Tribes are unique in the world.

In the sphere of Adivasis Gandhiji thought of sending large number of trained person unbound with spirit of service to every village and develop every village in a balanced way.

Notes and References

1. Lok Sabha debates, Sr. No. 10, June 41-42, 1995, Vol. 42, Lok Sabha Secretariat, Parliament of India, 1995.
2. Minocheher Rustom Masani and Ramaswamy Srinivasan (1985), Freedom and Dissent: Essays in Honour of Minoo Masani on His Eigthtieth Birthday, Democratic Research Service, http://books.google.com/books?id=v861AAAAIAAJ, retrieved 2008-11-25, "... The Adivasis are the original inhabitants of India. That is what Adivasi means: the original inhabitant. They were the people who were there before the Dravidians. The tribals are the Gonds, the Bhils, the Murias, the Nagas and a hundred more. ..."
3. Mohandas Karamchand Gandhi (1968), The Selected Works of Mahatma Gandhi : Satyagraha in South Africa, Navajivan Publishing House, http://books.google.com/books?id=cApuAAAAMAAJ, retrieved 2008-11-25, "... The Adivasis are the original inhabitants ..."
4. Acharya, Deepak and Shrivastava Anshu (2008): Indigenous Herbal

Medicines: Tribal Formulations and Traditional Herbal Practices, Aavishkar Publishers Distributor, Jaipur- India. ISBN 978-81-7910-252-7. pp 440.

5. Robert Harrison Barnes, Andrew Gray and Benedict Kingsbury (1995), Indigenous Peoples of Asia, Association for Asian Studies, ISBN 0924304146, http://books.google.com/books?id=-8eBAAAAMAAJ, retrieved 2008-11-25, "... The Concept of the Adivasi: According to the political activists who coined the word in the 1930s, the "adivasis" are the original inhabitants of South Asia ..."
6. Louise Waite (2006), Embodied Working Lives: Work and Life in Maharashtra, India, Lexington Books, ISBN 073910876X, http://books.google.com/books?id=gLm6WmbFsA0C, retrieved 2008-11-25, "... The scheduled tribes themselves tend to refer to their ethnic grouping as adivasis, which means 'original inhabitant.' Hardiman continues to argue that the term adivasi is preferable in India as it evokes a shared history of relative freedom in precolonial times ..."
7. Govind Sadashiv Ghurye (1980), The Scheduled Tribes of India, Transaction Publishers, ISBN 0878556923, http://books.google.com/books?id=9qt2e8xc-M4C, retrieved 2008-11-25, "... I have stated above, while ascertaining the general attitude of Mr. Jaipal Singh to tribal problems, his inisistence on the term 'Adivasi' being used for Schedule Tribes ... Sir, myself I claim to an Adivasi and an original inhabitant of the country as Mr. Jaipal Singh ... a pseudo-ethno-historical substantiation for the term 'Adivasi' ..."
8. Labour Bureau, Government of India
9. New Book: Anthropology of Primitive Tribes in India
10. Bharathi, K.S., The Social Thought of Gandhi (Nagpur: Dattsons Publications), 1995.
11. Chaudhury, Sukant K., Patnaik, Soumendra Mohan, Indian Tribes and the Mainstream (New Delhi: Rawat Publications), 2008.
12. Kapoor, A.N., Gupta, V.P., A Dictionary of Gandhian Thought (Delhi: Ambe Book Publishers), 1995.
13. Sahay, B.N., Srivastava, B. K.,Vidyarthi, L.P., Gandhi and Social Sciences (New Delhi: Bookhive Publishers), 1970.

Gandhi on Peace, Conflict and Conflict Resolutions

Sumit Narula

There is very popular saying that "Villains don't fall from the skies, neither do they pop out of the ground like evil spirits. They must be seen as symptoms of society and therefore every citizen is responsible for their existence."

War and peace, love and hate, bad and good... we have opposite conceptions for most things in the human existence. But what do we really have as an opposite conception for violence? As long as we lack a truly concrete definition in our mind, we are not capable of expressing it in daily action. Ahimsa - the sanskrit definition for non-violence also stands for universal love, compassion. Despite the many conflicts in India, ahimsa is a far more established definition in the East than non-violence is in the West. The main difference is that we more or less consider it as a technique, a method, or just the absence or freedom from violence, whereas in India ahimsa stands for a whole philosophy of life, a way of living. The origin of ahimsa goes back to 3.000 B.C., to Buddha and the Buddhism, and to Lord Mahavira, the founder of Jainism. Jain means a conquerer, not a conquerer of countries or treasures, but a conquerer of the self. One who has mastered his own desires. There are approximately 10.000 jains in the world today, belonging to a branch of hinduism that has no bloodshed on it's conscience. But unlike the Tibetan Buddhists they have not suffered any major oppression.

What Gandhi did in the 30s is that he developed the ancient hindu philosophy of ahimsa, into a social and political tool, not only to make India independent but also to uplift the self-confidence of every Indian, in his constructive programme for social, religious, political and economic justice.

NON-VIOLENT RESISTANCE

When Gandhi started his commitment back in South Africa, the English press referred to the struggle as a method of "passive resistance", a term responsible for that deep-rooted misinterpretation of non-violence as a form of passivity. Actions of non-violence is on the contrary exactly what he says - actions which are non-violent. Gandhi said that the root of every Violence or Conflict is Untruth and that the only permanent solution of Conflict is Truth. Consequently, to resolve conflicts, he conceived a novel technique which he called Satyagraha. It's made up of two sanskrit words, satya (truth) and agraha (firmness) or, Unwavering search for the Truth. And since the only way of getting to Truth is by Non-violence (or Love), it follows that Satyagraha implies an Unwavering search for the Truth using Non-violence. And therefore Gandhi emphasized that Satyagraha is the most potent method of ensuring an endurable Peace. Therefore, Satya means "that which is", which is undestroyable, or 'truth', and 'agraha' means holding on to something. So satyagraha literally means holding on to the truth, and offer non-violent resistance, even at the cost of your own life.

In this context Gandhi further said that.

Truth is God;
Non-violence is Love in Action; and

Peace, the result of enduring conflict resolution, is the Fruit of Satyagraha.[1]

The one who offers satayagraha is called a satyagrahi. It's almost impossible to estimate the number of satyagraha campaigns in India during Gandhis' lifetime, they where several hundred linked together, and even today satyagraha is performed by local villages in great amount, when the corruption in India gets too serious.

THE SOUL-FORCE

The force of violence is mechanical, physical, while the force of non-violence is mental and spiritual. Gandhi also referred to satyagraha as the soul-force. The main thing when you offers non-violent resistance is to distinguish between the wrong-doer and the wrong-being-done. That means you oppose the injustice, but without loosing sight of the human being inside the aggressor or the opponent.[2] Adam Curle, a negotiator and peace mediator between guerilla leaders and governments in South America, Africa and Asia says that "the term non-violence is just as insufficient as calling love non-hate. And he goes on to explain that " to say 'I non-hate you, darling', would seem like a fairly lukewarm expression."[3] "We can't control our thoughts and emotions completely. Perhaps we don't express them in words; but they more or less arise spontaneously. It's easy to verify this. Try to observe or memorize how your thoughts jump from one subject to another and ends up somewhere it couldn't be predicted, as a link in an hidden chain of associations. These associations dominate a greater part of our mind, and is connected to hidden dreams and memories. They bring us moments of anxiety, depression, happiness, fear and self-satisfaction. We are not aware from one moment to another of who we are. We are not experiencing our own presence. When we are angry, we are the anger. When we are depressed, we are the depression. We are not aware of ourselves as a special phycho-physical unite. We are not aware of the basic foundations for our existence, the origin we share with others which relates us with everybody. Our instinct of self-preservation is strong and prevent us from recognizing the facts that links us to other human beings. But still, we notice that something is missing, that something in our lifes is unsatisfactory."[4] He further said that:

"We try to compensate this by building a false identity, we can call it the "I" or the ego. This image of myself, that I call "I", and which I think is a constant, is really a constantly changing collections of moods, impulses, thoughts and imaginations. Yesterdays "I" are not todays "I". Although some characters in all those different "I's" are more permanent than others and stands for some continuity, our image of the "I" is an illusion. That "I" which appears in the company of friends, when we want to make an impression on people, with people we feel afraid of or dislike, people we love, when we are happy, depressed - all these are different, separate personalities, masks we put on or off. But unlike actors we are not aware that we do it.

"We create images of an "I" with bits and pieces of our life, which we hope shall make an attractive and pleasant impression. The cornerstone in this image may very well be a special talent or quality which we ourself-consider of great value. But that which satisfy us, not necessarily satisfy others- and then we feel that the "I" lets us down.

"When this happens we experience what we can call an crisis of identity. We automatically try to rebuild the broken defence system of the ego. We blame the damages on the circumstances or other people - they are stupid, have bad taste, the show envy, etc., etc. At the same time, we rebuild our "I" so it can handle any further attacks. When the damages are too serious to handle, we become what we call depressed.

"These states of minds that occur then, are harmful for all human relationships, especially for those that demands a great inner strength and sensibility, such as mediation, peacekeeping and active non-violence. There you need a calm mind, which will not be affected by the need and fears from an unsatisfactory ego, and which is capable of creating a serious communication with others, a contact with their common origin. A disturbed mind just tend to influence others with its own anxiety."[5]

INDIVIDUAL NON-VIOLENCE

Well, how do we react when we are faced with violence - physical violence, mental violence or social violence? The first impulse can be anger and a strong sense of revenge, to meet violence with violence. Another reaction can be to give up, out of fear. That would mean a form of cowardice which turns away from injustice, and which according to Gandhi is worse than revenge, because it let's the violence continue unstopped.

No, we must first establish that we are not conducted by a depressed ego, and than realise that we and the one who threaten us have a problem in common. We are faced with the danger of being hurt in larger or smaller extent, while the aggressor is faced with the moral danger of hurting another person.

What's that for some sort of moral danger, you may ask. Well, the danger is that the aggressor may develop a violent behavior that narrows his possibilities of reaction, and may lead to both bad reputation and painful revenge. For the moment he's naturally not aware of this. Therefore we must not only try to prevent violence, but to do it in a way that makes him understand that his methods will hurt him just as much as it will hurt us. To do this is the very core, the essence of non-violence. It's a kind of technique which uses the violent energy of thc aggressor to turn upside down on his self-understanding.

RECOGNIZING NON-VIOLENCE

"I have found that life persists in the midst of destruction", remarked Gandhi when thousands of sikhs were massacred in Amritsar in India 1919. "And therefore I came to the conclusion that there exists a force that is stronger than violence. But history don't recognize non-violence. If two brothers quarrel and become friends again, this do not become history. But if they need the help of a lawyer or hurt each other seriously it will certainly be recorded in the books. Non-violence is that everlasting force which upholds the universe. History just becomes a notebook of the interruptions in that continuing flow."

According to Gandhi the aim of education is to build character. But what we do, both in the East and the West, is to produce money-making machines, not thinking human beings. If we made thinking human beings the world wouldn't look like this today.

WASTE OF HUMAN BRILLIANCE

There are many inner conflicts which had led many peace movements to protest movement rather than that social movement Gandhi advocated. The world consume 2 million dollars every minute on military expenditure, but its not mainly a question of a waste of money but with the human brilliance.

All this power could be used for something constructive. There are many forms of violence and Gandhi saw poverty as the worst form. 35.000 children die every day due to malnutrition and lack of social care.

TO HANDLE CONFLICT

Before coming to the resolution or handling of conflicts we must understand what is conflict?

Conflict involves a person's struggle with him/herself, another person, or a thing. It is a problem or disagreement- a situation that needs resolution. Conflict is present in every person's life. It is inescapable. However, conflict can be dealt with creatively, if a person has the right tools. Actually they are only a clash of interest and opinions. They are not the real problem. There will always be different thoughts and ideas. We are different! It's a beauty in this.

The question is not conflict itself, it is how we handle conflict. And there are only two ways - through violence or through non-violence. If conflict is handled properly they can lead to growth in institutions, they can lead to growth in personal relationships. But we have the war system of today, because we - that is adults living in democracies - have decided, that when there will be a conflict we may use violence to resolve it. We shouldn't confuse the habitual with the natural.

Conflict resolution is the process of finding a solution to a conflict. There are several methods of conflict resolution. Some result in win-lose solutions, while others can be win-win. Through programs like peer mediation, kids learn to go for the win-win solution!

There are many different ways of resolving conflict. The three most common ways are fight, flight, and flow.

In a fight, two or more people are aggressive with one another. Fighting can be done with words, weapons, or fists. There is a battle of some sort, and there will be one winner and one loser.

In a flight situation, one person walks away from the conflict. The problem is left unresolved, again with one winner and one loser. Common "flight" language includes: "talk to the hand", "never mind", "just forget it", "whatever", etc...

In a flow situation, both people walk away from the conflict satisfied with the solution, which they have reached together. Conflict resolution encourages everyone to "Go for the flow" and create win-win solutions![6]

NON-VIOLENT DEFENSE

Non-violence is a science. It does not mean just sitting around feeling good about the world. Without analysis, research and proper training you can't practise it. We have constructed a perfect violent defense system. But we haven't put so much as one dollar a day aside, on systematic training in non-violent defense.

And there is such a defense. In USA we have the Civilian-Based Defence Association, where Professor Gene Sharp has been doing research on the issue for over 30 years. In The Politics of Non-violent Action, a regular encyclopaedia on non-violence, he systematically describes 198 specific actions, including historical examples. The Indian Society of Gandhian Studies founded by Acharya J. B. Kripalani and Lok Nayak Jaya Prakash Narain, currently under the Presidentship of Professor Jai Narain Sharma, Department of Gandhian Studies, Panjab University is doing tremendous job towards spreading Gandhi's principles and ideas and how they can be used in our day-to-day life.

THE PEACE ARMY

Actually, the first seeds of non-violent defense was already spread by Gandhi, at the ashrams and communities where thousands of people from all different nationalities and religions lived together. Gandhi talked about a Peace Army, Shanti Sena.

"O, misers, your speech is not backed by sena", it says in the Vedas. Meaning is has no power, it will not carry. Literally sena means a band of people assembled to do or die. The idea occurred in 1914, while Gandhi struggled in South Africa and the world got ready for the first world war. What is a winning army really, Gandhi asked himself. The armed chariot that wins the victory of Rama in Ramayana is not of the ordinary kind:

"Courage is it's wheels; character it's banner; self-discipline and good will it's horses, with mercy and spiritual balance as it's reins."[7]

This was the equipment suitable for the non-violent soldier. In the 20s Shanti Sena became a part of the Indian struggle for independence and fostered fearless and passioned co-workers. Says Gandhi: "Satyagraha brigades can be developed in every village and block in the city. They must remain free from political intrigue, but with good judgement and a will to serve."

Several of western friends of Gandhi was inspired. Dr Maude Royden in an open letter of London Daily Express in 1932, asked for voluntaries for a peace army. It would serve as a buffer between the fighting Japanese and Chinese forces in Shanghai.[8]

MARTIN LUTHER KING JR IN INDIA

After Gandhi's death Shanti Sena went into decline. Vinoba Bhave, the spiritual inherent of Gandhi, revived the idea in the end of the 50s.

March 2nd 1959 eight hundred satyagrahis gathered for a march from Ajmer to Gagwana. One of the participators was Martin Luther King. At the camp after the march King asked Vinoba about the possibilities for satyagraha in the nuclear age.

We no longer can afford conflicts of mental attitudes, Vinoba answered. Courage, vision and faith are necessary elements for a mutual disarmament. I feel that two forces will shape the human life hereafter, those of spirituality and those of science. But a third force should cement these two together.

Shanti Sena expanded and included disaster relief after floods, refugee services, work with Himalayan bandits, and racial riots. The Shanti Sena also became internationally active and collaborated with people in Cyprus, Africa, Pakistan and Bangladesh.

UNARMED PEACEKEEPING FORCE

In 1971 Vinoba formulated a proposal for an "Unarmed Peacekeeping Force", presented to the UN. The idea resulted in the "Cyprus Resettlement Project" of 1972-1974.

Shanti Sena got several follow organizations in the west. Peace Brigades International was established in Canada 1981. They train escorts to threatened human rights activists in different parts of the world. Peace Brigades have offices in 14 countries.

CIVIL THREATS

Most peace researchers today agree on that the major military threats are decreasing, that after the end of the Cold War, what we are witnessing is a large number of civil wars, within countries, not war between countries. They also agree on that the so-called civil threats are increasing. Civil threats, that is environmental disasters, terrorism, xenophobia and racial violence. But defending human rights and the environment requires a completely new kind of defence.[9]

Björn Hettne, peace researcher at the University of Gothenburg, in an article recently warned for a potential risk of civil war. There are a number of trustworthy indicators of a society on the edge of a breakdown, and two of them are: 1, when the largest group of people with a common interest, is fairly small, and 2, when the difference in standards of living increase in the society.

"We lived on the belief that we had a rather low level of conflict in Sweden," Björn Hettne remarks. "But the main solidarity is declining, in favour of the interest of your own group of people. There is a lack of security, which expresses itself in violence."[10]

Hettne's opinion is that you need more psychological research, less soldiers, and a lot more active civilians.

In that perspective, there is an urgent need to develop the same self-confidence in our society, as Gandhi managed to do in India in the 30s. More than anything else he enlightened his people and made them feel faith, trust and courage. You can't live on mistrust and discourage. Your need, faith, trust and courage as well as you need food and water. Then you don't need any violent walls to surround you. With faith, trust and courage, non-violence becomes reality and not just a longing or a wish.

Notes and References

1. Sharma, Jai Narain, Satyagraha, Gandhi's Approach to Conflict Resolution (New Delhi: Concept Publishers), 2008.
2. Bandyopadhayaya, Jayant, Social and Political Thought of Mahatma Gandhi (Bombay: Allied Publishers), 1969.
3. Curle, Adam, Another Way: Positive Response to Contemporary Violence (N.J.: Jon Carpenter Publishing) 1995.
4. *Ibid.*
5. *Ibid.*
6. Avruch, Kevin, Peter W. Black, and Joseph A. Scimecca (eds.), Conflict Resolution: Cross-Cultural Perspectives (London: Greenwood Press), 1991.
7. Shanti Sena.
8. London Daily Express in 1932.
9. Aron, Raymond, Peace and War: A Theory of International Relations (London: Transaction), 2003.
10. Tidwell, Alan, C., Conflict Resolved? A Critical Assessment of Conflict Resolution (London: Pinter Publishers), 1999.

Gandhi's Vision: A Search for Peace and Security

RANJAN BALA

In a world pervaded with violence and terror, the struggle for peace and security must begin in everyday life. Peace and security have always been among humanity's highest value, for some supreme end. The concept of peace and security is as old as human knowledge of society. The quest for peace and security has been a central motive in the life of man from the first moment of his entrance in the worldly scene. Mankind has been searching for an ideal society, where men can lead a happier, worthier and more rewarding life. Peace and security continues to be a powerful wish, desire and a passion with millions as well as a conviction deeply felt and aspired too. All nations long for it. Leaders negotiate for it yet it remain must elusive than ever.

Conflicts and tensions of all sort are mounting up. Highly sophisticated weapons are being pilled up on the name of a better life. The number of nuclear basis are increasing day by day. A void loom large and various insecurities has grippled humanity. The problem of human life at the present juncture of world history is peaceful and secure survival of mankind. Will man in society survive peacefully? Will he be able to contain the seeds of conflicts and violence that he has himself sown in the pursuit of civilization and turn them into instruments of change and reconstruction towards a new and different peaceful secure order?

Admist of numerous evils in the world, we need an inclusive vision that makes life meaningful, peaceful and secure in all the fields of human endeavour - viz. social, economic, political and cultural. We need a philosophy that is value based, humane, just participatory and the one that is feasible and practical.

We can achieve a peaceful, secure and just world order only by following the doctrine of Ahimsa (non-violence) - a word most dearest to Mahatma Gandhi. To him, the cut of love, sacrifice and truth can save the human race from annihilation and convert this hell of world into heaven. Gandhi was the man, who laid down his life for spreading the message of love and Ahimsa. He was of the firm belief that violence can never overthrow the violence.

Albert Einstein had once said "we need an essentially new way of thinking if mankind is to survive. Men must radically change their attitudes towards each other and their views of the future force must no longer be an instrument of politics...... Today, we donot have much time left, it is up to our generation to succeed in thinking differently. If we fail, the days of civilized humanity are numbered"[1]

In contrast to the conflict laden world, Gandhi stands for non-violence, love and fearless human spirit. Gandhi was the first person to have successfully practiced non-violence on a large canvas in socio-political life of man for him, non-violence stood for an alternative vision of life that promised peace and security for all.

The prevailing definition of peace is "absence of violence". Peace denotes bombs not falling on Bergrades, missles are not falling, Hindus and Muslims are not rioting, blood not driving by the crips spraying bullets. Peace is the reduction or absence of violence in all its kinds. Noted scholar on peace John Galtung[2] described this kind of peace as Negative Version of peace. This definition of peace in

Gandhi's opinion was at once two facile and arbitrary to be taken seriously. Gandhi rejected outrightly the literal meaning of peace as inadequate and unacceptable. The peace, "you find in stone or in grave" was utterly meaningless and futile."[3] He also said that "Anything would be better than living death of the grave."[4] For Gandhi, peace meant elimination or destruction of all kinds and forms of tyranny, it was a positive condition conclusive to the realisation and preservation of human dignity and social justice. Peace was noting if it was not an absolutely a positive value. Peace is a nobler goal towards a just world order. Peace Gandhi insisted "must be just."[5] Shortly after the world war II, Gandhi wrote, "Peace must be Just. In Order to be that, it must neither be punitive nor vindictive, the fruits of peace must equally be shared."[6]

Gandhi also rejected the western conception of "peace through war". He strongly believe that we can't bring peace in the world through war. War can never brings peace. Weapons can't provide any sort of security. Gandhi felt clearly that war was just not a means to peace. In fact, his deep rooted conviction had made him steadfastly declare that he was an "uncompromising opponent of violent methods even to serve the noblest of causes."[7] War for him is illegitimate and morally indefensible means for achieving peace. Peace concluded through war is a temporary affairs for Gandhi, things attained by love and peace were impresihable, lasting in contrast to those gained through the force of arms or other brutal methods. To vanish war, Gandhi said, "We have to eradicate possessiveness, greed, lust and egotism from our own hearts. We have to carry war within ourselves to vanish it from society."[8] There can be no peace for individuals or for nations without practicing truth and non-violence to the uttermost extent possible for man. Peace can be bring only by peaceful means.

In contrast to the western viewpoint, i.e. to 'bring peace through war'. Gandhi suggested a more effective way to bring peace, i.e. 'peace through non-violence' (Ahimsa). Non-violence is a weapon, a technique and a method which man can adopt to fight the battles of the world. It is the principle of human existence being a force of truth. Gandhi wrote that

"Non-violence is the greater force at the disposal of mankind. It is mightier that the mightiest weapon of destruction devised by the ingenuity of man."[9]

The word ahimsa literally means non-injury, or more narrowly non-killing and more widely harmfulness, the renunciation of the will to kill and of the intentions to hurt any living thing, the abstention for hostile thought, word and act. As early as 1916 Gandhi distinguished between negative and positive meanings of ahimsa.

"In its negative form it means not injuring any living being whether by body or mind, I may not, therefore, hurt the person at any wrong doer or bear any ill will to him and to cause him mental suffering. This statement does not cover suffering caused to the wrong doer by natural acts of mine which do not proceed from ill-will..... ahimsa requires deliberate self-suffering, not a deliberate injuring of the supposed wrong doer.... In its positive form, Ahimsa means the largest love, the greatest charity. If I am a follower of Ahimsa, I must love my enemy or a stranger for me as I would my wrong doing father or son. This active Ahimsa necessarily included truth and fearlessness.[10]

Gandhi thus extended the meaning of ahimsa to include all moral virtues, similarly he stretched himsa far beyond its ordinary usage, all unfair and foul means come under the category of himsa.

This lead to so much confusion about Gandhi's views on non-violence that it is often equated with cowardice. Gandhi himself had said, "where there is a choice between cowardice and violence I would advice violence. Non-violence and cowardice go ill together."[11]

Gandhi in reply to a question—"Is not non-violence resistance by the militarily strong more effective than that by the militarily weak? Says this is contradiction in terms. There can be no non-violence offered by the military strong ...... what is true is that if those, who are at one time strong in armed might, change their mind, they will be better able to demonstrate their non-violence to the world and therefore to their opponents. Those who are strong in non-violence will not mind whether they are opposed by the militarily weak or the strongest.[12] Strength does not come from physical capacity. It comes from an indomitable will. In most cases, violence is the expression of fear. It is due to fear complex that man arms himself or attack others. Thus at the bottom, violence is really the expression of an inner sense of weakness. Even the nations armed themselves out of fear of each other force issued when people are under the spell off ear. Fear breads hatred. The very first step that nations must take towards ensuring peace was to dispel fear and along with it, mistrust.

Gandhi declared that "peace will never come until the great powers courageously decide to disarm themselves...... I have an implicit faith—a faith that today burns brighter than ever, after half a century's experience of unbroken practice of non-violence ..... that mankind can only be saved through non-violence."[13]

In Gandhian ideal society, there is no room for weapons. Security for Gandhi is not merely strategy and technique of defeating an invading army. It is not an international wrestling among nations with weapons of mass destruction. For Gandhi, security is a holistic phenomenon. It is a matter of opting for a way of life. Highest form of security is possible only in a civilized, gentle and a non-violent world. It is morale and faith in God and Truth that leads to real sense of security.

Peace through security is the essence of modern conception of security. But for Gandhi, security is possible through peace only. The major difference in these two view points is primarily that of emphasis. Gandhian perspective considers security as a natural corollary of peace. Security without weapons is necessary as an ultimate aim. Weapons bring inherent and increasing sense of insecurity. Real security is when one does not even have to think of armaments. One can walk down the streets without the feeling of any terror, or to be safe on the roads one does not need any policemen. It is not the weapons but human beings who are the real significance. Everything else is secondary. The western conception of security is stockpiles of weapons provide a sense of security replete with threats of complete human extinction. Security is possible through stockpiles of weapons more and more.

With this type of culture in the world, humanity has reached at a critical point, where people can do anything and can give birth to many "Black Tuesday" (September 2001). Not only the citizens of USA. But of the whole world were shattered and shocked. The world watched silently when terrorist dismantle the world trade centre towers and killed countries innocent persons and the fear in the heart of most powerful nation of the-USA a superpower in a world, which looked like a helpless crying child. The huge arms can't be able to bring a small amount of security to the USA. Then, why the world is mad in the Arms Race? State can't be the provider of security said Gandhi. Gandhi regarded state as a "soulless machine."[14] The state represent violence in a concentrated and organized form. "The individuals have souls but as the state is to soulless machine, it can never be weaned from violence to which it owes its very existence."[15] Gandhi rejected the concept of state centric security. Can disarmament brings peace and security to the world? Disarmament means an action of disarming, to deprive of means of attack or to divest of hostility, etc. In broad sense, it implies the reduction or limitation of the size, equipment, armament and armed forces. The problem of controlling the arms race has attracted the attention of world more than century. The idea of disarmament was also mooted in 1920 by the former President of America, Woodrow Willson. The arm race has posed a serious threat to peace and security of the world, even the space surface was misused with star war kinds of programmes. What a dilemma it is! This type of thinking needs transformation.

"However one judges the desirability of peace or legitimacy of (at least one) wars, it should be clear that peace and war exist on a continuum at violent/non-violent national behaviours and that they constantly fluctuate. Neither should be taken for granted, and neither is humanity's natural state. The human condition—whether to wage war or to strive to build an enduring peace—is for us to decide."[16]

At this stage, we have the choice of two risk the one lies in continuing the mad atomic race with its danger of an unavoidable war in near future. The other is renunciation of nuclear weapons. The first hold no hope of a peaceful and secure survival. The second does, we must risk it.[17] For years, Gandhi campaigned for the view that peace and security was a mater of justice rather than strength. The world over a true peace depends not upon gun power but upon pure justice. Armaments were both a symptom of force and a temptation to use force. Instead of talking of a mere restriction of armaments, their quantity and quality. Gandhi pleaded passionately for complete, universal disarmament. In a column in *young India*, Gandhi said,

> "Total world disarmament, the only material safeguard for peace, should be the outward and visible sign of that inward mental disarmament on which alone outward peace can secure. So long, however, as one people is actually subjecting another to itself by superior military might even the very first step towards this inward mental disarmament has not been taken."[18]

If the great powers disarmed themselves, feel Gandhi, they would not only escape the ravages of war but also cover themselves in glory, restore sanity to the world and earn the eternal gratitude of posterity. By the same token, Gandhi Ji suggested that it would be disastrous if India, after attaining its freedom, were to join the arms race. According to Gandhi, it would be a miracle if the great powers accepted his ideal, but he also add that miracles have happened before and may happen again perhaps with the power shown by him in non-violence peace.

In the non-violent ideal state of Gandhi, size and role of police and military has to be limited to dealing with thieves, robbers, raiders from without and a few emergencies only. It would be better if police and military perform largely the role of a body of reformers. Gandhi looked forward to a world where "no state has its military."[19]

Real holistic security for Gandhi is possible only through:

- Non-violence
- Non-stealing
- Truth

- Non-possession
- Chastity

for a peaceful and secure world order Gandhi suggested four pillars

- It should be non-violent.
- It must be non-exploitative and based on justice.
- It has to be based on the reform and regeneration of individuals.
- It must work its way up to the global of international level through reform or non-violent reorganization (including democratization) at other levels of polity, such as local or national.

What Gandhi is emphasizing here related very closely to UNESCO aphorism that is: "Since war begin in the minds of men it is in the minds of men that the defence of peace must be constructed."[20]

The way we had cultivated the culture of violence in young generations, the same way, we will have to cultivate the culture of truth and non-violence in young ones. Peace is less costly and more meaningful than war and violence.

Notes and References

1. David P. Barath and Charles P. Webel, Peace and Conflict Studies (New Delhi: Sage Publications), 2002.
2. Galtung, John, Peace by Peaceful Means: Peace and Conflict Development and Civilization (New Delhi: Sage Publication), 1996.
3. Tendulkar, D.G., Mahatma (New Delhi: The Publications Division, Ministry of Information and Broadcasting, Government of India), 1960, Vol. 6, p. 169.
4. The Collected Works of Mahatma Gandhi (New Delhi: The Publications Division, Ministry of Information and Broadcasting, Government of India), 1960, Vol. 15, p. 310 (herein after CWMG be used).
5. *Harijan*, Vol. 6, New York, Garland, 1973, p. 290.
6. CWMG, Vol. 25, p. 424.
7. *Ibid.*, Vol. 17, pp. 439-441.
8. Pyarelal, Mahatma Gandhi, The Last Phase (Ahmedabad: Navajivan Publications), 1956, Vol. 2, p. 138.

9. *Harijan*, 05-09-1936, p. 734.
10. Iyer, Raghavan N., The Moral and Political Thoughts of Mahatma Gandhi (New Delhi: Oxford University Press), 2000, pp. 179-180.
11. *Harijan*, 15-07-1939, Vol.VII, No. 23.
12. Iyer, Raghavan, The Moral and Political Thoughts of Mahatma Gandhi *op. cit.*, pp. 448-450.
13. *Harijan*, Vol. 6, p. 295.
14. *Young India*, Nov. 1928, No.2.
15. *Ibid.*, p. 3.
16. Pasricha, Ashu, Peace Studies, The Discipline and Dimensions (New Delhi: Abhijeet Publishers), 2006, p. 25.
17. Schweitzer, Schweitzer, Peace or Atomicwar (Bombay: Asia Publishing House), 1958, p. 8.
18. CWMG, Vol. 48, p. 158, Vol. 47, p. 277.
19. Gangal, S.C., Gandhian Thought and Techniques in the Modern Word (Delhi: Criterion Publication), 1988, p. 100.
20. UNESCO Preamble.

Mahatma Gandhi: A Life for Non-Violence

Kiyanoush Ghalavand

Gandhi, being the 'practical idealist' that he was, always spoke of truth and non-violence, never of non-violence alone. Within the meaning of his 'practical idealism', the practice of non-violence became, in other words, an exercise in the art of the possible.

Non-violence and truth were one interpenetrated whole it mosaic in which each patch of colour lent meaning to the other Gandhi never spoke of non-violence in the abstract but only as it related to some concrete situation. Of course, like all human beings, he did at times, especially in his later years, indulge in the luxury of generalizing from particular events. But as a rule his awareness of reality, painfully acute at all times, tended to overmaster the natural human gravitation towards romanticism.

Gandhi was never tired of saying that his whole life has been a series of compromises. Though he undoubtedly regretted this as who wouldn't? nevertheless it was not his way to let himself he consumed with remorse and frustration on that account. All life is a compromise. Human perceptions, no less than human sensations, are subjected to the law of dvandva or what may be called the hot cold, good bad, syndrome. Violence and non-violence are no exception to this rule. Pure non-violence, as much as pure violence, is an impossible stance for human beings and human institutions. Neither would exist for a second on such a diet. The kind of permanent, enduring peace that man has been seeking since the dawn of creation is a will or the wisp. War and peace, conflict and reconciliation, are two aspects of the on-going human process of social, political and psychological evolution. The evolution is not, as it is commonly misperceived, from war towards peace, but rather from one kind of war and peace towards another kind of war and peace. It is a relative, not an absolute evolution.

Perhaps this point needs to be amplified somewhat, to fore-stall any suspicion of casuistry on our part. That forms of war-fare 'evolve' (in the primary sense of that word) is nowhere more apparent than in the nature of modern nuclear war itself. No nation, unless it is quite mad, prepares for a nuclear war in order to fight it. But rather in order to ensure that such a war will never take place. This is the essence of the modern concept of nuclear deterrence which, whether we like it or not, continues to preserve the world, despite endless provocations, from the horrors of a third World War. While our ancestors sharpened their swords in order to use them at the first opportunity, whether for defence, or depredation, we pile up our bombs in order never to have to use them. The evolution is from secrecy to openness on the one hand, and from the Janus faced concept of defence and attack to that of deterrence on the other.

Gandhi lived well into the dawn of the nuclear age. He also lived through the Nazi Tyranny. But faced with these, bizarre happenings he fell into the generalizations that all great men resort to at times of stress and dismay. For once he let go of his hold on truth and unconvincingly argued that non-violence still was the answer both to Auschwitz and Hiroshima. It is more than probable that Gandhi, had he lived long into our nightmare age of the Chinese Red Guard, the Viet Cong and the genocidal American bombing of Vietnam, would have characteristically owned his error and shown us where and how our doctrinal moorings had to be readjusted.

But in his absence, it devolves on us who claim to be working towards the revolution he left unfinished, to make those necessary readjustments.

If, on the other hand, we continue to look upon non-violence as an absolute concept, not subject to the exigencies of history or to the evolutionary, trial and error nature of all human ideas, we, thereby achieve only what each one of the great religions hams achieved in the past a progressive fossilization. Doctrinal purity is a meaningless obsession when our aim is to achieve certain well defined social and political goals. In this the followers of Gandhi at any rate most of them are different from Gandhi in a very vital sense, though few dare to admit the difference. With Gandhi it saint to the manner born the achievement of the secular goals of political freedom and social justice was always subservient to the religious goal of moksha, or self-realization. If the former had come, in the way of the latter and had proved an obstacle in the path of his well set spiritual journey (which they fortunately did not), Gandhi would have had little hesitation in discarding them. For him therefore, non-violence became in consonance with Hindu tradition both the means as well as the end. This can hardly be said to be the case with the bulk of present day Gandhian.

The spiritual overtone in Gandhian non-violence, exceedingly though it is when non-violence is practiced primarily spiritual ends and only secondarily for the achievement of the secular goal of social change, nevertheless has led to certain inner compulsions which have reduced its acceptability to modern societies. This is unfortunate, for the importance of the Gandhian orientation lies precisely in the successful manner in which he showed how the heavenly Ganga of non-violence can be brought down to earth, and tamed for worldly ends. Among these inner compulsions, probably the most serious was the need lie felt (no doubt genuinely) to make sweeping generalizations about non-violence and, in the process, to ignore the essentially finite nature of all human instruments.

Gandhi's greatness as a leader and thinker lay in his

transformation of the individualistic message of non-violence into it success technique for direct mass action. Mahavira, Buddha, Nagesena and Santideva have conceived of Ahimsa as a tenet ofpersonal action and motivation. But Gandhi transformed it also into it social and political technique. He, thus, attempted to apply the theory of himsa enunciated by the old Indian teachers and prophets on a social and political plane. The supreme concept, according to him, which is necessary for the reformation of politics, is non-violence.

Violence is a comprehensive category and is manifested both at the personal and the institutional levels. Evil thoughts, sentiments of revenge and brutality, verbal pugnacity, and even accumulation of unnecessary things represent examples of personal violence. Falsehood, trickery, intrigues, chicanery and deceitfulness are also forms of violence, according to the comprehensive connotation given to the term by Gandhi. Physical punishments, imprisonment, capital punishment and wars represent examples of violence committed by government. Economic exploitation and strangulation of others are also manifestations of violence. Even excess of emulation and competition can become species of violence. Non-violence or Ahimsa is, hence, necessarily, equally comprehensive and represents the total neutralization of violence in all forms.

Ahimsa is not merely the negative act of refraining from doing offence, injury and harm to others but really it represents the ancient law of positive self-sacrifice and constructive suffering. Gandhi interpreted it as signifying utter selflessness and universal love. The ultimate aim of Ahimsa is even to love the so called enemies or opponents. In 1930, Gandhi said that he would suck the poison out of a dying enemy of hi s if he was a victim of snake bite. Ahimsa, thus, is equivalent to positive compassion and love."[1] It even implies the cultivation of gladness and felicity involved in suffering for others. Ahimsa is implicitly latent in all human beings because all are sharers in the divine spiritual reality and its culmination is the negation of self-subsistent particularity and a realization of the feeling of love and substantive unity with the whole of creation.[2] it is the substitution of arrogance, antagonism and alienation by love.

Hence Gandhi wrote in his Autobiography, "I must reduce myself to zero. Ahimsa is the farthest limit of humility."[3] The supreme vocation or man is the purposive evolution, of Ahimsa as universal positive love. Ahimsa, as thus conceived by Gandhi, is a profound social import. Aristotle had said that friendship is the cohesive bond of communities. Gandhi also pleaded for brotherly ethic and believed that Ahimsa has, almost an obligatory and compelling power to bring peace and unity to the world.

He also interpreted human history in terms of the slow evolution of Ahimsa. Like some of the western anthropologists hr says that "our remote ancestors were cannibals." That was, succeeded by stage of chase the life of wandering hunters. The third stage was of agriculture which marked the growth of civilized stable life. Man "founded villages and towns, and from member of a family he became member of a community and a nation. All these are signs of progressive ahimsa and diminishing himsa. Had it been otherwise, the human species should have been extinct by now, even as many of the lower species have disappeared."[4]

It may appear surprising to several students of Gandhism to find speaking here as an adherent of the school of evolutionary anthropology rather than one deriving his theory of social origin" from the Purusha Sukta or the Puranas. He regarded the proem of human evolution as a vindication of the superiority of Ahimsa as love. "It is my firm faith that man is by nature going higher," he, wrote.

The practice of Ahimsa requires faith in the reality and compassion of God and deep self-introspection, the votary of non-violence has to cultivate the acquisition of freedom from envy, hatred, malice, lust, cupidity and uncharitableness." This leads to the acceptance of an elevated standard of virtues. The code of vows or Vrata has to be followed by the non-violent Satyagrahi and has to become the standard for cultivation by others. The acceptance of the norm of non-violence would thus almost amount to a moral transvaluation of values. The law of love, if courageously practiced" is bound to lead to the elevation of the accent, quality and character of politics and civilization.

Gandhi believed in the thorough practice of the ideal of

Abhayam or fearlessness along with non-violence. He was always stressing for practicing Ahimsa it is essential to shed all fear. The votary of Ahimsa only has one fear of God. As he pursues the he realises the eternal Atman and feels absolute indifference towards the temporary pleasures of the world. He sheds the attachment for the mortal physical frame. "Violence is needed for the protection of things external; non-violence is needed for the protection of the Atman."[5] Ahimsa or positive creative love can be practiced only on the basis of fearlessness and it may even be said that perfect Ahimsa means absolute fearlessness. It is the path of the brave. He pleaded only for the heroic non-violent action of the brave and was never attached to the non-resistance offered by the weak. He wanted the cultivation of courage as a preparation for life, but he wanted this courage to be expressed non-violently and not violently. He insisted on the development of that moral courage and strength which proceed from an indomitable will. He was in Noakhali on November 27, 1946: "The only real guarantee is to be sought in the personal courage of individuals. Everything else depends on it."[6] The operation of Ahimsa is the exercise of soul-force and it is a gospel of strength, according to Gandhi. It proceeds from moral and spiritual strength. It is the strongest force known and it is a force of the subtlest kind, according to Gandhi. It is a demonstration of the resolute strength of the heroic soul which refuses to hurt any body because every living creature is essentially a spirit and fundamentally one with himself. Ahimsa is the farthest removed from a false masquerade for one's weakness.

There is a solid concern for the actual and the concrete in Gandhi's saying that the sword is not the sign of strength but the symbol of fear and weakness. Fear generates suspicion and sometimes even arrogance. The accumulation of fear results in the formation of complexes. Sometimes it may produce aggressiveness. A greatly disturbing situation of our times is the growth of perverted and maladjusted personalities who are prone to being exploited by demagogues who raise bogeys and scares of different kinds and play upon the fear of the people. Gandhi teaches the psychological efficacy of fearlessness based on spiritual faith as the way to counteract the blighting influences of political coercion, group jealousies and rivalries and individual appetites.

Fearlessness is acquired by perfection of personal character and by deep faith in the existence of God. A believer in the reality and kindness of God cares only for truth, faith in the creative and beneficent power of the Spirit provides to man a firm, determination to fight all factors of injustice even at the cost of the sacrifice of one's life.

Gandhi was a perfect devotee of civility and humility, but he explicitly, unconditionally and categorically stated that if the only actives were cowardice and violence he would choose the latter. He was not tired of repeating that fear or cowardice should have no place in the national dictionary. He wrote:

"The truth is that cowardice itself is violence of a subtle and therefore, dangerous type, and far more difficult to eradicate than the habit of physical violence. A coward never risks his lilt. A man who would kill often risks it. A non-violent person's life is always at the disposal of him who would take it. For he knows that the soul within never dies. The encasing body is ever perishing. The more a man gives his life, the more he saves it. Thus non-violence requires more than the courage of the soldier of war. 'The Gita definition of a soldier is one who does not know what it is to run away from danger."[7]

Non-violence, hence, is to be regarded as, the summit of bravery Gandhi pointed out that he could no more preach non-violence to a cowardly man than be could tempt a blind man to enjoy healthy scenes.

Gandhi wanted India to follow the doctrine of non-violence not because she was prostrate due to political subjection. He affirmed that India had an imperishable "soul" which could rise above all weaknesses. But after Independence, nevertheless, Gandhi, a little pessimistically and with some amount of mortification, said that India had adopted only the non-violence of the weak because once the British power was out of the picture, the people engaged in unrestrained and intensely violent slaughter and internecine struggles. He confessed, "I have to hang down my head in shame." Gandhi wrote: "I have already said that the non-violence that was offered during the past thirty years was that of the weak .... India has no experience of the non-violence of the strong."[8] He stuck, however, to his faith in the moralization and spiritualization of politics and remained thoroughly devoted to the principle that increasing adherence to Ahimsa alone would emancipate mankind from all kinds of conflict and evil.

Gandhi preached the gospel of Ahimsa both for the East and the West. But in their different situational contexts Ahimsa implied somewhat different things for them. For India, Ahimsa as a social and political technic meant a pooling together of the energies of the people for the work of national liberation. It implied the elimination of petty local jealousies and group, caste and communal discriminations and persecutions and notions of regional superiority. It also signified the notion of the realization of a national community based on suffering, tolerance, self-abnegation and the neutralizations of fissiparous trends. For the western world, the Gandhian philosophy of Ahimsa mainly appeared as a gospel of renunciation. In 1947, Gandhi wrote that if Europe was to save itself from suicide something along the lines of non-violence had to be adopted. Non-violence applied to international politics signified a spiritual substitute for struggle and war and the consequent repudiation of "blood and iron" and "the mailed fist." It, thus, meant the negation of the cults of power, stratagems, exploitation, enslavement, economic imperialism, and war. But it was to be only a moral substitute for war and not the tame acceptance of status quo. In face of the advancements in nuclear energy, Gandhi, stood for the resort to techniques of love because he was deeply concerned with the survival of man.

As a spiritual and ethical idealist, he believed in the moralization of public administration to make it patterned, more and more, on the basis of non-violence. He wanted to reform the structure of modern political life. If swaraj could be achieved by non-violence then, the swaraj polity had to be increasingly based on the principle of Ahimsa. Hence he emphasized the application of honesty, integrity and beneficent purpose in public administration.[9]

The world is swept by the wind of violence. This storm which ravages the harvest of our civilization did not break out from a clear sky. Centuries of brutal national pride, whetted by the idolatrous ideology of several religions and crowned by a century of inhuman industrialism, rapacious plutocracy and a materialistic system of economics where the soul perishes, stifled to death, were bound to culminate in these dark struggles where the treasures of the West succumbed. It is not enough to say all this was inevitable. Each people kill the other in the name of same principles, which hid the same covetousness and Cainish instincts. All be they Nationalists, Fascists, Communists, members of the oppressed to use the force, while refusing this right to others. In the past might dominate right.

The true characteristic of faith is not to deny the hostility of the world, but to recognize it and to believe in spite of it! Faith is a battle. And our non-violence is the most desperate battle. The way to peace is not through weakness. We do not fight violence. No much as weakness. Nothing is worthwhile unless it is strong, neither good nor evil. Absolute evil is better than emasculated goodness. Moaning pacifism is the death-knell of peace; it is cowardice mid lack of faith. Let those who do not believe, who fear, withdraw. The way to peace leads through self-sacrifice.

One thing is certain: either Gandhi's spirit will triumph, or it will manifest itself again, as were manifested, centuries before, the Messiah and Buddha, till there finally is manifested. In a mortal half god, the perfect incarnation of the principle of life which will lead a new humanity on to a new path.

Notes and References

1. *Harijan*, 17-8-1934.
2. *Ibid.*, 29-6-1940.
3. M. K. Gandhi, An Autobiography or The Story of My Experiments with Truth, Ahmedabad, Navajivan Publications, 1975
4. *Harijan*, 21-7-1940.
5. *Ibid.*, 18-8-1940.
6. *Ibid.*, 27-11-1946.

7. *Young India*, 18-12-1924.
8. *Harijan*, 29-6-1947
9. V.P. Varma, The Political Philosophy of Mahatma Gandhi and Sarvodaya, Agra, Lakshmi Narayan Agarwal, 1959.

Index